PRACTICAL CRIME SCENE PROCESSING AND INVESTIGATION

CRC SERIES IN
**PRACTICAL ASPECTS OF CRIMINAL
AND FORENSIC INVESTIGATIONS**

VERNON J. GEBERTH, BBA, MPS, FBINA *Series Editor*

PRACTICAL CRIME SCENE PROCESSING AND INVESTIGATION

Ross M. Gardner

CRC PRESS

Boca Raton   London   New York   Washington, D.C.

**HV
8073
G228p
2005**

Library of Congress Cataloging-in-Publication Data

Gardner, Ross M.
Practical crime scene processing and investigation / Ross M. Gardner.
       p. cm. — (Practical aspects of criminal and forensic investigation)
    ISBN 0-8493-2043-7
     1. Crime scene searches. 2. Criminal investigation. 3. Evidence, Criminal. I. Title. II.
   CRC series in practical aspects of criminal and forensic investigations.

HV8073.G32 2004
363.25'2—dc22
                                          2004041408

Visit the CRC Press Web site at www.crcpress.com

Dedication

To my wife Karen, for her patience and understanding,

and to

the men and women of the United States Army Criminal Investigation Command, past, present, and future, for their dedication to excellence.

Foreword

I feel very comfortable in saying that criminal investigators throughout our law enforcement community universally agree that the importance of quality crime scene investigations cannot be overemphasized. Criminal investigators must be able to identify and collect items of evidentiary value left at the crime scene in order to better piece together events surrounding the crime and to identify perpetrators and sometimes victims.

It is essential, then, that crime scene personnel take all means necessary to ensure the integrity of evidence collected in order to avoid legal restrictions that may prevent the introduction of such evidence at trial or the development of a solid case for prosecution.

The content of this book speaks to issues in crime scene processing that are important, addressing techniques and applications that apply. It tells you what you need to know, what you need to do, and how to do it.

The methods and procedures used in crime scene processing, as presented here by Ross Gardner, combine the collective knowledge of other experts and practitioners in the field as well as his own practical experiences garnered over more than two decades of work as an active criminal investigator and some four years as a police chief. I had the pleasure of serving as his executive manager for six and one-half years during his special agent investigator tenure.

I am convinced that it is essential that all officers and investigative personnel have a solid understanding of professionally accepted crime scene protocols in order that their agency can take full advantage of today's sophisticated laboratory techniques and technologies. This book can play a significant role in helping responsible, concerned individuals realize that objective.

Eugene R. Cromartie
Deputy Executive Director/Chief of Staff
International Association of Chiefs of Police
and
Major General (Ret)
United States Army Criminal Investigation Command

Preface

This is not a book about crime laboratory techniques. It will not go into depth about the G-C-A-T order in DNA or discuss how mass–gas spectrometry works at the crime lab. This is not a book about criminal investigations. It does not have chapters on burglary crimes or sex crimes, and it does not discuss how to develop functional investigative timelines or talk about interviews and interrogations. This is not a book about behavioral science; there will be no in-depth discussion of serial vs. mass murders or differentiating of organized vs. disorganized crime scenes.

The subject of this book is crime scene processing — practical proven methods and procedures to be used at *any* crime scene. It includes concepts and investigative procedures that anyone charged with the responsibility of processing a crime scene should understand. These methods and techniques are field-proven by people who have been using them, not someone who simply read about it in a book once. To teach these methods, we will deal with forensics, investigative procedures, and a myriad of other subjects. Nevertheless, the focus will remain on what crime scene investigators do, how they actually do it, and how to decide in what order they will do it.

I make no claim that these ideas and concepts are my personal brainchild. The procedures described here are the consolidated knowledge of the literally hundreds of mentors, peers, and instructors I've encountered over the past 29 years. From municipal departments to federal agencies, from Scotland Yard to the Finnish Bureau of Investigation, each of the individuals I've encountered has added, in his or her own way, to our collective understanding of functional crime scene procedures. These are proven techniques, methods I have employed in day-to-day criminal investigations over the past 24 years. They are the real deal, and they work. I certainly intend for this book to serve as a functional reference for those new to crime scene processing. I expect it also will be used as a handy refresher for those engaged in crime scene processing as a part of their daily duties. Unfortunately, there are also many participating in the process who, simply put, have never been taught the basics. Hopefully, this book will aid those individuals as well. The contents are a knowledge base of many capable and competent subject-matter experts.

If one were to choose the entertainment industry as a subject-matter expert, as many lawyers do, it would appear that crime scene processing is simple, absolute, and written in stone. Accordingly, any dummy can do it perfectly, each and every time. As these sources would have it, evidence should never be damaged or destroyed through processing techniques, and nothing would be degraded. Of course, this logic has one major problem — Hollywood producers are not bound by any rules associated with reality. Amazingly enough, Hollywood rules, and many lawyers seem content to say, "Well, I saw it on *CSI*, so that is how it's done." I liken this thinking to the old joke about incest and the resulting DNA in a family tree. Every time a lawyer watches *CSI*, his or her understanding of forensics and crime scene practices becomes more and more warped. Yet every time these lawyers open their mouths in court, they present themselves as somehow "in the know." That is amazing in and of itself, because across the years I have spent a lot of time teaching lawyers (defense and prosecution) about forensics and crime scene practices, and I am continuously flabbergasted to find that few receive *any* in-depth training on police practices or forensics in their formal education. They are left to learn about crime scene practices and forensics on the fly! Nevertheless, lawyers continuously espouse comments, concepts, and opinions about "how" it is really supposed to be done. As a result, a number of myths about crime scene processing abound. It is important that we debunk a few of these myths.

First and foremost, there is no one-and-only "right" way to process a scene. There is a clear and specific purpose for why we process the scene: it is to collect as much evidence as possible in as functional and pristine a condition as is possible. By achieving that, we hopefully define more effectively what did or did not happen in the situation being investigated. Every action we take is directed toward accomplishing this purpose. There is certainly a basic sequence of effort directed at the crime scene. Investigators routinely assess, observe, document, search, collect, and analyze the scene, in that order. So there are rules to the game, just not hard and fast rules. If there are rules, then there are clearly "wrong" things to do in a crime scene. Yet no two scenes are the same, and every scene presents unique problems that must be overcome. Competing interests routinely occur in the process, and that presents contradictions that the crime scene investigator must overcome. In the end, it is only by considering the overall purpose, by reviewing the optimum sequence of effort, and by understanding the associated forensics that the scene investigator can reach an appropriate decision on what to do. Even then, there is no guarantee that their decision will be right, given the 20:20 hindsight available at trial.

An equally important myth to debunk is the notion that there are perfect crime scenes or perfect crime scene processors. The scene begins to degrade from the moment the event begins, throughout the course of the crime, and continues right through the arrival and processing by police and forensic scientists. It is impossible for the scene to do otherwise. Granted, every procedure we discuss is directed toward collecting the evidence and its associated context in as pristine a condition *as possible*, but scene degradation is a fact of life. We use every mechanism available to limit this degradation, but we must accept that it will occur.

These myths negatively impact the way crime scene investigators operate, and they are often used as a distracter at trial. Far too often, crime scene investigators say, "Oh, the scene was disturbed. There is no reason to even try to process it." That kind of thinking is ridiculous. There may be scenes that are so disturbed that little if anything of value will be found. But until the crime scene investigator tries, there is no way to know what he or she might find. Lazy investigators routinely use this excuse to keep from doing their job. At trial, the myths comes into play as well, where crime scene investigators are put on the defensive because something was damaged or lost through the processing. Why be defensive? Embrace the reality and tell it like it is: "We tried something, it failed. Would you have preferred, Mr. Lawyer, that I had not tried at all?" This answer cannot be used as a routine excuse for poor procedures or haphazard effort on our part, but just the same, we cannot allow unknowledgeable people to get away with painting the Hollywood version of crime scene processing for the court. Hollywood's version of crime scene investigation is fantasy and always has been.

What drives the Hollywood hype is, however, rooted in forensic science. Edmund Locard's Principle of Exchange states simply that "every contact leaves its trace." With every new advance in technology, forensic science increases its ability to do more with the evidence. Things unimaginable 10 years ago are commonplace today, such as recovering and identifying DNA from the residue on a postage stamp. Each change increases our ability to prove Locard far more accurate than perhaps he ever thought possible. Although the technology is constantly changing, the underlying process of dealing with the crime scene has not changed at all. Documentation, collection, and analysis still require the same basic skills. Between the time this book is sent to the publisher and the day it is published, there is no doubt that some new fingerprinting method or forensic technique will be forthcoming. For that reason, this book will not concentrate on every specific technique available. Instead, it will concentrate on the basic procedures that do not change with time and on the basic techniques and skills necessary at most crime scenes.

When I said that these procedures could be used at *any* crime scene, I meant that in every respect. From the household burglary to the triple axe murder, it is not whether we should apply all of these techniques to every crime we investigate, but rather a function of whether we can. I guarantee that if you *could* apply all of these procedures and practices to each and every crime you investigated, your solve rates would astound you. Between 1980 and 1999, while I was serving in the USACIDC, our organization routinely had a 69% solve rate on felony property crimes worldwide. Why? Not to say it was the only factor, but there was a simple rule that the agents lived by. Lift all latent prints found and submit all lifts to the crime lab. It didn't matter that you thought it was smudged or that it was only a partial finger. All prints were collected, sent to, and evaluated by the crime lab. Burglary or murder, it didn't matter. As a result, we solved crime. It was anything but a secret; we simply had the resources to conduct fingerprint evaluations at that level. But that is an oddity. Imagine asking your county or state lab to provide you the same service. You would get laughed out of the building. Now it is a matter of: "Is it AFIS quality?" If not, then sorry. Whether in the form of investigative resources, money, or time, resources are what drive the investigative train. In a perfect world, where resources were not an issue, we could apply these methods across the board at every scene and be far more successful at identifying and stopping criminals.

Unfortunately, we live in a far from perfect world. Sure, at the homicide scene we pull out all the stops; we employ all the gadgets and gizmos. But I guarantee that the smash and grab at a local business or the fast-food robbery will not get the same level of attention. Resource-driven, the crime scene supervisor has to make hard decisions about exactly what they will or will not do. In order to make those decisions intelligently, those processing the scene have to understand forensics and the underlying purpose behind the techniques used in crime scene processing.

Even in an imperfect world, there must be some standard of what "minimal scene processing" entails, particularly if we are to meet our duty to society. Once defined, that standard must be met. Are a couple of Polaroid photographs and no attempt to lift latent prints at the fast-food robbery really a sufficient effort? Perhaps, if you feel that testimonial evidence is more reliable. This book will not presume to define that standard in detail. Through discussions of photography, sketching, evidence collection, and report writing, it will certainly suggest where that minimum standard may lie. In the end, given the resources available and the crime encountered, each crime scene investigator or supervisor must objectively evaluate their effort and set that standard for their own organization.

Once you get past the Hollywood hype, past the limitations of our organizations, and past the drama-queen lawyers of the courtroom, this business is really quite simple. Crime scene investigators seek to establish what happened and provide the justice system with factual information on which to base justice decisions. We have no sideline agendas, no master to serve but the truth. When it is all said and done, the crime scene investigator simply has to look in the mirror and ask, "Have I done my job to the best of my ability? Have I secured and documented the evidence that might help prove the facts more effectively to the judge and jury?" If the answer is yes, then we can all sleep well. If not, then perhaps we need to work a little harder at enhancing our skills and abilities.

Acknowledgments

This book is a compilation of knowledge gained over 29 years of involvement in law enforcement. No one person can take credit for the ideas; I certainly cannot, as no one person defined them. They are the combined knowledge of many years of service by thousands of dedicated, often anonymous people. This book is a testament to their excellence.

If we are honest with ourselves, we have to accept that any skill or success we achieve in life is very much a product of those who mentored and chose to teach us. I simply cannot begin to mention all of the outstanding police officers and criminal investigators I have encountered over the years who took an interest in me. But I recognize that my success is very much a product of their effort. Each and every one of you has my heartfelt thanks.

I certainly owe a great debt of gratitude to the men and women of the U.S. Criminal Investigation Command, supervisors, peers, and subordinates alike, who through the years taught, cajoled, and beat proper techniques into me. Jim Smith, Tom Coster, Phillip McGuire, Bob Jones, John Jones, Bill Middleton, Willie Rowell; the names are endless of outstanding criminal investigators who shared their experience and knowledge as crime scene experts. I still believe and uphold that part of my agents' oath that said, "I shall at all times seek diligently to discover the truth deterred neither by fear nor prejudice." Nothing in my career has given me greater pride than being counted among the individuals who share the title of USACIDC Special Agent.

Along the path, I also encountered a vast number of experts outside of the CID, like Detective Investigator Wichanski and Detective Sergeant Vickery of the Metropolitan Police Academy in the U.K. Both were dedicated and capable criminal investigators sharing their knowledge with students at the Scenes of Crime Officer Course at New Scotland Yard. There is no doubt in my mind that they set a fire in me at an early age, one that would continuously fuel my desire for excellence in the investigative organizations I worked for. This book is very much a product of the beliefs and ideas they put into play in 1985.

I also owe a debt of gratitude to all of the individuals who specifically assisted in creating this book. My specific thanks go out to the following individuals for assisting me:

Tom J. Griffin and Chris Andrist, authors of *Mass Crime Scene Handbook*, for their outstanding insight and knowledge on mass scene situations.

John Anderson for his encouragement and support of the project.

Special Agent Mike Hockrein, St. Louis FBI. As a foremost expert in gravesite recovery, Mike gave significant input and reviewed critical sections of the text to ensure that it defined the best methods.

Captain (Ret.) Tom Bevel, Oklahoma City Police Department, for his review of the bloodstain pattern and crime scene analysis sections. Tom has always been a mentor and supporter, and I have learned immeasurably from my association with him.

Sergeant Steven Ray, Cpl. Rex Duke, and Officer Faith Case, Lake City Police Department, for their assistance in creating photo figures used in the documentation chapters.

Detective Sergeant Bruce Wiley and the San Jose Police Department for their insight in dealing with landfill recoveries. SJPD's experiences and success in dealing with this complex scene will serve us all.

Special Agents Don Houseman, Mike Maloney, and William Herzig of the Naval Criminal Investigative Service (NCIS), who have always supported and assisted me in every endeavor.

Bud Veazey, Fox-5 News, Atlanta, and Pete Scott, *Atlanta Journal-Constitution*, for their insight into journalism operations.

Of course a number of individuals provided photographs and figures to help demonstrate or explain the techniques. My thanks go out to: Herb Leighton, Maine State Police; Roy Heim, Tulsa Police Department; Brian Steel, Steel PC; Special Agent (Ret.) Don Hayden; Kelly Fite; Kim Duddy and the Washington State Patrol Crime Lab; Ranger John A. Martin, Texas Rangers; Nikon Inc.; Special Agent Laura Delong, Oakland FBI ERT; Special Agent (Ret.) Steve Chancellor; Det. Craig Gravel, Captain J. Becker, and the Oklahoma City PD Crime Scene Unit; DA Wes Lane, Oklahoma City, OK; Mike McGuffey, Covington PD; and Tom Faith of Totally Ballistic.

About the Author

Ross Martin Gardner worked in law enforcement for nearly 29 years. The vast majority of that period was spent with the U.S. Army Criminal Investigation Command, performing duties as a Special Agent and as a Command Sergeant Major. In 1999, Special Agent Gardner retired from the military to take a position as chief of police in a small suburban Atlanta police department. He served in that position until 2003, when he quit public service to become a full-time consultant and instructor.

Gardner holds a master's degree in computer and information systems management from Webster University, a bachelor's degree in criminal justice from Wayland Baptist College, and an associate's degree in police science from Central Texas College. In 1985, he attended and graduated first in his class from the Scenes of Crime Officers Course, New Scotland Yard. Between 1988 and 1996, he served as an adjunct professor for Central Texas College. He is a member of a number of professional associations and has served in a variety of positions, including president of the Rocky Mountain Association of Bloodstain Pattern Analysts (RMABPA), president of the Association of Crime Scene Reconstruction (ACSR), chairman of the Education Committee for both the RMABPA and the International Association of Bloodstain Pattern Analysts (IABPA), chairman of the Taxonomy and Terminology Committee of the FBI Scientific Workgroup on Bloodstain Pattern Analysis (SWGSTAIN).

Gardner is certified as a senior crime scene analyst by the International Association for Identification and is an active instructor in crime scene processing, crime scene analysis, and bloodstain pattern analysis. Throughout his career, he has taught for police agencies (national and international), police academies, law enforcement professional associations, and trial counsel professional associations. He has also written a number of articles. Gardner has qualified as an expert in bloodstain pattern analysis and crime scene analysis in both state and federal court. In 1997, Gardner cowrote the text *Bloodstain Pattern Analysis: with an Introduction to Crime Scene Reconstruction* with CPT (Ret.) Tom Bevel of the Oklahoma City Police Department.

Editor's Note

This textbook is part of the "Practical Aspects of Criminal and Forensic Investigtion" series. This series was created by Vernon J. Geberth, New York City Police Department Lieutenant Commander (Retired), who is an author, educator, and consultant on homicide and forensic investigation. This series has been designed to provide contemporary, comprehensive, and pragmatic information to the practitioner involved in criminal and forensic investigation by authors who are nationally recognized experts in their respective fields.

Contents

Introduction

1

Crime scene processing is an inherent task and duty associated with most criminal investigations, for rarely does one encounter a crime without some kind of crime scene. Crime scene processing consists of an examination and evaluation of the scene for the express purpose of recovering physical evidence and documenting the scene's condition *in situ*, or as found. To accomplish this, the crime scene technician engages in six basic steps: assessing, observing, documenting, searching, collecting, and analyzing. These steps, and the order in which they are accomplished, are neither arbitrary nor random. Each serves an underlying purpose in capturing scene context and recovering evidence without degrading the value of either. Any way you look at it, this is not an easy task, since the mere act of processing the scene disturbs the scene and evidence. From these efforts however, the investigator will walk away with important items of physical evidence and scene documentation in the form of sketches, photographs, notes, and reports. All of this information plays a significant role in resolving crime by providing objective data on which the investigating team can test investigative theories, corroborate or refute testimonial evidence, and ultimately demonstrate to the court the conditions and circumstances defined by the scene. This is a task that is easily said, but it is not so easily done.

Action without purpose is folly and, simply put, becomes wasted effort. This is true in any endeavor, so it is imperative that before pursuing the actions an investigator conducts in the crime scene, the investigator must understand his or her mandate. Crime scene processing is a duty in every sense of the word. Crime scene processing is not something the technicians do because "they were told to," but rather because they have a responsibility to do so. If the investigator fails to recognize this duty and its ultimate purpose, many of the procedures used at the scene might appear meaningless and therefore unnecessary. But each has an underlying purpose in seeking to recover both evidence and scene context. What follows in this chapter is a discussion of the conceptual and theoretical ideas behind crime scene processing. As we will discover, there is no single "right way" for the crime scene technicians to conduct themselves at a scene, but there are certainly a number of wrong ways.

No matter what action a crime scene investigator takes, ultimately s/he will be asked to defend that action in court. Opposite the investigator will be a counsel with little, if any, understanding of the process or practice of crime scene investigation. What the counsel is likely to have however, are excerpts from various references on crime scene investigation, with no contextual understanding of what they mean. To stand the test of cross-examination and not allow a counsel to misrepresent these references, the crime scene investigator must be able to articulate the reasons why a certain action was taken over some other course of action. Without this ability, the counsel will likely sway the jury that the police failed in their duty. So it is not enough that a crime scene investigator can process the scene, he or she must understand the underlying theory in order to weather such storms in court.

Even before we can speak to the conceptual issues of crime scene processing, we must ask and answer an even more basic question. Why does this duty to society exist? What is the true function of the police and the investigator in a free society? Many will say, "It is to see that justice is done." The police are clearly a significant player in society's efforts to seek justice. Yet the police are only one player in a convoluted criminal justice system, and unfortunately the search for justice in that system is oftentimes confusing. Despite the confusion of the system, the role of the professional police and crime scene investigator is really quite clear.

Police Goals and Objectives

The true role of the police, and thus of the crime scene investigator, is very well defined with little, if any, ambiguity. In a free society, the police have two basic goals:

1. The prevention of crime and disorder, and the preservation of peace
2. The protection of life, property, and personal liberty

This mandate ultimately defines why police act as they do and why the role of the crime scene investigator is so important to the criminal justice system. In order to achieve these two goals, the police apply five basic objectives:

1. *Crime prevention:* Prevention includes the actions and efforts designed to keep crime from occurring in the first place. Crime is not singularly a police problem; it is a societal problem. Community programs, youth programs, proactive patrol techniques, and participation in neighborhood watches, all of these actions are directed toward preventing crime from occurring.
2. *Crime repression:* When prevention fails, the police then seek to repress the criminal by actively investigating crimes and attempting to identify those responsible. A criminal investigation is clearly rooted in our crime repression activities. If the police fail to stop a crime, they must investigate the crime fully and impartially and, if possible, identify those whom they believe are responsible. Once identified, the police are then responsible for apprehending the criminals and bringing them to justice.
3. *Regulating noncriminal conduct:* The police act to control general behavior patterns, such as compliance with city ordinances and traffic regulations, in order to prevent chaos.
4. *Provision of services:* As any police officer knows, when there is no one else to call, a citizen will call the police. From helping stranded motorists to looking for lost children, the scope and breadth of the services provided by police is very broad.
5. *Protection of personal liberty:* This is perhaps the single most confusing aspect of the police role in society. Police have a mandate to protect citizens from unwarranted police interference of their personal liberties. In effect the police must

actively control their own behavior to ensure that their methods and practices abide by the Constitution and the law.

Crime repression and protection of personal liberty are both related to the criminal investigation and the processing of the crime scene, and thus they are important objectives. The police must proactively investigate the crimes reported to them and do so in a manner that is consistent and respectful of the law and the liberties of those they encounter. Even with these objectives in mind, significant confusion still arises in this mandate, and it relates specifically to concepts of duty, truth, and justice.

When presented with grotesque and unimaginable crimes, those responsible for the investigation almost always feel an extreme sense of urgency and, oftentimes, a very personal sense of duty to resolve the investigation. Ego or pride, disgust with the kind of human that would act so inhumanely, or empathy for the victims themselves can build a stress that few outside of the profession will understand or even recognize. Unfortunately, overpersonalization of the event in the investigator's mind can also warp his or her sense of duty. Remember always that the true duty is to remain professional and objective and, through this professionalism, to resolve the investigation. Without objectivity, police end up acting on emotion, and that can lead to a subjective nightmare.

As for our beliefs on truth and justice, the two words are often bandied about as if they were somehow synonymous. Truth is simple fact, without regard to agenda and subjective factors. Truth is the old Joe Friday routine: "The facts, ma'am, just the facts." The suspect was last seen with the victim. This is Smith's fingerprint. The victim's DNA (deoxyribonucleic acid) is on the clothes of the subject. These are all examples of facts. These facts in and of themselves rarely define an absolute truth about crime. It is through consideration of the totality of these facts that the investigator is able to draw some ultimate conclusion.

Justice is different, however, and a bit more complex. Justice is the process by which "each receives his due." It is society, in the form of judges and juries, who defines justice. They do so using facts and evidence, but as most police officers know, the jury is not always privy to every piece of information. Whether it is because the police failed to collect it legally or because some prosecutor does not want to "confuse" the jury, the jury acts based only on the knowledge and information presented to them. It is also important to understand that in order to be fair, justice considers the needs of three different entities: the victim, society, and the accused. Thus, for all of these reasons, the course of events suggested by justice may well be in conflict with those suggested by the pure truth! This presents an interesting and oftentimes perplexing problem to the investigator. It becomes distracting to try and understand why the justice system acts as it does, particularly in light of all of the information the investigator may know. All of these distractions can lead to disillusionment and create significant ethical issues.

Nevertheless, the purpose of the criminal investigation still remains first and foremost a search for truth, even if the investigator does not always understand or in all cases agree with the administration of "justice." The bottom line is that the police seek to objectively define what happened and who was involved, and to do so in a manner that is lawful and does not violate the rights or liberties of those being investigated. Furthermore, the police are expected to seek this truth as objectively as possible without regard to any personal agenda. As professional investigators, we have as much of a duty to refute an allegation as we do to try and corroborate it. Our master then is the truth and only the truth. Professional ethics demands an absolute adherence to this mandate.

There will certainly be moments when an investigator will be dismayed by what society thinks "justice" is, but the investigator must always remain cognizant of his or her specific role in seeking justice. Investigators are not, nor have they ever been, the judge and jury. When the police begin to view themselves as such, the result is something that can only be characterized as a police state, far from our concepts of democracy. The police must do their job as intended. If they seek and bring precise and objective information of the crime scene to the justice system, and if they do so without any agenda beyond seeking the truth, then the probability increases that true justice will be served.

Case Example: Facts vs. Agenda

In the late evening hours on a rainy December evening, a sheriff-elect returned home to join his family. He was to be sworn in as the sheriff of a major metropolitan county within days. He parked his car on a cul-de-sac, as there were two vehicles of friends and relatives already in his driveway. He began walking east to the residence with several bags. His son observed this approach from the residence. He reported that as his father arrived at a point adjacent to the opening between the two cars in the driveway, the sheriff looked in a direction away from the driveway (to the northwest) and then turned in the same direction. The son reported hearing a number of gunshots, but he saw no one in between the cars while making his observations. The son ran for his father's weapon and observed nothing further.

At that moment a neighbor, in the house immediately north of the victim's home, was looking out her window. She observed a man dressed in black moving from the north side of the sheriff's lawn to the south (toward the sheriff's walkway and driveway). Her line of sight prevented direct observation of the vehicles and the driveway, but she did hear multiple gunshots and observed a single individual dressed in black run to the street. There he got into the passenger door of a small two-door sedan, which drove off. She provided specific information regarding characteristics of this vehicle.

When the shooting stopped, the family rushed from the residence to find the sheriff on the south side and at the east end of the driveway, close to the house. The sheriff-elect died of multiple gunshot wounds.

A crime scene examination was completed and significant evidence located. (See Figure 1.1.) Around the car that was closest to the street, police found three 9-mm casings. The first was beneath the vehicle by the left rear tire. The next was found on the north side of the vehicle, adjacent to the driver's door, and the third was located on the north side, adjacent to the front left tire. Between the two cars in the driveway were the three bags the sheriff was carrying as he approached the house. Six more 9-mm casings were located in and around the grass at the south edge of the property. No shell casings were located east of the second vehicle in the driveway or to the east beyond the final location of the victim. The sheriff collapsed at the southeast corner of this vehicle. Three feet east of his position, two bullet fragments were located in the grass.

Of interest as the investigation developed, the mailbox was located to the west of the residence on the north side of the driveway and sidewalk, and it was surrounded by large bushes that would provide concealment from observation of anyone approaching from the street.

Forensic analysis of the casings indicated that the weapon used was a Tek-9 or similar weapon and that only one weapon had deposited all of the shell casings in the scene.

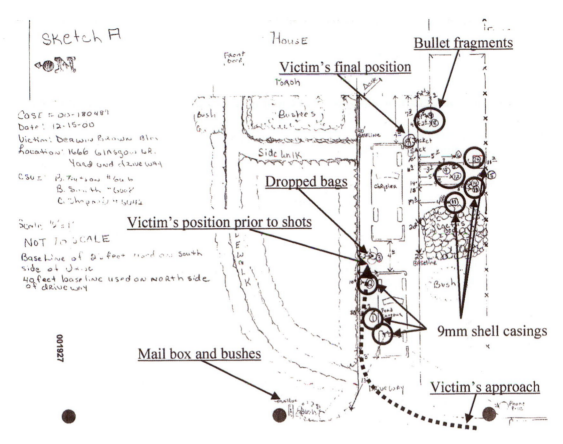

Figure 1.1 A crime scene sketch depicts the location of shell casings and the victim's position as observed by his son. The dropped articles support this positioning. The cluster of 9-mm casings on the north side of the car in the driveway speaks clearly to the position of the shooter at the initiation of this assault. This is in clear contradiction to the story provided by the coconspirator. (Figure courtesy of Steel Law Firm, P.C.)

The case remained unsolved, with significant media attention and open speculation focusing on the outgoing sheriff as a possible suspect. A year after the event, a suspect was arrested in another homicide. The suspect was an ex-deputy with close ties to the outgoing sheriff, who was rumored to be behind the killing. The district attorney (DA) offered this suspect a deal to turn state's evidence in the sheriff-elect's murder, with one significant stipulation. The suspect could not be the primary shooter. With that exception, the suspect would serve one year on all charges, including the subsequent homicide. The suspect accepted the offer, and from the suspect emerged a tale of conspiracy involving late-night meetings with the outgoing sheriff in which the primary communications regarding the conspiracy were written on notes that were then eaten by the parties involved. This set in motion a conspiracy involving three other men. The ex-deputy claimed that three of the conspirators approached the home through a tree line from a frontage road to the northwest of the cul-de-sac. A fourth man remained in the car on the frontage road, several hundred yards away. The ex-deputy positioned himself near the residence mailbox, dressed in black. The "real shooter" was positioned between the two cars parked in the driveway, crouching so as not to be seen. The sheriff-elect arrived, and as he approached the space between the cars, the shooter stood, shooting the victim immediately from this position. The ex-deputy and the third conspirator watched from relatively concealed positions. A second self-confessed conspirator, who was also granted full immunity with the same stipulation, claimed to have been the getaway driver for the four. He claimed to have parked on the frontage road, while the other three committed the hit. Unfortunately, the two men had a short opportunity to talk before the second conspirator was interviewed, but even with this assistance, they couldn't seem to make up their minds as to who was actually present during the meeting when the entire conspiracy began. One claimed he was alone with the outgoing sheriff; the second claimed he was present with his friend.

Despite these minor issues, the DA went forward with his "star" witnesses in an attempt to obtain murder convictions against the two remaining conspirators. He lost this case completely. Not put off by the loss, the DA then proceeded with a case against the outgoing sheriff for masterminding the assassination.

From the beginning, there was clear and specific information available to the DA based upon the crime scene. The two witnesses independently indicated that the avenue of attack was from the northwest, which was corroborated by the evidence. The Tek-9, if held in a normal orientation, will eject its casings to the right and slightly rearward. The presence of shell casings to the west of the victim's reported position before the shooting — and the fact that they were found on the north side of the driveway — clearly suggested a shooter operating from a point northwest of the victim. If the shooter were positioned as the ex-deputy claimed, there was simply no logical way to explain the presence of these casings. They should not have been there. The strewn belongings and ultimate position of the victim indicated an attempt to flee or take cover from the attack, in which the victim moved south between the cars on the driveway and then continued east to his final position. Once again, the clustering of shell casings on the south side of the second car suggested a weapon being fired from a position west of the victim. All of this evidence suggested a pursuit that moved from a point northwest of the driveway and ending with the shooter firing west to east. If the ex-deputy was being truthful, the victim would literally have had to run through the shooter, but the ballistics and pathology failed to support that contention.

The neighbor as a witness was concise. Before the shooting, she placed an individual on the east side of the mailbox and bushes, which was northwest of the victim. One man ran from the immediate scene, not three. That person was observed getting in the passenger side of a car parked on the cul-de-sac, not the frontage road. The victim's son was precise in indicating his father looked and turned to the northwest immediately before the shooting began. The initial wounds were directed from the front of the victim and not his back. There really was little question regarding the crime scene evidence; the shooter fired on the sheriff-elect from the northwest and pursued him to his final position.

Given the totality of information available, it was significant that the ex-deputy had not only placed himself northwest of the sheriff-elect, he put himself in similar clothes and acknowledged that the car used in the murder was exactly as that described by the neighbor a year before the deputy was arrested. All of this begs the question: why was the DA so willing to ignore this evidence and accept the clearly incongruent tale of events described by the ex-deputy?

No objective evidence exists to answer this question. As is often the case, was the DA simply incapable of understanding the forensic evidence? Just the same, it is apparent that to call the ex-deputy on the crime scene issues and challenge him based on that evidence would suggest that he was untruthful. If untruthful in any part of his story, then any claim of having committed the murder at the order of the outgoing sheriff would suffer from a credibility issue. Whatever the case, the truth regarding who shot the sheriff fell victim to the situation.

The lesson in this example is simple. It shows how logic can be twisted and warped when an individual strays from using the truth as the agenda. A rookie crime scene technician could have seen through the logic errors in the ex-deputy's story, but ultimately the facts and evidence were ignored. Remember always that crime scene technicians cannot go about their business with the same cavalier attitude to truth as the law profession does. People's lives are significantly affected by the decisions the police make. If there is to be justice, then truth must underlie all aspects of the investigator's decision making processes.

Evidence Defined

Evidence can be defined as anything that tends to prove or disprove a fact in contention. In any investigation, the evidence presents itself as either testimonial evidence or physical evidence. Each is important, and each plays a role in helping the jury come to a decision of guilt or innocence.

Testimonial evidence is collected through the interview and interrogation of witnesses, victims, and suspects or subjects. It is often illuminating in understanding motives or in explaining those things found at the scene. But testimonial evidence has a major flaw in terms of its consideration: it is offered by human beings, and humans are subjective creatures. Victims, witnesses, and subjects all bring agendas and perceptions to the table. At times, these agendas and the associated subjectivity include outright lies. Perjury is not unknown, with individuals presenting alibis for suspects who were otherwise caught on videotape at the crime scene, or with relatives protecting their own because "I can't believe Johnny would do such a thing."

More often than not, the nature of this subjectivity is far less deceitful. It revolves around our ability as humans to perceive and remember events. The robbery victim who describes the gun forced into her face as "huge," when in fact it was a .22 caliber, is not lying to us. From her perspective, the gun was huge! The witness who overhears another witness describe some detail of a subject, which he himself did not see, may internalize that information and later change his testimony after convincing himself that he too observed this trait. How many convictions based on eyewitness identification have been overturned and proven incorrect through DNA? Are we to believe these victims lied about the identity of their attackers? This is doubtful. Simply put, if investigators place all of their stock in testimonial evidence, then they have missed the boat. Victims, witnesses, and subjects are all capable of distorting facts, sometimes for purpose, other times without even knowing they have done so. Does that mean we ignore the testimonial evidence? Certainly not, but the investigator must always recognize the importance of physical evidence in evaluating testimonial evidence. This is a lesson lost on many in the criminal justice system.

What are the virtues of physical evidence? Physical evidence takes the form of specific items found at the scene that are often collected for subsequent analysis and presentation. Sometimes physical evidence is not "collected" at all, but merely documented through photography or sketching. But in either case, it is real, it is tangible, and it cannot be denied. The physical evidence never lies. It is what it is, although we can certainly misinterpret its meaning. That failure, however, is still human in origin; the fault does not lie with the evidence. Whether it is the ambiguity of the involved science or the subjectivity of the officer, jury, or lawyer involved, it is only the human element that prevents us from understanding the true nature of the physical evidence. Properly considered, the physical evidence establishes a framework of facts that are irrefutable by anyone. The physical evidence creates a scaffold of objective knowledge that will guide and support the investigator's overall understanding of the crime being investigated. This framework will serve as a reference to which the investigator can compare the testimonial evidence, allowing him or her, in many instances, to corroborate or refute the information presented. When the investigation becomes mired in subjective information, this objective framework will be a ready reference to return to for clarity. Together, the physical evidence and any testimonial evidence that ultimately stands the test of time will allow some level of insight into the overall event.

However, the concept of physical evidence involves more than the mere collection of things. Each scene encountered tells a story. Each scene demands consideration of issues evident through observations made by the investigator's senses of sight, smell, and touch. Thus a complete consideration of physical evidence demands that investigators be critically observant. The information available in these simple on-scene observations can often be significant.

The Interpretive Value of Evidence

The value of an item of evidence is not based solely on its mere presence in the crime scene. Crime scene analysis demands that the investigator consider the interpretive value of the evidence. Crime scenes are often likened to a jigsaw puzzle. The police arrive at a scene generally devoid of answers but containing numerous artifacts. Each artifact is, in effect, a piece of a puzzle. Unfortunately, the police do not have all of the pieces to the puzzle, nor do they have the luxury of referring to a picture on the box containing the puzzle pieces. The crime scene technician is left to ponder innumerable questions regarding the scene. For instance, is a given artifact part of the puzzle to be solved, or is it perhaps related to some event that occurred hours or days before? Just as the addition of each piece to a jigsaw puzzle brings clarity to the overall picture, the consideration of each artifact in the scene brings knowledge to the event being investigated. Chisum and Rynearson commented on this interpretive value of evidence when they noted that "the full meaning of evidence is a function of time and the item's surroundings."[1]

In other words, the value of evidence is far more an issue of context than it is of mere content. Merely owning the pieces of the puzzle is not enough. The investigator must be able to place the pieces in the overall picture. For example, the presence at the crime scene of a bloody shoe mark that is identified with some specific individual is significant. The ability to distinguish that shoe mark as having been made at or near the time of a beating, for example by evaluating the disturbed spatter beneath the shoe mark, is of far greater value. In the same fashion, the physical location of the shoe mark in the scene, which perhaps contradicts an explanation offered as to why the shoe mark is there, is of equally important value. This aspect of context and the interrelationship of evidence to the scene and other items is a major reason why the crime scene technician documents the scene through sketches and photographs. Lacking the ability to functionally place an item of evidence back into the scene, the value of these interrelationships would be lost.

Case Example: Scene Context and Interrelationships

A husband returned home in the middle of the day and discovered his wife beaten to death. Overwrought, he claimed to have begun attempts at CPR and immediately notified the police. EMS (emergency medical service) technicians arrived moments after the 911 call and found him on the floor, bloodied from top to bottom. The scene investigation and subsequent autopsy indicated that the woman was bludgeoned with an object that had distinct angled corners. Despite significant effort to locate anything remotely similar, the police failed to find such an object at the scene. They certainly failed to locate anything similar that was bloodied. In the examination of the dress shirt worn by the husband, a number of odd bloody pattern transfers were located, as seen in Figure 1.2. These patterns clearly indicated that some object with distinct angled edges, while bloody, was in contact with the husband's shirt. The angles and edges of this unknown item had similar dimensions to the angles and edges evident in the pattern of injury on the victim. The bloody pattern transfer, however, was a positive and not a negative, so contact with the injury itself could not explain its creation. The husband claimed that the pattern transfer was simply a bloody mark caused by his actions while performing first aid.

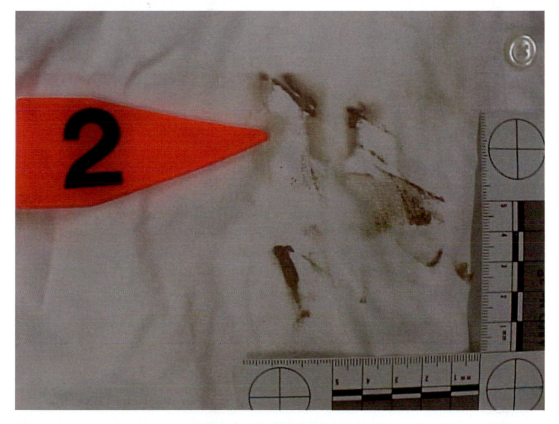

Figure 1.2 Bloody pattern transfers on a husband's shirt. The patterns show he was in contact with a bloody object. He claims not to have left or altered the scene and to have been alone. Yet the bloody object is not present in the scene. If he is truthful, this demands that someone else altered the scene. But that also demands that the husband was present in the scene before the alteration. His story cannot explain this contradiction.

Although the husband could present reasonable explanations for being bloody, the pattern transfer was a major contradiction. The police arrived on the scene while he was still inside; nothing was removed from the scene; and they certainly did not overlook a bloody weapon. The husband was alone, claimed to have come home alone, and made no claim of having left the scene for any reason. So nothing could have left the scene between the time the police were notified and their arrival. Granted, lacking a recovered weapon, there was no way to verify that the pattern transfer resulted from a "weapon." Yet the husband was clearly in contact with a bloodied item that was no longer present at the scene. The mere fact that the husband was bloodied was certainly expected and arguably explained in a variety of ways. But the fact that he was bloodied by something that was no longer present in the scene was significant, because no explanation offered could clear up this contradiction.

The husband being bloody was not an issue until it was examined in light of the scene context. In the crime scene, context is everything. It is only through context that the police derive conclusions. Forensic analysis may define specific facts about an item of evidence, but that can only tell us part of the story. Possession of data is meaningless unless we put it to work and look beyond the tree to see the forest.

In considering this context of the evidence, Rynearson and Chisum offered that such context might manifest itself in a number of ways. They classified these manifestations as:

- Predictable effects
- Unpredictable effects
- Transitory effects
- Relational detail
- Functional detail[2]

Predictable effects are those changes to the scene or evidence that occur with some rhythm or regularity. Based upon this regularity, such evidence provides the investigator a factual reference or, at the very least, an inference as to the actual time of the crime. Classic examples of predictable effects are found in forensic entomology, in which the stage of insect activity at a homicide scene allows the entomologist to establish the approximate period since death. Other examples include the onset of rigor and livor mortis in the body, which in a stable environment follows regular and somewhat predictable timelines following death.

Unpredictable effects are changes that occur in an unexpected or random fashion. Unpredictable effects alter the original scene and the evidence. If unrecognized, such effects can cause significant misinterpretation of the scene. A classic example of an unpredictable effect is found in the entry of police or EMS into a crime scene. Oftentimes they open doors or turn on lights and then fail to report such actions. The subsequent observation by the crime scene technicians of these postincident changes often results in incorrect premises regarding when the crime occurred or the manner of entry or exit by the perpetrator. Other examples include the disturbance of an item of evidence, moving it from one location to another, or even the haphazard opening of a revolver's cylinder by the technician. As Chisum and Rynearson commented, such changes can be disastrous to the overall investigation, as the original context of the evidence is lost forever.[3] The order in which the investigator processes the crime scene is accomplished in part to prevent creating or including unpredictable effects in the crime scene documentation and subsequent analysis.

Transitory effects manifest themselves at the crime scene in a number of ways. Oftentimes they are fleeting. Unlike the body, the gun, or the bloodstains, transitory effects fail to stand out to the investigator. It is only through deliberate observation that transitory effects are noted. Examples of transitory effects include the heat of a burning or burnt cigar or cigarette, the presence of ice in a glass, or odors of chemicals or colognes that are present when the first officer arrives. A technological example of a transitory effect is the heat signature of a tire on a roadway. When evaluating significant crashes or fatality accidents, a handheld thermal-imaging device allows the crime scene technician to differentiate new and old tire marks on a roadway. Ultimately, time and environment will destroy any transitory effects present in the scene. A failure to observe, smell, or feel such evidence in the early stages of the scene will result in the loss of such information. Many of the actions and processes we expect first responders to accomplish and make note of upon arrival at the scene are directed toward identifying such evidence.

Relational details manifest themselves through the investigator's ability to physically place items in the scene. Examples of relational details would include the presence of a void pattern on a wall surrounded by spatter, a clustering of shell casings on grass, the presence of a weapon in close proximity to the victim, the recognition that a gunshot wound is distant vs. close. Through relational details, the investigator is able to establish a correlation between various objects. Significant in our understanding of relational detail is the belief that the item was actually at a given location at the time of the event. Those arriving at the scene or those processing the scene often displace easily moved items, changing and destroying the relational information. In an exterior crime scene, the position of small items can also be changed as a result of wind, rain, or water flow. The crime scene sketch and associated measurements allow the scene investigator to document these relational details. It is rare that the scene processor will recognize every relational aspect that may subsequently be at issue during trial. This is one reason that the measurement and fixing methods such as triangulation and baseline techniques should be applied to all items of evidence, not just those the scene processors think are important at the time. These measurements are often seen as laborious and unnecessary, but without them, information to prove or disprove a relational detail may be lost.

Functional details manifest themselves in the operating condition of items in the scene. Is the weapon capable of operating in a normal fashion? Was the clock alarm set for a specific time? Did the deadbolt operate normally? All of these are functional details. Each tells the investigator something about what was possible or impossible given that specific item. Functional details assist the investigation in a variety of ways. They can disprove specific allegations (e.g., "I dropped the gun and it just went off") or help define when the crime occurred (e.g., the alarm was set to go off automatically at 5 A.M.).

Using Rynearson and Chisum's five effects is a functional and appropriate method of evaluating the information and evidence present in the scene. The author, along with Bevel, offered an additional approach to evidence observations when discussing crime scene reconstruction.[4] When considering each item observed in the scene, the investigator should ask three questions about that evidence:

1. What is it and what function did it serve?
2. What relationship does it have to any other items of evidence or to the scene itself?
3. What does it tell us about timing and sequencing aspects?

How an item is used in the scene is not always congruent with what the item actually is or how it was originally intended to be used. Just as important, recognizing the nature of the item will assist the investigator later when he or she begins looking at relationships and decides whether the item is foreign to the scene. Knowing this prevents the investigator from wasting investigative effort at some future point. The first consideration then is to identify the item, if possible, and consider its use, function, or purpose in the scene. Consider the example of an empty wax paper roll that is found in the kitchen area of a suspicious fire. A wax paper roll in a kitchen is not unexpected. This is certainly an item one would find in many kitchens. Is it merely a pre-incident artifact left by the kitchen owner? That is certainly possible. If true, the item lacks evidentiary value and will likely be left without further examination or processing for fingerprints. Pursuing the "what function did it serve" portion of the question, however, forces the investigator to examine other possibilities. The fact that the roll is empty and located in an area between two sources of low burn is of interest, since wax paper is an effective "trailer" that allows the arsonist to spread fire in a scene with little if any subsequent residues. The nature of this residue is such that it might easily be overlooked. The consideration of the wax paper as an arson trailer and any subsequent effort to resolve the issue may result in locating additional evidence. Considering why the item was present in the scene changes the investigator's perspective about the item from one of a pre-incident artifact of no importance to one in which the item may have significant evidentiary value.

Most crime scene investigators have heard of or seen the forensic linkage triangle in one form or another (Figure 1.3). The function of the forensic evidence linkage triangle

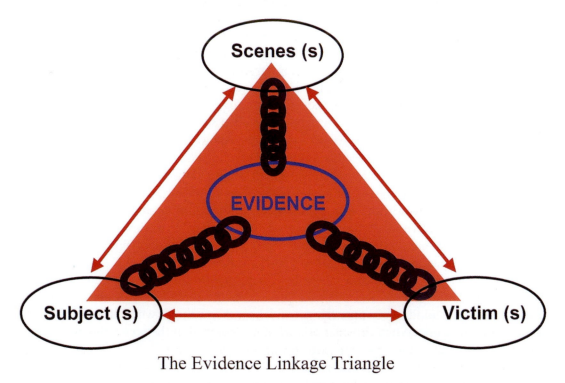

The Evidence Linkage Triangle

Figure 1.3 The forensic linkage triangle reminds us that items of evidence are used to establish specific links or relationships between the suspect(s), the victim(s), and the scene(s).

is to remind the investigator that each item discovered must be considered as a mechanism of linking the scene, the victim, or the suspect in some form or fashion. Ultimately, every piece of evidence is considered against this concept to determine whether any links exist and if they are of evidentiary value. The nature of these links may or may not serve to illuminate investigative issues. This is particularly true in our consideration of trace evidence. For example, in a suspected domestic homicide that occurs in the victim's residence, the presence of fibers consistent with the clothing of a "suspect" spouse has little evidentiary value. Both had access to the home and routinely interacted with each other, therefore transference of fibers would be an expectation. On the other hand, in a stranger rape, in which the suspect is located hours later and fibers consistent with the victim's sweater are located on the suspect's clothing, this link has obvious evidentiary value. Every item of evidence must be considered to see if some link between the three entities is possible. If the links exist, the investigator must then consider whether it has evidentiary value or is explainable through some other innocent mechanism.

After considering relational issues, the last questions deals with timing and sequencing aspects. Timing and sequencing are two distinct concepts. Timing aspects allow us to place the time of the crime in some form or fashion. Sequencing aspects help the investigator decide how or in what order the crime occurred.

Some classic examples of timing aspects at a crime scene are meals that are in preparation or completed; the condition of stomach contents of homicide victims; and alarms, clocks, or timers that are set but have yet to go off. The pathologist will often provide significant timing aspects through the consideration of body temperature or the evident stages of livor and rigor mortis. All of this evidence suggests the relative or actual time of the crime.

Sequencing aspects tell the investigator in what order certain events occurred as the crime proceeded. Crimes are not instantaneous events. Criminals must approach the scene, act within the scene, and then depart. The consideration of the various items of evidence will lead to a definition of what are often referred to as "time snapshots" of the crime, specific moments when specific actions occurred. One of the most critical elements of crime scene analysis is the process of logically ordering these snapshots in order to understand how the events proceeded. It is sequencing information that allows the investigator to do this. Sequencing information can present itself in almost any format. Examples of sequencing information include the disturbance of a bloodstain pattern by a shoe mark or hand print; the order in which a series of items are recovered from the floor; or the manner in which radial cracks emanate from a series of bullet holes in pane glass. Each example allows the investigator to understand the order in which specific events occurred. By considering all of the sequencing information, the crime scene investigator is able to objectively sequence a majority of the events composing the crime. Together, timing and sequencing aspects provide significant information to the criminal investigation, and neither type of information should be overlooked.

Each approach described allows investigators to evaluate the evidence and information they find within the scene. By identifying Chisum and Rynearson's effects, or by pursuing the three questions (what is it, what relationship does it have, and what does it tell us about timing and sequencing), the investigator adds clarity to the overall understanding of what the scene represents. Crime scene technicians cannot simply be garbage collectors. They must know what they are looking for, and they must understand what each piece of the puzzle tells them. As important as it is to the job to understand what we are looking for in the crime scene, it is equally important to understand what we are trying to prevent from occurring while at the crime scene. This leads to consideration of the question, "What does a good crime scene examination entail?"

Good Crime Scene Examinations and Scene Integrity Issues

Every action taken in the crime scene has some level of destructive effect on the scene. This is a given and something that cannot be escaped. Scene degradation occurs from the moment the crime begins and continues until the last officer turns off the lights and leaves the scene. Actions of suspects, witnesses, the first responding officers, EMS, the environment, and certainly those of the crime scene processor will result in the disturbance and alteration of the scene. Given this understanding of the inevitability of scene alteration, the basic goal of any processing methodology is to limit the damage and recover as much evidence and context from the scene as possible. No one has yet defined the one and only "right" way to process a crime scene, but any good processing methodology will demand the following five basic ingredients:

1. Knowledge
2. Skills and tools
3. A methodical approach
4. Flexibility
5. A coordinated effort

First and foremost, those responsible for examining the crime scene must understand what they are trying to accomplish. Knowledge on the part of the crime scene investigator is critical. As previously discussed, the scene processor is more than just a collector of things; the investigator must seek the interpretive value of the evidence. By understanding what he or she is looking for, what the lab can do with the evidence, and what questions should be asked, the investigator will not overlook information and evidence. Beyond knowledge, the processor must also have the skills and tools required to recover evidence. Examples of skills and tools that may be necessary to achieve the result the investigator seeks include competency with the available camera equipment and the ability to conduct fingerprint recovery or casting of impressions. Whatever approach is used to process the scene, it must be methodical. To be methodical, the method must be all-encompassing and purposefully regular. Without a methodical approach, steps are often forgotten or overlooked. Some processors find the use of investigative checklists a functional means of maintaining this regularity. An outstanding example includes Geberth's *Practical Homicide Investigation Checklist and Field Guide.*[6] As positive a tool as checklists are, rote compliance with a checklist can be as dangerous as not using one. Therefore, the scene investigator must maintain a level of flexibility in dealing with each new scene. Flexibility on the part of the investigator is critical. Each scene presents its own challenges. The investigator will have to make hard decisions when presented with fragile evidence or competing or con- tradicting interests. For example, basic crime scene methodology tells us that we should photograph evidence before collecting it. But what if the evidence is a shoe mark in the soil outside a burglary homicide, and the investigator realizes a storm is moments from breaking? If a downpour occurs, the evidence will be destroyed, so the investigator must act promptly to preserve or collect the mark before that happens. The investigator must always recognize when it is necessary to break from routine in order to achieve the desired end result.

Case Example: Flexibility and the "Wrecking Crew"

Late in winter in Alaska, a body was located in the woods. It lay supine in a snow bank, with portions of the head showing above the snow. As normal excavation techniques progressed, immediate investigative concerns were noted due to the fact that a blood flow was observed moving up the nose of the victim. The final position of the victim was clearly not the only position of the victim subsequent to wounding. The initial excavation resulted in identification of the individual, who had been reported missing several months before. With obvious concern as to the likely movement of the body after wounding (suggesting a dump site or subsequent scene alteration), processing continued.

When all the snow had been removed, it was apparent that the body would not be easily recovered. A number of freeze and thaw cycles had occurred in the months after the individual's disappearance, and the body now lay in a thick layer of ice. This layer encased the entire body and clothing, and it was 4 to 6 in. in depth. In an effort to free the body, heavy-duty heater/blowers were used to loosen the ice all around the boundary of the body. Following several hours of effort using the heaters, as well as attempts to chisel around the body, the investigators were no closer to freeing the body than they were before. The heater was damaging the clothing on the body to the point of burning small sections that were exposed too long.

As evening fell and the temperature dropped, it was clear that some extraordinary method was needed. Part of the overall problem lay in the fact that the body itself was a block of ice, frozen solid by long-term subarctic exposure. The crime scene investigators, partly out of studying the situation and partly out of desperation, chipped a deep hole along the high side of the body, large enough to insert a long-handled 2-in. flat-bladed pick. The blade of the pick was then forced into this hole, and outward leverage was applied to the handle. To say the least, a number of raised eyebrows were observed, and guffaws were heard as the technique was applied. Where the body had refused to budge through all the prior attempts, in a matter of seconds a slight pop was heard. Then the body popped from the grip of the ice, intact and none the worse given the odd method of retrieval. The two investigators, although vindicated in their method, were subsequently tagged as the "wrecking crew."

As in this example, occasionally the investigator will be presented with a problem that defies normal practice and procedure, an issue or situation that is not mentioned in any textbook. Nevertheless, some action must be taken, and the crime scene investigator cannot be afraid to take a calculated risk. Flexibility in practice allows the investigator to see through the problem and find a solution.

Last, but certainly not least, of the necessary ingredients for a good scene examination is the need for coordinated effort. A scene examination conducted without coordinated effort is unlikely to achieve the desired result. Each team member and those assisting in the processing must know what every other team member's responsibility is. Coordination ensures that all actions are taken in the proper order and that important aspects of the scene examination are not sacrificed without prior consideration.

If the investigator is to achieve the goal of crime scene processing, which is the collection of the evidence and scene context in as pristine a condition as is possible, then these five basic ingredients of good scene-examination practice must be combined with an understanding of basic scene-integrity concerns. The crime scene technician's methods must consider three specific scene-integrity issues:

1. The addition of material to the scene
2. The destruction of material in the scene
3. The movement of material in the scene

Addition of material results in what are referred to as postincident artifacts. In effect, the authorities end up creating evidence that was not there to begin with. These postincident artifacts can obscure the investigator's understanding of the crime and are often used successfully by defense counsel to cast doubt about the guilt of a suspect or to support some alternative theory about the event. Examples run the gamut of shoe marks to blood trails. Officers, EMS technicians, supervisors, almost anyone can end up adding artifacts to a scene. Individuals walking in from a wet exterior may leave shoe marks on floors and carpets, intermixing with the shoe marks of concern. EMS or first responders who attempt first aid often create blood trails and bloodstain patterns through their manipulation of the body. Hours into a late-night crime scene, it would be unusual not to observe coffee cups that were not there before processing began. The addition of material is always a concern. *Every contact does leave a trace.*[7] Therefore, any effort directed at processing the scene must consider this issue, and investigators should actively seek to eliminate any action that creates unnecessary postincident artifacts. At the very minimum, the crime scene investigator must distinguish between those items that are postincident artifacts and those that are actual evidence related to the event. It is this consideration that requires the responding officers and investigators to ask and determine who did what to the scene prior to their arrival. Later chapters will discuss isolating the scene and establishing collection points for evidence and equipment, all of which are directed at preventing the addition of material.

Destruction of material results in the loss of an item's evidentiary value. There are numerous examples of the destruction of evidence. Officers arriving at a burglary scene early in the morning are likely to encounter a dew trail caused by the approach or departure of the subject. By the time the investigator arrives, it is unlikely this dew trail will remain, having been trampled by well-meaning officers searching the area. A classic example of destruction occurs when a homicide victim is placed into the body bag. Prior to this action, there are often bloodstain patterns on the clothing or exposed skin surfaces. During transport in the body bag, residual bleeding occurs, which contaminates the body bag itself. As a result, saturation and contact stains end up on the clothing and victim, obscuring forever the original patterns of interest. Another example of destruction occurs when, by focusing too quickly on the primary scene, investigators miss evidence on the periphery. As additional resources arrive in the form of more people and vehicles, this peripheral evidence is trampled and lost. Many of the investigative beliefs on how and when to deal with fragile evidence, as well as the necessity of using an established methodology, are directed at preventing the destruction of material in the scene.

Movement of material is the last scene-integrity issue. Movement is often the result of investigative processing techniques, but when such movement is unchecked and unrecognized, it clouds the investigator's understanding of the crime scene. In effect, movement of material significantly changes the relational aspects observed by the crime scene investigator. A classic example of movement of material occurs when an officer encounters a weapon. SWAT officers often demonstrate a special penchant for kicking weapons from the hand of a suspect, despite the apparent fact that the suspect is dead. Consequently, by the time the investigators arrive, the weapon is 15 ft from the suspect. If no one takes responsibility for this action, it leaves open the argument that the suspect was shot after giving up and putting down the weapon. Similarly, patrol officers have been known to take a suicide weapon from the vicinity of the body and place it on the opposite side of the room. The investigator arrives and, without recognizing this change, perceives what was a suicide as a likely homicide. The opening of doors, the opening and closing of window shades, the turning on or off of lights and appliances, all of these actions change the scene. It is not uncommon in the photographic documentation of a crime scene to observe a single item in various locations. Counsel will use these contradictory photographs to challenge the appropriateness of the crime scene processing or to claim that the resulting false relational links prove some alternative theory. As the police arrive, or as a result of processing the scene, many of these movement actions are necessary. But each unrecognized movement creates false relational links. The crime scene investigator must know when these changes were made, by whom, and for what reason. A golden rule for the crime scene investigator is simply, "Know who did what."

Case Example: The Compassionate Officer

Police officers checking a remote campsite discovered a woman strangled and sexually assaulted. Investigators were called to the scene and, upon arrival, found a scene clearly in disarray, with the body lewdly displayed and the ligature still in place around the victim's neck. The woman's upper body was exposed as well, and her legs were spread and positioned open with the knees bent up and off the ground. This position was clearly a post-homicide act by the perpetrator. Oddly enough there was a small piece of clothing that was neatly folded and placed across the vaginal area. Given the disarray of the scene and the disrespect shown to the victim subsequent to her death, this item made no sense in the overall picture.

Scene processing continued in a normal fashion, but the clothing modestly placed across the victim's crotch remained a significant issue, particularly given the placement of the body. While interviewing the first responding officers, one of the younger officers admitted his role in altering the scene prior to the arrival of investigators. He was dismayed and disgusted by the perpetrator's actions at leaving the victim as she was. He felt it his duty to offer her, in death, some modicum of modesty. Therefore he chose to place the clothing over her crotch before the world arrived and saw her as he had found her. In his eyes it was only proper and appropriate that she be given this respect.

It is often a specific action taken by a responder at the scene that changes the scene. As in this example, the change may not have been necessary, yet it did occur. The crime scene investigator always seeks to identify and understand why these changes happen. By understanding the three scene-integrity issues as they relate to the techniques and approaches of scene processing, and by applying the five basic ingredients to good scene examination, the crime scene investigator is more apt to make good, defensible decisions when faced with difficult choices at the scene.

Investigative Ethics

The investigator's role in repressing crime was defined as simply conducting objective investigations. This is done in an effort to define who did what, and why. The crime scene is clearly a source of significant information in this pursuit, and the crime scene technician or crime scene investigator is thus likely to remain actively involved in any future trial associated with the event investigated. How does the investigator maintain objectivity and remain true to the profession throughout the search for justice?

First and foremost, it is important to understand that the investigator has no personal stake in what he or she finds in the scene. Sir Arthur Conan Doyle once wrote a line in which his fictional character Sherlock Holmes states, "I can only find evidence Watson, I cannot change it." This is a true statement about the crime scene investigator. Until we look, we do not know what we will find. Once we find it, we cannot ignore it simply because we do not like what it tells us. But more importantly, the crime scene investigator really should not care what he or she might find. If the goal is truth, then how that truth plays out is of little consequence to the investigator. Sure investigators will all have pet theories and suspicions, but if they are true to their profession, then they will remain open and objective, certainly willing to consider new evidence. Investigators must report their findings objectively and truthfully to whomever needs to know, no matter how those facts impact on their personal beliefs.

This idea of neutrality is often lost in the profession of policing because of the close association of the police with the DA's office and the desire of the police to protect the citizenry from "bad guys." Rookies are often heard to comment that "my job is to put people in prison." Granted, the police are the ones who initially deny individuals their freedom through arrest. But in no book on law enforcement will the investigator find "putting people in prison" to be a responsibility of the police. This is a function of justice, not law enforcement. The job of law enforcement has always been to bring people to justice. The nuances between these two statements, although perhaps minor in form, are major in context. The failure of police to recognize those differences often leads to significant failures in the justice system.

Will investigators believe in the guilt or innocence of the individuals they investigate? One would hope so. Otherwise, why would they send cases forward to the DA's office? Belief in the involvement of some individual in a crime is not a bad thing, so long as that certainty does not cause the investigator to sway from procedures or alter testimony. What we do not know as investigators can always hurt us, and simply put, investigators rarely know everything about how or why an event occurs. The author was once involved in a case in which an alleged police expert argued that the police had only the responsibility to investigate a crime to the standard of probable cause. Once that standard was achieved and the suspect arrested, it was then the duty of the DA's office to carry on the investigative process. But it is important to note that *probable cause is not the investigative standard.* Granted, the police can arrest at that level, but the professional investigator's standard has always been to investigate to the point of beyond a reasonable doubt. That is the standard of the court, so why would we pursue anything less? Truth is only achieved through detailed study and analysis. Investigators may not achieve that standard in every investigation, simply because they lack specific evidence to really know everything they need to know. Nevertheless, it must remain the standard they pursue.

The investigator will never have every piece of the investigative puzzle. To prevent that lack of knowledge from affecting their role in the criminal justice system, investigators must follow good investigative ethics. Such investigative ethics demand that investigators collect and document the evidence as they find it. The investigator cannot pick and choose what to report. Just because a particular item of evidence does not conveniently fit into the pet theory of the hour does not mean that it is unimportant or unrelated. This is a particular concern in the early stages of the investigation, when many initial subjective theories abound.

Investigators must consider all viable theories until they are excluded. They cannot proceed with tunnel vision. Excluding an alternative theory, such as one supported by an alibi, may work out fine in the early stages of the investigation, when no one is there to challenge the investigator. Sooner or later, however, someone — most likely a defense counselor — will force the investigator to consider those alternative theories. The wrong time to deal with and rationally argue for or against such a theory is clearly while testifying at trial. The investigator should have considered whether a theory or alibi is viable long before the state enters into trial. If the crime scene investigator is truly objective, there will be few if any alternative theories presented by counsel that have not been taken into consideration. Granted, that will not prevent counsel from raising issues, but the investigator cannot effectively argue such theories for the first time while sitting in the witness chair. The environment of a courtroom is far too emotional and far too antagonistic for on-the-spot objective evaluation.

Another critical aspect of investigative ethics is the need to treat all facts the same. The investigator cannot differentiate in how he or she documents the information obtained. It is rare that there is not some form of exculpatory information present in the crime scene, something that suggests someone other than a particular suspect is responsible. These contradictions are expected and they are nothing to be afraid of. Investigators must report exculpatory information and not subjectively exclude it from their report. Once again, investigators do not know what the scene will tell them, and they have no personal stake in what the evidence ultimately says. So nothing defined by the scene is bad.

The last consideration of investigative ethics is that investigators can never let any lawyer, defense or prosecution, tell them what they know. Investigators must factually and objectively report the information that they have obtained. How the lawyers choose to use the information is their business, but they do not get to define what the investigator knows or what he or she has found.

In a book directed at law enforcement officers, it would seem unnecessary to state that altering testimony, engaging in perjury, or creating false evidence is clearly outside the scope of an investigator's duty. Unfortunately, the fact of the matter is that this message must be made, and it is a message that we must make again and again at every level of law enforcement. Perhaps as a result of some warped sense of duty or out of sheer frustration and disillusionment with a system that seems to make no sense at times, crime scene investigators and analysts have altered evidence, manufactured evidence, and failed to testify truthfully. Although still rare, these failures call in question the integrity of every single law enforcement officer. As a result, even an honest mistake becomes the fodder of conspiracy theories by lawyers out to make a buck through civil suit or groups out to further some agenda.

There was once a very basic attitude in law enforcement, "Better that ten guilty men go free, than one innocent man go to jail." That belief seems for some reason to have gone by the wayside. Our fears over the inhumanity we see day to day and our desire to stop it, and the ever-growing chasm between law enforcement and the citizens we serve: both factors may have indirectly affected our beliefs. Despite the confusion, despite the chaos of our system, and despite the personal dilemmas we face daily, investigators must always remember that small integrity and objectivity failures will ultimately lead to larger integrity and objectivity failures. It can never be stated too loudly nor too often that investigators must remain objective and true to their profession.

Summary

The system of justice may be convoluted, but the role of the crime scene investigator in that system is straightforward. The investigator seeks to establish the truth regarding a given event or crime by objectively pursuing this truth without regard to any other agenda.

Truth is defined by the collection of evidence, factual information that allows us to draw some conclusion about an event. The crime scene investigator realizes the significance of physical evidence in defining this truth. Unlike testimonial evidence, physical evidence does not lie. We as humans may well misinterpret what the physical evidence is telling us, but that is our own fault. Physical evidence will aid both the investigator and the jury in corroborating or refuting much of the testimonial evidence. Used properly, physical evidence establishes a foundation of objective information that few, if any, can refute.

To understand why investigators take the steps they take in collecting this physical evidence, one must understand the underlying conceptual ideas behind crime scene investigation. Oftentimes the investigator is faced with competing interests and difficult choices. Whatever action s/he takes must be defensible in court. It is not enough to have taken the action; the investigator must articulate why. Understanding these principles allows the investigator to make difficult decisions when faced with contradicting requirements.

The collection of items at the scene, the mere ownership of physical evidence, is not the end-all of crime scene processing. The crime scene investigator must realize the interpretive value of evidence, which depends on the context in which the evidence is found. This context is manifest in five effects or details: predictable effects, unpredictable effects, transitory effects, relational details, and functional detail.[9] The consideration of each manifestation adds additional information to our understanding of the crime and brings us closer to the truth.

In pursuing this context or the interpretive value of the evidence, the investigator must also ask three questions about each item of evidence found. What is this item and how was it used? What relational links will this item establish between the scene, the subject, and the victim? In what way will this item define the time of the crime or sequence the events associated with the crime? Once again, by looking at more than mere content and by considering the context in which the evidence is found, the investigator will find that far more information is available in seeking the truth of the matter.

However, in pursuing the end result of the crime scene processing — the collection of as much physical evidence in as pristine condition as possible — it is imperative that the investigator realize there are many means to this end. There is no one "right" way to process a crime scene. When evaluating methods, the investigator must consider that any good processing methodology will include five key ingredients. These are *knowledge* on the part of the investigator, the *skills* and ability to accomplish what the knowledge defines must be done, and a *methodical approach* that defines in what order it will be done. *Flexibility*, or the ability to adapt to the requirements of a given crime scene, is another key ingredient. The fifth ingredient is the need for *coordinated methods*, where the efforts of all participants mesh to maximize the information extracted from the crime scene. When these five ingredients are combined with an understanding of the three scene-integrity issues, the investigator can functionally and reasonably choose between different courses of action at the scene. The investigator knows that his or her methods must prevent, whenever possible, the addition of material into the crime scene, the destruction of material in the scene, and the movement of any material in the scene. Each in its own way will damage the investigator's understanding of the crime or event being investigated.

Finally, with all of these issues in mind, the investigator recognizes the need to have a strong sense of ethics. Crime scene work often presents significant personal ethical dilemmas. Any of several factors — a sense of duty, a belief in the guilt of a particular individual, or simply disgust with a system that often allows half-truths to be presented to the jury — can warp the investigator's purpose. Investigators must never allow such issues and their associated dilemmas to lead them to stray from their professional duty, which is to remain an objective seeker of truth.

Suggested Reading

Bevel, T. and Gardner, R.M., *Bloodstain Pattern Analysis: with an Introduction to Crime Scene Reconstruction*, 2nd ed., Chap. 2, Crime Scene Reconstruction, CRC Press, Boca Raton, FL, 2001.

Nordby, J.J., *Dead Reckoning: the Art of Forensic Detection*, Chap. 1, Method — the Andrews Case, CRC Press, Boca Raton, FL, 2000.

Chisum, W.J. and Rynearson, J.M., *Evidence and Crime Scene Reconstruction*, Section III, Reconstructing Crime, Rynearson, J.M., Ed., Shingletown, CA, 1989, p. 93.

Chapter Questions

1. What is the basic goal of crime scene processing?
2. The police utilize five basic objectives in seeking their goals of preventing crime and disorder and protecting the life and liberty of their fellow citizens. Which two of the five objectives are more closely related to the crime scene investigation and why?
3. Why is physical evidence more objective than testimonial evidence such as eyewitness accounts?
4. The interpretive value of evidence is a function of what?
5. Rynearson and Chisum (1989) identified five ways in which context manifests itself in the crime scene. What are they?
6. Bevel and Gardner (2001) defined three questions that the investigator should ask about evidence. What are they?
7. Describe and explain the forensic linkage triangle.
8. Any good crime scene examination requires five key ingredients. What are they?

9. Describe and explain the three crime scene-integrity issues that the investigator considers.
10. What is the standard that the investigator uses when pursuing a solution to crime, and why is this standard necessary?

Notes

1. Chisum, W.J. and Rynearson, J.M., *Evidence and Crime Scene Reconstruction*, Rynearson, J.M., Ed., Shingletown, CA, 1989, p. 93.

2. Ibid., p. 93.

3. Ibid., p. 94.

4. Bevel, T. and Gardner, R.M., *Bloodstain Pattern Analysis: with an Introduction to Crime Scene Reconstruction*, 2nd ed., CRC Press, Boca Raton, FL, 2001.

5. Ibid., p. 36.

6. Geberth, V.J., *Practical Homicide Investigation Checklist and Field Guide*, CRC Press, Boca Raton, FL, 1997.

7. Saferstein, R., *Criminalistics: An Introduction to Forensic Science*, 6th ed., Prentice Hall, Englewood Cliffs, NJ, 1998, paraphrased as presented by Edmund Locard.

8. Doyle, Sir Arthur Conan, *The Complete Strand Version of the Adventures of Sherlock Holmes*, Wordsworth Editions, Ltd., Hertfordshire, UK, 1996, p. 982.

9. Chisum, W.J. and Rynearson, J.M., *Evidence and Crime Scene Reconstruction*, Rynearson, J.M., Ed., Shingletown, CA, 1989, p. 93.

Understanding the Nature of Physical Evidence

2

Throughout this text, one particular theme will be evident: physical evidence has a greater power and ability than testimonial evidence in defining what happened at any crime. This is not to say that testimonial evidence should be ignored or excluded, but an understanding of physical evidence will provide an objective foundation for any subsequent theory of the crime. Physical evidence is what it is, and it is tangible. Presented with DNA (deoxyribonucleic acid) evidence from the scene or a photograph of the condition of the scene, only a fool would argue that the DNA was not really there or that the scene looked other than as depicted in the photograph. To gauge testimonial evidence, all we have is our perception of the individual. Does she appear honest? Did he have the ability to perceive what he reported? Any witness is capable of unconsciously misperceiving events or, for that matter, purposely misrepresenting events based upon some personal agenda. This is a well-established fact in the study of criminal investigation. Understanding this, we do not exclude testimonial evidence, but we certainly seek corroboration of testimonial evidence through some objective means. That means is called crime scene analysis, which is the end result of any effort directed at crime scene processing. The more physical evidence recovered, the more likely a functional and objective theory of what transpired during the crime will be forthcoming.

In 1933, Luke S. May commented in his text *Scientific Murder Investigation* that "before [the detective or investigator] can successfully conduct a search for evidence, he must know what he is searching for."[1] Never were more accurate words written, for in order to collect physical evidence, the crime scene technician must first recognize it. In the past, that was a relatively easy process. Items such as fingerprints, bloodstains, shell casings, or weapons stood out at the scene, leaving little doubt that they might serve a function in solving the crime. But with each new advent in technology, the capability of forensic science increases. Now, even the slightest trace of evidence (e.g., saliva on a stamp) has the ability to provide clear and specific information to the investigation.

Before the crime scene technician can expect to process a scene for evidence, s/he must have a working knowledge of the nature of physical evidence, what a crime lab can do with it, and how best to collect it. This in no way presupposes that they are experts in every discipline of forensics, but lacking this understanding, the technician is likely to overlook evidence or collect it in an inappropriate fashion. Crime scene examination is very much a discipline involving, as Bruce Wiley says, "lab rats and field mice."[2] Both must understand each other's role; both must work together in order to achieve truth. Therefore, it is incumbent in the job for the crime scene technician to take an interest in all aspects of forensics and to try to remain current. An effective means of accomplishing this is to get involved in the various professional forensic associations.

Class and Individual Characteristics

Not all evidence is created equal. Some evidence provides specific and detailed information for the investigation, while other evidence provides only limited assistance. Based on specificity, the characteristics presented by all physical evidence can be classified in two categories: class characteristics or individual characteristics.

Class characteristics describe traits or characteristics of evidence that allow the item to be compared with a group. Tuthill and George defined class characteristics as "characteristics that are common to several objects."[3] Class characteristics serve forensics best in eliminating possibilities. Depending upon the similarities or differences of the class characteristics, items can often be excluded as belonging to a group. Class characteristics may include size, color, common manufacturing patterns, or taxonomic classifications. By comparing the class characteristics of a questioned item to a known item, should any one of the class characteristics fail to match, the forensic scientist can effectively establish that they are not of common origin. For example, consider the recovery of a piece of glass from a suspect's clothing. The color and refractive index (the manner in which the glass bends light) can be compared with a sample of known glass from the crime scene. If the forensic scientist discovers that either characteristic does not match, then s/he has effectively established that the two items are not of common origin. On the other hand, if both characteristics match, that does not prove the items are of common origin. In that instance, they simply cannot be excluded as having come from a common origin. In other words, it is possible that the suspect glass came from the scene, but it is also possible it came from some other broken glass somewhere totally unrelated to the scene. Class characteristic evidence is routinely presented in court, but it must always be properly represented. Class characteristic evidence is also widely used as a screening mechanism by the forensic scientist.[4] As a screening tool, exclusion at the class-characteristic level prevents wasting time and money on a more-detailed examination of other additional characteristics. For example, if screening of a blood sample finds a specific antigen (a class characteristic) in the known sample but this antigen is absent in the questioned sample, then the two samples are excluded as having a common origin. The exclusion is objectively established between the two samples, and there is no need to pursue an expensive and time-consuming DNA examination.

Individual characteristics make up the second category. Individual characteristics allow the forensic scientist to compare the item with a specific object or person and include or exclude it as having originated from it. Tuthill and George define individual characteristics as "unique," resulting from natural variation, damage, or wear.[5]

The classic example of individual-characteristic evidence is the fingerprint. Fingerprints result from natural variation in human beings, and no two fingerprints are the same. Presented with a fingerprint in the crime scene that is compared with a known fingerprint of an individual, the fingerprint examiner will either include or exclude the individual as having left the print. There is no in-between, no gray area.

Of course, if something interferes with the examination, even when dealing with individual characteristics, it is possible to have a "no conclusion is possible" result. This latter situation is an inconclusive result due to having insufficient detail to make the comparison.

Individualization, the examination of individual characteristics, is a primary goal of forensics. It is powerful evidence to conclusively state that this blood, this fingerprint, this hair came from this individual. Of course, the power of this evidence is directly related to the context in which the crime scene technician finds it. Evidence considered outside of context is of no value. For instance, DNA is often touted in the press as a panacea for crime solution, and it is certainly effective evidence. But the presence of matching DNA alone does not prove a crime. If it did, then every male in the world should shake in fear at the possibility that his lover might become the victim of a sexual murder and his DNA might be discovered on the body. If the mere presence of DNA establishes a crime, then we may as well send the juries home and start rounding up all the husbands and lovers. No matter what evidence is available, no matter what its characteristics, it is only by considering all evidence and the context in which it is located that solutions to crime are found. Thus every piece of available evidence in a scene has function, and the crime scene technician cannot afford to haphazardly collect or preserve it.

The list of forensic disciplines is a long one, including everything from forensic anthropology to forensic toxicology. This chapter considers some of the more common forms of physical evidence discovered at the crime scene that is evaluated by the forensic scientist, including fingerprint evidence, serological and biological evidence, trace evidence, firearms evidence, tool-mark evidence, shoe and tire impression evidence, document evidence, general chemical evidence, and computer forensics. For further insight, there are a number of texts available that deal with the full scope and specific processes used in all of these forensic disciplines.[6,7]

Before turning to the specifics of the various categories of physical evidence, it is important to define and describe several concepts that relate to a number of these evidence categories. These concepts are: Locard's Principle of Exchange, cross contamination, and mechanical fit.

Edmund Locard, a French criminologist, is considered by many to be the father of the modern crime laboratory. *Locard's Principle of Exchange* is stated simply: *every contact leaves its trace*. Locard believed that whenever two objects came in contact with one another, material from the first would be transferred to the second, and material from the second would be transferred to the first. This principle is the underlying theory behind trace-evidence examination. It is directly applicable to our actions in crime scene processing and the theories underlying crime scene analysis. One has to wonder if Professor Locard truly understood just how correct he was. Would he be surprised by our modern ability to find DNA in minute quantities? Given the technology revolution, the true question in forensics today is, "How far will technology go in allowing us to recognize these contact traces?"

Cross contamination is directly associated with Locard's Principle of Exchange and is caused by inappropriate handling of evidence. It is particularly problematic in trace-evidence examinations and serology examinations. By exposing one item of evidence to another, evidence from the first is passed to the second, and vice versa. Consider the following example. In collecting rape evidence, the investigator often deals with the victim in the blind, not knowing at first why she is there or what she will say. In many instances, the victim identifies a perpetrator within a short period, and the investigator talks to a suspect on the same day. If the investigator were to set the victim in a particular chair prior to collecting her clothing, a transfer of fibers from the clothes to the chair would occur. If the investigator were then to bring the suspect into the same office and set him in the same chair prior to collecting his clothing, there is a possibility that fibers from the victim's clothes could transfer from the chair to the suspect's clothes. This is cross contamination. It is the responsibility of the crime scene technician to isolate evidence and use validated collection techniques to prevent cross-contamination issues.

Finally, *mechanical fit* or "fracture matching" is a unique form of evidence. Mechanical fit is where an item is damaged and pieces are deposited in the scene. These pieces, when collected, are preserved in their original shape and condition. When the source object is located and examined, it may be possible to see exactly where the piece broke off from the original object. (See Figure 2.1.) Because the breakage is accidental, it is also random, which makes it possible to individualize a specific piece to a specific item.

Fingerprint Evidence

Fingerprints are one of the most common forms of evidence sought in the crime scene. The use of fingerprints as a mechanism of identification dates back to the 17th century. In the field of forensics, fingerprints have been an integral part of crime solution for over 100 years. Fingerprint evidence provides individual characteristics. An analyst can identify or exclude an individual print by comparing ridge details and their associated minutiae in the questioned print with a known inked fingerprint of an individual. (See Figure 2.2.)

Fingerprints develop in the human fetus at about 12 weeks. To date, no fingerprints from different individuals have ever been found to match. This is a significant fact, considering that fingerprint analysis has been studied for over 100 years and that automated fingerprint identification systems (AFIS) routinely catalog and compare hundreds of thousands of fingerprints. Fingerprints are classified and stored in these systems using the modified Henry System, developed by Sir Edward Henry in India in 1894. The taxonomy for ridge detail includes three basic ridge patterns: loops, which make up approximately 65% of all patterns; whorls, which make up approximately 30% of all patterns; and arches, which make up the last 5% of all patterns. There are subdivisions within these patterns: plain and tented arches; ulnar, radial, and double loops; and plain, central pocket, and accidental whorls.

Fingerprint examination and identification is based on both the ridge detail and the minutiae present in the patterns. Ridge identification is based on at least 15 different ridge characteristics, including ridge endings, bifurcations, short ridges, enclosures, ridge dot, ridge break, angular formations (deltas), overlap, spurs, bridges, trifurcations, crossings, changeovers, ridge pinch, and loops. In modern forensics, the identification of a fingerprint is no longer based on an arbitrary point system (e.g., finding eight or ten similar points). A point system was first suggested by Edmund Locard as a guideline, and point systems were routinely used in fingerprint identification up until 1973. Today,

Figure 2.1 Mechanical fit is a method of individualization. An item can be associated with a specific source based on the unique way the two fit together. The unique damage of the metal razor blade shown in this photograph and the position of the staining on both sides of the break produce a form of mechanical fit.

fingerprints are identified and individualized based upon "finding agreement of individual characteristics — with no unexplainable dissimilarities."[8]

The fingerprints found deposited in the crime scene consist of approximately 98% water. The remaining 2% is a combination of grease, oil, salts, and amino acids. In the scene, fingerprints can exist in three basic forms. Latent prints are considered to be the generally invisible prints created by the deposit of normal body secretions. Patent prints are fingerprints caused by the deposit of contaminants (e.g., bloody or greasy finger marks) that are visible to the naked eye. Plastic prints are fingerprint impressions where a print has been deposited in a soft surface such as wax.

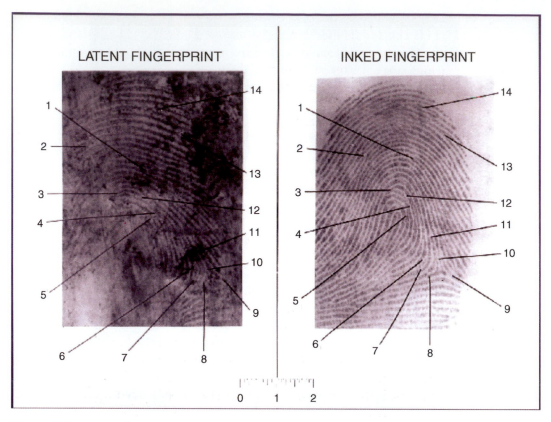

Figure 2.2 Latent fingerprints are compared with an inked fingerprint of an individual in an effort to identify or exclude a person as a source. The latent-print examiner looks at a variety of physical characteristics (minutiae) in the print to determine whether there is a match. (Figure courtesy of Special Agent [Ret.] Don Hayden. With permission.)

The crime scene effort directed at locating and recovering fingerprints is very much dependent on what surfaces are examined. The nature of the surface (e.g., porous, nonporous–smooth, nonporous–rough, or other special conditions) determines what techniques are used. Chapter 9 provides a detailed discussion of the various surfaces the technician is likely to encounter and crime scene techniques available for developing prints from those surfaces.

There are several important considerations the crime scene technician should take into account when processing a scene for fingerprints. First and foremost, the methods for lifting fingerprints on-scene represent only a fraction of the techniques available for recovering fingerprint evidence. Using chemical enhancements and a variety of alternative light source (ALS) technologies, a crime lab can recover fingerprint evidence in situations where on-scene techniques could not possibly recover functional evidence. For this reason, in serious cases the technician should never be in a rush to forego lab examination in lieu of the speedier on-scene techniques.

A second consideration is that fingerprints are quite enduring. Far too often, technicians arrive on scene and, because someone has touched or moved items in the scene, they do not even attempt to recover fingerprint evidence. Granted, fingerprints from these postincident actions are likely to be recovered, but in and of themselves they will not eliminate fingerprints from the participants of the crime. Fingerprints have been found in circumstances where one would never imagine the possibility of fingerprint evidence existing, for example, smooth objects directly exposed to flame and heat. Almost every advancement in modern fingerprinting relates to recovering latent fingerprints under difficult situations and on poor surfaces. When presented with these difficult surfaces, the technician should coordinate with a supporting fingerprint analyst before presuming that fingerprint evidence cannot be recovered.

A final consideration is that there really is no way to accurately predict when fingerprints will be deposited. Any number of conditions might prevent a fingerprint from occurring on a surface that otherwise would be expected to hold prints. Simply put, the technician is not to be surprised by the lack of fingerprints.

Serology and Biological Evidence

Serological and biological evidence present the investigation with both class and individual characteristics for comparison. Biological evidence can exist in the form of blood and other body fluids such as spittle, semen, vaginal secretions, or any other any DNA source such as bone or tissue. Prior to the introduction of forensic DNA techniques, wet-bench serology was directed primarily at class differences in human blood. These class differences included the specific blood type (A, B, O) as well as variations in blood antigens. Differentiations in antigen systems were based on the Lewis system, the Rhesus system, and a host of enzyme markers, including phosphoglucomutase (PGM), erythrocyte acid phosphatase (EAP), and peptidase A (Pep A). All of these characteristics were class characteristics, but underlying them were a number of studies that set probabilities for finding the particular characteristic in any given population. Wet-bench serology provided a description of the questioned blood sample, compared that sample with any known blood samples, and then offered a backdrop of statistical evidence documenting the frequency of the expected markers. The statistics developed from this type of examination ranged widely, with the low end of the range being as few as 1 in 200 (meaning that 1 in every 200 people tested would demonstrate this particular characteristic in their blood). In other instances, the examination would offer much higher discrimination, such as 1 in 200,000. Statistics of this nature were hardly useful to the fact finder. Regardless of the numbers, the statistics still provided only a class comparison that was excellent for eliminating suspects but left the jury to ponder the circumstantial probability when the evidence indicated inclusion in a group.

In addition to evaluating blood in this fashion, serologists have long been able to identify the presence of sperm and semen by testing for acid phosphatase or by microscopic examination for sperm cells. They can also determine if saliva is present by testing for the presence of amylase or starches, and they can distinguish between other body fluids such as urine, vaginal secretions, or fecal matter.

With the onset of forensic DNA evaluations, all of these tests have taken on a more significant role, since individualization is now possible as well. The existence of deoxyribonucleic acid (DNA) was first reported in 1868. The structure of DNA was later discovered by Watson and Crick in the 1950s.[9] This understanding of DNA structure would ultimately lead to the most significant scientific revolution in history, changing medicine, microbiology, and forensics.

It is important to understand that the following discussion of DNA techniques examines DNA from the nucleus. Nearly every type of cell in the body has a nucleus, including cells found in skin, organs, bone, and muscle. In blood, however, only white blood cells have a nucleus. Red blood cells shed their nucleus during their early formation. Each nucleated cell has a single nucleus, and each nucleus holds 23 pairs of chromosomes. At conception, each parent contributes one half of these 23 pairs, creating a completely distinct set of chromosomes in the offspring. Within each of these chromosomes are approximately 100,000 genes that define every trait of the organism. The basic subunits of these genes are guanine (G), cytosine (C), adenine (A), and thymine (T). These substances always pair in specific combinations, with G always pairing with C, and A always pairing with T. The variable combinations and order present in the chromosome (consisting of over 3 billion base pairs) are the result of natural variation through heredity. With the single exception of identical twins, every individual's DNA can be distinguished from the next individual's.

In 1984, Alec Jefferys, an English geneticist, made a significant breakthrough in his study of genetics in seal populations. He found a mechanism of mapping variable regions of the DNA molecule, allowing him to compare the DNA of one source with that of another. In time, Jefferys recognized the possibilities of his discovery and carried this research into the study of how genes evolve in humans. After further study and development, a technique known as restrictive fragment length polymorphism (RFLP) was integrated successfully into forensic work in the U.K. RFLP was used in 1987 to resolve the homicides of Lynda Mann and Dawn Ashforth in the town of Narborough, England. This case was detailed and made famous by Joseph Wambaugh's book *The Blooding*.[10] As a forensic tool, RFLP was certainly important. It evaluated several loci, and from this comparison it was able to provide significant discrimination between samples. Typical discrimination for RFLP examinations were 1 in 5 million, a far cry from the lower discrimination provided by wet-bench serology. In many instances, individualization was statistically possible. As a result, DNA was coined as the "genetic fingerprint" by the press and received significant hype. Having been rushed into the venue of forensics, DNA technology received a significant challenge in the late 1980s but ultimately weathered the storm. An offshoot of these challenges was the development of DNA guidelines, which helped eliminate some of the poor work demonstrated early on by some labs. Beyond its role as the "genetic fingerprint," DNA significantly broadened the range of samples that could be compared. Previously, serology was primarily concerned with blood and other body fluids. Using DNA, any sample that contained nucleated cells had the potential for individualization.

RFLP's downfall as an investigative tool was its reliance on large and undegraded samples. The typical biological sample recovered from a crime scene is both small (e.g., 1- to 2-mm-sized bloodstains) as well as degraded from being exposed to environmental conditions. RFLP required a significant amount of genetic material to make an evaluation, and since each cell only holds a single nucleus, there is only so much material available. Nevertheless, DNA analysis using RFLP technology proved to be a windfall to criminal investigations, allowing science to more effectively include or exclude individuals accused of crimes.

Given the limitations of RFLP in forensic work, a new technique known as polymerase chain reaction (PCR) was developed. PCR allowed the scientist to copy the DNA structure in small samples, quantities too small to allow for RFLP techniques. By making copy upon copy (literally millions of copies of the original material), enough genetic material was created to allow a DNA examination. PCR techniques examined a completely different gene area than RFLP, known as the HLA DQA1. Unfortunately, the statistical discrimination produced by PCR under these circumstances was significantly lower than that presented by RFLP. Although PCR technology allowed evaluation of much smaller samples, it was not uncommon to have statistical results as low as those found in the old-style serology. Oftentimes, PCR results ended up being nothing more than an expensively produced class characteristic, a far cry from a genetic fingerprint.

To resolve this problem, the next major breakthrough in forensic DNA was the development of short tandem repeat (STR) technology. STR combined concepts of PCR but created statistical discrimination that was higher than that developed through RFLP. Thus degraded and small samples could be examined to the point of individualization. STR statistics routinely exceeded 1 in 6 billion, so much so that few laboratories report higher numbers and simply refer to such a conclusion as identification. With this technology, samples as small as the amount of saliva deposited by licking a postage stamp have resulted in individualizations. Using STR, the ability to evaluate such small samples is significant, but it also presents a greater potential for cross contamination of samples during collection. There is no doubt that as technology advances, crime labs will develop additional guidelines on the collection and handling of DNA evidence.

Another recent advent in DNA technology is that of mitochondrial DNA analysis (mDNA). Mitochondria are organelles in each cell. They are the true powerhouse of the cell, where the production of adenosine triphosphate (ATP) occurs. Because of their critical role in producing ATP, these organelles exist in numbers within each cell, and each mitochondrion is a source of mDNA. Mitochondrial DNA is not the same as DNA from the nucleus. It consists of some 16,569 base pairs, forming a loop structure.[11] The mDNA is inherited singularly from the mother. Because of the manner in which it mutates, it can be compared through a maternal line of related individuals over several generations. Thus, given a questioned sample of mDNA, such as a hair or bone from a decomposed body, the mDNA of any maternally related relative can be compared with the sample to determine if they are related. This kind of evaluation can be particularly effective in missing-person cases, where there is no standard DNA sample of the missing person. In such an instance, an mDNA sample from a mother, grandmother, or sister can be used instead. The use of mDNA is quickly gaining popularity in hair analysis. As the text will discuss, typical trace hair analysis is limited by its ability to discriminate samples, and very few questioned hairs found in the crime scene provide sufficient root material to allow for a standard DNA analysis. An mDNA analysis, however, is routinely possible with hair, providing a far more objective exclusion or inclusion of an individual to a questioned hair.

Biological evidence in the crime scene is routinely encountered in one of two volumes. There is either a large volume — represented by stained articles, tissues, or fluids — or there are trace amounts. The following are general guidelines for the collection of biological samples. Because of the variations in approaches, the technician should always coordinate collection techniques with the supporting crime lab.

When presented with volume amounts, the crime scene technician generally collects the stained articles (e.g., clothing) and, after air drying the item, submits it for evaluation to the crime lab. In some instances, where the stained item is not of evidentiary value (e.g., a bloodied chair), a sample of the volume is taken, and the sample alone is

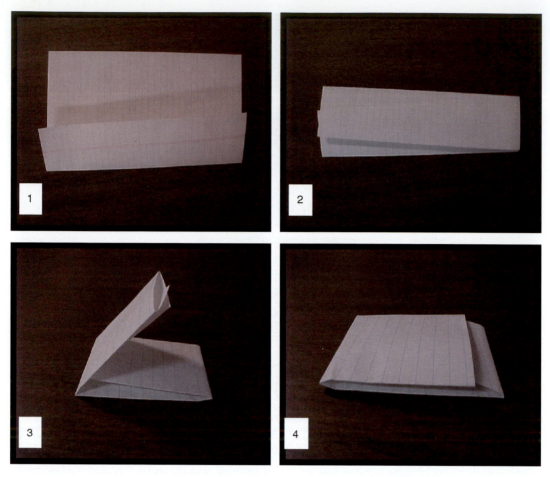

Figure 2.3 The pharmacist's fold is an effective way to collect samples of small substances (e.g., dried blood, paint chips, etc.). It is produced by folding the two outer thirds of a paper in toward the middle, but at a slight angle. This results in a fold where one end is slightly larger than the other. The folded paper is then folded in thirds again, but this time lengthwise. The smaller of the two ends is then inserted into the larger. The pharmacist's fold prevents particles from escaping the fold. This is then sealed inside another appropriate container.

submitted for evaluation. In a dry form (e.g., dried blood), samples can be cut out or scraped into a pharmacist's fold using a clean razor blade. The pharmacist's fold (Figure 2.3.) is then secured and placed in another envelope that is sealed with tape. If the volume is wet (e.g., a pool of fluid), the technician moistens a sterile swab with the sample and then air dries the swab. Once air-dry, the swab is double-sealed in envelopes or any other suitable container.

At the scene, stained articles such as clothing are collected in whatever fashion is necessary and taken to a drying room. Placing bloodied clothing in plastic at the crime scene is a necessary evil, since there are no other options. There are no drying chambers on scene, and the technician cannot hang the clothing on the back porch and wait for it to dry. The clothing must be contained, as the blood represents a biohazard. If the technician places the bloody item in paper bags, the bags can become saturated, resulting in inadvertent blood contact through the bag to other items. Handling the evidence in this fashion represents both a biohazard and a potential cross-contamination issue. Of

Figure 2.4 Items such as clothing recovered for serology and DNA evidence should be packaged to prevent blood or other fluids from being transferred from one point on the item to another. This is accomplished by folding the item in paper, in such a manner that no direct contact occurs. Once seized at the scene, these items must be returned to a drying room, air dried, and then repackaged for shipment to the crime laboratory.

course the clothing should not be wadded up and simply tossed in a plastic bag. This kind of treatment will result in postincident artifacts and may cause cross contamination of a stain or DNA from one area of the clothing to another. Poor handling of this nature can result in losing important scene context information. Whenever possible, lay the item out flat on clean paper, and then fold the paper in to enclose the clothing without placing cloth against cloth (see Figure 2.4). Once this is accomplished, the item is enclosed in any viable nonpermeable container (e.g., a plastic bag) and taken to a drying room or chamber as soon as practical. There it is removed and allowed to dry completely before repackaging it in paper using the same technique. Biological samples should never be containerized for the long term in plastic or nonbreathable containers. No matter how dry the technician thinks the item is, mold and bacteria can develop and degrade the sample.

Trace amounts of biological evidence represent a greater challenge. First and foremost, they must be recognized. The use of an alternative light source (ALS), which is discussed in Chapter 9, may help in locating trace amounts of fluids like urine and semen. Once located, samples are collected in the same fashion as volume samples. If possible, the area in which the trace biological sample is found should be collected (i.e., the area cut out or the entire article seized). If this is not possible (e.g., bite marks on a corpse), a sterile swab is used to collect as much of the trace sample as possible.

Given the ability of STR to work with extremely small samples, it is imperative that the technician consider any likely source of contact with DNA in the scene and then consider collecting these items. It is also important that cross contamination be excluded. Samples should be collected independently using clean instruments. Technicians should change gloves in between handling different items, and they should never chance the introduction of foreign DNA (e.g., by licking the adhesive of an evidence envelope).

Trace Evidence

Trace evidence consists of a wide variety of materials. The nature of trace evidence is typically that of class characteristic, but in some instances it may provide for individualization. Trace evidence is encountered in the crime scene in the form of hairs and fibers, glass, paints, and soil. Using a variety of instrumentation, including the comparison microscope, infrared spectrometry, automated refractive index systems, and scanning electron microscopes (SEM), the forensic scientist can compare these trace amounts to known samples.

Hairs and Fibers

Using classic trace-evidence examination, hairs can be distinguished first by species, and in the case of human hair, by the general race (Caucasian, Negroid, Mongoloid) as well as the general location of the body from which the hair originated (head, pubic, facial, axillary). Examination of the structure of the hair — its diameter, scales, medulla, cortex, and pigment — will allow the hair to be compared with a known hair sample. Hair analysis by the trace-evidence examiner is most often a class-characteristic examination. In some odd and rare instances, such as the use of hair treatments or peculiarities produced by repetitive dyes, it may be possible to establish individualization of a hair to a known sample. Trace-evidence hair examinations are quickly being replaced by mDNA analysis because mDNA provides far more objective data.

Fibers, like hairs, are classified first by their originating source (e.g., naturally occurring, manufactured, or synthetic). Manufactured fibers offer additional areas for discrimination. Dye and composition peculiarities can be examined through elemental analysis using an SEM, and optical differences can be evaluated using both microscopy and infrared spectrometry. Trace-evidence analysis of fibers routinely results in class-characteristic determinations, but it can also lead to individualization.

Hair and fiber transfers usually result from contact between people, objects, or clothing. Depending upon the source, this transfer may be limited in number. It has been suggested that 90% of any transferred hairs or fibers are lost in the first 8 hours following the contact. Thus, depending upon the circumstances, only a small number of fibers or hairs may be left for recovery. In terms of collection on scene, hairs and fibers should always be considered as fragile evidence. Once the technician spots a hair or fiber, it should immediately be documented and then collected. Without fail, after seeing a single hair or fiber in the scene or on a corpse, the technician will step away for a moment only to return and find the evidence gone. Whether lost due to some incidental contact or because it simply fell to the ground, fiber evidence routinely disappears. Collect hairs and fibers upon discovery. In instances where there are several trace hairs or fibers, these are best collected by an instrument such as tweezers and placed into an envelope. The envelope is sealed on all edges and placed into a second container. The propensity for fibers and hairs to literally disappear cannot be overstated. Double-seal these items after collection to prevent their disappearance between the scene and the crime lab. The use of an alternative light source (ALS) is also effective in locating trace fibers. Any number of fibers may fluoresce under different wavelengths of light, aiding in their detection by the crime scene technician. (See Figure 2.5.)

In some instances, a general search for hairs and fibers is initiated on a surface such as upholstery, car seats, floors, or other items. The two most common methods for search and collection are taping and vacuuming. In taping, wide clear adhesive tape is cut in 8- to 10-in. lengths. Holding the two opposite edges, the technician applies the adhesive side of the tape to the surface in question and lightly applies pressure. This is done in very much the same way that one uses tape to remove lint from a suit. This single piece of tape is used to cover a specific area until its tackiness is reduced. It is then applied adhesive side down to a piece of transparent plastic (e.g., a document protector) and, if necessary, secured in place. Using a transparent plastic backing allows the trace-evidence examiner to conduct a visual examination and prevents the tape from sticking, as it would if the technician used a more porous backing such as paper. The process is repeated as many times as necessary to cover and collect loose fibers or hairs from the surface in question. Numerous tapings from a general area (e.g., a chair) can be placed on a single document protector, so long as each piece of tape is marked so it can be related back to a specific location (e.g., front, back, or seat). Separate backings should be used for distinctly different areas, such as when shifting from a passenger seat to a driver's seat. This prevents any potential cross-contamination issue. Once collected, the backings should be sealed in paper envelopes, once again keeping evidence collected from distinctly different areas in separate envelopes.

The forensic vacuum is another matter. Some crime labs hate them, while others support their use. The problem associated with a forensic vacuum is that the technician gets it all: dirt, dust, dried cheese whiz, anything and everything is picked up along with the hairs or fibers. When searching for hairs or fibers, the best advice before employing a forensic vacuum is to check with the supporting crime lab.

Glass

Examination of glass from the crime scene is typically directed at one of three basic determinations: glass type determinations, direction of force determinations, and sequence of force determinations. Type determinations compare a glass fragment with a known glass sample in an effort to determine if it can be excluded or included as having originated from a common source. Direction of force determinations evaluate the radial fractures present in the first concentric ring of glass fractures in an effort to determine in which direction force was applied to pane glass. Sequence of force determinations evaluate situations where multiple bullet defects in glass are arranged in close proximity to one another and their radial fractures meet. By considering the termination points of the radial fractures, it is possible to establish a sequence or order of the shots.

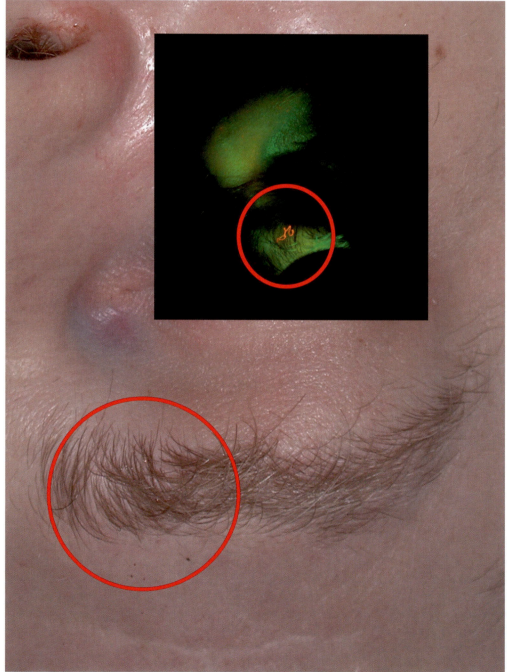

Figure 2.5 An alternative light source (ALS) is an effective tool for searching for fibers. Many fibers are nearly impossible to see in natural light but will fluoresce under different wavelengths of light. In the photo, the small fiber mixed in with the eyebrow of the victim is not visible. The inset shows the same area when viewed with an ALS. (Figure courtesy of Special Agent [Ret.] Don Hayden. With permission.)

All glass is not the same. A variety of "recipes" are used to make different types of glass, and even a general style of glass, such as pane glass, is different from sample to sample. As each batch of glass is produced, it may have a distinct mix of ingredients, slightly different from that of a previous batch. The temperature variations the glass is exposed to as it is manufactured can also result in variations in the properties of the glass from one sample to the next. Basic properties such as color, thickness, and curvature may be evident from one glass source to another, and each offers a means of visual discrimination between two glass samples. Optical properties of the glass, specifically the manner in which it allows light to pass through it, are defined by the various manufacturing variations. This quality is referred to as the refractive index (RI) and is easily measured in the crime lab on even the smallest sized glass fragments. All of these characteristics (the various physical properties and RI) are class characteristics, allowing the examiner to exclude specific glass fragments as having come from a specific source. As with any class-type evidence, a match of the class characteristics simply indicates the two glass samples could be from a single source.

A variety of glass evidence can be found in the crime scene. Pane glass is often fractured in burglaries or rapes, broken bottle glass may be involved in aggravated assaults, and glass from automobile lights and lenses may be present in hit-and-run accidents. Fragments of glass can be found on suspects when they have been in close proximity to pane glass breakage. As the pane of glass is fractured, the glass does not merely move in the direction of the force. The pane will reach a point of stress where the glass fails. As failure occurs, the pane will rebound. In the process, a cloud of oftentimes micron-sized glass fragments are expelled into the surrounding area, both in front of and behind the point of fracture. Therefore, an individual breaking the glass is likely to be caught in this glass cloud, and small fragments can be located in the hair, on the surface of clothing, and in particular in the seams and crevices of clothing or shoes.

In instances of pane glass breakage, the suspect's hair should be combed with a clean comb, seeded with cotton. Anything falling from the hair is caught on a clean examination paper. The paper along with the comb and cotton are secured using a pharmacist-style fold and then sealed in another container. The clothing of the suspect is collected as well, with the suspect undressing over a clean examination cloth. Both the clothing and the examination cloth are handled carefully during collection to prevent dislodging small fragments. Any item suspected of holding glass fragments should be thoroughly sealed to prevent inadvertent loss of the small fragments. When collecting other types of glass for type determinations, the technician should collect samples of all broken glass in the scene. Each sample should be marked as to its specific location in the scene as well as a warning that the item is sharp and fragile.

When presented with lens or light breakage at a hit-and-run accident scene, all fragments at the scene should be recovered. In addition to comparing the class characteristics of the particles to any suspect vehicle, it is also possible to individualize the fragments to a suspect vehicle through a mechanical fit. In this instance, the manner in which a fragment breaks off from its source may allow it to be placed back in the original item at a specific location. Mechanical fit elevates a class characteristic to the level of individualization.

Determining direction of force is a simple process and can be accomplished by the crime scene technician. It can always be repeated by the trace-evidence examiner, but the evaluation is straightforward and anyone properly trained can accomplish it. The purpose of the evaluation is to establish in which direction force was applied to a pane of glass. By understanding the direction of force, the technician can often identify staged scenes, such as those associated with alleged arson and burglary cases. The method of evaluating direction of force is referred to as the 4R Rule. This rule states that **Ridge** lines on **Radial** fractures are at **Right** angles to the **Rear**.

The first consideration in conducting the 4R Rule evaluation is to locate radial fractures that are within the first concentric fracture. Radial fractures radiate out from a central point in the fracture. Concentric fractures encircle the central area of the fracture at various distances. Together, the radial and concentric fractures create a spider web effect, as seen in Figure 2.6. The fragments from the inner concentric fracture tend to be pie shaped with a relatively narrow terminating side on one end. This is not always the case, however, and in some instances the technician may have to reconstruct the glass on scene or at the lab in order to locate an appropriate radial fracture. It is important to locate the interior radial-fracture fragments, since evaluating radial fractures found on second- or third-tier concentric fractures may not be accurate. An obvious consideration in this evaluation is in knowing what side of the fragment was facing out and what side was facing in. This is best accomplished on scene by examining the remaining

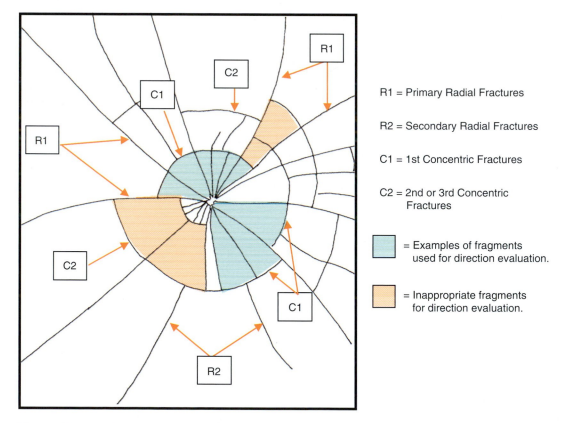

R1 = Primary Radial Fractures

R2 = Secondary Radial Fractures

C1 = 1st Concentric Fractures

C2 = 2nd or 3rd Concentric Fractures

= Examples of fragments used for direction evaluation.

= Inappropriate fragments for direction evaluation.

Figure 2.6 An important aspect of evaluating glass fractures is in locating primary radial fractures. These are the fragments made up by the first concentric fracture and the radial fracture lines extending out from it. The fragments colored in green would be appropriate fragments for evaluating direction of force. The fragments colored orange would not.

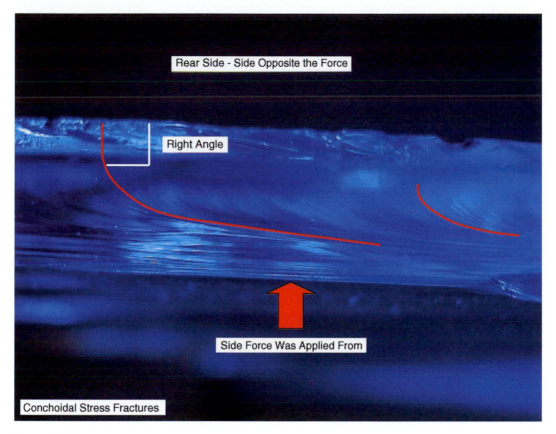

Figure 2.7 The 4R Rule says that Ridge lines on Radial fractures are at Right angles to the Rear. The ridge lines are the curving conchoidal fractures seen in this side view of a piece of glass. The red lines have been added to better illustrate the hard-to-see conchoidal fractures. The fracture lines will be at a right angle to one side of the glass and nearly parallel to the opposite side. Where they appear at right angles is the side opposite the force.

fragments, particularly any remaining in the window pane. Residues and contaminants from the surface facing inside will look and feel differently than those facing the outside.

Once an appropriate radial-fracture fragment is located and a determination of inside vs. outside is possible, the technician turns the fragment and looks at it in profile. Conchoidal fractures will be obvious in the edge of the fragment. These fracture lines will lie parallel to one side of the glass, and on the opposite side they will lie at nearly a 90-degree angle (a right angle). The side of the glass where the conchoidal fractures lie at right angles is the rear of the glass, the side opposite the force. The side where the conchoidal fractures lie nearly parallel is the side where the force was applied. (See Figure 2.7.) The technician may find it necessary to turn the glass fragment in the light or seek different lighting to see the conchoidal fractures clearly.

In instances of multiple bullet defects in pane glass or windshields, examination of the termination of radial fractures will allow, in some instances, a sequencing of the shots. Additionally, by examining the bullet defect itself, it will be possible to determine in which direction the bullet was moving. Both of these evaluations are described and explained in a discussion of trajectory analysis in Chapter 10.

Paints and Polymers

Paint and other polymers are encountered in a variety of crime scenes. Hit-and-run accident scenes account for a significant number of paint analysis requests. It is also possible to encounter situations in which trace amounts of paint are deposited on a suspect, victim, or object during the commission of a crime. In such instances, the investigator may wish to determine if the paint is similar to some known paint sample. Paint is manufactured in a wide variety of types for different functions. Above and beyond the color of the paint or its basic type (enamel, latex, etc.), the ingredients and chemical makeup of the paint may offer a means of discrimination. In circumstances involving full- or partial-thickness paint chips, the sequence and layering of the various components (primers, base coats, and clear coats) can offer a method of discrimination as well. The trace-evidence examiner uses a variety of instrumentation, including fluorescent microscopy, infrared spectrometry, gas chromatography, and the scanning electron microscope to look for and differentiate the various differences between samples.

Paint samples represent the true trace-evidence sample, as there is rarely very much material present. Paint transfers and paint chips should be collected in their entirety. When recovering a paint transfer on a solid object such as a paint trace on a fender or bumper, the technician should try to cut beneath the transfer in order to get the full thickness. As a last resort, the sample can be scraped from the object. Paint chips represent another opportunity to make a mechanical fit, therefore larger paint chips should be collected carefully and packaged so they are not further damaged. Small chips or scraped transfers can be packaged in clean pill bottles or in pharmacist's folds.

Known samples of paint are collected from any source the technician believes is involved in the transfer. If the known standard is recovered using a tool to chip it off, full-thickness chips should be collected, and the technician should ensure that a sufficient quantity is collected. If at all possible, it is better to cut a small section from the known sample to ensure that a complete standard is recovered.

Soils

Soil is a complex mixture of inorganic and organic substances, and it can vary significantly, even across a single backyard. This variation may not be evident by mere visual examination (e.g., color or consistency), but it will become evident through analysis of the content and quantity of the various minerals and substances. The trace-evidence examiner looks at the content of the soil, seeking environmental variations that will allow one sample to be compared with another. Environmental contamination or unique environmental settings can lead to variation from sample to sample. One useful approach is to evaluate pollens contained in a sample. Plant pollens are easily identified by their structure, and the presence or absence of a specific pollen type in the soil may allow the examiner to exclude the soil as having originated from a particular source.[12]

Known samples of soil from the scene can be placed in small, clean, pint-sized paint cans. Generally, a minimum of $1/2$ to 1 cup of material is suggested for any analysis.[13,14] Samples should be taken from a variety of probable contact locations, such as points where participants walked, fought, or where tires rolled through. If the technician collects footwear or tire impression evidence, soil samples from the immediate vicinity of the marks should be collected as well. Known samples from the crime scene should be collected as soon as possible to prevent subsequent contamination or change. The soil should always be collected to an appropriate depth. For instance, if tire marks at the scene penetrate to several inches, the technician should recover soil to a similar depth.

Trace amounts of soil may be found on clothing, shoes, or tools used at a crime scene. Vehicle tires, wheel wells, undercarriages, floorboards, and pedals can also hold trace amounts of soil.

Trace amounts of soils should always be collected in their entirety and preserved in a container that will preclude loss. When trace amounts of soil are found on shoes or clothing, the technician should not attempt to remove the soil. The entire article should be packaged to prevent loss of any material and submitted for examination. If possible, soil samples should be allowed to air dry before final packaging. Situations involving safes or safe insulation may be encountered as well. Both trace and known samples of insulation should be collected and preserved in the same fashion as soil samples.

Gunshot Residues (GSR)

During a firearm discharge, a significant level of burned and unburned residue is discharged along with the bullet. These residues eject from the barrel, from the cylinder gap in revolvers, and during ejection of the cartridge in pistols. GSR residue contains trace amounts of three primary elements, antimony, barium, and lead. In the past, atomic absorption analysis (AAA) and neutron activation were the primary methods of evaluating whether these three elements were present on individuals involved in shooting incidents. Crime scene technicians would routinely swab the hands of victims and suspects who were believed to have fired weapons and submit these swabs for subsequent analysis. Unfortunately, neither negative nor positive tests were considered to be of probative value by the forensic scientist. False positive results were a common occurrence, since the three elements in question were found in other circumstances. Just the same, for a number of reasons, individuals who had handled a firearm would test negatively. An additional concern was that the presence of the residue simply indicated that the individual was in the vicinity of the discharge. The mere presence of GSR did not effectively place a weapon in the hand of the suspect. At the present time, AAA evaluations are not typically utilized in the U.S. Evaluation of GSR residues is still possible using the scanning electron microscope (SEM). The trace-evidence analyst still seeks to locate barium, antimony, and lead, but rather than finding these three elements in combination with each other, the SEM seeks unique particles that contain all three elements. This distinction is important, as research indicates that the three elements will occur together in a single particle only in gunshot residues. There is still a recurring concern as to what the presence of these elements in a given context proves. Some labs have assigned minimum threshold levels for the presence of these particles, while others believe that when they achieve certain thresholds, this is verification of "holding" the firearm. It is likely that continued research in this area may change the application and direction of this type of evidence. Given a lack of consensus, the technician should seek the advice of the supporting crime lab in terms of how and under what circumstances GSR evidence should be collected. As GSR particles are not easily observed, when on scene, the crime scene technician may have to conduct a nitrate test on objects such as clothing or bedding in an effort to identify possible GSR residues. Once located, the object is submitted for further evaluation by the crime laboratory.

Firearm and Ballistic Evidence

Firearms evidence holds both class and individual characteristics. Firearms analysis considers the weapon and any expended casings, bullets, or unexpended cartridges in an effort to associate these items to one another. Firearms analysis is also directed at examining gunshot residues (GSR) on objects and making distance determinations when GSR patterns are present.

It is important for the crime scene technician to understand proper morphology when describing weapons and ammunition. Excluding black-powder weapons and specialty weapons or ammunition, the following descriptions are functional for a majority of weapons discovered at a crime scene. The typical ammunition is referred to as a cartridge, a single and complete unfired unit of ammunition. The cartridge is made up of the projectile, referred to as a bullet. Bullets are of varying calibers and weights and are most often described based upon their construction (e.g., full metal jacket, semijacketed, hollow point, wad-cutter). In the case of shotguns, the projectiles are generally made up of a number of shot pellets or a single lead slug, all of varying sizes and weights, depending upon the particular ammunition involved. Bullets are seated in the cartridge case or, as in the case of a shotgun, enclosed by the cartridge case. This casing consists of a metal or plastic-and-metal cylinder, which holds both the gunpowder and a priming mechanism to ignite the gunpowder. (See Figure 2.8.) Cartridges are either center fire or rimfire, depending upon the location of the primer mechanism. In center-fire cartridges, a small primer cap is seated at the center and base of the casing. The firing pin of a weapon, upon striking the primer cap, ignites the primer compound, which in turn ignites the gunpowder. In rimfire cartridges, the primer compound is manufactured into the rim of the casing. The firing pin, upon striking the rim of the cartridge, ignites the gunpowder.

Weapons can generally be categorized as handguns, rifles, and shotguns. Handgun weapons are short-barrel weapons designed to be fired with one or two hands. The primary handgun designs are the revolver and pistol. A revolver has a cylinder in which ammunition is manually inserted. Depending upon the weapon, a cylinder can hold anywhere from four to seven cartridges. With each pull of the trigger on a revolver, the cylinder rotates to deliver a cartridge into alignment with the barrel. In order for the cylinder to rotate freely, there is a slight gap between the cylinder and barrel, referred to as the cylinder gap. The cylinder gap is important from a crime scene perspective primarily because it will often create a distinctive gunshot residue pattern. Once fired, casings remain in the cylinder of the revolver until it is manually emptied. A pistol, on the other hand, has an ammunition magazine. Cartridges are inserted into the magazine, and the magazine is inserted into the base or lower receiver of the weapon. The upper receiver of the weapon consists of a slide and barrel that that move along a tongue-and-groove rail on the lower receiver. To use the weapon, the user must load the weapon. This is accomplished by inserting the magazine while the slide is to the rear and then releasing the slide, or by pulling the slide to the rear after inserting the magazine. The action of the slide, after it is released and moving forward, lifts a single cartridge from the top of the magazine and inserts it into the barrel. At that point, the pistol is ready to fire. When the trigger is pulled, the cartridge fires and a bullet is expelled. At the same time, the slide is forced to the rear, and a small ejector pulls the fired casing from the barrel, ejecting it out into the scene. As the slide returns

Figure 2.8 Typical cartridge components. Center left is a center-fire pistol cartridge (A). It is composed of a casing (a1), bullet (a2), and powder charge (a3). Rifle cartridges are similar in construction to the pistol cartridge. Center right is a shotgun cartridge (B). It is composed of a metal-and-plastic casing (b1), shot of varying sizes packed in white polyethylene filler (b2), a powder charge (b3), and a number of different paper and plastic wadding or shot shell cups. These act as a spacer between the powder and the shots and filler. Any of the components can be found in the scene. The spacers and plastic shot cup are also capable of creating secondary wounds. In close- or near-contact wounding, gunpowder from a weapon can cause stippling, where particles of gunpowder are embedded in the skin.

to its forward position, a new cartridge is lifted from the magazine and fed into the barrel, once again reloading the weapon. After the initial manual loading, this process is automatic unless a misfire occurs. Each time the trigger is pulled, a single cartridge will fire until the magazine is empty.

Rifles are long-barrel weapons designed to be fired from the shoulder. As with all firearms, they are manufactured in a variety of calibers. The term rifling refers to a series of grooves manufactured in the barrel of the weapon that give the projectile spin. This spin stabilizes the bullet in flight, making it more accurate. In the development of firearms, prior to this discovery, all long-barrel weapons had smooth bores. Thus the term rifle was coined to distinguish a rifled-bore from a smooth-bore weapon. In fact, all modern pistols and revolvers are manufactured with rifling as well. This rifling on the interior of the barrel is made up of projections (lands) and depressions (grooves) that will twist either right or left. Rifle ammunition is designed and described in the same manner as handgun ammunition. Rifles can be magazine fed or manually fed, and they operate on any number of different mechanisms. They can be a single shot (each time the weapon is fired, a casing must be ejected and a new cartridge manually inserted), semiautomatic (magazine fed, where each time the trigger is pulled, a cartridge is fired and another automatically inserted), or an automatic (magazine fed, where so long as the trigger is pulled, the weapon continues to fire until the magazine is empty).

Shotguns are long-barrel weapons designed to be fired from the shoulder. They differ from rifles in that they have smooth bores. Shotguns typically fire a number of lead pellets rather than a single projectile, although single-projectile ammunition in the form of shotgun slugs is available. Modern shotgun ammunition consists of the cartridge, the pellets or projectile, and wadding or shot shell cup. The shot shell cup is a plastic device that acts as both wadding and helps keep the shot shells from expanding inside the barrel. Both wadding and shot shell cups will behave as a projectile, but they do not have the same flight characteristics as the shot and therefore do not carry as far. As with rifles, shotguns can be manually fed ammunition or may have a magazine. Shotgun magazines consist of a tubular mechanism located below the barrel. Magazine-fed shotguns operate primarily by a slide action (a "pump" shotgun) that requires a manual effort to extract the old casing and reload a new one.

Evaluation of a firearm by the crime lab always begins with an operational check. Can the weapon be fired as intended or, for that matter, at all? Are all safety mechanisms operational? What is the trigger pull? Any abnormalities are noted by the firearms analyst, as they may be of importance in explaining some aspect of the scene or incident. Firearms by design and operation create or share a number of class characteristics with the ammunition they utilize. These class characteristics include the caliber of the weapon; the shape of the firing chamber; the location of the firing pin; the shape of any extraction or ejecting mechanisms; and the number, size, and direction of twist present in the lands and grooves.

Presented singularly with a bullet recovered at the crime scene, a firearms examiner can identify a list of possible weapons that could have fired the projectile based solely on the caliber and the number, size, and twist of the lands and grooves present. This can be valuable information when searching for a suspect weapon, significantly reducing the number of weapons that must be considered. Once a suspect weapon is located that matches the class characteristics of the questioned bullet, additional bullets are test fired from the weapon. The firearm examiner then compares the striations present on the test bullets with those of the questioned bullet. This comparison is not of the marks left by the lands and grooves, but rather of smaller striations that lie parallel to the land and groove marks. Remember that the creation of the lands and grooves is a manufacturing process, and although they may appear quite smooth, there are microscopic variations in their surfaces, which differ from weapon to weapon. Additional variations in these surfaces occur through normal wear on the weapon (e.g., firing of the weapon) or through poor handling or cleaning. As the bullet is forced through the barrel, these small variations in the barrel surface mar the soft lead or copper of the projectile, as seen in Figure 2.9. Comparison of these microscopic variations allows for exclusion or individualization of projectiles to the weapon that fired them. Pellets fired from smooth-bore weapons do not hold individual characteristics, although slugs and shot cups may hold some potential for comparison

Recovered casings can be examined for a number of marks. As the firing pin strikes the primer or rim of a casing, it leaves a tool mark with microscopic detail, as seen in Figure 2.10. In the case of semiautomatic and automatic weapons, the casing is explosively forced back against the breech of the weapon during operation. This may result in a breech-bolt mark across the base of the casing. In weapons with ejector mechanisms, whether

Figure 2.9 Bullet comparisons are accomplished using a comparison microscope. The question bullet and a known bullet from a specific weapon are viewed simultaneously (look for the small vertical line that separates the two images), allowing the forensic firearms examiner to compare the microscopic striations of each side by side.

fired by the weapon or manually ejected by the operator, the casing will be marked by the ejector and extraction mechanism. In addition to any class characteristics presented by these marks, all of these surfaces are likely to hold microscopic variations as well. Comparison of any one of these marks may allow exclusion or individualization of a casing to a weapon.

Any projectiles and casings located in the crime scene should be seized and containerized. These items should not be marked on directly by the crime scene technician, as this may mar or destroy microscopic detail. Items such as weapons should not be superglue-fumed prior to any ballistics examination, as this may mar microscopic details. Ballistic evidence should always be individually containerized and the container clearly annotated as to where in the scene the item was recovered. Far too often, technicians collect a number of casings and throw them all in the same container. If multiple weapons are involved in the shooting, significant scene context can be lost by this action. The container should also prevent the bullet or casing from rolling around or rubbing up against other hard objects, as this may also damage microscopic detail. Film canisters or small pill boxes are an effective container for bullets, bullet fragments,

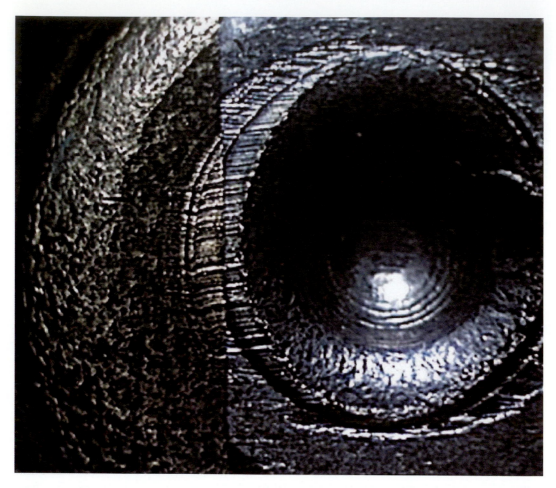

Figure 2.10 Casings are marked in a number of ways by a weapon. The two most common tool marks on the casing are the firing-pin mark and ejector marks. These marks are compared side by side in the comparison microscope. In this photograph, the two firing-pin marks indicate a match.

and casings. During recovery, the technician should not place metal tools such as knives and forceps in direct contact with these items. If bullets must be recovered from inside wood or other hard objects, specific care must be taken to not inadvertently damage the item as the technician removes the surrounding material. In the case of shotguns, all shot pellets and evident wadding should be collected. Because shot pellets do not have individual characteristics, they can be packaged together.

At the time of collection, any firearm in the scene must be made safe. This requires manipulation of the weapon by the crime scene technician. The technician should note the specific manner in which the weapon is or is not loaded. This includes, as in the case of a revolver, creating a cylinder diagram. The cylinder diagram demonstrates which cylinder was beneath the hammer and which specific casing or cartridge was in each cylinder. In some instances, a variety of different brands of casings or cartridges may be present in a weapon, providing important sequencing and scene-context information.

When presented with a gunshot residue pattern or a shotgun pellet wound pattern on clothing, skin, or other objects, the firearms examiner can conduct test firing of the suspect weapon to establish the distance of the weapon from the target when it was fired. These test firings require using similar ammunition as that used in the event. This is necessary because different ammunition may have different types of gunpowder with different flight characteristics and/or different amounts of gunpowder. The comparison is accomplished by firing the weapon into clean paper, from a variety of distances until a pattern of similar size and dispersion to the gunshot pattern or shot-pellet pattern is created. On occasion, the firearms examiner will conduct what are known as ejection studies. The purpose of this evaluation is to determine the distance and direction the weapon will eject a casing when held in any given orientation. Such studies have limited value, however, since the casings ejected from the weapon will roll when they hit the ground or ricochet off walls or other objects. In certain scene contexts, however, these determinations may be of some value to the investigative team.

Trajectory analysis is another area of ballistics that involves the firearms examiner, the crime scene technician, and the forensic pathologist. An examination of the trajectory of a bullet is possible based upon impacts in intermediate targets, the shape of the final defect, trace evidence on the bullets themselves (e.g., glass fragments or fabric), and information derived from the autopsy. Trajectory analysis will often provide specific information to the investigation. Trajectory analysis is explained in detail in Chapter 10.

Tool-Mark Evidence

Tool-mark evidence is usually the purview of the firearms examiner, although it is considered a distinct discipline. Tool-mark evidence presents both class and individual characteristics. Tools marks are formed by the interaction of various objects at the scene, creating three general categories of marks. These include striation, compression, and saw and drill marks. Striation tool marks are caused when the cutting edge of a tool is brought in contact with and slid against a target surface. An example is the scraping of a chisel along a door casing as it is forced into place. A compression mark occurs when a tool is forced into soft material. The side-to-side leverage of the chisel in the door casing will likely create a compressed tool mark. A hammer head against wood or gypsum board will create a compression mark. Tools with opposed jaws, such as bolt or wire cutters, create compression marks by forcing the tool edges into the target surface, cutting through it in the process. Saw and drill marks round out the categories.

Tools are manufactured through a variety of means, all of which create class characteristics. Besides characteristics such as size and shape, this may include mold variations or extrusion and milling marks from machining. These characteristics might be shared by several or several thousand of the same type of tools. Once the tools are employed, however, their individual history results in unique accidental variations on the tool edges. As with all forensic examinations, the tool-mark examiner begins with a comparison of class characteristics and then proceeds to these unique marks.

Tool marks in the crime scene present a challenge. As in the case of striations on a projectile, the most important tool-mark variations occur at the microscopic level. Poor casting of a questioned tool mark may or may not capture such information. A general rule of thumb is that whenever possible, the tool mark itself should be collected as evidence. Casting of tool marks at the scene is accomplished with commercially available products such as Microsil and Durocast, which are designed to capture the microscopic detail.[15] Use of these materials is discussed in Chapter 9.

At the crime scene, tool marks can be found in any number of circumstances. The internal mechanisms of a lock may hold striations from where lock-pick devices scraped against them. Doors, cash registers, and other objects that have been levered open will hold both striation and compression marks. Locks, chains, and wiring that have been cut will hold compression marks from the cutting edges of the tool used. On rare occasions, compression marks will be evident in bone during an autopsy. These are generally found in the form of marks caused by blunt force to bony areas (e.g., the skull) or where the tip of a knife blade was forced into underlying bone in a stab wound. In these circumstances, it is almost always necessary to recover the bone itself in order to make any comparison. Saw marks are encountered in everything from simple thefts to homicides in which the body is dismembered. At the time of recovery, both tool marks and suspected tools must be protected from additional damage. Tool edges and points are best protected by covering them (e.g., taping cardboard in place to cover the tooled surfaces). This will prevent the creation of additional marks on the cutting edges through rough handling at the evidence room or during transport to the crime lab. Once successfully cut from any object at the scene, a tool mark can be packaged in an appropriate container protecting it from further damage. If the tool mark cannot be cut out, then the larger object should be seized and the tool mark covered for protection. Any recovery effort by the technician will likely create additional marks on the item of evidence. Tool marks on the item should be marked clearly so the examiner can distinguish between the questioned tool mark and any postincident marks.

The use of tools at the crime scene also presents several opportunities to encounter mechanical-fit evidence. Oftentimes a tool is used by the perpetrator in a fashion totally unintended by the manufacturer. By using the wrong tool or using the tool in an incorrect fashion, breakage can occur. Tips of screwdrivers and chisels or pieces of saw blades may be present in the scene. If a suspect tool is later recovered, these pieces offer an opportunity to make an individualization of the tool to the scene evidence. A second mechanical fit associated with tools is based on paint. Many of the tools used in crime are not of the highest quality, and bargain-brand tools such as crowbars are often covered by thick enamel paint. When employed in the scene, this paint can chip off in large pieces. If the crime scene technician notes, recovers, and protects these paint chips, they also present an opportunity for individualization through mechanical fit.

An additional and very important aspect of tool-mark analysis is the restoration of serial numbers. Using a simple process, serial numbers that have been obliterated in metal can be visualized. The stamping of a serial number results in molecular disruption and change of the metal beneath the actual serial number mark. Even when the entire serial number has been removed, these changes may remain in the deeper sections of the underlying metal. The tool-mark examiner will grind down and polish the area where the serial number was, creating a smooth surface. Once this is accomplished, an acid is applied to the area. As the acid interacts with both the surrounding metal and the stamped metal, the serial number will become evident and can be read and photographed, as seen in Figure 2.11.

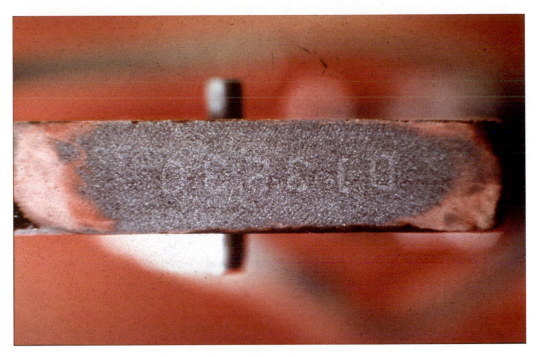

Figure 2.11 A serial number restoration on a weapon. Even after the metal has been filed, the metal beneath the serial number is changed. The tool-mark examiner first files and polishes the area where the serial number was and then applies a number of different acids to bring out the number.

Impression Evidence

Impression evidence is present at the crime scene in the form of shoe and tire marks, bite marks, tool marks, and plastic fingerprints. Tool marks and plastic prints have both been discussed and are handled by their respective disciplines. Bite marks are evaluated by a dentist trained in forensics.

Tire and shoe wear evidence is an independent discipline that evaluates both three-dimensional impressions, such as those encountered when a tire or shoe leaves an impression in soft dirt, and two-dimensional patterns such as shoe marks deposited in grease or dirt on a hard surface. Tire and shoe marks offer both class and individual characteristics. In tires, tread design, noise treatment, and tread-wear bars are all manufactured class characteristics that can lead to recognizing the type, brand, and even model of tire leaving the mark. Just as a firearms examiner can look at the characteristics of the lands and grooves on a single projectile and compare this to a database to identify possible weapons, a tire examiner can compare the class characteristics in the tire mark to several established databases, which will offer some indication of the type of tire that made the mark. These class characteristics are certainly important, but once a tire is sold, the individual history of each tire is unique. Accidental marks or variations in wear will offer individual characteristics that the tire-mark examiner can use for exclusion or individualization of a tire mark to a tire.

If enough tire marks are present at the crime scene, a variety of characteristics of the vehicle leaving the marks can be evaluated. This includes establishing the track width of the vehicle, which is often inappropriately referred to as the wheelbase. Track width is a measurement of the width across the front or rear axle. Given a dual set of tire marks (e.g., left and right side), track width is measured from either the outside tread to an opposite outside tread or from an inside tread to inside tread. Using this information along with the tread width of the involved tires, the examiner can establish a track width. Wheel base is a measurement from the center of the front hub to the rear hub, the distance between the two axles. Turning diameter is the diameter of the circle created when the front axle is turned to its full extent. In seeking these latter evaluations, the best advice is to contact the tire-mark examiner in order to properly record any details that may be required. Each represents a class characteristic that may be useful in limiting the list of suspect vehicles that need to be searched for or for excluding a specific suspect vehicle.

Shoe marks are evaluated by a number of manufactured class characteristics. Size and sole shape are both important, but tread design is a significant class discriminator in shoe marks. As with tire marks, major databases exist displaying the range of tread patterns encountered in footwear, identifying the type and brand of shoe they are associated with. With even a partial tread pattern, it may be possible for the shoe-mark examiner to focus the search for a suspect shoe to a single brand or model. As with all evidence, individualization occurs through a combination of accidental damage and wear and tear to the shoe. Each shoe has a unique history, and the accidental marks created by that history allow for the possibility of individualization of a shoe to a shoe mark or exclusion of a shoe to a shoe mark. (See Figure 2.12.)

Both shoe and tire mark evidence is documented at the scene using close-up photography and oblique lighting. Proper photographs typically offer the examiner greater detail for comparison than do plaster casts or other lifting techniques. Recovery of tire and shoe marks at the scene is accomplished through the use of plaster compounds for three-dimensional impressions. For two-dimensional patterns on hard surfaces, lifting media such as gelatin lifters, electrostatic dust lifters, or rubber lifters are used. The recovery of impression evidence using these techniques is discussed in detail in Chapter 9.

Bite-mark evidence is often encountered in the crime scene as well. Bite marks may occur on human skin as a result of assaults and homicides, perpetrators may eat food items in the scene and then leave the uneaten portions, or a perpetrator may clench something with his or her teeth and subsequently discard it. Food and other objects are seized and preserved by whatever means necessary. These items can be delivered complete to a forensic dentist for evaluation at a later date. Bite marks on human skin, however, are best documented by the forensic dentist. If this is not possible, it is imperative that close-up photographs be taken of the bite with an appropriate scale. The best scale is an American Board of Forensic Odontologists (ABFO) scale designed specifically for bite marks. (See Figure 2.13.) These photographs should be taken in such a manner that the film plane of the camera is aligned with the plane on which the bite mark is present. Holding the camera at odd angles to the surface will create distortion in the photograph that can interfere with any subsequent examination. Suspected bite marks should always be swabbed for both DNA and saliva.

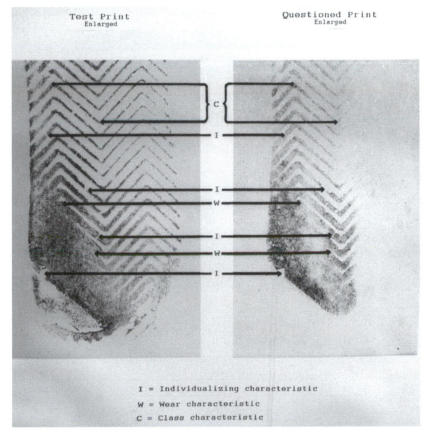

Figure 2.12 Shoe-mark comparisons include both class and individual marks. Class characteristics may identify a specific brand or model of shoe, but individual marks caused by the unique history (wear and damage) of a shoe allow the examiner to compare a show mark and associate it to a specific shoe. (Photograph courtesy of Kim Duddy and the WA State Crime Laboratory. With permission.)

General Chemical Evidence

The chemistry section of a crime lab is called on to consider different types of evidence in a variety of different crimes. They may be asked to conduct examination of suspected drugs, to identify some unknown substance located in the crime scene, to search for and isolate accelerant residues in fire scene evidence, or to isolate and identify toxins used in poisonings. With the efforts now directed at environmental crimes, chemical analysis will play a major role in identifying contaminants dumped or deposited in an environmental crime scene. There really is no limit to the questions that might be posed about some substance found or associated with a crime. Chemical analysis is accomplished using a variety of instrumentation, including gas chromatography, mass spectrometry, and infrared spectrometry.

In the crime scene, evidence that may require chemical evaluation is collected in its entirety unless there is a significant volume. Unknown dried substances can be packaged in paper bindles and enclosed in envelopes or other containers. Liquid samples can be collected using a clean pipette and contained in a sealable glass or plastic bottle.

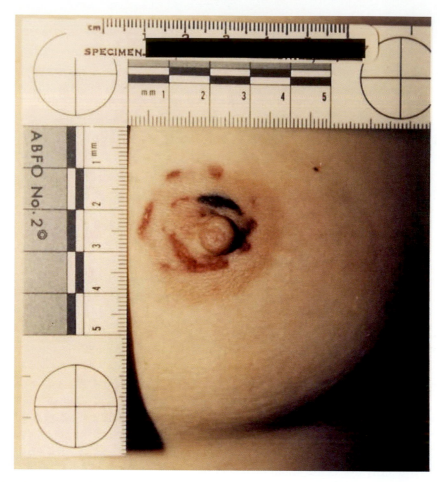

Figure 2.13 Bite marks in humans present difficulties in documentation. If a forensic dentist is not available to document the bite, photographs of the bite mark that include quality scales of reference are necessary. As with all impression evidence, it is important to hold the film plane of the camera as parallel as possible to the surface where the bite mark is located.

Evidence that will be examined for the presence of accelerants is always collected and sealed in clean, unlined paint cans or glass jars. Plastic is not impervious to petroleum products, so storing arson evidence in plastic has the potential for the trace amounts of the accelerant to interact with the plastic, thus eliminating or changing the evidence.[16] A functional short-term container for arson evidence is a nylon bag, such as those sold as roasting bags at the grocery store. These bags are impervious to accelerants, and the entire bag and contents can later be placed in and sealed inside a can or jar. When used, these bags must be double-sealed to prevent any vapors from escaping.

Document Evidence

The document section of a crime lab is called on to consider and evaluate a number of different types of evidence in order to determine if the evidence is a forgery or a tracing, has been altered in some fashion, or can be used to recover indented writings.

A forgery or questioned-writing examination considers a known writing, such as notes found at the crime scene, and attempts to identify the writer. This can include extensive writings or simple signatures. An integral part of any forgery examination is to determine if the writing is a tracing. Tracings are conscious efforts to copy a known writing. Because the act of tracing lacks fluid movement, a tracing cannot be identified to any writer. Alterations of writing can occur as changes in logs and ledgers, the amounts of financial instruments, or any other imaginable change. Alterations are often evident under an alternative light source (ALS), since different writing instruments were likely used in creating the original writing and the alteration. The inks in these instruments may fluoresce at different wavelengths, allowing the document examiner to quickly identify the nature of the alteration. Indented writings are most often recovered using an instrument known as an electrostatic detection apparatus (ESDA). When examined with the ESDA, indented writings can be found on documents that were located multiple pages beneath the original writing.

Document evidence is most often encountered in economic crimes, but any crime scene can present document-type evidence. The typical crime scene evidence will include ransom notes, hold-up notes, and alleged suicide notes. When discovered, all questioned writings are recovered and packaged in paper envelopes. If there is any issue of indented writings, the document is secured between hard cardboard to prevent damaging or adding to the indented writing. If a writing tablet is involved, the entire tablet is seized, as indented writings of drafts or additional documents may be evident on the remaining pages of the tablet. All document evidence should be protected for fingerprint evidence. Paper is an excellent medium for creating and retaining fingerprints, even after extended periods of time and handling. Writing instruments are of interest as well. Any writing instruments found at the scene and associated with the questioned document or alleged to have been used in the writing should be seized.

Computer Forensics

An associated concern of document evidence is the proliferation of computers in society and the departure of standard machines such as copiers and typewriters. In the past, document examiners routinely examined typewritten documents and documents created by copiers to include or exclude specific machines as having produced them. This capability still exists, but the need for such examinations is quickly becoming outmoded by the use of computers.

A forensic computer analysis section is usually a separate and distinct entity in any crime lab. This section of the crime lab conducts analyses of all types of computer media and systems when a need arises. Computer crimes run the gamut, including Internet fraud, pedophile investigations, and hacker attacks. This text is clearly not the venue to discuss computer crime investigation. Nevertheless, computer forensics is important, and computer evidence is routinely encountered in the typical crime scene. In a master's thesis in 1991, the author argued that criminal investigators would soon be overloaded by the sheer volume of computer-generated evidence found in normal investigations, without even considering true computer or Internet crimes. That belief is now a reality, and the computer forensics section is typically one of the most backlogged sections in any lab.

Computers are an integral part of our society, and we capture and store both personal and business data on them. The very documents described in the previous section are now created on computers and therefore exist not only as a physical document, but also as digital evidence. But digital evidence is quite different from other forms of physical evidence. The investigator could tear apart a computer, a disk, or a hard drive and never be able to lay hands on the evidence. Files exist as invisible magnetic fields on the disk. The reason computers are so widely used is the ease with which we can store, retrieve, and change data. Thus an alleged "original" file could have existed in any number of prior conditions before it was recovered. Any ten-year-old knows how to change the time and date setting of an operating system, so time and date stamps of files are easily spoofed. Getting rid of computer files is not as easy as it might seem either. Unless directed effort is made by the operator, deleted files are not really deleted; the operating system simply tells the system that the file is gone and that the disk space occupied by the file is now available for use. Thus "deleted" information exists on the media if the examiner knows how to find it. Paging files and disk files write information in memory to specific areas of the disk, and that information will remain there until the system resources require that disk space. Computers are also amazingly inefficient in storing information, often using much larger areas to store a file than is necessary. These areas are known as "slack space," and many systems actually write data to the slack space at the time the file is created. This is random information that happened to be adjacent to the file in memory and has nothing to do with the file in question. Slack-space data can provide a context as to when a file was created. The idea of preserving evidence without alteration is a standard concept associated with evidence collection; unfortunately, as operating systems have developed, so too has their complexity. A DOS system would open a relatively small number of routine files at system startup. Windows, on the other hand, reaches out and touches a myriad of files during startup, writing to a number of files on the disk. So the mere act of starting a system has the potential, if not done correctly, of opening the investigator to challenges of having altered the evidence.

All of the foregoing issues and factors provide a convoluted and difficult context in which the computer forensic expert must work, but it also opens up the possibility of recovering a wealth of evidence. Some of the examinations conducted by a forensic computer analyst include determining content of drives and media; comparing data files; establishing when a file or action was created or conducted; recovering deleted information and files; and decrypting password-protected systems, files, or media. Computer-generated evidence can be found in any situation involving a computer-generated document. A computer may hold images of individuals or events that are of concern to the investigation or data related to a criminal enterprise, such as burglaries or frauds. There is no limit to the type and nature of computer-generated evidence that may be present in the scene.

Lacking training in computer crime, the technician should contact a supporting computer crime team before attempting to seize a computer in the crime scene. They can walk the technician through an appropriate shutdown procedure. Lacking this ability, the technician should use the following guidelines and document each step. If the computer is off, photograph its condition and all peripheral connections. Disconnect the power and then, using adhesive labels, annotate all connections and cables effectively so the system can be reconnected in the same configuration at the crime lab.

After all connections are labeled, remove the cables and package them, ensuring nothing is lost. Place clean or unformatted media into any open drive bays (disks and CDs) and then tape the bay shut. Secure and protect the system components from rough handling or any source of magnetic energy (e.g., radio transmitters) and remove them from the scene to a secure and appropriate location. Unless it is clearly unnecessary, seize all peripherals such as printers, scanners, and other external devices.

If the computer is running, the technician must try to ascertain whether a destructive program is operating. Pedophiles, hackers, and computer-savvy drug dealers have been known to set up destructive programs that they can initiate easily during a search warrant, allowing them to overwrite incriminating files. If there is any indication of significant disk activity with no underlying cause, disconnect the power immediately. If this is not a concern, photograph the screen and document the nature of any programs running on the system. After noting the nature of all programs running, disconnect the power cable from the wall, then label and package the computer as described previously. When disconnecting a system, look to see if there is an uninterruptible power supply (UPS) in use. If so, disconnect the power by disconnecting the computer at the UPS.

Forensic Pathology

Forensic pathology is a subject unto itself. An entire chapter on patterns of injuries could not do justice to the subject matter. There are any number of references that discuss the critical aspects of forensic pathology in detail.[17,18,19] In the context of this book, what is important is that the investigator understand that not all pathologists are created equal; they are differentiated by their training. A clinical pathologist generally works at a hospital and is concerned with determining the cause of death, i.e., an objective medical reason why the body ceased to function. A forensic pathologist is trained in additional skills, such as patterns of injuries, and speaks both to the cause and manner of death. The forensic pathologist also helps establish the interval of death (time since death). The manner of death is a determination of whether the death is a homicide, a suicide, accidental, the result of natural causes, or undetermined. The forensic pathologist considers both medical evidence as well as scene context to make these determinations. If the supporting ME (medical examiner) system does not have its own ME investigators, the crime scene technician must act as the eyes of the ME and provide him or her with clear and objective scene data. To serve in this role and to enhance the coordination between the ME and the scene investigators, it is imperative for a crime scene technician to seek and receive training in death investigation and patterns of injuries. This training will give the investigator a better understanding of any information developed by the forensic pathologist and allow him or her to incorporate that information into any subsequent crime scene analysis.

Summary

The crime scene technician never knows what kind of evidence s/he will find at a scene. In order to collect and use that evidence, the technician must first recognize the evidence, know in what condition it must be recovered, collect it in a useable format, and understand what the crime lab can do with the evidence. At the most basic level, physical evidence is distinguished by the specificity of its properties. Items may have class or individual characteristics. A class characteristic allows the item of evidence to be compared with another group of items and excluded from the group. Lacking exclusion, a class characteristic does not establish inclusion in the group, only the possibility of inclusion. An example of a class characteristic is a tread design on a shoe mark. An individual characteristic allows the item to be compared with another item and to be excluded or included as having originated with that specific item. Individual characteristics are unique characteristics, created as a result of natural variation, natural wear, or accidental damage. An example of an individual characteristic is the microscopic striations present on the barrel of a weapon.

There are a variety of different forensic disciplines, each specializing in examining different types of physical evidence. Any one of the disciplines might be of critical importance in answering questions of concern to the investigator or the judge or jury. No single area of evidence stands alone, and all of the various items of evidence must be collected and evaluated. The typical evidence encountered in a crime scene includes fingerprints; biological evidence, including any item involving DNA; trace evidence such as hairs, fibers, soils, paints, and glass; tool marks; ballistic and firearms evidence; impression evidence from tires and shoes; as well as general chemical evidence. Each category of evidence is examined by a forensic scientist or criminalist in an effort to define objective scientific knowledge about the item. Whenever possible, the forensic specialist uses the class and individual characteristics common to that category of evidence to establish or exclude an association with some other item of evidence.

Suggested Reading

DiMaio, V.J.M. and Dana, S.E., *Handbook of Forensic Pathology*, Landes-BioScience, Austin, TX, 1998.

DiMaio, D.J. and DiMaio, V.J.M., *Forensic Pathology*, CRC Press, Boca Raton, FL, 1993.

Fisher, B.A.J., *Techniques of Crime Scene Investigation*, CRC Press, Boca Raton, FL, 2000.

James, S. and Nordby, J.J., Eds., *Forensic Science: an Introduction to Scientific and Investigative Techniques*, CRC Press, Boca Raton, FL, 2002.

Spitz, W.U. and Fisher, R.S., *Medicolegal Investigation of Death*, Charles C. Thomas Publishing, Springfield, IL, 1980.

Tuthill, H. and George, G., *Individualization: Principles and Procedures in Criminalistics*, Lightning Powder, Jacksonville, FL, 2002.

Chapter Questions

1. Describe the differences between class and individual characteristics of evidence.
2. Of the available methods for DNA analysis, which is the best for individualization in forensic work and why?
3. Describe how tape is used to collect hair and fiber evidence at the crime scene.
4. When evaluating glass fractures for direction of force, which fragments can be used in the evaluation?

5. How is paint layering used to differentiate two paint samples, such as when comparing a paint sample from a hit-and-run to a suspect vehicle?

6. Comparison of soil sample is based on environmental variations from one sample to the next. What are some of the most significant forms of environmental variation?

7. How would evaluating crime scene evidence involving a pistol differ from that involving a revolver?

8. Rifling refers to what two manufactured components of a barrel?

9. How are bullets marked for evidence and why?

10. Of the two methods used to collect tool-mark evidence (collection of the entire item or casting of the mark), which is better and why?

11. What is the most significant class characteristic in shoe-mark examinations and why?

12. What type of containers are used to collect fire scene evidence, in which accelerants are believed to be present?

13. In terms of a forensic analysis, what is the difference between a forged writing and a traced writing?

14. What is the most appropriate response by the crime scene technician for collecting a computer for computer forensic analysis?

Notes

1. May, L.S., *Scientific Murder Investigation,* Institute of Scientific Criminology, Seattle, WA, 1933, p. 9.

2. Wiley, B., presentation to the Association of Crime Scene Reconstruction, Denver, CO, Oct. 23, 2003.

3. Tuthill, H. and George, G., *Individualization: Principles and Procedures in Criminalistics,* Lightning Powder, Jacksonville, FL, 2002, p. 58.

4. Ibid., p. 59.

5. Ibid., pp. 59–61.

6. James, S.H. and Nordby, J.J., Eds., *Forensic Science: an Introduction to Scientific and Investigative Techniques,* CRC Press, Boca Raton, FL, 2002.

7. Fisher, B.A.J., *Techniques of Crime Scene Investigation,* 6th ed., CRC Press, Boca Raton, FL, 2000.

8. Tuthill, H. and George, G., *Individualization: Principles and Procedures in Criminalistics,* Lightning Powder, Jacksonville, FL, 2002, p. 106.

9. Coleman, H. and Swenson, E., *DNA in the Courtroom: a Trial Watcher's Guide,* GenLex Press, Seattle, WA, 1994, p. xi.

10. Wambaugh, J., *The Blooding,* Bantam Books, New York, NY, 1989.

11. James, S.H. and Nordby, J.J., Eds., *Forensic Science: an Introduction to Scientific and Investigative Techniques,* CRC Press, Boca Raton, FL, 2002, p. 243.

12. Ibid., p. 272.

13. U.S. Army Criminal Investigation Command, *Crime Scene Handbook,* Dept. of the Army, HQS USACIDC, Ft. Belvoir, VA, 1999, p. 119.

14. Eltzeroth, R. and Elzerman, T., Eds., *The Crime Scene Technician Manual,* University of Illinois and Illinois Dept. of Law Enforcement, Springfield, IL, 1981, p. 302.

15. Microsil and Durcoast are registered trademarks of Kinderprint Industries and Sirchie Fingerprint Laboratories, respectively.

16. Fire Investigation Unit, Metropolitan Police Forensic Laboratory, *The Work of the Fire Investigation Unit*, London, U.K., p. 10.

17. DiMaio, V.J.M. and Dana, S.E., *Handbook of Forensic Pathology*, Landes-BioScience, Austin, TX, 1998.

18. DiMaio, D.J. and DiMaio, V.J.M., *Forensic Pathology*, CRC Press, Boca Raton, FL, 1993.

19. Spitz, W.U. and Fisher, R.S., *Medicolegal Investigation of Death*, Charles C. Thomas Publishing, Springfield, IL, 1980.

Actions of the Initial Responding Officer

3

In order to understand and ultimately achieve a solution to the puzzle that each crime scene represents, a number of different entities must work together. These entities include the initial responding officers, the crime scene technicians, the investigators, and the laboratory scientists. Each one of these groups plays a critical role, and each has specific responsibilities. How these groups interact in a given situation is organizationally driven; thus SOP (standard operating procedures) and custom will define specific responsibilities differently in different organizations. Some of the factors that will affect these differences include the size of the organization, technical capabilities internal to the organization, and preferences on the part of the supervisors involved. In whatever fashion an organization chooses to define responsibility, a failure of the groups to work together or a failure of any one group to do its individual part will hobble an investigation.

No single group's responsibility is as clearly defined or as often described in crime scene references as that of the initial responding officer. The role of the initial responding officer is critical, and prior authors such as Geberth[1] and Griffin and Slack[2] have effectively assisted in defining this role. Initial responding officers do not process scenes; processing is accomplished by the crime scene technician or investigator. Nevertheless, the initial responding officer sets the stage for a successful processing of the crime scene by bringing control to what is generally a chaotic situation. Crime scenes are not abnormal circumstances for the responding patrol officer. The responding officer's objectives at the crime scene are the same as they are in any critical incident: bring the site under control and coordinate resources.

Site control demands that the officer size up the situation in an attempt to define the full extent of the problem. The officer then mobilizes whatever available resources s/he may have in an attempt to achieve control without negatively impacting on any future operations. Finally, the officer seeks to isolate the area in an effort to prevent further injury or the escape of individuals. Once this initial site control is achieved and as the incident matures, the priority changes to establishing control of all of the resources present. This is accomplished by establishing entrance and exit routes to the incident, creating staging areas for resources, and creating effective liaison with supervisors who arrive to take control. With these basic thoughts in mind, let us explore the specifics of how this is accomplished at the crime scene.

Specific Objectives of the Initial Response

These basic goals of incident management that the initial responder is responsible for can be achieved and expressed in five specific objectives at the crime scene. To safely and effectively gain control of the scene the initial responding officer must:

1. Document the provided information
2. Not become a casualty
3. Provide for emergency care
4. Secure and control the scene and all those within it
5. Release the scene to the appropriate authorities (the investigating detective or crime scene technician)

Documenting Initial Information

Documenting the initial information might seem unimportant to the patrol officer responding to a crime scene, particularly given the presence of computer-aided dispatch and the fact that most departments record phone lines and radio transmissions alike. In actuality, though, keeping what was said and who said it straight at the onset of any crime scene investigation can be truly a critical skill. The responding officer should make written notes regarding what s/he was told about the situation and specifically identify who told them. A mass of chaotic facts often present themselves as the officer is en route and certainly as the officer arrives on scene. While the officer is traveling to the scene, there may be confusion on the part of dispatch as to the nature of injuries or who is reporting the incident, or even the specifics of where the scene is. As these "facts" are reported by dispatch, the officer often takes them at face value. This can result in false leads and initial confusion in reacting to the scene. Incorrect information may be repeated to arriving investigators, who then incorporate this information into the investigation. Days or weeks later, everyone involved is still trying to understand why or how that information was introduced into the investigation.

Upon the officer's arrival, witnesses or suspects are usually present. In the initial commotion and confusion, these individuals will interact with officers, providing additional information. What they claim to know in the heat of the moment may be at odds with what they claim to know at a later date. If their knowledge of some fact suggests guilt or involvement, they may ultimately claim that an officer on scene advised them of this piece of information. The ability of an initial responding officer to delineate who said what and at what point they said it can be critical when investigators are evaluating who actually knew what and when.

The responding officer's observations upon arrival are important as well. A significant consideration is for the officer to verify the location of the scene. Once again, this might seem unnecessary, since as police arrive, they naturally gravitate to or are led to a focal point. The cluster of EMS (emergency medical service) vehicles, a group standing around on the street, any unusual activities will lead the police to the incident in question. To the initial responder, the address itself rarely serves a significant role in locating the actual scene once s/he arrives in the immediate area.

Yet a failure to verify the scene can be catastrophic to the investigation. More often than not, investigators will require a warrant to conduct a search of the crime scene. For example, imagine officers who are dispatched to a scene in which the caller tells dispatch the address is 123 Smith Street. The officers arrive and, as expected, gravitate to the location of the activity, accepting what they received from dispatch as the address. As the crime scene technicians arrive, confusion is often still a part of the overall environment. In haste, the scene investigators accept the address as reported to them by the responding officer, without verifying it themselves. If the crime scene investigators then seek a search warrant based on "123 Smith Street," when in fact this turns out to be the caller's home address across the street, the evidence discovered through the technically incorrect warrant may be in jeopardy. Simple verification by those responding to the scene, to ensure that the address is as it was reported, will prevent this type of mistake from occurring.

Observations regarding the specific time of arrival can also play an important role, narrowing time frames of events that may have transpired. Just as important, responding officers should mentally note and later document what they observe as they approach the scene. Even with quick response times, in the intervening period between the reporting of the event and the arrival of officers, individuals may be leaving the scene, or for that matter, others may be arriving who are uninvolved. The ability of the responding officer to comment on arrivals and departures, to know what various people may or may not have been doing as the police arrived, or to describe vehicles observed leaving the scene all come into play as the investigative team develops additional information. Any one of these observations might prove critical in corroborating or refuting an alibi or claim by some individual.

Responding officers must use all of their senses as they arrive at the scene. Beyond simply looking with their eyes, they must be alert to sounds or smells, which are fleeting and transient but which may provide critical information. Odors in particular may come to the attention of the initial responding officer. Colognes, petroleum products, and burning tobacco products are all examples of smells that may be present as the first officer enters the scene. In all of the confusion and chaos, if the officer does not take the time to consciously attempt to identify such odors, this evidence will be long gone by the time the crime scene investigators arrive.

Officer Safety

Officer safety is a constant issue, one that plagues police administrators. In their desire to make a difference, officers (young and old alike) often rush headlong into a fray without considering the potential threats at the scene. Officer safety is an issue in both the patrol response of driving to the scene and the actions of police after they arrive. The only true caution that can be offered is to remember that the number of officers killed or injured each year driving is far greater than those attacked by suspects. If the responding officer never arrives on scene, s/he cannot help anyone.

The initial responding officer's consideration for personal safety at the scene must begin long before s/he arrives. The initial information presented by dispatch or an individual reporting a crime on the street is usually sketchy and incomplete. Oftentimes it is contradictory as well, leaving the officer wondering exactly what s/he is walking into. Whatever the case, whatever the information, the officer must consider potential threats before s/he arrives. Will a suspect be on scene? Will the relatives of a victim turn in anger on the emergency workers? What kind of hazards can I expect? These and other questions must be considered and hasty contingencies developed that will allow the officer to overcome any potential threat that presents itself. Three specific areas to consider are:

1. Is this a crime in progress, and are there suspects on scene?
2. Are there natural hazards present that can inhibit or harm first responders?
3. Are there man-made hazards present that can endanger first responders?

It is interesting to contrast the police approach to scenes with the approach taken by firefighters. Firefighters are far more conscious of hazards as they approach any situation. To illustrate that difference, an old joke asks the question of police officers, "Are you a firemen's blue canary?" The analogy refers to the early mining days, when miners often carried small songbirds into the mines as a biological early-warning system. If the bird keeled over, this might indicate a hazardous environment for the miner. The canary, although pretty, was expendable. Thus it is said that as the firefighters pull up to the scene, they look for three things. Is the engine running on the police car? Everyone knows that in their haste to arrive, the police jump out, leaving their cars running. If the engine is on, then the firefighters know there must be enough oxygen in the environment. They then look to see if the police officers are up and walking about. If so, then they know the environment is not toxic to humans. And lastly, they look to see if the police are smoking or burning flares in the scene. If so, then the firefighters know the site is not an explosive hazard. Only then do the firemen proceed. Perhaps slightly exaggerated in the context of the joke, the truth of the matter is that police have yet to develop a strong enough sense of personal safety. Police handle "in progress" calls with due care and caution, but there is a lesson to be learned from firefighters on risk management in so-called static scenes.

Of particular concern to any responding officer, particularly those who discover scenes of crime without being dispatched, is the presence of suspects in the scene. The officer can never presume that a situation is static and that all suspects are gone. As will be discussed later in this chapter, taking control of the scene in part requires identifying and controlling all witnesses and other involved parties found there. Once safety and lifesaving activities are in place, the officer will turn to controlling and limiting the actions of these people. Suspects, however, represent a higher level of concern and demand a higher priority due to officer-safety issues. Even before lifesaving can take place, the initial responding officer may have to make a protective sweep of a scene to ensure that a suspect is not lurking about. If officers encounter a likely suspect, for example a wife who rushes out covered in blood at a domestic assault, it is only prudent to take control of such an individual until everything can be sorted out. Granted, the individual may ultimately be identified as a witness and not a perpetrator, but officer safety can never be taken for granted.

Emergency Care

In crimes involving injury or death, an additional factor is controlling lifesaving activities and any medical authorities who respond. After ensuring that no immediate threat exists in the form of suspects and man-made or natural hazards, the responding officer's attention is likely to turn to caring for injured parties or those who may be in danger in the scene. Emergency medical actions, whether carried out by the police or EMS, come at a high price in terms of evidence preservation. What was once a relatively pristine scene will be littered with bandages, needles, gauze, and other residues after the EMS are through. The level of disruption is so significant that the aftermath is often referred to as the "EMS bomb." A constant theme in this book is the issue of not disturbing the crime scene unnecessarily. Evidence preservation is an absolute mandate for every law enforcement officer working the scene. Nevertheless, the rule regarding emergency care is simple and inviolable: *lifesaving always takes priority over evidence preservation.*

If they arrive before EMS, the initial responding officers must take steps to aid the injured and ensure that proper medical care is in en route. These actions will usually prevent them from acting on issues of scene preservation and control, but there simply is no choice. Even though the officers may not be able to personally act, that does not prevent them from directing others to act. If presented with a scene where lifesaving is the priority, the responding officer can direct witnesses or others present to take specific actions that may assist in protecting the scene. This certainly applies to additional officers as they arrive on scene. Often, all of the officers present get caught up in the lifesaving activity when, in fact, they are not all needed for that purpose.

Case Example: Damage Control

Responding to a "shots fired" call, two investigators and three patrolmen encountered an apartment where a street-level window was broken and a second-story window was open. The officers could hear moaning from the second-story window. Forcing entry and clearing their way to the second floor, they encountered a woman with a perforating gunshot wound to the abdomen on the floor and a man with a perforating gunshot wound to the chest on the bed. The woman was conscious; the man was not. A call for EMS went out as the group of officers began administering first aid to both victims. Two officers assisted the woman, while a patrolman and one investigator began CPR on the male. At that moment, the scene was relatively pristine, with numerous items of evidence lying about the room, including a gun on the bed, various bloodstains, a holster, and a pair of glasses. Knowing full well that the cavalry would arrive in moments, in the form of advance lifesaving units, the second investigator was charged with making note of where these items were. In a matter of minutes, no fewer than eight firemen and EMS arrived with two backboards to join the five officers already inside this small 12 × 12-ft bedroom. The male subsequently died of his injuries, the woman survived.

With 13 people providing care to two critical victims, the scene was overrun with medical residues. Even after cleaning up the obvious residue items, it was evident that the condition of the scene had changed dramatically. The evidence was still there, but the question was: "Where was it originally?" In the ensuing investigation, a significant issue revolved around the location of the weapon. Defensive wounds on the man's hands suggested that the woman had shot the man. An investigative theory developed in which it was believed that after shooting him, she turned the weapon on herself. Having failed to kill herself, it was believed that she had placed the gun near him to make it look as if he had been in control of the weapon all along. To consider and evaluate this theory, it was necessary to have some confidence about where the weapon was before the scene was disturbed. It was only as a result of the investigator's notes that the gun could be placed in the scene at the moment the police arrived.

The officer should make every effort to preserve evidence while tending to or assisting in lifesaving. Remember always that any effort is better than no effort. The officer does not simply have to accept the resulting damage to the crime scene. These efforts might include directing EMS into the scene as they arrive and advising them of areas that may be important. Some EMS technicians respond to these requests professionally; some do not. The officer can either take direct action or ask others to take action to protect, document, or collect fragile evidence as they await the arrival of EMS. When EMS are working on a victim, nothing precludes the officer from working in the background to try and preserve fragile evidence. Many patrol officers are equipped with a patrol camera or use a personal camera, which can be quite helpful. Upon responding to the scene, the officer might snap several digital or Polaroid pictures. These photos are typically forgotten by everyone, but they may include important details of the scene prior to any disturbance. Patrol officers should turn these photographs over to the crime scene investigators. If it is obvious that evidence will be destroyed by EMS efforts, the officer should act to collect it before the arrival of investigators. This is an acceptable option, although collecting evidence in the crime scene is the exception and not the rule for the responding officer.

Unless given the authority by law, police officers do not establish who is beyond medical help and who is not. This is clearly a function of the medical professionals. When EMS personnel arrive on scene and injured or dying parties are present, officers cannot hamper or prevent access to the scene in the name of evidence preservation. Officers must allow EMS personnel to assess whether medical intervention is appropriate and, if not, allow them to establish death.

Case Example: Death Isn't Always a Sure Thing

One spring in Alaska, two brothers decided to hike up a mountain in the Chugach Range, just outside of Anchorage. Both were tourists and had no understanding of the Alaskan backcountry or of the weather issues. They were not outfitted or dressed appropriately, and they presumed that they would achieve their goal quickly and return that afternoon. Although they began early, they found themselves deep in the woods as late afternoon approached. They turned back and began the difficult task of negotiating the woods as dusk set in. As the temperature dropped, both began exhibiting the effects of hypothermia. Well past sunset, one brother became unresponsive and was unable to continue. The second brother could hear cars on the nearby highway, so he left his brother and set out in hopes of finding assistance. The second brother made it to the highway, but all efforts to locate his brother throughout the evening failed. The following morning, after sunrise, an officer involved in the search located the first brother. An experienced officer, he checked the man and, based on all evidence, determined him to be dead. A subsequent autopsy verified that the man died of exposure and hypothermia. This was a sad and unfortunate story, but one that was not quite finished.

Within days of the event, a medically trained individual claimed in the local paper that the officer had caused the man's death. He based this claim on the fact that the officer sent the body directly to the morgue and not to the hospital. The individual claimed that the hypothermia the victim suffered would have created conditions similar to the mammalian diving reflex seen in cold-water drowning. Therefore, he claimed that, in the hands of proper medical authorities, the deceased brother could have been revived. As a result of this claim, the press clamored for more information, and the alleged mistake was front-page news for several days. In the end analysis, if the officer made any mistake at all, it was a procedural one in which he made the call of death rather than allowing a medical authority to do so.

In most jurisdictions, state law will define exactly who can pronounce death. Officers should know and comply with any such requirements to prevent placing themselves in a similar predicament.

Without disparaging our comrades in the fire and EMS services, officers should also recognize that, at times, the enthusiasm of EMS can get the better of them. There are logical exceptions when it is appropriate to slow or prevent an EMS from entering a scene, but the officer must use common sense in attempting to slow such individuals down. The officer also must ensure that such actions are not in contravention to local laws. Obvious instances where EMS can be slowed include scenes where there is putrefaction of the victim or where the head is in one corner and the body is in another. In these clear-cut death circumstances, the officer should stop the EMS or medical authority at the perimeter, explain the situation, and then lead one of the EMS crew into the scene to check the body personally. This allows EMS to accomplish its task without having to take the officer's word as to the condition of the victim. At the same time, it prevents unnecessary damage to the scene, since the EMS technician is led to the body in a controlled and deliberate manner.

Case Example: Curbing EMS Enthusiasm

In an army installation, soldiers gather every day for morning formation. This often occurs at or near dawn. One morning just before dawn in Washington State, a unit gathered for its morning formation as usual. As they were formed, the soldiers were facing a three-story utility building across the road. The first sergeant verified attendance and went about advising the soldiers of the various work details for that day's activities. As this occurred, the sun was rising. It soon became evident to the leadership that something had the soldiers' attention across the street. As dawn broke fully, this something was revealed to be a young man hanging by the neck from a fire escape ladder. The police were called and, in an abnormal circumstance, investigators arrived prior to EMS. The investigators climbed the building to check the victim. It was apparent he was dead and had been so for some time. By the time they completed this check, the body had been hanging from a choke chain for no less than 20 min since discovery. As investigators climbed back down, a siren was heard approaching in the background. Two ambulance attendants arrived a few moments later and immediately sprang from their vehicle. There was evident haste in their step, so the investigators explained the circumstance and the time lapse since discovery. Despite this information, the EMS rushed to climb the stairs and crawl out onto the fire escape ladder in the chance that CPR was in order. As there was little they could actually disturb in the scene, they were allowed to proceed.

The victim was hanging from the ladder just below the top floor, and the only way to attach heart leads was by reaching down from above. Of course, the only way to the top of the building was over the victim. One EMS clambered up the ladder with the heart monitor — a large, heavy, plastic orange box — slung over his shoulder. When the EMS swung his body out to negotiate his way over the victim, everyone watched as the heart monitor swung out wildly and slammed into the victim's face. Sheepishly, the EMS continued his climb, attached the heart monitor, and then enlightened everyone with the information that the patient was, in fact, dead. Needless to say, at autopsy the victim demonstrated postmortem injuries to the head.

The desire to make a difference affects everyone, and there may be times when the officer will not be able to talk sense to EMS. Whatever the circumstances, the responding officer's responsibility is always to present a professional demeanor and work within the guidelines of EMS as much as possible, recognizing that they too have a job to do. An attitude of teamwork and cool-headed effort will usually eliminate any issues or problems that arise.

When EMS arrive prior to the initial responding officer, it is imperative that the EMS personnel be questioned as soon as practical as to what they observed upon arrival, particularly the position of the victim and the condition of clothing on the victim. All of these scene aspects are likely to be changed by lifesaving activities. Questions should be asked about any actions taken by EMS to move or change the condition of the scene, as well as ensuring the full identification of all EMS who responded to the scene. Supporting EMS or firefighters are often the best source for this information, since they are not as focused on the immediacy of the victim and have occasion to observe the overall situation. The primary EMS are generally a poor source for the responding officer; besides being focused on the victim's care, they are usually quite busy and unable to break from their duties for even a few moments. Once identified, the primary EMS can always be interviewed in depth at a later time.

If the victim is alive in the crime scene and transportation to a medical facility is planned, whenever practical an officer should be assigned to ride along with the ambulance. This officer's responsibility is to document any dying declarations or utterances made by the victim and to collect any evidence removed from the victim in the course of lifesaving activities. The nature of such evidence may include personal effects, bullets and casings, trace evidence, or other items recovered during the initial examination, and this certainly includes the victim's clothing as it is removed en route or at the hospital. These items will be of considerable interest to crime scene investigators and may be critical evidence.

Secure and Control the Crime Scene

Once the scene is safe and lifesaving activities are underway or completed, the initial responding officer must seek to secure and control both the scene itself and anyone found there. The level of chaos encountered at the scene is often determined by the number of individuals present there. These additional parties may or may not have information relevant to the investigation. Many will be nothing more than "looky-lous" who happened upon the event and, having heard the commotion and choosing to investigate, inserted themselves in the midst of the mess. It is often difficult, if not impossible, at this initial stage to distinguish those who are relevant to the case from those who are not.

Rather than attempt to make this distinction arbitrarily, the initial responding officer should simply bring this group under control and isolate them. This action prevents additional onlookers from being mixed in with this group. That alone will make it easier to deal with this group once resources become available. Direct this group from the primary crime scene, isolate them from the onlookers if possible, and seek their cooperation. By explaining the need to identify and interview each of them, they are more likely to comply with requests to remain in the area. The individuals should be instructed not to discuss with each other what they may have observed. In instances where there are significant witnesses or additional victims known to the officer, those individuals should be isolated immediately.

Because controlling and ensuring continued control of this group will be difficult, it is imperative that at the very least everyone in this group be identified upon arrival. Having failed to do so, some may simply vanish into the crowd, never to be heard from again. A critical mistake the first officer might make when dealing with this group would be to make a knee-jerk decision as to who is and who is not relevant to the investigation. Many a significant witness has been chased away from the crime scene by the good intentions of officers who were trying to prevent a crowd from gathering. Be cautious in dealing with the crowd. The vast majority of citizens tugging on the officers' coat tails as they arrive have little if anything to offer the investigation. Yet among this mass of humanity there may be a critical witness who can point out the perpetrator, identify additional leads or evidence, and provide immediate assistance to the investigation.

As additional officers arrive on scene, dealing with this group should be a priority. The group should be fully identified. Those who are totally unrelated to the investigation should be released and returned to the area outside of whatever crowd-control barriers are in place. Those who are determined to be witnesses or additional victims should be briefly interviewed for critical details and then funneled to the investigative team. If additional suspects are located among this group, they too must be dealt with effectively, controlled, and brought to the attention of the investigative team. As it may be some time before any of these individuals can be fully interviewed, the officer must take steps to prevent cross-contamination of their individual stories. Whenever possible, conduct initial interviews outside of the hearing of the other witnesses, and afterwards, isolate each individual and give them a clear warning on the importance of not discussing their observations with others. Although most people will readily agree to this request, be cautious as the scene matures. Human nature and their natural inquisitiveness will quickly take over. Fifteen minutes later, the officer will return to find them discussing the event in detail. An important aspect of taking control of this group, as well as controlling the scene, is to remove these individuals from the primary crime scene. One thing that is certain is that the officer cannot allow them to take up residence within the crime scene itself.

What defines the primary scene? What area should the officer bring under immediate control? There are no easy answers. Every crime scene is different, and the initial responding officer must be observant. In deciding where to establish an initial perimeter, the officer should consider the following:

- Primary focal points
- Natural entry and exit points
- Secondary scenes

Primary focal points are easy. As the officer arrives, he or she will naturally gravitate to or be led to such points — a body lying in the middle of the room, the ransacked bedroom in a burglary, shell casings scattered across the floor of a convenience store after a robbery. Primary focal points always stand out to the responding officer. It is not difficult to figure out that these areas hold important evidence and should be included in the controlled area. But primary focal points are only part of the picture. The body lying in the living room may only represent its final position. The actual assault may have occurred on the front porch, with the body having been dragged back into the house later on. If the responding officer realizes this only after sequestering the witnesses on the front porch, it may be too late to prevent damaging or destroying evidence.

Natural entry and exit points are of particular interest as well. Perpetrators cannot appear and vanish from a crime scene. Just like the responding officer, they have to enter and exit in some fashion. The officer should look for natural entry and exit points and include them in the controlled area. By linking the focal points with natural entry and exit points, the officer will identify and include areas in the primary scene most likely to hold physical evidence.

A significant problem is that responding officers often overlook *secondary scenes*. Drawn to the focal point, officers do not always give enough consideration to areas on the periphery of the scene or along natural avenues of approach or departure. Such secondary scenes may include staging areas used by the criminals, locations where they loaded up goods subsequent to the crime, or areas where items were deposited as they fled. These areas are identified by the responding officer through critical observation and by considering the natural actions necessary to accomplish the crime. If the police do not look for secondary scenes on the periphery of the primary scene until after completing the crime scene examination, it is likely that these secondary scenes will no longer exist. Secondary scenes must be considered in the officer's initial scene assessment.

Once the primary focal points, their natural entry and exit points, and any nearby secondary crime scenes are identified, the responding officer will have a relatively defined area to secure. This initial scene assessment does not take long. It can be accomplished in a matter of minutes. In making this initial assessment, remember that it is always better to extend the perimeter well out from these areas of interest. It is much easier to decrease the secured area than it is to expand it. As the crowd grows, as the press congregates, and as additional police and fire resources arrive, all of them will encroach on the outer perimeter of the crime scene. If it becomes necessary to increase the secured area, it will be a logistical nightmare to move this mass of people and equipment out and away from the initial perimeter.

A significant caution is in order when defining this initial scene. The officer cannot allow artificial or even natural boundaries in the scene to unduly define the initial perimeter. This is particularly true in outdoor crime scenes. As officers arrive in any scene, there are natural and artificial boundaries present. An example of a natural boundary might include a hedgerow of thick thorn bushes on one side of the crime scene. Lacking any opening, the condition of the bushes and their mere presence may make it improbable that anyone moved through them. In that instance, the hedgerow might serve to functionally define that section of the scene perimeter. On the other hand, consider another natural boundary such as a stream that meanders through a field. The officer may arrive and visualize the water's edge as a boundary, simply because s/he has no intention of walking through it. But the depth of the stream itself may not have prevented a perpetrator or victim from having crossed it multiple times in the course of an event. In that case, it may be unwise and unwarranted to allow the streams edge alone to define some part of the perimeter. Man-made boundaries are perhaps more common as distracters when defining the initial perimeter. Invariably, crime scene tape is strung up along the boundary of a property, along the street at the edge of a property, or along some other artificial line. In most cases, it is not that the officer arrived and assessed the scene based on the focal points and natural entry and exits, but rather s/he arrived and, in a simplistic assessment, decided the scene was defined by the technical boundaries of the street, property, or whatever. If these initial boundaries are far enough back from the true scene, then all is well. But if this simplistic assessment is used in an extended crime scene, physical evidence is likely to be lost or destroyed.

Once the arriving officers have some idea of what area they wish to secure as the initial perimeter, the problem becomes one of actually creating a means of barring onlookers, witnesses, victims, and newly arriving officers from entering this area. The officer's presence and voice commands are the first tools used, but as the scene matures, these will quickly become ineffective. A physical barrier of some nature is usually necessary. In an interior scene, the physical barrier is often the confines of the room itself. The doorway to the primary focal point (e.g., a bedroom in which the murder victim is located) is manned to prevent others from entering. The door to the building can be used to secure the scene. Thus the entire building is defined as the initial perimeter. Securing an interior scene through this process is all well and good, but the officer must return to the three considerations described earlier, which include primary focal points, natural entry and exit points, and secondary scenes. Unless an officer arrived on scene and arrested a suspect inside the scene, the perpetrator will have had to have entered and exited the building or room in some manner. Entry and exits to these areas are themselves of interest and should be secured and subsequently searched for physical evidence.

The use of barrier tape, set up in an extended perimeter around the actual building, is a far more appropriate response. Even if it is later determined to be unnecessary, extending the physical barrier out away from the building will prove quite functional as the scene matures. This action will allow the unencumbered flow of necessary emergency service personnel in and out of the building, as well as eliminating a crowd of onlookers, press, or relatives from congregating at the door. Rolls of barrier tape should be carried by all patrol officers or, at the very least, by patrol supervisors. Barrier tape is relatively inexpensive and is the most effective way to quickly establish a visual perimeter on scene.

When the barrier tape is in place, the officer must establish a single entry/exit point and ensure that this location is manned. The individual manning this control point will be responsible for documenting who enters and exits the scene and for what reason. Ultimately, a crime scene control log will be established and maintained at this location as well. Additional officers may be needed to roam the outer perimeter and verify compliance with the police line established. The mere fact that the barrier tape says to stay out will have little impact on many in the crowd. Hard-headed onlookers, concerned relatives arriving on scene, and certainly members of the press will ignore the barrier's presence and pass through, around, and under it if given the opportunity. These individuals must be controlled to ensure scene integrity.

In considering overall scene integrity, the responding officer must protect the scene from more than just the EMS and other non–law enforcement parties present on scene. A significant group of individuals must be controlled and guarded against; this group is the police themselves. Police officers, from patrolmen to chief, represent a major threat to scene integrity. As any officer knows, police tend to swarm at significant scenes and calls. It is not uncommon to find officers from adjoining jurisdictions present on scene, ready to lend aid if needed. The mere fact that an individual is a police officer is not sufficient reason to allow carte blanche entry to the crime scene. Once some level of control is in place, with onlookers and witnesses removed, first aid in progress, and the scene generally safe and free of suspects, the tempo of police operations should slow down. Scene integrity becomes the priority. Only officers with specific purpose and missions should be allowed back into the scene. Officers on scene who are not directly involved in these initial concerns should be placed into service, assisting in crowd control, initiating neighborhood canvasses, maintaining perimeter control, or in organizing and directing arriving resources.

Of course, tact and respect should be used when asking these officers to leave the primary scene. In the minutes before the crime scene tape went up, everyone and their mother's uncle was probably inside the primary scene. Suddenly, in a matter of moments, everything had changed. In the chaos, these remaining officers may not have realized that this transition had occurred. Many an officer or assisting citizen's feelings have been wounded needlessly by tactless remarks as they were herded unceremoniously from the scene.

Case Example: Transition to a Secured Scene

Just before lunch, a man walked into a municipal police department asking to see an officer. The senior detective of the department happened to be present and began talking to the man. The man presented a video camera and proceeded to show the detective what appeared to be a decomposed corpse floating in a pond. He informed the detective he had just come from a neighborhood park where he had observed the body.

The detective and officers from his jurisdiction proceeded to the park. Sure enough, there in the water was a corpse. As it happened, however, the body was floating approximately 50 yards past the municipality's border, clearly in the next city's jurisdiction. The corpse was in an area frequented by school children and others during lunch. The second jurisdiction was immediately notified and their detectives advised of the situation. As the first officers awaited the arrival of the second city's detectives, they set up an initial scene perimeter to prevent the lunch crowd from happening upon the scene. The senior detective, as his training dictated, proceeded to take pictures of the scene. He was still actively accomplishing this task when his peer from the second jurisdiction arrived and was briefed. Without so much as a thank you, the newly arrived detective, whose crime scene it now was, walked up to the first detective and loudly asked, "Are you done? This is our crime scene and you need to leave." Of course, this was done in front of all of the officers present.

Was the second detective correct is asking the first detective to leave the scene? Of course he was. Taking control of the scene and turning over responsibility to the proper jurisdiction was necessary. But the first detective had secured the scene, and his efforts up to that moment were appropriate as well. The lack of respect shown to the first detective when asking him to leave left him fuming over an act that was not soon forgotten. A simple, tactful comment between the two and a "thanks" would have easily accomplished the transition more effectively without creating any animosity.

In the example, the two officers involved were senior detectives, but very often it is the patrol officers who become the target of such comments. The use of tact during the transition of the scene from the initial responding officers to the crime scene team is in order as well.

It is not just officers who are working secondary missions in the investigation that represent a threat. It is important to protect the scene from those officers directly involved in the primary crime scene activities as well. The primary scene is not a command post, and the responding officer should not take up residence inside the primary scene. Nothing will perturb the crime scene technicians more than arriving to find the responding officer seated at the kitchen table 5 ft from the victim's body, filling out an incident report. Encountered just as often are officers who, inside the primary scene, use the facilities or phones because they are handy, or are found eating, smoking, or drinking inside the inner perimeter. Protecting the crime scene from ourselves is an important and critical aspect of maintaining crime scene integrity.

Once the scene perimeter is established, the tempo of operations will slow significantly. In this lull, a number of considerations need to be revisited by the initial responding officer or any supervisor who may have taken responsibility for the scene. First and foremost, consideration should be given to enhancing the security of the scene. Are more officers necessary? Have sufficient resources been requested? Is more barrier tape needed? Officers should coordinate for additional manpower and equipment as required and not wait for the investigative team to make that decision. Another consideration is the presence of fragile evidence. Officers should reexamine the scene to ensure that there are no items of evidence in immediate danger due to current or impending operations. If fragile evidence is present, the officer should take action to protect and or collect the evidence to prevent its destruction. The last consideration is to ensure that the scene is contained. An officer should be assigned to reexamine the perimeter as well and ensure that all obvious secondary scenes and or avenues of approach and departure are secure.

If a crime scene entry log is not yet in place, this is the time to initiate one. The purpose of the crime scene entry log is to document who entered the crime scene and why. Although the patrol officers may not have a specific form available to them, a simple sheet of paper that identifies the name, agency, the reason for being at the scene, and time in and out will be more than adequate. More often than not, upon arrival detectives will task a patrol officer with this responsibility. There is no reason to wait for their arrival to initiate this action.

Release the Scene to Appropriate Authorities

Eventually a crime scene technician or detective will arrive to take responsibility for the scene. Whether this is a few minutes or a few hours depends on the operations tempo of the organization. Needless to say, there is usually a period of downtime as the patrol officer waits. This period is an excellent time for the officer to begin making notes regarding initial observations, his or her actions upon arrival, and details regarding any statements offered by individuals present on scene. It is also a good time for conducting further interviews of the firefighters and EMS personnel who may have arrived prior to the police.

Once the detective is on scene, passing of responsibility to the investigative team is not simply a function of two ships passing in the night. As the detectives arrive, the officers do not jump in their cars to rush off and answer the five calls that have been holding for an hour. The officer responsible for the scene, and certainly the initial responding officer, must brief the investigative team on all aspects of what s/he knows, what s/he found, and what s/he did upon arrival. It is best that this responsibility not pass from supervisor to supervisor as additional patrol resources arrive. This often happens, and the initial responding officer is returned to service. The chain of command can certainly function on scene, but it should do so in support of the initial responding officer. It is imperative that the initial responding officer debrief someone from the investigating team on all of the issues previously described.

When conducting this debriefing, the officer should assume nothing. All pertinent details and actions should be discussed. Do not assume that a witness will tell the crime scene team the same information or that the investigators will "figure it out on their own." If fragile evidence was recovered or photographs were taken by responding officers, ensure that the investigating team is made aware of this as well. Do not be surprised by a certain level of indifference on the part of some investigators or crime scene technicians. It is not uncommon for this group to look at the time spent talking with the patrol officer as wasted. That judgment is a critical error on their part, but in no way does this eliminate the responsibility of the initial responding officer.

The current status of the crime scene perimeter should be discussed as well, with particular attention paid to concerns or issues that might affect scene integrity. Oftentimes, patrol resources will be tasked with continuing the crime scene security or enhancing it as the investigative team performs its mission. Responsible supervisors should ensure that no one leaves their security post unless a proper authority has given authorization and a relief is in place. The time assigned to these security duties is perfect for the officer to use in order to catch up on notes of observations, actions, or other information developed as a result of the officer's investigation.

Once all of these actions are complete, the responsibility for the scene transitions from the initial responding officer to the crime scene team and detectives. From that point forward, the initial responding officers take on a support role, and the actual processing of the scene begins.

Summary

The initial responding officer is not directly responsible for the processing of the crime scene. The officer's actions, however, will set the stage for success by the crime scene team. The two basic goals of the responding officer are (1) to gain control of the site and (2) to manage the available resources effectively. At the crime scene, this translates into five distinct objectives, which include documenting all of the information that comes to the officer, not becoming a casualty, providing or coordinating emergency care, securing and controlling the physical scene and the individuals found there, and subsequently releasing the scene to the investigative team. Although processing and collecting evidence is not a specific responsibility of the initial responding officer, when presented with obvious threats to evidence integrity (e.g., fragile evidence), the initial responding officer must act to protect the evidence or to document and collect it before it is destroyed.

Suggested Reading

Geberth, V.J., *Practical Homicide Investigation*, CRC Press, Boca Raton, FL, 1996.

Griffin, T.J. and Slack, G.E., *Crime Scene Investigation*, AIMS Basic Peace Officer Academy, Greely, CO, 1999.

Chapter Questions

1. What are the two primary goals of concern to the initial responding officer when reacting to any critical incident?
2. There are five basic objectives the officer uses to achieve these goals. Identify and briefly discuss each one.

3. How might a failure to verify the address of a crime scene negatively impact in the investigation?
4. With regard to evidence preservation and emergency care, what is the overriding rule for the responding officer?
5. When is it appropriate to slow or stop EMS from entering a crime scene?
6. If tasked to accompany a victim to the hospital, what is the officer concerned with?
7. When confronted with numerous individuals at a crime scene who do not appear to be directly involved, what should the officer consider before chasing them off?
8. The area contained within the initial responding officer's crime scene barrier should include three things. Identify and briefly describe each of the three.
9. How might a natural or man-made barrier (e.g., a row of trees or a roadway) in the crime scene negatively affect what an officer includes in his initial crime scene boundary?
10. What is the purpose of a crime scene entry log, and when is it put in place?
11. During the on-scene debriefing between the initial responding officer and the crime scene team, what information should be provided to the team?

Notes

1. Geberth, V.J., *Practical Homicide Investigation; Tactics, Procedures and Forensic Techniques*, 3rd ed., CRC Press, Boca Raton, FL, 1996, pp. 39–68.
2. Griffin, T.J. and Slack, G.E., *Crime Scene Investigation*, AIMS Basic Peace Officer Academy, Greely, CO, 1999.

Processing Methodology

4

With the arrival of the crime scene technicians, responsibility for the scene transitions from the first responders, who attempted to control and protect the scene, to the investigators who have responsibility for "processing" the scene. *Process* is a very simple word that means "to submit something to a treatment or preparation." But what is this treatment and how is it accomplished?[1] The fact of the matter is that there is no one right way to process a crime scene. The methods and the order in which those methods are employed is a product of the situation and the resources available to the technician. Nevertheless, there is an underlying rhyme and reason to scene processing; there are certain sequences of procedures that must be employed throughout the overall process. Although it may appear to be a haphazard affair, there is a clear method to the madness in scene processing. To recognize both the necessity and practical application of this sequential order, we must revisit the basic goal of crime scene processing.

The purpose of processing the crime scene is to collect as much information and evidence as is possible, in as pristine a condition as possible. This evidence will serve to develop conclusions regarding how the crime transpired, who was involved, and perhaps the "why" of the crime. But this collection of evidence is more than simply the physical collection of things from the scene. Crime scene technicians are not mere garbage collectors picking up whatever residue they encounter. Cataloging the interrelationships of where items are in the scene, noting the physical layout of the scene, and documenting observation of things that cannot be physically collected are all integral parts of "collecting" evidence. Content and context of the scene are both important aspects that are easily disturbed.

Why is the order or sequence of the scene processing so important? Simply put, scene processing is a one-shot operation. You only get one chance to do it right. Once altered or damaged, you cannot put the scene back in place and try again. There are opportunities to reenter a scene after the fact, perhaps in search of some overlooked item, but even these instances are few. As the crime scene technician walks out the door and turns off the light, the scene is irreparably changed, its content and context forever altered by the efforts of the police. At this point the technicians either have what they need, or they do not. There are few second chances; there is no way to answer the question, "Oops, I forgot to take a picture of the chair before we moved it; was it facing east or was it facing west?" Any and all questions that might ultimately arise about the scene must be answered from the product of the crime scene examination. If a question cannot be answered from that product, then it is unlikely it will ever be answered. But what will the issues be? No one really knows. In the initial stages of an investigation, police rarely have any way to know what will be in contention at some future trial. There is no way to know what alibis or alternative theories may be forthcoming. The technician must be prepared to answer any and all questions. Any failure in scene processing, any failure to document the condition and context of the scene can have a devastating effect on the ability to solve a crime or provide an answer to the judge or jury at some future hearing. As the scene-processing model is introduced, many professionals may argue, "I don't do that. I don't need to! That is overkill." Overkill is a truism of scene processing. There is significant overkill in any valid scene-processing model. Given only one chance to do something, it is always better to overkill the process than underkill it. The methods employed by the crime scene technician must be methodical and systematic in order to be effective. You will only get one chance!

Crime scene technicians are not exempt from Locard's Principle of Exchange; every action the technician takes in the scene has an impact. Some actions are less intrusive; others are significantly intrusive, damaging the original content and context of the scene. Technicians, by their mere presence and certainly by their action in the scene, will create postincident artifacts and may damage the condition of evidence already there. There is no way to prevent adding, moving, or damaging evidence in the scene as it is processed; all the technician can do is limit the nature of this alteration. This is accomplished by beginning with the least-intrusive methods of processing, leaving the most-intrusive methods to the latter stages.

Basic Activities of Scene Processing

At any crime scene, the technician will apply the following actions to any evidence found there:

- Assessing
- Observing
- Documenting
- Searching
- Collecting
- Processing/analyzing

Assessing

Before any action can be taken at the scene, the crime scene technician must assess the circumstances in order to decide on a proper course of action. How complex is the scene? How extensive? What resources are required, and how will those resources be employed? Are there risks inherent to the scene? If so, how can the risks be mitigated? Assessment begins the processing task and defines what procedures will be employed. Assessment is an ongoing process as well. The technician continuously assesses the situation and adjusts the processing plan when necessary. This is a critical aspect of remaining flexible in responding and dealing with the crime scene.

Observing

The most basic aspect of crime scene processing is observation — looking and mentally registering the condition of the scene and artifacts found in the scene. On its face, observation might appear as nonintrusive, and in most instances it is not intrusive. But quite often, observation is conducted in conjunction with specific search efforts. To observe, the technician must move about the scene, which in and of itself presents opportunities of adding, moving, or damaging evidence. As the technician observes the scene, items of interest often present themselves. More often than not, this leads the technician to move other items to better observe some facet of an item of interest. So observation in and of itself can be any intrusive act. There are specific points at which the technician must consciously act only to observe and purposely limit moving into the scene or moving objects in an attempt to observe. Later in the processing model, after documenting the overall condition of the scene, the technician can take more-intrusive actions (e.g., exploratory search) to better observe specific aspects of items of evidence.

Documenting

Documentation entails a variety of efforts, which include written documentation of the technician's observation, photographing and videotaping of the scene, and the creation of sketches. As with observation, documentation can be a relatively nonintrusive act, such as carefully walking through the scene to photograph the scene condition as found. Just the same, documentation can be exceptionally intrusive, such as when documenting bloodstain patterns using techniques like the roadmapping method (see Chapter 6). In the same fashion, the creation of a rough sketch has little impact on the scene itself, but the ability to provide factual dimensions and measurements (e.g., fixing of evidence) requires significantly intrusive action on the part of the technician. The technician must enter and make precise measurements in and around objects and evidence. Every measurement presents an opportunity to change or damage the condition of the scene. So even the actions taken to document the scene demand an order or sequence based on their intrusiveness. These actions are not one and the same, and they are not accomplished simultaneously. Documentation of observations always precedes photography; photography always precedes sketching and measuring; close-up photography and special techniques such as roadmapping are always the last actions taken. Documentation is the critical component. It is through documentation that the technician backs up claims regarding the original condition and context of the scene. Initial documentation must capture the content and context of the scene *in situ* before any significant scene alteration.

Searching

The nature of any search and associated activity is always intrusive. During a proper search, items have to be moved so that their surfaces can be examined, and there is no way to do this without changing the scene. But the search of the scene is not always accomplished in one fell swoop. Initial searches tend to be visual more than physical, while later searches require significant movement, including dismantling and even removal of items from the scene. The overall method of processing the scene must incorporate and introduce these search methods, starting with the least-intrusive method and saving the more-intrusive activities for the latter stages of processing. Because of its intrusive nature, any physical search of the scene always follows initial documentation efforts.

Collecting

Physical collection of items in the scene is always an intrusive process. Once the technician removes an item from the scene, the context of the scene is changed forever. Some mechanisms of collection are far more intrusive than others. For instance, simply picking up a revolver from the scene has little impact on the rest of the scene. On the other hand, recovering a bullet from a wall or door creates significant disruption of the remaining scene. Unless dealing with fragile evidence, the technician always collects evidence after the observation and documentation phases. Once collected, an item cannot be placed back into the scene to create "scene documentation." If an item is moved prior to documentation, then the technician must live with the mistake and simply provide whatever written documentation is possible regarding its original location or condition.

Processing/Analyzing

The actual processing of items of evidence in the scene is a significantly intrusive action. Powder deposits, superglue fuming, or other chemical enhancement techniques for latent prints clearly change an item's original condition while also altering the scene. Luminol, fluorescein, or leuco-crystal violet enhancements of bloody prints and pattern transfers can alter the scene as well. Oftentimes, this alteration does not change the outward appearance of an item; rather, it introduces chemicals that can damage or alter the original condition of other evidence (e.g., DNA [deoxyribonucleic acid]). Whatever the mechanism, processing will alter the evidence being processed and, more than likely, alter the scene. Processing techniques for various items of evidence are almost always the last actions taken by the technician in the overall scene-processing methodology. Ultimately, all of these items of evidence must be analyzed to establish what each one defines in and of itself and what the various interrelated pieces may define about events that occurred during the crime. Scientific analysis is always an intrusive act.

The crime scene technician constantly considers every method and process employed at the scene in an effort to determine where in the overall sequence it belongs. Only by conscious effort and careful consideration can the technician hope to prevent unnecessarily altering or damaging the scene, its contents, and the associated context. Obviously, there are instances in which the rules are ignored. Consideration of fragile evidence, initial searches of the scene for a suspect, and lifesaving efforts all require immediate emphasis. But beyond these exigent situations, scene processing falls into an orderly and relatively simple sequence of events. In this simplest form, the order is to observe, document, search, collect, and process, all the while assessing the situation and remaining flexible. Interestingly enough, technology advances have not changed this order. Adherence to this basic order provides the greatest probability of achieving the underlying purpose of crime scene processing.

A Processing Model

There is no single, foolproof sequence or methodology the author can offer to ensure success. There are, however, a number of established and validated methodologies. The following is based on one such validated and functional sequence. It was developed by the U.S. Army Criminal Investigation Command (USACIDC), and it has been the basis of their crime scene training for over 30 years. As with most scene-processing models, it is presented in the context of a homicide, but it is easily applicable to less serious crimes by simply eliminating the unnecessary steps. The USACIDC model is presented in an abbreviated form, adjusted to account for organizational differences between various agencies. Although distributed in a variety of formats over the years, the full model was published in 1999 in CID Pamphlet 195-10, *Crime Scene Handbook*.[2]

The model incorporates the six basic crime scene actions: assessing, observing, documenting, searching, collecting, and processing. As the sequence develops, it will be obvious that there are various levels of these actions (e.g., multiple searches during a single crime scene processing). As discussed, the less-intrusive forms will precede the more-intrusive forms in the entire process. Here, the model is presented in a synopsized format primarily for consideration of the overall order of sequence. The specific activities and techniques involved in assessing, documenting, and processing crime scenes are described in detail in later chapters.

When applying any processing model to a scene, the investigator must be prepared to go back at any given moment to a prior step. This is necessary when the technician discovers previously unobserved evidence. For instance, imagine a situation in which the processing has proceeded to the collection stage and nothing new has been located. Every known item of evidence has been observed, documented (photographed and sketched), and examined (searched) to ensure that there is no other trace evidence associated with it. As a large item is collected from the scene and physically moved, the technician suddenly discovers a bloody fingerprint beneath it. The newly discovered bloody fingerprint now requires the same effort as all other previously discovered evidence. Thus the technician must stop the current step (collection) and return to the initial steps (observe, photograph, sketch, and search), acting on each step for this new item. In effect, this will bring the bloody fingerprint up to speed with the level of effort directed at the rest of the scene.

This going-back process is an integral part of scene processing. It happens all the time and at nearly every step of scene processing. The further one goes into the scene-processing procedure, the more intrusive are the search, collection, and processing actions and, thus, the more likely it is that the technician will encounter items that were not previously observed. As a result, technicians are routinely discovering new items of evidence. Throughout the overall scene-processing procedure, the technician must expect to stop the current step and return to the earlier steps of the sequence in order to deal with newly discovered evidence.

Step 1: Initial Notification

In the same fashion that the initial responding officer must carefully note what he or she is told, on scene the call-out to the investigative team requires the same consideration. As Bruce Wiley of the San Jose PD Homicide Unit says, "The call you got isn't the call you get!"[3] A dispatcher reports a shooting involving one victim, and the technician arrives to find a stabbing involving two victims. Rarely is what you find at the scene similar to what you think you will find. The investigator must make note of who called, what they reported, and how that individual became aware of the information. These contradictions may be significant at a later date, and the investigator must be able to identify the source of any misinformation. Whether talking directly to someone on scene or through a dispatch office, the investigator should ask what crime scene security measures are in place and then provide basic guidance. The more information provided in this initial call-out, the more adequately the investigator can coordinate a response.

Step 2: Coordination, Assessment, and Team Call-Out

A first consideration for the investigator is a legal one of jurisdiction. Verify that the scene is part of the local jurisdiction and, if necessary, make appropriate notification if there are multiagency issues. More often than not, the initial investigator will perform an on-scene assessment before initiating a call-out for a crime scene team. Once again, the issue is simply that what the technician thinks he or she has — based on the initial information — is often nothing like what is found on scene. Sometimes the scene is significantly more complex than anticipated, but just as often the scene is far less than what was initially believed. Requiring on-call resources to respond to a scene before it has been assessed can lead to a waste of time and effort. Just as the initial responding officer did, the first investigator on scene should make note of environmental conditions, verify the scene location, and seek out the initial responding officer.

Step 3: Conduct Initial Observations

Once on the scene, the investigator conducts an initial scan, looking specifically for victims, central-theme items, and fragile evidence. If lifesaving is necessary, then that takes priority over all other actions. If lifesaving is not an issue, the investigator looks for central-theme items, which might include a body or living victims, weapons, points of entry or exit, or perhaps a room in disarray. Central-theme items assist the investigator in trying to develop some understanding of what may have happened. Remember always that these initial impressions are just that, impressions based on incomplete information. Thus the investigator must be prepared to constantly reevaluate his or her beliefs as additional information becomes available. Too often, investigators suffer from tunnel vision and allow these initial impressions to become fixed despite the discovery of additional information or evidence. This refusal to consider other viable hypotheses of what happened can hamstring the investigation and hinder the administration of justice.

This initial scan will assist the investigator in making a thorough assessment of the scene. Once the initial scan is complete — and given that there is no requirement to provide first aid — the investigator must complete the assessment described in Chapter 5, acting on the scope and integrity of the scene (including additional security), defining team composition and resources, developing a viable search plan, and assessing what risks exist and how those risks can be mitigated. Any fragile evidence discovered during this step must be dealt with appropriately by the investigator, to include photographing, documenting, and collecting it in order to prevent its loss. Although an initial responding officer may choose not to act on a fragile-evidence issue, the investigator has an absolute duty to act. Ambivalence or laziness is not an acceptable reason for losing fragile evidence once it has come to the investigative team's attention. This does not mean that the investigator will be able to prevent the loss of all fragile evidence, but the investigator cannot simply ignore it.

Step 4: Deal with the Deceased

The investigator should check any apparent deceased victims for vital signs and identify who, if anyone, has already made a pronouncement of death. Many jurisdictions will have ME (medical examiner) investigators who have authority and responsibility for examining the body at the scene. This examination may include adjustment of position, clothing, and even the insertion of temperature probes. It is imperative to determine what actions were taken during lifesaving or during any ME examination. Fully identify these medical authorities and ensure that you understand all of the actions they may have taken. Seek the opinion of EMS, ME investigators, or doctors as to the nature of obvious injuries or reasons for death, but treat these opinions with a healthy dose of skepticism. The investigative team should then coordinate for release of the body and, if possible, coordinate the time and location of the autopsy.

Step 5: Photograph the Scene

By this point in the processing model, all actions necessary to ensure the well-being of possible victims have been taken. The scene is stable, and now there is no further reason to violate the scene for lifesaving purposes or to protect fragile evidence. The investigative team should now photograph the scene, using both still cameras and video equipment, if available. Initial photographs must include overall photos. These photographs will define the condition of the scene as the formal processing begins. Chapter 6 provides a detailed review of the photographic documentation necessary.

Step 6: Document Overall Observations

Unlike the initial observation and scan of the scene, overall observations by the investigator require significant effort. The best method is to use an eight-step descriptive set:

1. Quantity
2. Item
3. Color
4. Type of construction
5. Approximate size
6. Identifying features
7. Condition
8. Location[4]

Using this descriptive set, the investigator describes the scene in depth in a narrative format. This process is in depth without being intrusive. The investigator should accomplish the vast majority of observations from a point outside the primary scene, moving into the scene carefully only when necessary. As the scene has not been sketched and items of evidence have yet to be fixed, items are not moved during the overall observation step. The investigator makes the most detailed observation of the items as possible given their position, realizing that additional notes and observations will be necessary once evidence is collected and items are moved. This step is important, as it memorializes the condition of the scene in words, which will support the initial photographs.

This narrative description should include the building, room, furniture, fixtures, and items present within. Although this step will ultimately be synopsized in the crime scene report to a page or two, the actual notes of initial observations should deal with every aspect of the scene.

The phrase "in words" is an important distinction when conducting overall observations. Many investigators employ a recording device in this stage. Although practical, this also presents an opportunity for failure. Recording devices fail, and tapes get jammed or lost. Overall observations are best documented via handwritten notes. If you choose to use a recording device, then at least back it up with some level of note taking.

Step 7: Sketch the Scene

Creating a rough sketch, which includes notes on the room and furniture dimensions as well as evidence-fixing measurements, is the next step of the processing model. The prior observations and efforts to photograph the scene did not require any movement of articles in the scene, thus everything should be in the same position as when found, with the obvious exception of items moved during lifesaving or fragile evidence collection. The investigator now creates a rough sketch of the scene depicting the orientation and relationships of the various articles in the scene. This document will support the notes and photographs. Chapter 7 describes in detail the various methods used to create the sketch, and as the reader will discover, sketching requires movement of items in the scene, since the investigator cannot measure accurately without occasionally moving items. For this reason, measuring and fixing of evidence is always conducted after completing initial photography and recording overall observations.

Step 8: Conduct a First Recheck

To this point in the processing model, all search efforts have been visual, with the investigator looking for any items he or she feels are important. Each item discovered, as well as the general scene, has been photographed, described in notes, and sketched. During this recheck, the search continues in a visual mode in which the investigator rechecks for any items or critical observations that may have been overlooked. Anything found during the recheck will require the investigator to return to the earlier steps in order to complete the photos, the overall observations, and the sketching steps.

Step 9: Release the Body

Unless undue exposure of the body in the scene is a problem (e.g., a body lying in the middle of a busy highway), there is no investigative reason to rush the body from the scene. Therefore, the body should remain in place throughout the photography, overall observational, and sketching processes. Once these actions are complete, the body is released from the scene to the appropriate authorities. Before moving the body, preserve fragile evidence on hands or feet by bagging them with paper bags. Physical examination of the body is a must, including examination with an alternate light source (ALS). If items are observed (e.g., fibers, abnormal blood drops, or broken fingernails) at any point during the examination, they should be collected immediately. An investigator who turns a back on these items will find that they have a habit of disappearing. Make sure that the clothing and body condition are adequately documented *in situ* before placing the body into a body bag. This should include photographing both the front and back of the victim. As a result of movement and passive blood flow from wounds, once the body is inside the bag, blood will tend to saturate or smear unstained areas. This action can obliterate gunshot residue or bloodstain patterns of interest. Whenever possible, keep an investigator with the body until it is signed into the morgue in order to maintain a physical chain of custody.

Step 10: Collect Items of Evidence

At this point in the scene-processing model, the condition and location of all items that were evident in the scene have been documented. It is now permissible to begin moving items that the investigator intends to collect as evidence. Each item is examined for further trace evidence, and the areas beneath the item are examined for additional evidence that was not evident before removal. Controlled close-up photographs of the evidence are taken in addition to any photographs previously taken as it lay in the scene. Each item is documented on an appropriate evidence custody voucher and the item marked for identification. If the item requires fingerprinting on scene, this should be accomplished before it is placed into an evidence container. Keep in mind that if the item is collectable, a more appropriate fingerprint response is to return the item for superglue fuming in a controlled environment (e.g., a fuming tank). In this case, the investigator need only secure the item in a manner that will preclude smudging or smearing any latent prints during transportation to the office or laboratory.

Step 11: Conduct a Second Recheck of the Scene

The second recheck is a far more intrusive act than any prior checks or searches. At this point, all known evidence has been collected and is safely containerized or removed from the scene. Now is a good time to utilize an ALS (alternative light source) in an effort to locate body fluids or trace fibers and evidence not evident in white light. Once that search is complete, efforts to obtain fingerprints from scene surfaces (e.g., walls and furniture) can begin without inadvertently contaminating other evidence. Fingerprint searches at the scene are not arbitrary. The investigator must consider how the perpetrator interacted with the scene and then pursue fingerprinting in these areas. The investigator will also begin exploratory searches of the scene during this step. Items are moved, removed, or dismantled in the scene in an effort to determine if there is additional evidence on, inside of, or beneath them. As these additional actions are taken, new evidence is likely to be located. With each new discovery, the investigator must stop and return to the earlier stages of the processing model in order to completely document the newly found evidence.

Step 12: Conduct a Third Recheck of the Scene

During the third scene recheck, the investigator ensures that all exploratory searches were sufficient and that no areas have been overlooked. In terms of rechecking the scene, the investigator continues to recheck the scene until the recheck is negative. This is also an excellent time to review investigative checklists, ensuring that all necessary steps have been completed and the investigator is not forgetting some specific aspect of the scene. Once this action is complete, advanced techniques such as chemical enhancements (e.g., luminol or amido-black enhancement) or external ballistic examinations can be undertaken without fear of damaging other evidence.

Step 13: Check Beyond the Scene

Although checked during the initial assessment, the scene perimeter and outlying areas should be thoroughly checked again by the investigative team to ensure that no evidence has been overlooked. Blood trails leading from the scene may suggest areas where a luminol search is necessary, which in turn could lead to secondary scenes at some distance from the original scene. This is a good time to photograph the exterior of the scene and approaches to the scene. In investigations of serial homicides, these photographs are often of importance to a criminal profiler.

Step 14: Conduct an On-Scene Debriefing of the Investigative Team

Before releasing or relinquishing the scene, the investigative team should spend a few moments reviewing their efforts. Investigative checklists can be checked, and crime scene products (e.g., narrative notes, sketches, and photos) can be checked against one another to ensure that all information is documented and that information has not been skewed. This is a time to question what was done by the team and what was not done. If something was not done, then ask, "Why not?"

Step 15: Release or Secure the Scene

Once a scene has been released, the technician cannot return to the scene without a warrant. Therefore, it is imperative to be confident that all appropriate effort has been completed. Keeping a scene only requires manpower. Particularly when dealing with scenes early in the morning, it is often a good idea to hold the scene until someone with a clear head can review the scene documentation. When releasing a scene, whenever possible, release it to an appropriate individual (e.g., resident, manager, or employee). Be sure they understand that the police are done and that responsibility for security of the scene now lies with the individual.

Step 16: Process and Package Evidence

On scene, the investigator cannot always package evidence for the long term. Items bloodied and still wet must be dried and packaged at a later date. The investigator may not have the best container on scene and might choose instead to use an adequate interim container. Once the investigator returns to the office, s/he can take steps to locate the best packaging and then repackage the evidence. Evidence vouchers should be checked against scene documentation to ensure that everything is annotated properly (e.g., room and directions). As the investigator works these issues, s/he can begin formalizing any analysis plans. What items need to go forward to the lab for what purpose? What latent-print methods are appropriate given the items that need processing? These are all questions that must be considered and answered.

Step 17: Conduct a Formal Debriefing

A formal debriefing is usually conducted within 24 hours of the completion of scene processing. All of the available primary parties sit down and revisit the investigative effort. This debriefing often serves as an outlet for considering and validating possible hypotheses and for ensuring that all aspects of the scene processing are understood and shared with the investigative team. If possible, individuals such as the ME investigator or initial responding officer should be invited to attend this meeting as well.

This model is applicable to all crime scenes, from the simplest to the most complex. In simpler scenes and less severe crimes, the steps associated with bodies obviously are excluded. But the overall sequence as described is appropriate to all crime scenes, whether they be misdemeanors or felonies. The model sets the stage for the technician to leave with as much evidence as is possible. The issue will never be whether these methods should be applied to all crimes scenes. If we could, we would, because it would help solve crimes. The problem is one of resources; simply put, this model cannot be applied in its entirety at every scene.

Summary

This book cannot set a minimum standard methodology for every police agency. There are simply far too many variations in manpower and equipment resources. Each organization and each technician must understand the basic methodology and apply it as conscientiously as possible given their particular circumstance. Whatever means they use at the scene, it must include in some fashion the six basic processes: assessing, observing, documenting, searching, collecting, and processing/analyzing. If the scene context is to be captured in as pristine a condition as possible, then the sequence of the method must follow the prescribed order as well. Haphazard behavior in the scene, or wandering about throwing a little dust here and there, is a charade. The technician might as well not be there. Without order and process, evidence will be lost unnecessarily. So if a technician chooses to be present at a crime scene and take responsibility for "processing" a scene, then that individual should choose, as well, to bring some method to the madness.

Suggested Reading

Crime Scene Handbook, CID pamphlet 195-10, HQS USACIDC, Ft. Belvoir, VA, 1999.

Chapter Questions

1. Why is sequence of order so important in crime scene processing?
2. What are the six basic processes accomplished during crime scene processing?
3. In terms of intrusiveness and alteration to the scene, how might the step of documentation alter a crime scene?
4. Explain why it is necessary for the crime scene technician to be prepared to return to an earlier stage of the processing model?
5. Pick any object in your immediate vicinity and, using the eight-step descriptive set (step 6), describe the item as completely as possible.
6. During the first recheck of the scene, are the methods used for the recheck visual or physical?
7. Prior to placing a corpse in a body bag, what are some of the documentation efforts the technician must take?
8. Rechecks of the scene are continued until when?
9. There are three debriefings that occur during a crime scene processing: the initial debriefing by the first responding officer to the crime scene team, and two that occur after all of the primary documentation and collection activities are complete. When, where, and with whom are these debriefings conducted?
10. In terms of the crime scene processing goal, why is the phrase "in as pristine a condition as possible" an important distinction for the crime scene technician?

Notes

1. *New Webster's Dictionary,* Lexicon Publication, New York, 1990, p. 321.

2. U.S. Army Criminal Investigation Command, *Crime Scene Handbook,* CID Pamphlet 195-10, HQS USACIDC, Ft. Belvoir, VA, June 1999, pp. 14–36.

3. Wiley, B., case presentation to the Association of Crime Scene Reconstruction, Denver, CO, Oct. 2002.

4. Ibid., pp. 21–22.

Assessing the Scene

5

Once the investigative team takes control of the scene, the true task of assessment begins. This assessment considers a number of logistical and technical aspects of scene processing. These considerations will ultimately define the actions of the crime scene team as well as identify additional resources that may be necessary. The team must complete this assessment before initiating any direct scene processing and after receiving a debriefing by the initial responding officer. If the investigative team fails to address these issues or fails to seek out the initial responding officer and simply starts processing, in all likelihood evidence and information will be lost, and personnel may be exposed to undue hazards.

The purpose of the debriefing and assessment by the investigative team is to consider the following issues:

- Scope of the scene
- Scene integrity and contamination control
- Team approach and composition
- Search methods to be used
- Personal protective measures

Additional considerations of the team may include dealing with mass scene and mass-casualty situations as well as interacting with media representatives.

Debriefing the Responding Officers

Upon arrival at the scene, the crime scene team must seek out the initial responding officer. Once found, this individual should be interviewed to determine the following:

Scene scope and nature: The initial officers should clearly define the scope of the scene, identifying specific boundaries and reasons why areas were included or excluded in the initial perimeter. The general impressions of the officer regarding the nature of the crime and specific observations that led to those impressions should be sought and considered by the investigative team. If the officer discovered specific items of evidence, these should be pointed out to the investigator. Information regarding how the crime came to the attention of the officer (e.g., dispatched or flagged down) and the specifics of what that information entailed should be sought.

Changes to the scene: The initial officer should quickly highlight significant changes to the scene by the police, fire, or EMS (emergency medical service) personnel. If items were moved, lights turned on, doors opened, or bodies were moved, the investigator must know that these actions occurred. The specific methods of entry by the police into the scene and any items that were inadvertently touched by the police or observed being touched by others should be identified.

Status of involved parties: The status of victims, significant witnesses, and any suspects should be made known to the investigator. Live or near-death victims may have been transported; suspects may have been detained; or individuals claiming to be witnesses may be present. As a result, the investigators or crime scene team may have to act immediately to evaluate if there is physical evidence (e.g., bloodstained clothing, gunshot residue tests, and trace evidence) present on these individuals. Particularly when dealing with bloody scenes, all witnesses claiming to have discovered the body should be examined by the crime scene technicians in an effort to determine if there are inappropriate bloodstains present on their clothing. Any statements to officers made by the involved parties should be shared as well. This will ensure that the crime scene team is able to recognize disparities, if they exist, as they process the scene.

Scene security: The initial responding officer should describe the steps taken to secure the scene, including those efforts the officer feels are necessary to enhance security. The initial responding officer may be aware of an area on a perimeter that is open or weakly secured. Any crime scene entry logs created by the initial responders should be identified so that they can be attached to the crime scene team's entry/exit log. If a specific scene integrity threat (someone who has already demonstrated an attempt to violate the perimeter) exists in the nature of a relative or media representative, the initial responding officer should ensure that the investigative team is aware of this threat.

The crime scene technician should listen carefully to all of the information provided and seek clarification of any issues that are not clear. While the technician must resist being misguided by seemingly wild theories, s/he must cautiously consider all of the information presented.

Case Example: Things Are Not Always as They Initially Appear

Responding to a report of a body dumped in the woods, the Maine State Police encountered what appeared to be a woman's body wrapped in a blanket and tied with ropes (Figure 5.1). The only portion of the victim exposed at the scene was a leg clad in fishnet stockings. From all apparent evidence, the Maine State Police felt that they were dealing with the dump site of a sexual homicide.

When checked by the initial responding officers, the exposed leg of the victim certainly appeared human, and when touched it felt much as a corpse should feel. Since it was clearly evident the body was dead, the scene was not disturbed, and a careful scene examination began. But as the investigators examined the scene and the "body," it also became evident that all was not what it appeared to be.

Figure 5.1 A scene that was originally believed to be a body dump site by the initial responding officers. Directly in front of the barrel is what appeared to be a body wrapped in a blanket, which was then tied by rope. Extending out of the blanket and evident in the photograph was a leg clad in fishnet stockings. (Photo courtesy of Deputy Chief Michael Ferenc and Detective Herb Leighton of the Maine State Police. With permission.)

The "victim," it turned out, was a doll anatomically correct in every facet (Figure 5.2). She showed obvious wear and tear, including evidence of previous attempts at restoration (e.g., reattachment of a breast). Investigators subsequently determined that this lifelike, human-feeling doll was available from a company in the West and sold as a sex toy for a price tag of several thousand dollars. The police ultimately concluded her predicament in the scene was either a dress rehearsal for future scenes or an artifact of a demand by a wife to dump the offending "friend." Interestingly enough, her head was not found, perhaps retained as a fond reminder of better times.

Investigators are not often presented with as convincing a false scene as the Maine State Police were, but the truth is that when investigators arrive at a scene, they are often provided with inaccurate information. The crime scene team cannot presume anything while being debriefed; at the same time, they must evaluate everything they are told in light of what they can see.

Once the debriefing is completed, the initial responding officer can be released to carry on other duties or assist in security of the scene. If the officer is released for other duties, s/he should be reminded of the importance of documenting his or her findings, actions, and observations in the incident report. The crime scene team should also coordinate to receive copies of these reports as soon as they are available.

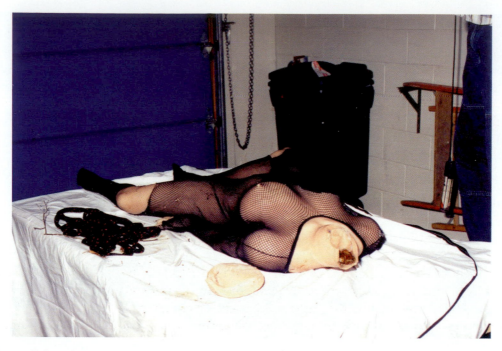

Figure 5.2 The "victim" from the scene in Figure 5.1. This doll was anatomically correct in every aspect and had a fleshlike look and feel. Although this is an extreme case, it illustrates that the initial impressions of those on scene are often incorrect. The crime scene team must evaluate all information independently. (Photo courtesy of Sgt. Steven Drake and Detective Herb Leighton of the Maine State Police. With permission.)

Scene Scope and Boundary Assessment

The crime scene investigators must reassess the boundary of the crime scene perimeter to ensure that all areas of concern are secured. The crime scene team uses the same criteria as the initial responding officers when considering where to place the boundary in the scene. These criteria include primary focal points, avenues of entry and exit, and secondary scenes. Although they use the same criteria, it is not uncommon for the boundaries to change once reassessed by the investigators. This occurs for a number of reasons. First and foremost, the crime scene team applies the criteria with a far more critical and experienced eye. They will often recognize a minor nuance in the scene that suggests expanding the perimeter or see evidence that was not immediately evident to the patrolmen. Another factor that affects reassessment is the general condition at the scene. By the time the crime scene team makes its assessment, the scene is far more stable. The chaos encountered upon the arrival of the initial officers is no longer a major factor, since the individuals encountered on scene are now under control, and any associated fire or EMS activity has declined. Often, additional lighting systems are in place as well, increasing everyone's ability to view the scene. All of these factors allow the crime scene investigators to evaluate the entire circumstance more effectively, particularly the issue of secondary scenes on the perimeter. Just as important, all of the fragmented information provided by various participants has now funneled to the investigative team, allowing them to better understand and evaluate what areas are or are not involved based on testimonial claims.

If the scene boundary requires expansion, the crime scene investigator should act on this requirement immediately. As this occurs, the initial responding officer may still be present. The crime scene investigators should not admonish or criticize the decisions of these officers, realizing that various factors may have prevented them from recognizing the true scope of the scene. They should, however, offer comment on why the expansion was necessary and mentor the officer as a mechanism of developing that officer's knowledge and experience base.

Scene Integrity and Contamination Control

Remember always that the basic goal of scene processing is to collect as much evidence as possible in as pristine a condition as possible. Therefore, the crime scene team must carefully consider how its impending actions will affect scene integrity. As processing begins, a number of individuals will actively move in and around the scene, resources and equipment will be needed inside the scene, and evidence will ultimately have to be removed from the scene. With these actions in mind, the investigator must consider establishing access routes to be used by the crime scene team, determine how the team will manage access to the scene, and establish how they will ensure scene isolation to prevent unnecessary contamination or destruction.

As the team arrives on scene, the initial perimeter is likely to consist of a single barrier put in place by the responding officer. Although adequate for its initial purpose, a single barrier is not sufficient for long-term scene integrity. A single barrier allows no buffer distance between what may be evidence and the crowd of onlookers (Figure 5.3).

In considering scene isolation, the crime scene team should employ multilevel isolation and containment. Two perimeters should be established, which in effect will create three areas of access (Figure 5.4). The inner perimeter boundary extends around the area considered to be the actual scene, as previously described. Access into this inner area is limited to those who are conducting the scene processing. A second perimeter, placed beyond the inner boundary, will create a working area surrounding the actual crime scene.

This working area serves multiple functions, and entry to it is controlled as well. Only law enforcement officials or others who are on scene in an official capacity should be present inside of this boundary. The buffer this boundary creates removes the onlookers from the immediate area of the crime scene. The area will serve as an excellent staging point for equipment. Items such as camera cases, bulky equipment, or investigative kits that are required in the scene but are not currently in use can be placed here. The working area also serves as a trash collection point for debris, in particular the gloves, Tyvek suits, and booties used for personal protection of the crime scene processors. Last but not least, the working area also provides a secure area for evidence collection. As items are brought from the scene, they are often collected at a single point before being placed in a vehicle for transportation to the evidence room. By establishing a specific evidence collection point in this area, away from the outer perimeter but within the secured area, evidence integrity is not violated.

Whether this second perimeter is placed inside or outside of the initial perimeter created by the responding officer is scene and situation dependent. If the initial perimeter is far enough out from the primary scene, there may be more than adequate room to insert an additional perimeter inside of this first barrier. On the other hand, if the initial perimeter

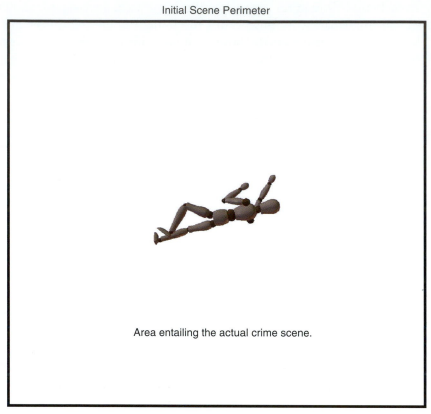

Initial Scene Perimeter

Area entailing the actual crime scene.

Area outside controlled perimeter where
onlookers and media may gather.

Figure 5.3 The use of a single scene perimeter is typical of the initial responding officer's effort. Although functional in the early stages, a single perimeter leaves onlookers and media in too close a proximity to the scene. A single perimeter provides for no buffer between these people and the actual scene and evidence.

barely contains the primary scene, the additional perimeter will have to be placed outside of it, demanding that onlookers and vehicles be moved further back. Everything outside of the outer perimeter is unsecured and uncontrolled. Here relatives, onlookers, and press are likely to gather. This outer boundary will always require the greatest level of effort and manpower on the part of the officers securing the scene.

If necessary, additional perimeters can be established to create even more defined access control. As an example, the addition of a third perimeter creates a second working area. Access to the innermost working perimeter might be limited to scene processors and used for evidence collection and equipment staging. Supervisors requiring briefings and other authorized officials or investigators not directly involved in the scene processing could then be limited to the second working perimeter. This increases the isolation of the scene, providing greater security at the evidence collection point, and prevents inadvertent entry to the scene by those supervisors who have no true business inside. There are limitations for establishing these additional levels of containment. The first limitation is ensuring that everyone understands who should be where in the scene, and the second limitation is in actually manning and controlling the various perimeters.

Outer Scene Perimeter

Inner Scene Perimeter

Area entailing the actual crime scene.

Working area, evidence holding area and staging point for equipment,
it also provides a physical buffer between the actual scene and
unauthorized individuals.

Area outside the controlled perimeters where onlookers and media may gather.

Figure 5.4 Multilevel containment of the scene is accomplished by using a minimum of two perimeters. The inner perimeter encompasses the actual scene. A second perimeter (the outer scene perimeter) in effect creates a buffer zone and work area for the crime scene team. It moves the crowd and media back from any evidence or areas of interest and is an effective staging area for equipment and personnel.

The use of multilevel isolation can be effective as the size and scope of the scene increases. In major crimes or situations involving mass casualties, multiple perimeters established at varying distances from the scene might be necessary to control and ensure scene integrity. The actual distance between each perimeter in any crime scene is dependent on the needs of the investigation. The best advice in terms of defining the distance between perimeters is to know why the perimeter is in place. If it is designed to keep the media from having a direct line of sight into the scene, that will demand a far greater distance than a perimeter simply designed to keep the media at a safe distance.

When using multilevel containment, never create more perimeters than are functionally necessary, and certainly no more than can be manned effectively. It is far better to have one perimeter that no one can violate than to have three perimeters manned by weak security that anyone can violate. Keep in mind that the innermost perimeter may require only limited security (e.g., one officer maintaining the entry log). If the organization is properly trained in advance and applies that training at each scene, the inner perimeter will likely be self-regulated.

No matter how many perimeters are created, once the purpose of the perimeter is defined, it is imperative that all parties be held accountable for respecting its purpose. This includes other police officers. It is often amazing to see the number of people present inside the barrier tape at a crime scene. Few, if any, will have purpose, and more than likely they will be standing around with their hands in their pockets (Figure 5.5). Status as a police officer, rank, or political position should play no part in defining who may pass a perimeter. The uniform division commander cannot enter a perimeter designed to keep everyone out (except for the actual crime scene processors) simply because he or she outranks the detectives. Similarly, the deputy chief does not need to walk through the crime scene just because he or she has to brief the chief in the morning. Perimeters have purpose, and that purpose will effectively guide the crime scene team in deciding who should or should not pass beyond the perimeter.

There are supervisory and political realities for those engaged in crime scene processing. Not all supervisors understand or, for that matter, care about crime scene integrity. They often believe their need to know overrides evidentiary issues. In trying to ensure

Figure 5.5 Once a perimeter is established, everyone is responsible for respecting its purpose, including emergency service workers and police. Far too often, everyone in uniform assumes they have purpose inside the perimeter. As in the case of this bombing scene, despite the presence of a perimeter, the inner perimeter is often filled by people without a specific purpose.

scene integrity, the crime scene team may find itself involved in politically incorrect actions. Balancing the competing interests and duties of everyone at the scene and applying a true team effort is necessary. Simply put, keeping a supervisor in the know does not always demand giving that person access to the scene. Explaining that to the deputy chief at 3 A.M. in a chaotic scene can be a task. Nevertheless, criminal investigations are fluid events, so it is imperative that supervisors and those with political responsibilities be kept informed. They need factual information and often need to understand scene nuances. Without this information, it will be difficult to deal with the press or ensure that senior officials are informed. The most effective approach is for the senior leaders in an organization to sit down and establish these access policies before an event. In the heat of the moment, interdepartmental confrontations can get out of control without established policies. Coordination, a standard approach to scene containment, and department-wide training before the incident will usually prevent "turf" issues from developing.

Three techniques for handling supervisors or politicians are (1) to enforce the use of standard personal protective measures, (2) to enforce the use of scene entry logs, and (3) to consider creating walking routes or observation points for authorized visitors. If everyone in the scene is required to use proper protective clothing (e.g., Tyvek, booties, and masks) without exception, this alone will remind those who are nothing more than "inquiring minds" that the scene is not particularly safe. If this hint is insufficient, then the requirement and inconvenience of putting on all of this protective clothing may be enough to make these individuals reconsider their need to be inside the scene. Requiring these individuals to log in on the scene entry log is often effective as well. If your name appears on the entry log, the probability of being called as a witness in future hearings and trials increases dramatically. Supervisors tend to want to arrive and leave anonymously; they generally do not like their names to be included in reports. Finally, the creation of established walking routes is an effective way to allow supervisory and political entities limited access to the scene. Such walking routes are generally created after completing the initial documentation. The route must be cleared of any items of evidentiary value and should be clearly marked. A member of the crime scene team should accompany anyone given access to the scene via a walk route.

Managing Access

Once the perimeters are in place, the next concern is to identify access points in the perimeters (where team members may move in and out of the scene) and to decide what scene entry logs are necessary. Defining the access routes into the scene is not as simple as it might appear. Just because the front door is right there does not mean that it is the best choice for access to the scene. Entry and exit points for the crime scene team are not defined solely on ease of access for the team. Other considerations are in play as well. The primary considerations are:

- What avenue of approach or departure did the perpetrator utilize?
- Will the access point expose operations to unnecessary media scrutiny?
- What access points are available?

Each of these considerations is important, and each must be evaluated in its own right. You will recall that access routes used by perpetrators are important areas. They are typically rich in physical evidence and therefore are areas in which scene integrity must be maintained. These areas are likely to hold footwear marks (both patent and latent), fingerprint evidence, and a variety of post-incident bloodstain patterns. Tromping the primary scene processors through this area can result in the degradation of any number of items of physical evidence. In this instance, an alternative entry point for the processing team is warranted, at least until the entry/exit can be properly processed and any evidence present collected.

The second concern in defining the entry point is media scrutiny. Once containment is in place and a routine established, the team's entry point may receive a significant amount of media interest. It offers a good backdrop for video clips, as it is a point of police activity. Items are moved out of the scene through this location, and often supervisors and processors will interact here. At any significant scene, expect the media to direct standoff audio and imaging devices at this location. The more exposed the entry point is to the media, the more difficult it may be to prevent unintentional information leaks. The only functional way to prevent this kind of media interest in an exterior scene is the use of sheer distance between the media and the access point. But if the media are equipped with specialized equipment, even that may fail. When operating in buildings, there are other options for preventing undue exposure. For instance, if the team uses a side or back door, one physically isolated from the main street and onlookers, it is less likely that media representatives will be able to observe or film the removal of bodies or evidence. If this is not possible, the use of crime scene screens (Figure 5.6) or the simple act of closing a door may limit this kind of invasiveness.

Figure 5.6   Crime scene screens are an effective way to limit the invasiveness of the media's cameras and to provide a victim with some level of final dignity. These screens can be self-constructed for under several hundred dollars.

Case Example: With Standoff Technology, You Are Never Out in the Middle of Nowhere

In 2002 the Georgia Bureau of Investigation (GBI) encountered a mass scene involving a crematory in which the operator — rather than cremating remains — was simply discarding the bodies throughout his multiacre facility. Ultimately, more than 300 bodies were found scattered across the property. The sheer magnitude of the situation, as well as the community outrage, created significant national and international media attention. In developing a scene response, a significant area surrounding the property was placed off-limits. This effectively prevented the media from directly photographing on-scene operations.

At one point during the scene processing, it was necessary to retrieve several remains from a ditch in a wooded section of the property. For all intents and purposes, the investigators working this detail were out in the middle of nowhere. Despite the isolation of this scene, photographs of a corpse being hoisted from this ditch were soon circulating on the Internet. A subsequent investigation identified the photographer, and it was determined that the photographer had shot the photos without violating the scene. The photographer simply walked onto an adjoining property and, from a significant distance, employed a standoff still-camera lens. Thankfully, good sense and ethics prevented the photos from being published in any newspaper or magazine, but the incident illustrates that the scene processor is never really alone.[1]

The crime scene team is often presented with a situation in which there is only one entry point into the scene. This is common in apartment buildings, hotel or motel rooms, and other small buildings. It is also possible that additional entry points to the scene are unreasonable or unsafe for some reason. In such situations, the crime scene team will have to utilize the main access. If this is the case, it will demand that the team process this area appropriately before allowing it to be used as an access to the primary scene. A point-to-point search method (as described in the Search Patterns section later in this chapter) can be quite functional, allowing a work path to the primary scene to be cleared in advance.

After defining the points of access on the perimeter, the crime scene team must decide how they will document access control using the crime scene entry-control log. The entry-control log is a simple document (Figure 5.7) that identifies who entered the scene, when they entered, what their purpose was, and when they departed.

At a minimum, the perimeter that defines the true scene should have a crime scene entry-control log. This is the area of greatest interest, and defense counsel is apt to question who had physical access to the actual scene and, therefore, access to evidence. Issues of who may have been in an outer staging area are far less likely to be of significant interest to anyone. Depending upon need and circumstances, crime scene entry logs can be used at additional perimeters (e.g., outer perimeters or at a press briefing area established in an outer perimeter). A caution is in order when considering the use of entry logs at the additional perimeters. Be careful not to create an unnecessary gauntlet of bureaucracy that scene processors must survive while trying to do their job. If team members have to sign in and out every 15 ft, this will lead to disgruntled officers and tempt individuals to try and bypass such security. Controlling access to any given perimeter does not necessarily require the use of a written entry-control log. The primary

Crime Scene Entry Log

Time In	Name/Unit	Reason at Scene	Time Out
1750	SA Brown – Homicide	Scene Processing	
1759	Smith/ME Investigator	Scene exam	1823
1800	H. Jones – CS Unit	Scene Processing	
1800	L. Marshall – CS Unit	Scene Processing	
1817	Chief Kyle	Scene visit	1833
1817	Maj. Darren – PIO	Update by Homicide	1833

Figure 5.7 The crime scene entry-control log is intended as a means of providing a running record of everyone who entered the scene, when they entered, why they entered, and what time they left. This allows the crime scene team to more effectively answer questions regarding crime scene integrity at judicial proceedings.

purpose of the entry-control log is to keep track of who was inside the actual "crime scene." Establish scene-entry logs at those areas necessary to document that information and then enforce their use.

If an entry-control log was created by the initial responding officers, it should be attached to the formal crime scene entry-control log and kept as a complete record of access to the event. Some authors have suggested adding names and times from the initial responding officer's entry log to the crime scene team's formal entry log. The entry log should stand on its own, a contemporaneous written record of what happened. It is unnecessary to go back and recreate entries on the team's formal log or to try and recreate a log that was never established in the first place. The court may view adding entries to "complete the record" as inappropriate. Simply ensure that the responding officer or someone in the investigative team documents in their supplemental report any information regarding who may have been inside the scene in these early stages and retain any written logs provided.

Defining Team Composition

The composition of the crime scene team is first defined by whether the team's approach is one of area or function. In the area approach, a single team handles all activities associated with processing. In a functional approach, the team leader designates different teams to do different activities. Which method is chosen is based primarily on the nature and scope of the scene. A simple burglary involving a single room requires far less effort and logistical support than a multiple murder scene, where bloodstain patterns or bullet trajectories throughout multiple rooms may be in question.

Using the area approach, a single group of scene investigators is responsible for all processing for a given area in the scene. The area in question may be the entire crime scene or a small section (a zone) of a larger, more complex crime scene. The group will document its area of the scene through photography, measure and sketch the scene, search for and collect latent prints and other physical evidence, and conduct any other associated activities involving that area. The area approach is very typical in small police departments, where specialization is not an option and manpower resources are limited.

In a functional approach, crime scene teams are developed to handle specific functions within the entire scene. Examples could include a documentation team, responsible for photographing, sketching, and measuring the crime scene; or a fingerprint team, responsible for processing all appropriate scene surfaces for latent prints. When using the functional approach, it is not as important how one breaks down the different activities (e.g., how many different teams you create to do different jobs), but it is important in what order the teams are staged through the scene. The basic order of procedures that were discussed in Chapter 4 must be adhered to. The supervisor cannot decide to send the latent team in prior to the arrival of a photography team, as such an action would violate the basic rules of documentation and scene integrity.

Some of the other factors to consider before making a determination of area vs. function include:

- Single or multiple scenes
- Order of activity involving specialty examination needs
- Available resources (equipment or personnel)
- Physical size of the scene

Not every crime is confined to a single scene. In a murder, there may be an assault scene and then a dump site for the body. In the burglary, you may find multiple homes or businesses burglarized on a block during a single event. Whatever the case, the more scenes you must deal with simultaneously, the more difficult it is to direct resources to them. The sheer logistics of moving teams or providing equipment at each scene may deter smooth operations. In a multiple-scene situation where equipment resources are not at issue, an area approach may be the more advantageous method. The area approach reduces the issue of transporting multiple functional teams to each scene.

The more complex the crime scene is, the more likely it is that specialty examinations may be necessary. Classic examples of specialty examinations include analysts conducting bloodstain pattern evaluations, reconstruction teams attempting to define external ballistic issues, or perhaps a unique latent-print issue that requires an on-scene chemical enhancement by a crime lab team. Additional examples might include the need for on-scene computer forensics, or addressing the safety issues involved in dealing with a methamphetamine lab. Specialty examinations must be considered in terms of the overall order of processing as well as whether the primary team has the skills necessary to conduct the activity. If a team lacks specific training in a specialty, that will demand locating appropriately skilled analysts. Bringing those individuals into the situation will then force the team into a functional team approach.

The physical size of a scene may force the issue of an area vs. functional approach. If the scene is too large, size alone may prevent effective movement of the functional teams through it in a timely fashion. In that instance, zones may have to be assigned to different teams and an area approach applied. This is particularly true in mass crime scenes or mass-casualty situations.

Resource availability is also a significant factor in considering which method to use. Manpower usually underlies any standard operating procedure for an organization's response to the typical crime scene. When faced with a significant scene, consideration must be given not only to the availability of people but also equipment. Are sufficient trained individuals present to create separate area teams? If there are enough people, is there enough equipment to properly outfit each team? If equipment resources are at a premium and there is not enough to go around, a functional approach may be the answer. There simply is no single right answer to apply. The team must assess the situation, considering the scene as well as the availability of resources. Use of a standard approach established by SOP (standard operational procedure) or organizational custom (whether based on area or function) may be more than adequate in a simple scene. As the complexity of the scene increases, any number of these considerations may force the crime scene team into a different approach.

No matter what method is ultimately chosen, the respective team members will engage in certain basic activities at every crime scene. These include photography, sketching and measuring, searching, and the collection of evidence. Each of these activities will be discussed in detail in later chapters, but a general understanding of how many people it takes to conduct these activities is necessary in order to properly plan and staff the teams in the first place.

Photography teams require a minimum of two people. An attempt by a single individual to take the photographs and maintain the photo log is likely to result in error. With two team members, one operates the camera, while the second is responsible for creating and ensuring the accuracy of the photo log. The second team member (or a third member if available) also assists by setting up scales and photo placards in the scene as the photographer creates the various photos necessary (e.g., with and without scale photos or evidence close-ups). A sketch and measurement team generally requires three people. Two members are needed to effectively operate the measuring device, while a third creates the rough sketch. If a fourth member is available, this person can act as a scribe and document each measurement on paper. If only two members are present, it is certainly possible to measure and create a sketch, but the flow of the process is not as effective and the accuracy of the sketch may suffer. Evidence collection teams require a minimum of two team members. The primary member is responsible for collecting the evidence, physically bagging and tagging it. The second member is responsible for creating the evidence log, documenting what was taken, when it was taken, and where it was found. If necessary, a single team member can accomplish both aspects, but once again the process is not as effective as when accomplished by two people, and the accuracy of the evidence log may suffer. It is not uncommon to find crime scene technicians who create their evidence log after the fact. In other words, they collect multiple items, then return to the office and create the evidence log. Although functional, this process often leads to mistakes. This is particularly true when dealing with multiple items that are similar (e.g., shell casings), but which were not fully marked on scene. This approach is discouraged. It is far better to create a written evidence log on scene, to prevent misidentifying or in some fashion misrepresenting where an item was located.

Defining the proper number of search team members is more difficult. As the next section on search methods will explain, what the police are searching for and in what environment they are searching for it will force a number of issues with regard to the number of searchers involved. In the "typical" crime scene search, a minimum of at least two search team members should be involved. A single searcher, no matter how methodical that person may be, is always capable of overlooking something. Because we tend to see and perceive things differently, two sets of eyes operating over the same territory will usually prevent inadvertently missing items of evidence.

Crime Scene Search Considerations

Eventually a search of the scene will be required to locate any evidence that is present. The specific method the crime scene team chooses to conduct the search is really unimportant so long as the method employed is methodical and systematic.

The word *methodical* is defined as "marked by ordered and systematic habits or behavior."[2] Methodical then, at least in the author's consideration, is the application of established procedures and practices. The word *systematic* is defined as being "purposefully regular."[3] Thus the approach used to conduct the search must be based on established practice and routinely conducted in a purposefully regular fashion. From the application of a methodical and systematic approach, the end result will be an all-encompassing and detailed search in which little if anything will be overlooked. What the crime scene team cannot do is meander about in the scene, moving from one point to the next, wherever fancy and mindless focus lead them.

Whatever search method is used, there are a number of factors to consider regarding the area or search swath that a single searcher is responsible for at any moment. This width, i.e., the size of the strip or swath the searcher is viewing at any given moment, is affected by the following factors:

- Nature of the ground being searched
- Lighting conditions
- On-scene environmental conditions
- Size of the item being searched for

The nature of the area being searched will have a significant impact on the swath a single searcher can evaluate. For example, a cluttered room with items strewn about on the floor is far more difficult to examine thoroughly than a clean, well-swept industrial floor. Similarly, searching an asphalt parking lot is far easier than searching through a field of knee-high grass (Figure 5.8). Since the crime scene team does not get to choose the site of the crime, all they can do is adjust the size of their search swath to the terrain they encounter.

The time of day and ambient lighting conditions can severely hamper the ability of even the best searcher. It is not uncommon to walk into a crime scene and find a single 40-watt bulb burning in a corner with no other lighting available, natural or otherwise. Crime scene technicians often carry 100-watt bulbs in their crime scene kits and use these to replace the existing bulbs in the scene. Although this practice will enhance the lighting conditions, it will not resolve all issues. The poorer the lighting conditions in the scene, the smaller the width of area the searcher can effectively monitor. On the other hand, if lighting conditions are favorable or if additional lights are brought in, the searcher can

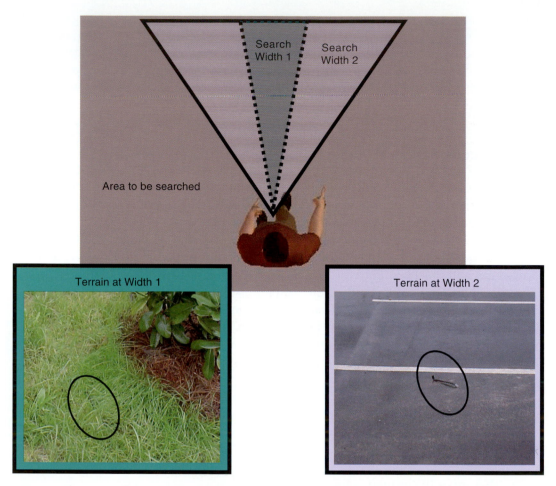

Figure 5.8 The area or swath that a single searcher can evaluate at any given moment is a function of many things. As in this case, when the search involves terrain such as high grass, the swath of area being searched must be reduced. On the other hand, when searching an area such as asphalt, the searcher can increase the swath size.

widen this swath, allowing the coverage of more ground in a shorter period. See Figure 5.9 and Figure 5.10.

Above and beyond the ability to put sufficient light onto the area to be searched, the kind of light available is a factor as well. The most important tool of the crime scene searcher is clean white light. Fluorescent lights, standard house bulbs, and flashlights are all helpful. They will certainly increase the illumination in the scene, but they do not always allow the searcher to see the scene cleanly. Natural white light produced by the sun, and mimicked by a variety of unfiltered alternative light source (ALS) systems, allows the crime scene technician to see and perceive the scene much more accurately. For example, in Figure 5.9, note the presence of a yellow tint in the light produced by the flashlight. That yellow tint affects the reflection of color for every item in the scene. The ALS used in Figure 5.10, however, produces a far more natural light that reflects the colors more accurately.

Lacking an ALS, work lights and spotlights are one optional way to increase ambient light in both interior and exterior scenes. These systems may include halogen work lights, industrial lighting systems with generators, or spotlights mounted on vehicles (Figure

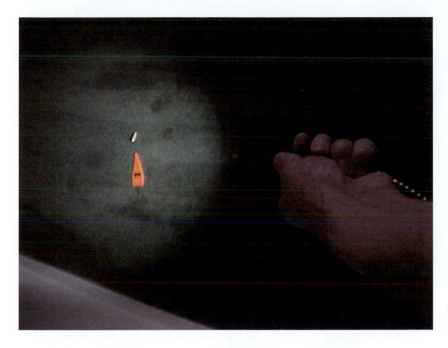

Figure 5.10 With the use of a portable alternative light source (ALS) system, the same area as in Figure 5.9 is illuminated with far better results. The beam of light produced by the ALS allows the searcher to check a broader area effectively in a single glance.

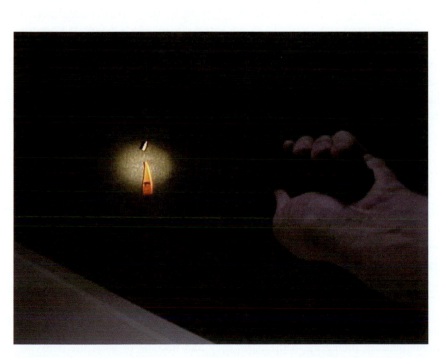

Figure 5.9 Ambient light and available light will affect the area that can be searched by a single searcher. In this instance, a flashlight provides effective lighting, but the beam obviously limits the area under observation.

Figure 5.11 Additional lighting systems are available to increase lighting in dark interior scenes and to help illuminate low-light exterior scenes. These may include halogen work lights (foreground) or vehicle-mounted spotlights. Often the crime scene team can also procure large industrial lighting systems from the fire department as well.

5.11). Halogen work lights are the most common approach for the crime scene technician. They can be purchased at any hardware store for a minimal cost, but they do come at a price in terms of application in the scene. First and foremost, they usually increase the ambient temperature in the scene, particularly in enclosed rooms. As a result, it becomes difficult to work in close quarters with one of these lighting systems while wearing protective garments. Second, the work lights often produce a glare that may actually reduce the ability of the searcher in some areas. Nevertheless, lacking the availability of any other lighting system, these work lights set up easily and provide significant additional lighting. By installing a power converter in the investigator's vehicle, one designed to convert the car's 12-V dc system to 110 V ac, halogen light systems become mobile as well.

When considering exterior scenes, particularly large-scale exterior scenes, the investigative team may find that there is no other option than to wait for daylight before conducting the search. In many instances, work lights and industrial lighting will simply not fulfill the lighting requirement, at least not in sufficient fashion to ensure a good-quality search.

Case Example: Waiting for Dawn

Just after midnight, in 1981, a Washington State fire crew responded to a brush fire in a recreational area. As the fire crew worked the field fire, they repeatedly found themselves tripping over items beneath their feet. In the dark, they had no clue of what the items actually were. Once the fire was under control, they took a moment to investigate and, to their surprise, determined that they had been fighting the fire on top of what appeared to be a body. The investigators called to the scene discovered a severely decomposed body, essentially consisting of skeletal remains. As the scene was examined with flashlights and additional lighting, bones were found scattered across an area of no less than $1/4$ acre.

The scene was in a field, $1/2$ mile from the nearest street, with no ambient light whatsoever. Even with the additional lighting present on the fire truck, most of this area was pitch black. Although no one really wanted to spend the rest of the morning waiting for dawn, the senior investigator realized that there was no other course of action. The crime scene team went into hold and waited for sunrise. When dawn arrived, a reassessment of the scene quickly expanded the area involved from the $1/4$ acre evident the night before to an area that easily encompassed a full acre. Small bones and artifacts were scattered from one end of this field to the other. Interestingly enough, even in the light of day, the head of the body was never discovered.

The team could easily have begun processing the scene the night before. Indeed, there was significant discussion and peer pressure suggesting this course of action. This "get on with it and get home" attitude often appears on scene. But the senior investigator, a wise and experienced crime scene investigator, realized that the effectiveness of a nighttime search would have been severely limited. Using the lighting available that night, he knew it was impossible to be confident of the actual scene limits or the quality of the search. Waiting for dawn and natural light was the only valid option available.

On-scene environmental conditions will certainly affect the ability of the searcher. In interior scenes, temperature extremes, odors, and other environmental factors can interfere with the ability of the searcher. In exterior scenes, rain, snow, or other inclement weather may limit the ability of the searcher. Clothing and equipment intended to limit the impact of such conditions will also affect the visual ability and stamina of the searcher. The concentration and focus of any searcher is always negatively affected as the environmental conditions worsen. The most appropriate way to respond to such conditions is to decrease the width of the swath being searched.

On occasion, the crime scene team may be required to search an area for a specific item, rather than conducting a generalized search for any and all evidence. In this instance, the size of the item being searched for will clearly impact on the width of area a single searcher can evaluate. Looking for a shell casing in a manicured lawn is a far different activity than looking for a .40-caliber pistol in the same lawn, as illustrated in Figure 5.12 and Figure 5.13.

As conditions and the situation change in the scene, the searcher must adjust the size of the search swath accordingly. Particularly when conducting an initial search, when the searcher has no idea of what s/he may or may not find; the smaller the width of the search swath, the better is the search.

Search Patterns

There are five basic patterns for conducting a detailed crime scene search:

1. Circle or spiral search
2. Strip and line search
3. Grid search
4. Zone search
5. Point-to-point search

Figure 5.12 Oftentimes a search is directed at a specific object. The nature of the object will force issues as to how wide of a search path a single searcher can evaluate. In this instance, a single .40-caliber shell casing in a manicured lawn is difficult to see, even close up.

One significant point is worth emphasizing when utilizing any of these search patterns. As they have developed over time, these techniques are generally described in any number of books on crime scene methods. But as defined, the descriptions suggest a two-dimensional process. The crime scene search is a three-dimensional process. As simple as this may seem, it is a point that must be made. Whether using a strip, circle, or zone, all of the surfaces that come into the swath of the searcher (e.g., undersides of cabinets, ceilings, table legs, trees, and shrubs) have to be examined.

Circle or Spiral Search

The circle or spiral search is an effective method that is widely employed in interior scenes. The searcher begins on the outside of the area or room and then, moving in a slow circle, searches in a spiral pattern inward, as seen in Figure 5.14. As was previously discussed, the width of the swath or area being evaluated with each spiral is scene dependent. The circle search is also employed in reverse, by moving outward from a primary focal point or the center of a room. The only critical consideration in the circle search is managing the pace of the search. As the circle closes, the searcher often begins moving along the path of the spiral at a faster pace. The searcher has to consciously slow his or her speed as the area remaining to be examined narrows. Whether moving inward or outward, the searcher must maintain a pace that allows a full evaluation of the area in question.

Figure 5.13 If the object of the search is a weapon in the same manicured lawn, the situation is radically different. Searchers must modify their approach to the search to meet the conditions and situation.

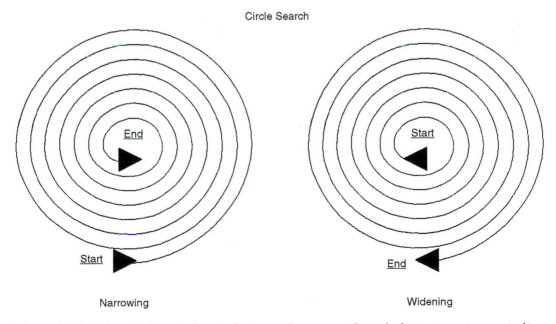

Figure 5.14 The spiral or circle search. A searcher moves through the scene using a spiraling pattern.

Strip and Line Search

The strip search is also a very effective technique. It is most often used in exterior scenes when a large area is being evaluated. Classic scene examples include yards or parking lots. A strip or swath size — one that can be functionally evaluated by a single searcher given the scene conditions — is designated by the crime scene team. The area is then subdivided into similar strips. In extremely large areas, the team can physically designate the strips by marking them with engineer tape or string. This action prevents searchers from fading from a given lane. In most circumstances, searchers are simply held responsible for visually maintaining their bearings. The searcher begins on an outer strip and moves down that strip. Upon arriving at the end of the area in question, the searcher reverses direction and evaluates the next adjacent strip. This process is repeated until the entire area has been evaluated, as seen in Figure 5.15.

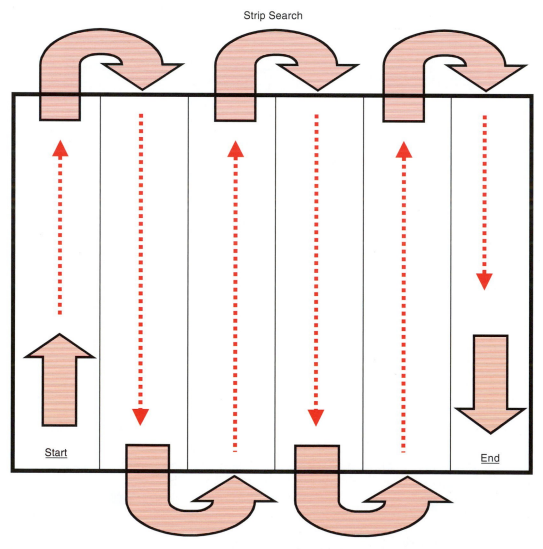

Figure 5.15   In the strip search, a searcher divides the area in question into functional strips or lanes. The searcher starts at one end of the scene and begins searching each strip, reversing direction at the end of a lane and searching the next adjacent strip until all areas have been evaluated.

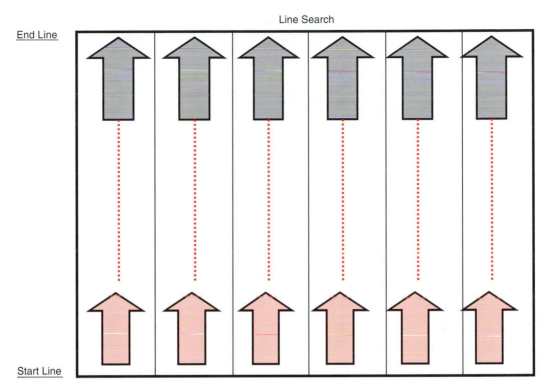

Figure 5.16   The line search is a variation on the strip search. It is effective when dealing with uneven terrain. A group of searchers is lined up along the lanes and moves in a single direction from a start line to an end line. Each searcher is responsible for evaluating a single lane. To keep the line moving, as items are encountered, the evidence is flagged and a team comes in behind the searchers to process the evidence.

A line search is a variation on the strip search. The primary distinction between the two methods is in the number of searchers. In the strip search, one or two searchers may start on the outside lanes and move back and forth until all ground has been covered. In the line search, a large group of searchers line up on the lanes and move down the strips together in a single direction, each evaluating their particular lane, as seen in Figure 5.16. The number of searchers necessary is, of course, scene dependent. This method is particularly useful in dealing with exterior scenes over uneven terrain. The most critical consideration for the search team is to move the group together as a single entity. Searchers should remain on line, moving at the pace set by the slowest searcher. One method that allows the search to proceed in a timely fashion is to flag items of evidence as they are found. Once flagged, the line of searchers continues on, and a crime scene team comes in behind the line to process the item. Whether in a shoulder-to-shoulder formation or at arms length from each other, any staggering of the individuals in the line is likely to result in an area being overlooked or in one end of the line pivoting the entire line. Such a motion will drag the entire formation off course from the intended area. To prevent this, the line search usually requires one or more supervisors to monitor and direct the pace of various parties in the line. On even terrain or in urban environments, the line search is easy to control. The more uneven the terrain, the more difficult it will become to control. Unfortunately, as the terrain gets rougher, the line search may be the only effective way to confidently search such an area.

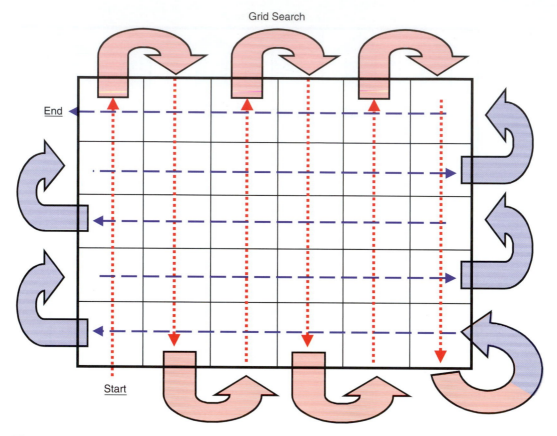

Figure 5.17 The grid search is also a variation on the strip search. Instead of a single group of lanes, two groups are established at 90-degree angles to each other. Starting at one end, the searcher moves along the first group in the same fashion as a normal strip search. When the searcher reaches the end, s/he begins the second look over the same terrain, following the second set of lanes. This results in one searcher checking the area twice from two different perspectives.

Grid Search

The grid search is another variation on the strip search. Rather than limit the search area to strips oriented in a single direction, the area is divided into two sets of strips or lanes that run at 90-degree angles to each other. Once subdivided in this fashion, the searcher treats each set of lanes in the same fashion as in a normal strip search. Starting on an outer lane, the searcher moves up and down the lanes until s/he reaches the far side of the area being evaluated. At that point, the searcher begins a second search using the second set of lanes, which lie at right angles to the first (Figure 5.17). What the grid method creates is a second look by a single searcher over all of the ground being evaluated. Simply changing the direction of the search, in and of itself, often changes the searcher's perception of the area, ensuring a more effective search.

Zone Search

The zone search is used in two variations. The first variation of the zone search is particularly effective when dealing with small confined spaces, areas that are not easily searched

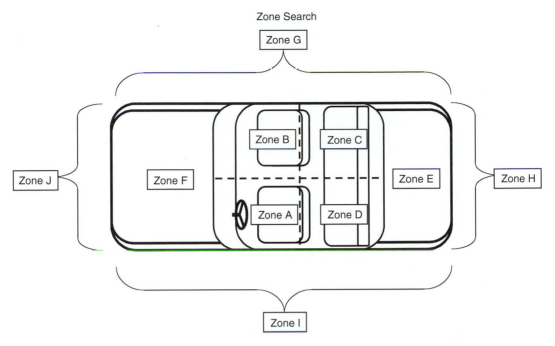

Figure 5.18 One variation of the zone search is to break down an area that is not easily checked with another patterned search into small, defined areas. The searcher checks each section independently before moving on to the next.

by a patterned movement (e.g., a spiral movement). The classic example of a zone search is the vehicle search. The areas in question in the vehicle are broken down into zones, and the searchers deal with each one individually. For example, in Figure 5.18 the inner compartment of a car can be broken down into four areas or zones (Zones A to D). The crime scene technician checks each area thoroughly and independently of the other sections before moving on. This process will generally result in sufficient overlap to prevent items from being missed that may lie in between or under the seats near an adjoining zone. The hood and trunk are each considered an independent zone (Zones E and F) and are dealt with accordingly. If the exterior of the car is under scrutiny for fingerprints, paint chips, bloodstains, or some other type of evidence, each side of the vehicle becomes a zone (Zones G to J). The utility of the zone search is that it prevents the searcher from indiscriminately moving from one point of interest to another. It forces the searcher to consider each area independently and reduces the probability that an area will be overlooked.

The second variation of the zone search is to subdivide a larger scene into manageable pieces of ground that the searcher can then check with some other search method (e.g., strip or spiral). As depicted in Figure 5.19, these zones are often defined by the geography of the scene. In the figure example, the yard is broken down into eight zones (Zones 1 to 8). Each zone is assigned to a team to be checked independently using a strip, circle, or grid search. If directly involved, the house is defined as Zone 9, which another team will evaluate.

A more formal approach to subdividing an area is to physically grid off the zones. Although this can be done with engineer tape or crime scene barrier tape, it is often more effective to simply stake the grid intersections. The grid intersections created are then assigned a letter and number system. Each individual zone can be identified by the associated intersections that define its perimeter, as seen in Figure 5.20. This method is par-

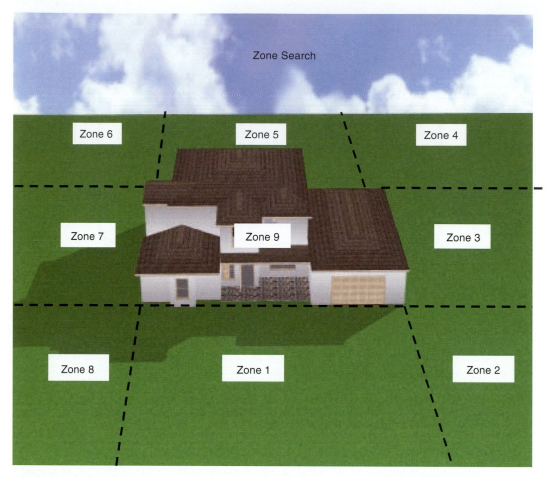

Figure 5.19 Another variation of the zone search is to break a large area up into smaller areas to be searched independently by different teams. Once the area has been broken down and assigned, the team uses another search pattern (e.g., strip or grid) to check these smaller zones.

ticularly effective in dealing with large exterior crime scenes involving significant amounts of evidence, situations involving scattered remains, or even aircraft crashes. The zones and associated grid allow the area to be effectively subdivided, which allows for more effective command and control by a supervisor when assigning and verifying that areas have been searched. It also provides for a more thorough search and easier identification of where in the scene the various items of evidence are found. Using the measurement techniques to be described in Chapter 7, the evidence is fixed using the intersections of the smaller zone as a reference. This significantly reduces the span of measurements necessary for fixing evidence in these large, expansive scenes.

Point-to-Point Search

Point-to-point search methods are rarely practiced in the U.S., at least in any effective manner. The point-to-point method is taught in the "Scenes of Crime Officer's Course" at the Metropolitan Police Academy in Hendon, England. In the point-to-point search, the crime scene investigator determines in what order s/he wishes to deal with primary focal points and evidence. Following that priority, a path is cleared to the first focal point (e.g.,

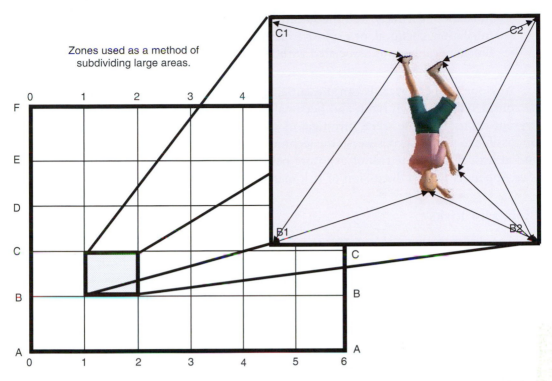

Figure 5.20 In extremely large scenes, zones can be formally assigned and a grid established using stakes and/or barrier tape. The use of barrier tape is not as functional, as searchers must move around the tape. The use of stakes is effective and has been employed by the FTSB (Federal Transportation Safety Board) at aircraft crashes. The teams use each intersection as a reference point for evidence-fixing measurements.

the body in a homicide) and an area cleared around this point. That particular focal point is dealt with accordingly, and when it is completed, the team clears a path to the next focal point. This process is repeated until all areas have been dealt with and processed. The application of proper point-to-point search methods is a far cry from entering the scene and allowing the team to move randomly through the scene. The primary distinction is that walk and work paths are cleared from and to each point of interest, and the team does not stray from these cleared areas. Throughout the author's career, he can recall no instance in which he observed a point-to-point search conducted as defined above. Lacking practice in this method, the point-to-point search routinely breaks down into a haphazard affair.

Personal Protective Measures and Hazard Identification

Once the search method and approach are defined, the crime scene team must consider safety issues. A significant level of effort has been directed at informing crime scene investigators on the issues of biohazards. Biohazards are clearly important, but the nature of hazards at the crime scene is not limited to biohazards. The full scope of hazards includes:

- Biohazards from blood and other body fluids
- Structural hazards found in fire and explosion scenes
- Chemical and inhalation hazards found in fire scenes

- Inhalation, chemical, and fire hazards from on-scene processing methods
- Inhalation, chemical, or explosive hazards associated with drug labs
- Biochemical hazards associated with terrorism

Any one of these hazards can present significant health and safety issues. Each must be considered in its own right, and personal protective measures should be employed to prevent exposing crime scene investigators to potential hazards. In most instances, it is impossible to prevent exposure, so the technician must apply risk-management techniques and at least mitigate the risk of exposure before directing team members into the scene. (See Appendix B for a discussion of risk management.)

Biohazard Risks

Biohazards are the most common concern of crime scene investigators, particularly when dealing with violent crime or death scenes where the technician is likely to encounter blood, urine, fecal matter, sputum, or vomit. The primary biohazards associated with such situations are HIV and hepatitis. HIV, or the human immunodeficiency virus, is responsible for AIDS (acquired immune deficiency syndrome). The HIV virus attacks white blood cells known as CD4 T-cells in the host, reducing the ability of the host to fight off other infections. Following infection by HIV, if the CD4 cell count falls below a certain level, the individual is considered to have AIDS. In the past, any HIV infection would almost certainly lead to AIDS. Although there is still no cure for HIV exposure, currently there are a number of treatments that help keep the infection from progressing to AIDS. HIV is transmitted primarily through contact with blood, semen, and vaginal secretions. Avenues of infection in the crime scene run the gamut from needle-stick injuries to direct exposure of open wounds and mucous-membrane contact (e.g., eyes, nose, and mouth). A critical concern regarding HIV is its survivability in a dried form. The only literature available suggests that the virus can remain active for up to 3 to 5 days in a dried form, and when wet, the virus can survive for even longer periods.[4] The HIV transmission risk appears relatively low for most crime scene exposure, with studies suggesting an infection rate of less than 1% in cases involving blood contact with an open wound. Studies of mucous-membrane exposure suggest an even lower infection rate of less than 0.1%. However, these same studies suggest that the risk increases as the volume of infected blood involved in the exposure increases.[5]

Hepatitis A (HAV), hepatitis B (HBV), and hepatitis C (HCV) are additional threats present in biological fluids. HAV and HBV are less severe than HCV. HAV is transmitted primarily through oral or fecal routes, while HBV is transmitted through direct and indirect contact with infected blood or body fluids. This includes needle-stick injuries or other minor injuries caused by infected articles in the crime scene. In terms of efficiency of infection by HBV, contact with infected blood is more likely to result in infection than with other body fluids.[6] Of particular concern is the fact that HBV can survive in dried blood at room temperature for periods up to 1 week.[7] Both hepatitis A and B result in a variety of symptoms that affect the individual, including fever, malaise, nausea, jaundice, and abdominal discomfort. Untreated, either form of the disease can lead to more significant complications and even death.[8] Both are on the rise in the U.S. population. There are preventive treatments for both hepatitis A and B, in the form of inoculations. In the

U.S., OSHA regulations (OSHA 1910.1030) direct employers of at-risk employees to pay for such inoculations when requested by the employee.

Hepatitis C (HCV) is the more severe form of the three viruses. HCV attacks the liver and leads to serious liver problems or death. There are no preventive treatments for hepatitis C. Exposure routes for the disease are similar to HBV, with direct or indirect contact with infected blood the primary exposure risk at the crime scene. Studies show a less than 2% incidence rate of infection following exposure of open wounds to HCV infected blood and an even lower incidence rate for mucous-membrane exposures. There have been no reported cases of infection from exposure of intact skin with HCV-infected fluids.[9]

Any of these biohazard exposures can occur while assisting in first aid, handling the injured or dead, or through a variety of mechanisms involved in processing the scene. The crime scene technician can reduce this threat in a number of ways. If at all possible, individuals with preexisting open sores, cuts, or abrasions should not work a scene where a biological hazard is present. If this is not possible, such injuries must be thoroughly protected and isolated above and beyond the normal use of protective equipment. When involved in searching or engaged in activities involving tools, the crime scene technician should use extreme care, as needle-stick injuries and evidence-collection accidents represent a significant exposure avenue. During the collection of biological samples, in particular when scraping dried stains, only those individuals necessary for the operation should be present. These individuals should wear an appropriate particulate mask with safety goggles to eliminate exposure of mucous-membrane tissue from airborne particles. Activities such as eating, drinking, smoking, or the application of makeup are also discouraged in any biohazard scene.

Another concern for the technician is postprocessing exposure through contamination of crime scene equipment and clothing. The use of personal protective equipment (PPE) in the biohazard scene, to include shoe booties, is critical. This prevents the technician from carrying to their home, office, or car any contaminants on their footwear. Favorite pens or notebooks should not be utilized inside the crime scene either. It is better to use disposable pens and paper pads. Once processing is complete, these items are disposed of to eliminate any possible cross-contamination issue. Any durable items or equipment exposed to biohazards in the scene must be decontaminated. Durable equipment can be washed with a 1:10 dilution of bleach and water. Items such as plastic photo tents or scales can be cleaned with less-caustic commercial alcohol solutions.

Technicians should establish a biohazard collection point at the working perimeter. This should be a location convenient to the access point of the primary scene. The collection point should have large plastic trash bags (taped open) to help eliminate excessive handling of contaminated items by crime scene technicians. Fresh PPE (e.g., Tyvek, booties, and gloves) should be present here as well, making it easy for technicians to change gloves and booties when exiting and reentering the primary scene.

Crime scene supervisors should make exposure prevention their primary strategy for protecting their workers. The next step of prevention is vaccination from HBV for any technician who routinely processes biohazard scenes. Finally, if prevention fails and an accidental exposure occurs, the individual should seek medical assistance in order to obtain the most appropriate treatment. The CDC (Centers for Disease Control) indicates that timely reporting of possible exposure is very important for effective treatment. The individual should seek treatment in hours, not days.[10]

Current guidelines suggest the following as on-scene first-aid procedures following a suspected exposure. In situations involving mere contact, wash the area involved with soap and water or an antimicrobial wash. Exposed mucus membrane tissues should be flushed with water. Although prior guidelines suggest allowing needle-stick injuries or other wounds to bleed freely for a moment, there is no evidence to suggest that this action will reduce the probability of infection.[11] If possible, wash and rinse the wound with soap and water or an antimicrobial solution. The injured party should then seek medical assistance and report the incident to supervisors.

Structural Hazards in Fire and Explosion Scenes

Structures damaged as a result of fire, bombs, or explosions represent a significant threat to the crime scene processor. What may appear as structurally sound may actually be a severely weakened building. Additional weight or pressure on a wall or floor can lead to collapse or cave-in. The expertise of the firefighters on scene will serve as a primary line of defense for the crime scene technician. Prior to initiating interior operations in such a building, the crime scene supervisor should verify the safety of the building with the fire marshal. In severe situations, the crime scene technicians may have to call on the expertise of a structural engineer to determine if the scene is safe, and if it is not, determine how to make it safe. See Figure 5.21.

Chemical and Inhalation Hazards in Fire Scenes

One of the primary health concerns in the fire scene is the inhalation of dusts and gases. Scene processing, in particular the process of removing debris, will expose the technicians to significant levels of charcoal dust. Beyond the sheer amount of dust the technician may breathe in, contaminants present in the dust can increase the health risks. In older buildings, it is not uncommon to find asbestos material, and some scenes may contain burned wood treated by arsenic or other chemicals. Once burned, these contaminants become an integral part of the dust circulating in and around the scene. The primary control measure to prevent exposure to dust is for the technician to wear a proper particulate mask.

Inhalation, Chemical, or Fire Hazards from Scene-Processing Techniques

Many of the techniques the crime scene technician may use on scene also represent potential hazards. The first and foremost advice for the technician is to ensure that s/he understands all associated safety concerns of any collection techniques employed in the crime scene. A number of chemical enhancement techniques can expose the technician to chemicals for which the full health implications are not yet known. An example of this problem was the old presumptive test for blood using benzidine. These tests were routinely used at the crime scene for a number of years, until benzidine was determined to be carcinogenic. A variety of new tests have since replaced the benzidine derivatives, including leucomalachite green and phenolphthalein. Although these replacements are not considered carcinogenic, they are still active chemicals, and the technician should guard against direct skin exposure or inhalation of vapors.

A number of current fingerprint techniques also pose a scene hazard. The use of ethyl cyanoacrylate (super-glue vapors) or iodine fuming — both of which are common and functional crime scene techniques — can expose the technician to inhalation irritants when

Figure 5.21 Fire scenes always represent a significant scene hazard. The fire burned beneath this floor, resulting in several weakened areas. These weak spots are not always readily evident. If the crime scene team fails to ask the fire marshal to examine the scene before processing, they may find themselves breaking through floors or having ceilings fall onto them.

used in unventilated areas. Inhaled iodine fumes are not only an irritant, but are also toxic. Solvent-based fingerprinting methods such as ninhydrin and amido-black represent a possible fire hazard. In the instance of amido-black, the best precaution is to use only water-based procedures at the crime scene.[12] The use of solvent-based techniques can lead to oxygen depletion in the working area, resulting in an asphyxiation hazard.[13] Standard powder-and-brush applications represent a minor inhalation hazard from airborne particles, leading to respiratory irritation. Specialty powders such as aluminum powder present a greater risk due to the finely milled size of the aluminum particles. Wearing a particulate mask will reduce this type of hazard. When using aluminum powder in confined spaces, a breathing apparatus may be necessary to provide adequate protection to the crime scene technician.[14] Simply put, the list of hazards from scene processing is anything but limited. New techniques and procedures are discovered and tested routinely, and crime scene technicians should ensure that they understand any possible health risk before attempting these techniques in the field.

The primary exposure control for the technician consists of knowing how to use these techniques properly, wearing gloves and PPE to prevent direct exposure of exposed skin and eyes to chemicals, and wearing masks or breathing apparatus when employing these techniques. The suggested guidelines for using any on-scene solvent technique include having a second team member observe the procedure from a well-ventilated area. This person is responsible for monitoring and aiding the scene processor should something go awry.[15] First aid for exposure to spills or splashes of chemicals applied in scene consists of washing the affected area in cold running water. If any level of irritation, soreness, or complication persists, or if the identity of the chemical is unknown, the technician should immediately seek medical assistance.

Chemical and Bioterror Hazards

Drug labs represent a significant hazard to law enforcement. For example, the chemicals and solvents utilized in methamphetamine labs can be toxic to humans both from contact and or inhalation. At varying stages of production, these labs are literally bombs waiting to go off. In any situation involving a suspected drug lab, the initial responding officers and crime scene team should egress from the area immediately and await assistance from a team properly trained and equipped to enter and make the scene safe. Under no circumstances should the team attempt to handle the scene independently, unless previously trained and equipped to do so.

Finally, with the realities of terrorism, crime scene investigators must consider and approach the mass-casualty scene and suspected anthrax scenes carefully. By definition, crime scene technicians who become casualties have failed in their mission. Procedures and SOPs should be established for dealing with anthrax scares, and those responsible should practice these techniques so they are comfortable recovering evidence while operating under these conditions.

Personal protective equipment (PPE), illustrated in Figure 5.22, is the primary safeguard for many of these crime scene hazards. Goggles or safety glasses help prevent contact from splashes of chemicals or blood. Goggles will usually provide some level of protection of mucous membrane tissues from airborne particles as well (e.g., when scraping dried bloodstains for serology samples). Face masks and particle masks prevent inhalation of dust and other nontoxic irritants such as latent-print powders. A Tyvek suit creates a liquid-impervious barrier that will help protect the technician's clothes from chemical and biohazard contact. Rubber gloves provide the same protection for the technician's hands, guarding against contact with chemicals or biohazards. Booties provide some level of splash and contact protection for the technician's shoes and boots, eliminating cross-transfer issues when they leave the scene. Depending upon the hazards present, any or all of these PPE items may be necessary. Remember that the crime scene technician's strategy is one of prevention. *Prevention is always preferred over treatment!*

Considerations for Mass Crime Scene and Mass-Casualty Situations

Mass crime scenes in many respects are no different than any other crime scene, at least in terms of the basic actions necessary to document and process them. Size and complexity, however, will force a number of issues and may stretch the capability of any single organization to handle the scene independently. A mass crime scene will often demand a multijurisdiction response. The major concerns of the mass crime scene lie in the facts that (1) personnel from these multiple jurisdictions must somehow operate as a cohesive

Personal Protective Equipment (PPE)

1. **Goggles/eye protection** - splash and mucous membrane tissue protection.

2. **Face/particle mask** - inhalation protection.

3. **Tyvek suit** - impervious to liquid contaminants.

4. **Rubber gloves** - impervious to liquid contaminants.

5. **Booties** - splash and contact protection for footwear.

Figure 5.22 Standard personal protective equipment (PPE) may consist of goggles or eye protection, particle masks for the face or mouth, a Tyvek suit, rubber gloves, and booties. Each has a purpose, and each serves to protect the crime scene processor from a variety of on-scene hazards.

team and (2) the available resources will quickly be depleted. Scenes such as the bombed-out Murrah Building or the Columbine High School shooting are an unfortunate reality. This reality demands a level of proactive effort on the part of those responsible for providing crime scene response *before* an incident happens.

The following discussion is based primarily on the efforts and lessons learned in the Columbine High School shooting in Littleton, CO. Tom Griffin and Chris Andrist coauthored the publication *Mass Crime Scene Handbook*, which is based on their experiences as well as the experiences of many others who worked the Columbine scene.[16] Griffin and Andrist offer a variety of key considerations on preparing for and handling these types of scenes. Not unlike the "typical" crime scene, mass crime scenes first and foremost require a level of prior coordination, but this coordination extends beyond the limits of a single organization. Processing the mass crime scene will demand capabilities and personnel from any number of the local or state agencies. Without some level of pre-event coordination, these agencies will be left to learn how to work together on the fly.

Prior coordination begins at the executive level and involves the primary organizations responsible for dealing with a mass scene or mass-casualty situation. These parties may include, but are not limited to, the following:

- ME or coroner's office
- Chiefs of police for local agencies
- Sheriff
- District attorney
- State police and investigative agencies
- Local FBI
- HAZMAT officials
- Explosive Ordinance Disposal (EOD)
- Fire and rescue services[17]
- Local emergency management officials

These and any other relevant entities should meet and seek to develop a standard implementation of the incident command management system (ICMS). They should consider possible scenarios, discuss risk management for critical targets, and decide who the primary responders should be and what each organization should handle. These efforts are generally executive-level discussions defining organizational responsibilities, establishing mutual aid agreements, and dealing with similar issues, but they can be expanded to include tabletop exercises (e.g., *Abbottville Training Simulation*[18]). Whenever possible, police executives should include senior investigators and crime scene technicians in these training opportunities. Although tabletop exercises do not allow for scene-specific training, they do allow the senior leaders of investigative and crime scene teams to better understand their role in the ICMS.

Pre-Event Considerations of Crime Scene Supervisors

Once the basic issues are resolved at the senior level, the subordinate leaders who are most likely to lead and direct actual operations in a mass scene must work out additional issues. Their considerations may include:

Identification of specific technical skills in local agencies: This requires a skill assessment of the various personnel assigned to the organizations involved. Who is trained in what areas? What specific skills are available if required?

Identification of resources available in the local area: What investigative equipment can the local agencies muster if needed? What is the typical day-to-day stock level of investigative supplies? Is an equipment reserve necessary for a mass scene (e.g., personal protective equipment, barrier tape)? If needed, who will create and maintain this reserve? If required, where in the local area can heavy equipment, additional lighting, and other atypical equipment be located?

Identification of likely staging areas: Where would resources be sent in the instance of a mass scene? It is better to consider and identify in advance possible staging areas, rather than wait for the situation to arise.

Consideration of a scene-access identification system: Access control is much more critical at the mass crime scene. Who will control access to the scene and how will they control it? This issue is complex in a scene where multiple jurisdictions are operating and not everyone may know each other. Identification systems can be devised in advance, and with the availability of computer and lamination systems, these control methods can be taken to and managed at the scene. In a typical scene, inner perimeters tend to self-regulate themselves, but in the typical scene members also know to challenge anyone they do not recognize. At the mass scene, not only do you have a large number of people present who may not know each other, you also have significant media interest. Without a functional badge system in place, unauthorized individuals can violate perimeters without being recognized. In the recent past, there have been more than a few incidents involving media representatives who apparently left their ethics at the door and actively sought to infiltrate scene security. Developing a plan without considering some kind of ID or pass system at the mass scene is an invitation for failure.

The scope and nature of any scene will dictate the crime scene team's response, and this is certainly true for the mass crime scene. It would be nice to believe that prior to any mass scene or mass-casualty event, coordination could be accomplished that would eliminate all issues, but it is unlikely that such coordination could consider and deal with every possible scenario. Much of the coordination necessary to actually deal with a scene will have to wait until after callout and the initial scene assessment. The two primary concerns will be team formation and standardization of techniques.

Team formation deals with all of the issues discussed earlier in the chapter. For instance, will the team approach be one of area or function? What equipment do the teams require, and is that equipment available? If an "available personnel roster" is not already in place, one will be necessary to identify who is actually available from the various agencies to assist. How will the teams collect and store the evidence? Is each jurisdiction responsible for evidence, or will the primary jurisdiction ultimately take all evidence? Whatever decision is made, it will impact on the forms used and coordination required. Team leaders and team members will have to be assigned, and each team must have a team designation (e.g., a letter or number). That team identification should be something that can easily be annotated to photo placards, evidence vouchers, sketches, and other associated team products.[19]

Standardization of techniques across the various teams is a critical aspect for creating seamless teams and producing a consolidated scene documentation package. What conventions will be used on sketches, on photo logs, and for marking evidence? If Team A, operating in Zone 1, uses evidence items 1 to 45 for their sketch and Team B uses the same numbers for the adjoining Zone 2, there is a likelihood of confusion. Andrist and Griffin offer that an effective method is to liberally overestimate the number of evidence numbers and assign them to each team.[20] This approach will eliminate any possibility of duplication. A standard annotation of film rolls is necessary as well, with teams using a similar initial photo placard that clearly identifies the subject of the photographs. Consideration of both a team and zone number may be necessary, since teams may process more than one area within the overall scene. The methods of taking crime scene measurements and the general terminology used to describe the scene must be standardized. Is everyone clear on the difference between a bullet, a casing, and a cartridge? If one team operates on a baseline method while another operates on triangulation, that may lead to confusion. Are measurements for three-dimensional reconstruction necessary? If so, are teams applying the same measurement process? If they do not, the individual trying to put the different teams' effort into one product will end up pulling his hair out.

Standardization at the working-team level will present the greatest challenge and require the highest level of effort from those attempting to coordinate the situation. If this effort is well thought out and managed properly, the end result will be good scene documentation, where the efforts of one team will seamlessly fit with the efforts of another.

Practical On-Scene Considerations for the Mass Scene

There is no foolproof way to prepare anyone for the demands of the mass crime scene. But experience has shown that there are practical techniques that may make the job easier. Andrist and Griffin offer a variety of additional suggestions that will assist in controlling and dealing with the mass scene. These include:

- Dropping body placards at the time of the initial scene assessment. This will assist in tracking bodies throughout the scene processing and prevent confusion once the teams actually enter and begin processing.[21]
- Sending in a video and photo crew before introducing any of the teams into the scene. This is an effective method of documenting the scene before significant disturbance and provides a valuable briefing tool for supervisors.[22]
- As furniture is encountered, marking and labeling legs and chairs, then marking their position on the floor. This will allow the scene to be reassembled quickly after scene processing.[23] Such reconstruction may be necessary for analysis and theory testing.
- Having on-scene or near-scene counseling available for team members.[24]
- Establishing an effective chain of command that allows issues to be addressed in both directions.[25]
- Planning and conducting briefings and updates for team members, both in the course of the event and as a matter of double-checking documentation after the event.[26]

Managing the Media

Although managing the media is not a true logistical or technical consideration, it is a critical crime scene skill. The scene investigator must employ this skill throughout the scene investigation. How well the investigator actually manages media issues is very much a function of the quality of the media–law enforcement relationship that exists in the jurisdiction. Unfortunately the relationship between the media and law enforcement can often be characterized as tenuous at best. Law enforcement often doubts the media's sincerity in providing a true "public service," and the media tend to view our behavior as repressive and unnecessary. In the candid words of one media editor, too often they encounter an officer at the scene whom they view as having the "Barney Fife" syndrome. So there always seems to be a certain level of distrust, which is bridged only by the efforts of professionals on both sides of the relationship.

In order to deal effectively with the media and prevent inappropriate release of information, it is imperative to understand something about how the media operate and the nature of the ethical guidelines they work under. The typical news crew consists of a reporter and video journalist operating from a news truck as an autonomous team. Technology in the form of satellite and microwave communications allows the team to shoot, edit, and direct-feed completed stories from the field. The reporter usually acts as the crew chief and producer for this team, but is backed up by a managing editor or executive producer at the station. Unless dealing with a live feed, producers and editors have the final editorial decision on what is or is not broadcast. In sensitive cases, the executive producer or editor may even seek legal advice before deciding what is airable and what is not. Editorial guidelines usually prevent the airing of video feed involving bodies, body parts, or large blood pools. With that said, news editors quickly acknowledge that they expect their video journalists to be aggressive in getting complete video coverage of the scene and activities around it. Just because it is not typically shown on air does not mean the video journalist is not going to shoot such scenes. If the editor feels that graphic video serves a function in telling a story, then s/he reserves the right to show any video that was shot in a public setting.

As for their technology capability, any news crew outfitted with a mast on their vehicle may also have access to a remote camera mounted on the mast. Once raised, this camera allows the team to shoot video feed around obstacles (e.g., fences, bushes, or even crime scene screens). Of course, the ever-present news helicopter is outfitted with standoff video capability as well, which allows the camera to peer right down on top of the scene.

Ethically, news crews are instructed and expected to comply with all lawful requests and directives by law enforcement officials, in particular respecting crime scene barriers. If issues arise as to the legality of some request by the police, managing editors prefer that the issue be raised at a higher level than the on-scene authorities. In this fashion, the news media avoid creating a specific problem by arguing with the police on scene.

With this information in mind, the crime scene supervisor should approach the news crew with a cautious attitude. Expect them to respect crime scene boundaries and comply with lawful requests. If they fail to do so, the problem is likely to be with the individual and not the station. If a specific problem arises where an individual from the media violates the crime scene boundaries, the crime scene supervisor can begin by taking the issue to the reporter. If that fails to resolve the situation, a call to the station may be all that is necessary. If there are critical considerations in the scene that should not be released, such as hold-back details, the supervisor can approach the news crew as well. The news reporter will act as a go-between for such requests, but the editors and producers back at the station have the final say in deciding whether they will agree to such requests. "Deals" worked out between the crime scene supervisor and reporter may or may not be recognized when the final cut is made back at the station.

The news media prefer when a department has an assigned public information officer (PIO), simply because the probability of developing a good working relationship increases when you have fewer individuals interacting in the relationship. Obviously, what the media want from the PIO is as much information as possible. They prefer that the information be confirmed and not be pure speculation, but, oddly enough, they acknowledge that they will often ask for speculation on the part of the individual serving as the PIO. The media routinely call the PIO the "gatekeeper" in this relationship, meaning that if we, as the police, are willing to say it, then they, as the media, are willing to print or broadcast it. Thus the role of the PIO is critical. This is not a job to be relegated to a rookie or to an inarticulate member of the force. The PIO must use caution when releasing information, ensuring that what is released is appropriate from an investigative standpoint as well as being accurate. Coordination of effort on the part of investigators, senior supervisors, and the crime scene supervisor is necessary to ensure that only necessary information is released. The manner or words a PIO uses when relating this information must be carefully chosen to prevent inappropriate perceptions from viewers or the reporter. When practical, these releases should be written and handed out at the time of the interview. This helps prevent the PIO from going off on a tangent and ensures that a historical record exists of exactly what was said. A standard operating procedure defining the PIO's duties should be in effect long before the PIO says a word, with clear guidelines on how the jurisdiction intends to deal with new releases.

What the media desires from the police in this relationship is even-handed and equitable treatment as professionals, accompanied by an understanding that they too have a job to do. Another critical aspect from the media's perspective is that law enforcement should not carry grudges. The media often encounter stories involving alleged and even verified malfeasance by police or public officials. They have a responsibility to ask hard questions and show both sides of a story, even if it does not serve the best interests of the police department. What they report is that entire departments or an individual officer will often remember such stories and act vindictively at some later date.

A police department must seek a professional and mutually supportive relationship with the media. Operating as antagonists is not the answer, for at some point in the future the police may need the assistance of the media in some fashion. Nevertheless, it can be difficult to work with the media, simply because they expect so much and are willing to give back so little. Ultimately, the individuals who work together on the street will define how good or bad the relationship is between these two entities. Caution is always in order when dealing with the media, but professionalism is a must, which includes recognizing the media's public-service role. The technician may not always agree with this point of view, but it is a reality and a necessity.

Summary

Once the investigative team arrives, a myriad of assessment actions are necessary before initiating scene processing. These actions will define how the crime scene team will operate, help identify the level and nature of the resources necessary to do the job, and help prevent unnecessary exposure of crime scene team to the variety of hazards that may exist.

First and foremost, a debriefing of the initial responding officer is necessary. This debriefing will allow the crime scene team to understand the extent of the scene itself and any alterations that were made to the scene by responding officers, EMS, and others. The debriefing should identify the status of individuals who were on scene, which in and of itself may require further action on the part of the crime scene team.

After conducting the debriefing, the crime scene team must re-access the scope of the scene and adjust the crime scene barriers if necessary. Often, the initial responding officer will not recognize subtle nuances that suggest expanding a scene, or faced with chaotic conditions or the lack of light in the scene, the officer may not realize the full scope of the scene boundary. The crime scene team is responsible to ensure that the full scope of the scene is recognized and protected.

Once the full scope of the scene is evident, the crime scene team must ensure that scene integrity is maintained. The initial responding officer will usually establish a single crime scene barrier, but a single barrier only provides minimal protection. The use of a second barrier by the crime scene team will create multilevel isolation that will ensure that the onlookers and other nonpolice personnel are sufficiently isolated from the actual crime scene. Protection of the scene integrity from onlookers and the media is only half of the picture. The creation of these barriers is also intended to limit the number of police or investigative personnel who may enter the scene, including supervisors. The purpose of a barrier must be respected by everyone once it is established and in place. As a general rule, only those individuals who are actually processing a scene are allowed inside the interior barrier of the crime scene.

Barriers are intended to keep unauthorized individuals from the actual scene and evidence. The crime scene team should expect, however, that counsel will raise the question as to who in law enforcement was allowed access to these areas. The use of a crime scene entry log provides a written record of each individual who entered the primary crime scene. It defines who entered, when they entered, when they left, and what their purpose in the scene was. In multilevel containment, where there are multiple barriers, a crime scene entry log is not necessary for each and every barrier. Only the barrier that defines the actual scene, and perhaps the evidence-holding area, must have an entry-control log. The crime scene team must ensure that an entry log is established and maintained for this area.

Before initiating any processing of the scene, the team leader must decide if they will deploy their resources in an area or functional approach. In the area approach, a single team handles all activities associated with the processing of the scene. In a functional approach, the team leader designates different teams to do different activities (e.g., documentation team, latent-print team, or evidence recovery team) and, using an ordered approach, stages each team through the scene. A variety of factors can affect the team leader's decision, including organizational custom and SOP, size and complexity of the crime scene, and the availability of equipment and manpower resources.

Once a team search approach is defined, the team must then decide on a search method. This decision is based on a variety of factors as well, including but not limited to the nature of the ground being searched, the lighting conditions at the scene, and on-scene environmental conditions. The more disorderly a scene is, the more difficult it may be to search effectively. Similarly, the surface area of a scene may create a significant hindrance to effective searching (e.g., knee-high grass as compared with asphalt). The crime scene team has no control over what area they must search; therefore, in response to these factors, the team will have to adjust the size of the area that a single searcher is responsible for at any given time. Narrowing the search swath that a single searcher is responsible for is the only way to increase the effectiveness of a given search.

The methods most often employed in a crime scene search include the spiral or circle search, the strip or line search, the grid search, the zone search, and finally the point-to-point search. Each method has its unique pros and cons, and no single method must be employed in any given circumstance. Spiral and circle searches are very effective in an indoor or small exterior crime scene. Strip, grid, or line searches are often employed in large exterior scenes. All of them are effective mechanisms, but the line search is the best choice for a situation involving large areas over uneven terrain. The zone search is the most common search used when dealing with small confined spaces that are not easily searched using a patterned search method (e.g., spiral or strip). The zone search is particularly useful when searching a car. Zone searches are also used effectively to subdivide a large crime scene into smaller, more manageable portions, which are then searched using a standard technique such as a strip or grid. The point-to-point method, although an effective process, often breaks down into a haphazard affair. Properly done, the searcher creates cleared paths to and around the areas being searched. Whatever method the crime scene leader designates to use for the search, it must be methodical and systematic. This will ensure an all-encompassing search where little, if anything, is missed.

The crime scene team may face a variety of hazards in a scene. Biohazard scenes represent a significant risk. The crime scene team may be exposed to blood or body fluids that represent exposure risk for HIV, HBV, and HCV. Any one of these viruses represents a significant risk to the health of the crime scene team. There are also inhalation risks when employing chemicals, dusting for latent prints, and when evaluating arson or bomb scenes. Structural hazards exist in arson, bombed, or collapsed building scenes, all of these situations demanding that someone clear the area before initiating operations. Fire and explosive hazards from the use of solvent-based forensic techniques are a concern, and these hazards are especially problematic if the scene involves a drug lab. Crime scene teams must assess the level of risk and, using good risk management techniques, establish methods to reduce or eliminate these risks before entering a scene.

Any and all of these issues affect how the team will process the scene. Each area must be considered and acted on before initiating on-scene processing. Often, a standard approach defined by organizational custom is more than adequate for the crime scene team to employ, but as the complexity and severity of a given scene increase, SOP and custom may not be enough. The crime scene team must be prepared to consider and employ a variety of different techniques and methods in order to accomplish their mission.

Two additional concerns that can affect the crime scene team are dealing with mass crime scenes and the media. The mass scene or mass-casualty situation is a problem that requires "before the event" planning, in which the organizations most likely to work together must plan and organize for the probability of such an event. Once the event does occur, the most critical aspect will be in coordinating the organizations and individuals involved into cohesive crime scene teams whose work product can be integrated into a coherent whole. This will require significant on-scene effort and planning by the crime scene team leaders.

To deal effectively with the media, the crime scene team must understand how the media operate. A professional approach, recognizing that the media have a true public-service function, combined with a cautious attitude will help ensure that both investigative needs and media requests are considered and met whenever possible.

Suggested Reading

Andrist, C. and Griffin, T., *Mass Crime Scene Handbook*, self-published, Denver, CO, 2000.

Police Scientific Development Branch, *Fingerprint Development Handbook*, Home Office Policing and Crime Reduction Group, Heanor Gate Printing Ltd., Derbyshire, U.K., 2000.

Chapter Questions

1. What is the primary concern of scene assessment by the crime scene technician?
2. Why is the use of a single crime scene barrier ineffective?
3. How can enforcing use of personal protective equipment (PPE) help control scene integrity with regard to any police supervisors on scene?
4. When setting up crime scene teams, what are the two basic approaches to team composition and how do they differ?
5. Identify and describe three of the four factors that affect decisions about team composition.
6. Identify and describe the five basic patterns used to search a crime scene.
7. What are the variations of the zone search and when are they used?

8. Why is postprocessing exposure to biohazards a problem and how might it occur?
9. When presented with a possible drug lab, how does the crime scene technician respond?
10. Why is it important to establish standard team processing techniques at a mass crime scene?

Notes

1. Bankhead, J., presentation to the Georgia Association of Chiefs of Police (GACP), Savannah, GA, Aug. 2002.
2. American Heritage College Dictionary, 3rd ed., Houghton Mifflin, Boston, 1993, p. 858.
3. Ibid., p. 1379.
4. Bigbee, D., *The Law Enforcement Officer and AIDS*, 2nd ed., U.S. Govt. Printing Office, Washington, DC, 1988, p. 10.
5. U.S. Department of Health and Human Services, CDC, Updated U.S. Public Health Service Guidelines for the Management of Occupational Exposures to HBV, HCV and HIV and Recommendations for Postexposure Prophylaxis, *Morbidity Mortality Wkly. Rep.*, 50, June 29, 2001, pp. 7–8.
6. Ibid., p. 4.
7. Ibid., p. 3.
8. GlaxoSmithKline Biologicals, Twinrix Hepatitis A and B Twin Threats Twin Defense, Rizensart, Belgium, 2002.
9. U.S. Department of Health and Human Services, CDC, Updated U.S. Public Health Service Guidelines for the Management of Occupational Exposures to HBV, HCV and HIV and Recommendations for Postexposure Prophylaxis, *Morbidity Mortality Wkly. Rep.*, 50, June 29, 2001, p. 6.
10. Ibid., p. 16.
11. Ibid., p. 17.
12. Home Office Policing and Crime Reduction Group, Police Scientific Development Branch, *Fingerprint Development Handbook*, Heanor Gate Printing Ltd., Derbyshire, U.K., n.d. p. 51.
13. Ibid., p. 10.
14. Ibid., p. 76.
15. Ibid., p. 9.
16. Andrist, C.G. and Griffin, T.J., *Mass Crime Scene Handbook*, self-published, Denver, CO, 2000.
17. Ibid., p. 2.
18. Abbottville Training Simulation is a trademark name of Command School Inc.
19. Andrist, C.G. and Griffin, T.J., *Mass Crime Scene Handbook*, self-published, Denver, CO, 2000, p. 4.
20. Ibid., p. 6.
21. Ibid., p. 5.
22. Ibid., p. 5.
23. Ibid., p. 9.
24. Ibid., p. 8.

25. Ibid., p. 6.
26. Ibid., pp. 7–11.

Crime Scene Photography

6

Documentation of the crime scene is truly the most critical element of scene processing. Without good documentation, it is often difficult to explain or make understandable to a jury any observation made by the technician. Without good documentation, it can be difficult if not impossible to weather a well-thought-out cross examination. If there is no supporting documentation that clearly and concisely demonstrates the points the crime scene technician is trying to make, counsel will effectively argue that the technician was mistaken. Documenting the condition of the scene is a core element of proving what did or did not happen at the scene. Without proper documentation, it may be impossible for even the investigators to arrive at a conclusion regarding what did or did not occur. Unfortunately, documentation of the scene is one of the least understood processes of crime scene examination, which routinely results in an incredibly poor documentation product.

What does crime scene documentation entail? Documentation has four key elements:

1. Notes
2. Photographs/video
3. Sketches
4. Reports

Each element plays an important role; each serves to memorialize what the scene condition was, what the investigator observed, and what the investigator did. No single element stands alone; no single element can replace another element in and of itself, but often one element can serve to answer a question that another element is unable to. Together, these four key elements support one another and provide everyone with a clearer picture of the exact nature of the scene. This chapter and the next two chapters provide an in-depth treatment of each area of documentation, illustrating what must be done to document a scene properly and how best to do it.

To say that a picture is worth a thousand words is absolutely true in terms of understanding crime scenes. Put a crime scene technician on the stand and ask him or her to describe the general aspects of some part of the scene. There is no doubt that a competent technician can give an effective description. But in order to describe that small part of the scene, it might take 5 or 10 min of direct testimony, and even after the testimony, it is doubtful that the jury would equally and fully comprehend everything the technician was describing. Give that same jury a single photograph, one that is clear and in focus, and instantly every juror viewing the photo would comprehend the nature of that portion of

Figure 6.1 An overall photograph of a bathroom, with an evident item of interest present on the countertop. This photograph provides the viewer with a visual reference point.

the scene. Graphic information is far easier to comprehend and integrate than testimonial information. Our eyes serve as our window to our comprehension of the world and our surroundings. Without even thinking about it, we see and incorporate interrelationships between objects and spatial relationships of the scene itself, and literally in the blink of an eye, we take in details of color, texture, and any number of other characteristics. Pictures tell the story of the crime scene far better than any other form of evidence.

Crime scene photography, then, is the bread and butter of the crime scene documentation. Crime scene photographs are intended to lead the viewer of the photographs through the scene, from an overall perspective right up to the details of specific items of evidence. See Figure 6.1 through Figure 6.3. Such photographs serve to highlight and make understandable the crime scene report. Even without the report, someone viewing the photographs should comprehend significant details and aspects of the scene.

As important as they are to comprehending the scene, the technician can never take too many photographs. This is particularly true in a significant scene (e.g., a homicide). City managers and police chiefs are often quick to complain about the costs of film and film processing, but remember that the technician has only one chance to process the scene. There are no second chances, no opportunities to return and shoot a picture that was forgotten. By cutting a corner over a few cents worth of film, the technician can be

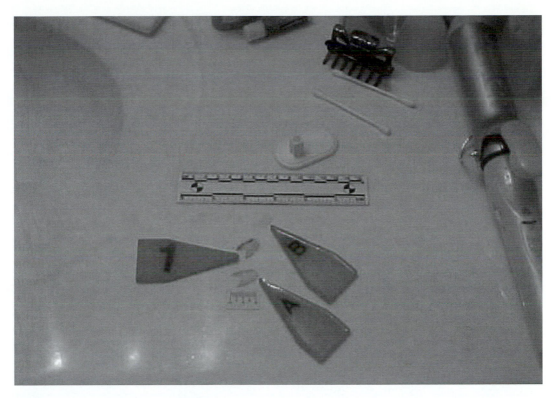

Figure 6.2 An evidence-establishing photograph of the evidence depicted in Figure 6.1. The viewer now recognizes the item of interest and can relate the evidence back to the overall photograph by associated articles and landmarks.

assured of paying for that shortcut three times over in aggravation or in an inability to answer some important question arising from the scene. *Film is the cheapest thing at a crime scene!*

Recurring Problems in Crime Scene Photography

The fact that crime scene photographs are important is hardly a revelation. It has been true throughout the history of criminal investigations. Despite the recognized importance of crime scene photographs, it is an area of documentation that routinely is lacking in content. From homicide scenes in which the total crime scene photographs (including the autopsy) equals a single roll of 36 exposures, to photographs so woefully out of focus that they are of little value, the same mistakes appear over and over again in investigative documentation. Improper photography can be blamed on two areas. The first is a lack of understanding or practice with the photography equipment. Whether using digital cameras, large-format cameras, 35-mm cameras, or instant cameras, the technician must feel confident in the use of the available equipment. A lack of confidence generally manifests itself in terms of poor focus, bleached-out colors, or insufficient lighting. This chapter addresses some basic issues related to lighting and focus that are applicable across the entire spectrum of photography equipment. Beyond understanding these basics, the tech-

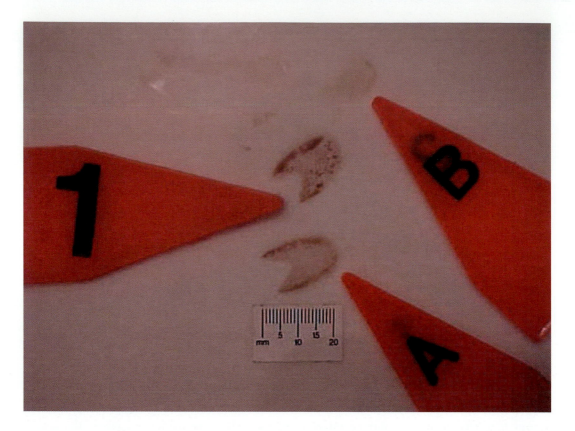

Figure 6.3 A close-up photograph of the evidence allows the viewer to see details of the bloody fingerprints. Combining Figure 6.1 through Figure 6.3 allows the viewer to know what s/he is looking at and where it is in the scene. The photographs lead the viewer to the evidence.

nician must be practiced with the equipment s/he is using. A homicide scene is not the time or place to read the owner's manual for the first time. The second area of concern is a lack of understanding of what the photographs are intended to depict. In nearly any crime scene reference, terms such as *overall, mid-range,* and *close range,* or *overall, evidence-establishing,* and *evidence close-up* photographs are utilized. Unfortunately, few references explain the purpose of each type of photograph and how the technician goes about creating them. As a result, the technician ultimately takes a number of photographs at the scene that create significant comprehension problems, including:

- Identification problems
- Orientation problems
- Confusion problems
- Incomplete documentation

Identification Problems

Photographs can be created in which the viewer has absolutely no idea of what the item is or why the photograph was taken. In viewing the photograph, some object may be apparent, but there are no supporting photographs to help the viewer see the evidence better. Looking at such photographs, the viewer asks questions like "What is it?" or "What size is it?" These problems are eliminated by creating evidence-establishing shots as well as proper evidence close-up shots that clearly and fully depict the object in question.

Orientation Problems

Photographs can be created in which there is no way to distinguish left from right. The viewer is left to ponder and guess where the object actually is in the scene. One of the greatest failures of crime scene photography is the absence of good evidence-establishing shots. These photos serve to orient the viewer as to where the item of evidence is in the overall scene by including some visible landmark. With appropriate landmarks in the evidence-establishing shot, orientation is easily understood. Orientation issues are often significant at trial, because orientation in the scene can change the conclusions drawn from the evidence. Figure 6.4 is a classic example of an orientation problem. Photographs of small items like bloodstains without the proper supporting photographs can leave the viewer wondering not only where the bloodstain is in the scene, but wondering which way is up as well.

What is the orientation?
Which way is up?
What surface is this?

Figure 6.4 A photograph producing an orientation problem. Looking at the photograph, the viewer asks, "Where is the surface this bloodstain is on?" and "What direction is up or down?" Direction and orientation in the scene can be of great significance, so other photographs must provide the viewer with enough information to clearly orient the object in question.

Which photo was first?

Figure 6.5   Multiple photographs of the same area showing the scene in altered conditions can create confusion or become a distracter at trial. Is the coffee cup part of the original scene, or is it a post-incident artifact? Photo logs help clear up issues of this nature.

Confusion Problems

Photographs can be created showing the scene in altered states or conditions. The obvious question becomes, "Which photograph depicts the scene best, and who altered the scene in the first place?" In Figure 6.5, is the coffee cup part of the scene, or is it a post-incident artifact left by the chief of detectives? The use of a photo log helps eliminate many of these problems and prevents wild and unsupported claims by counsel at trial. Confusion also arises from shooting poorly referenced photographs of a number of similar items (e.g., shell casings, bloodstains, or fingerprints). If shooting photographs of four shell casings (items A through D), the photographer must be able to discern which photograph is item A as opposed to items B through D. Photo logs combined with numbered or lettered photo placards will help eliminate this type of confusion.

Incomplete Documentation

Problems also arise from incomplete documentation. Ultimately, all critical aspects of the scene have to be documented through the crime scene photography. Far too often the technician realizes, too late of course, that no photograph of a critical item or condition was taken by anyone. Adherence to a systematic photography technique as well as a standard processing model will usually eliminate significant mistakes of this nature.

Types and Purpose of Crime Scene Photographs

Crime scene photographs are used to support and enhance an understanding of the scene and the investigative report. They should graphically capture the condition and orientation of the overall scene, the location, orientation, and, if possible, the spatial relationships of different areas in the scene to one another as well as to the various items of evidence found in the scene. Finally, they should allow the viewer to see the necessary detail of specific items found in the scene. All of this can be accomplished with three basic types of photographs:

- Overall photographs
- Evidence-establishing photographs
- Evidence close-up photographs

Although there may only be three "types" of photographs, not every item of evidence or point of interest at a crime scene can be adequately captured with only three photographs. At times, it may be necessary to shoot a number of overall photographs, evidence-establishing photographs, and even a number of close-up photographs in order to illustrate all of the important detail of a single item.

Overall Photographs

The purpose of overall photographs is to depict the general condition and layout of the scene. The technician seeks to capture how the scene is oriented, where major visible landmarks are (e.g., doors, furniture, bodies), and the condition of the scene prior to significant alteration. For the latter reason, overall photographs are the first photographs taken. These photographs are often exposed with a wide-angle lens (e.g., 28-mm lens) to allow the photographer to capture a wider area in a single photo. The use of a 28-mm lens will lead to a slight level of spatial distortion, but rarely enough to affect the quality of the photograph or prevent its use at trial. The use of extreme wide-angle lenses, such as a "fish-eye" lens, can enhance the ability of a single photograph to capture a larger area, but as the field of view increases, so too does the distortion. For this reason, a fish-eye lens is not appropriate for overall crime scene photography situations.

Overall photographs are normally discussed in terms of shooting the room or the scene itself. For instance, one effective method of taking overall photographs is to go to a corner of the room or scene and take a photograph across the area to the opposite corner. (See Figure 6.6.) The photographer repeats this process for each corner of the scene, resulting in four photographs that will generally provide overlapping coverage of the entire area. (See Figure 6.7 through Figure 6.10.) This process captures significant detail, but often not everything. Within any scene there may be a number of areas with various items of evidence or conditions that the photographer seeks to capture. Additional photographs of a more defined area can be taken as well, the sole purpose of which is to establish the initial condition and orientation of that area alone. Figure 6.11 is an example of an overall photograph of a bloodstain pattern on the floor. The photograph is not intended to depict close-up detail of the bloodstain, but rather the pattern's overall orientation in the scene and the entire pattern. This kind of overall photograph is related to the technique in bloodstain pattern analysis called *roadmapping*.[1]

Figure 6.6 Overall photographs are exposed so they overlap each other. A typical procedure is to go to the corners of a room and take a photograph in each one, looking to the opposite corner.

Figure 6.7 An example of an overall photograph. Evident landmarks include the desk, the white shelf, and the dark chair.

Figure 6.8 A supporting overall photograph. Additional landmarks include the computer and the brown chair.

Overall photographs are taken in two distinct iterations during crime scene processing. The first occurs prior to the introduction of any scales, photo placards, or the like. These photographs are best for eliminating any issue regarding alteration of the original condition of the scene. If some question exists as to where an item was (e.g., whether a drawer was open or not), these initial overall photographs depict the scene prior to any invasive processing activity. Later, as the technician identifies specific areas and items of evidence, photo placards are introduced, and a second set of overall photographs is created to aid in understanding overall orientation. (See Figure 6.12.) In scenes involving multiple rooms or widely dispersed areas, additional overall photographs may be necessary to properly orient the viewer as to how one room relates to another. (See Figure 6.13.)

Evidence-Establishing Photographs

Evidence-establishing photographs, also referred to as mid-range photographs, serve an important role in crime scene photography. Oftentimes the evidence in the scene consists of small items or objects, many of which will not even appear as recognizable objects in the overall photographs. Provided with only an evidence close-up photograph of such an item, the viewer has no means of determining where in the scene this item was. The evidence-establishing photographs are taken in such a fashion that the item is framed in conjunction with some other obvious landmark evident in the overall photographs.

Figure 6.9   A third supporting overall photograph. The desk, computer, and brown chair are all evident as well as the closet door behind the chair. The position of the red rug in the room is fully understood as well, and additional items of evidence (e.g., the holster at the base of the desk) are evident.

Figure 6.10   The final supporting overall photograph. The white shelf is evident along with the entryway to the room. Combining all four figures (Figure 6.7 through Figure 6.10), nearly every major landmark in the room is evident, and the overall orientation of the items in the room is understood.

Figure 6.11 An overall photograph of a bloodstain pattern. This photograph is intended to demonstrate the pattern's position in the room near the entryway and the extent of the pattern, but it is not intended as an evidence close-up photograph.

Figure 6.12 A second series of overall photographs should be taken after the introduction of photo placards. This helps identify areas of interest. For example, the item associated with placard 1 was not evident in the original overall photograph. Without the placard, the viewer would have no idea the item was even there.

Figure 6.13 Overall photographs can also demonstrate the relationship of one area to another. In this photograph, the doorway, red rug, and white shelf from the scene documented in Figure 6.7 through Figure 6.10 can be seen in the background of another area containing a body and a revolver.

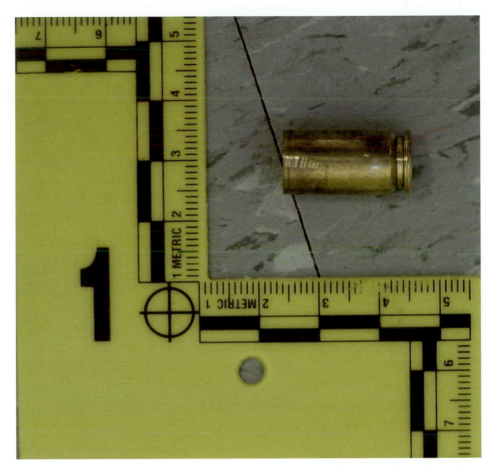

Figure 6.14 A close-up photograph of item 1, an expended shell casing. Alone, this photograph provides the viewer with no reference or understanding of where in the scene it is. Combined with an evidence-establishing photograph (Figure 6.15), its relationship is understood.

Particularly when dealing with a number of similar items (e.g., shell casings or blood-stains), it can be difficult to ensure that the evidence is "recognizable" in the establishing photograph. The use of photo placards is the most effective means of eliminating this difficulty. Figure 6.14 demonstrates not only why the evidence-establishing photo is so important, but also how the photo placard enhances the viewer's understanding. Given only Figure 6.14, a close-up photograph of a shell casing, the viewer has no way of knowing where on the green tile floor this casing is. The addition of a placard identifying it as item 1 and the creation of an evidence-establishing photograph (Figure 6.15) allow the viewer to see the position of the casing in relation to the chair. This effectively places item 1 in this area. Now compare Figure 6.15 with Figure 6.8, an overall photograph of the same area. In the overall photograph, one can clearly see the relationship of the rug, chair, and desk, allowing the viewer of Figure 6.15 to understand the relationship of item 1 to the overall scene. The casing, however, is not distinctly evident in Figure 6.8. The combination of an overall photograph and evidence close-up photograph, in and of themselves, is not usually enough to effectively orient the viewer. The evidence-establishing shot is necessary to properly orient this item. In some instances, the introduction of photo placards can actually decrease the number of photographs needed. If the placards are clearly evident in

Figure 6.15 An evidence-establishing shot of Item 1. The evidence-establishing shot includes landmarks (e.g., the brown chair, the rug, the desk corner) as well as providing a recognizable view of the item. Combined with Figure 6.12 and Figure 6.14, no one can argue that item 1 is anything other than a shell casing or where that casing is in the scene.

the second series of overall photographs, then additional evidence-establishing photographs may not be necessary.

Commercially manufactured evidence placards are cheap and available from a number of suppliers, but there is no requirement that the technician use commercially produced items. The crime scene technician can easily create disposable placards using a variety of products. One of the easiest methods is the use of 4 × 6-in. index cards and a bold marking pen. Index cards can present a minor issue, specifically in outside scenes. The technician must find a means of weighting them down so that they remain in place and do not blow about in the wind. Another easy placard method for outside scenes is to use grading flags and adhesive bold stencil letters, as seen in Figure 6.16. These placards can be produced for no more than a few dollars and are reusable.

A final note on using photo placards: early on, the crime scene technician must initiate a numbering or lettering system for any evidence discovered. Once an item is given a label (e.g., item A) and a photograph is created, the technician cannot arbitrarily renumber the evidence in the report or on the sketch. Doing so will create significant confusion for those viewing the photos and then reading the report.

At times, the technician may be presented with a situation that requires a series of evidence-establishing photographs. Items of evidence can be situated in the scene in such

Figure 6.16 A photo placard created from a surveyor's grading flag. The small orange pointer is a commercially available photo tool. Together, they demonstrate where the item is in the photographs. The addition of the ABFO scale adds a frame of reference as to size.

a fashion that there is no easy way to demonstrate their position. Figure 6.17 is an evidence close-up photograph of an expended bullet. Given the overall photographs of the scene (Figure 6.7 through Figure 6.10), the best guess for item 10's location might be somewhere on the surface of Item 8. The blue background evident in Figure 6.17 appears to be a color match to the jacket in the overall photographs. On closer inspection, however, the expended bullet is not on cloth, so where is it? Using Figure 6.18, the technician sets the stage by depicting the file box, with an evident bloodstain on the upper left side, that is sitting on the desk. Figure 6.19 shows the same box, without the top, and the addition of two new placards for items 9 and 10. Together, Figure 6.17 through Figure 6.19 allow the viewer to recognize that the bullet was found inside of another object.

In addition to defining where an item is, the evidence-establishing shot can also eliminate issues of orientation caused by subtle changes or mistakes introduced by the technician. For example, in Figure 6.20, based on the way the defect in the T-shirt and the photo placard are positioned in the close-up photograph, the viewer might interpret orientation of the vertical axis of the photo to be consistent with the lettering on the placard. The evidence-establishing shot shows the proper orientation of the emblem on the T-shirt and eliminates any misinterpretation resulting from the poor orientation of the placard.

Figure 6.17 An evidence close-up photograph of item 10. This item is in the same scene as depicted in Figure 6.7 through Figure 6.10, but where? Based on the background color, one might initially imagine it is present on the blue jacket, but that is not the case. See Figure 6.18 and Figure 6.19.

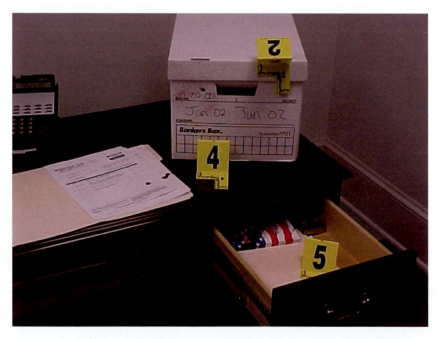

Figure 6.18 An overall photograph of the desk and a box in the scene. Placards 2, 4, and 5 act as landmarks and demonstrate the position of additional items of evidence.

Figure 6.19   An evidence-establishing photograph of Item 10. In combination with Figure 6.18, it is apparent from placard 4 that the box depicted is the same but is now lacking its cover. Placards 9 and 10 demonstrate the presence of additional evidence inside the box.

Evidence Close-Up Photographs

Evidence close-up photographs are exactly that, close-up photos. The technician should try to fill the frame of the viewfinder with the item of interest. Photographs taken from a distance of 3 and 4 ft away from an item that is $^1/_2$-in. in size are not "close-up," yet this mistake is one of the most common made in crime scene photography. The goal is to provide as much detail as possible in the close-up photographs while retaining the identity of the evidence. Figure 6.14 and Figure 6.17 are examples of close-up photographs. At times, placards may have to be repositioned in order to maintain the "recognizable" aspect of the close-up photograph. For instance, in Figure 6.21, by repositioning placard 2 from its original position on top of the file box to a point closer to the bullet defect, the technician can show the elliptical shape of the defect and still demonstrate its identity as part of item 2 (the bloodstain and defect). The technician should create close-up photographs both with and without a scale of reference. Although their presence is not absolutely necessary, counsel have argued that the mere placing of a placard in the scene somehow materially altered the essence of the photograph. Close-up photographs without the scale of reference or placard eliminate this kind of silly attack. Additional close-up photographs of each item of evidence can be completed after recovery from the scene. Back at the office

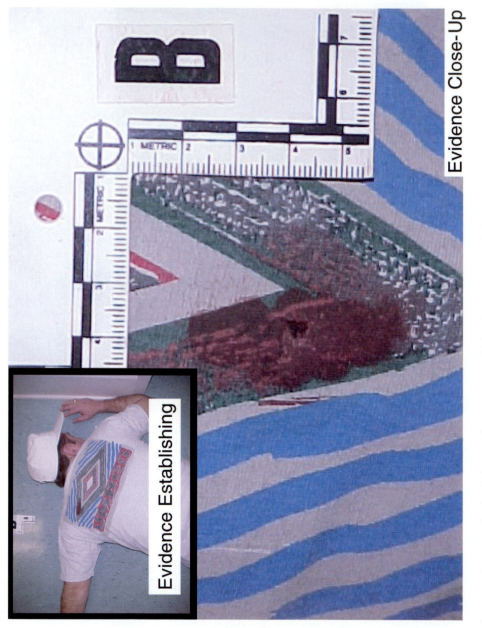

Figure 6.20 A close-up photograph of a defect and its associated bloodstain on a body (item B). A viewer seeing the placement of the placard on the body might presume that it is oriented up and down. The insert is an evidence-establishing shot of the area, which shows the true orientation of the T-shirt emblem.

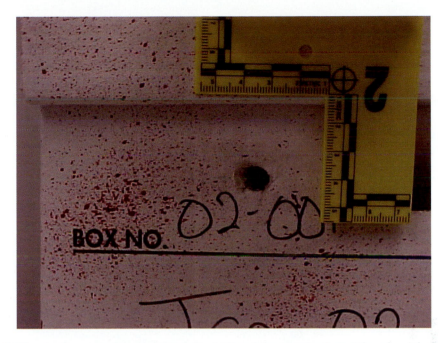

Figure 6.21   A close-up photograph of the bullet defect in the box. The placard was reposi-tioned in order to retain the item's identity and allow a photograph with greater detail.

or in the lab, where light and environment are controlled, quality close-up photographs may help highlight specific details such as serial numbers or small bloodstains found on an item of evidence.

As the crime scene processing progresses, certain aspects or conditions evident from the examination may become significant. Using a combination of the three basic types of photographs, the technician can demonstrate these aspects. For example, in order to graphically demonstrate the trajectory evident from the bullet defect in the file box, the technician might create an evidence-establishing shot of the defect (Figure 6.22) and combine that with the evidence close-up of the defect (Figure 6.21) prior to insertion of a trajectory rod. This places the defect in the scene and demonstrates its condition prior to an invasive process (rod insertion). Figure 6.23 and Figure 6.24 show the inserted rod, effectively demonstrating the general angle and direction of the trajectory. Additional photographs such as Figure 6.25 show the defect and trajectory rod from a position in the room along the indicated trajectory. Finally, using a laser trajectory kit, the technician can demonstrate the path of the trajectory more precisely, as seen in Figure 6.26.

The term *roadmapping* was introduced earlier in the chapter when discussing photo-graphs of bloodstain patterns. The roadmapping technique was developed by Toby Wolson as a documentation procedure for bloodstained scenes. It incorporates the three basic photographs in conjunction with a variety of placards and scales in order to accurately reflect the orientation, position, and detail of the various bloodstain patterns found in the scene. Bloodstains represent a significant documentation problem, since they are often so similar it can be nearly impossible to differentiate one from another. For instance, given two radiating spatter patterns of the same size on the same type of substrate (e.g., a basic white wall), it is difficult to differentiate the patterns when viewing close-up photographs. Roadmapping involves the introduction of a variety of labels and scales that become the

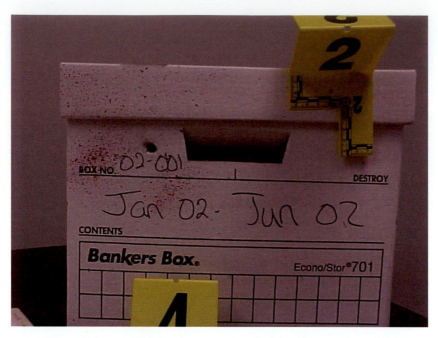

Figure 6.22   An evidence-establishing shot of the bullet defect in Figure 6.21.

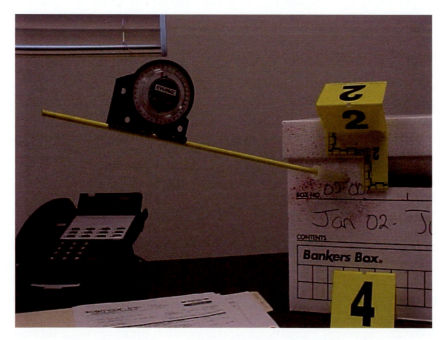

Figure 6.23   This evidence close-up is not of the defect but, rather, the trajectory defined by the defect. The photograph is taken as close as possible but still shows the entire aspect of the item of interest (e.g., the trajectory rod and the box).

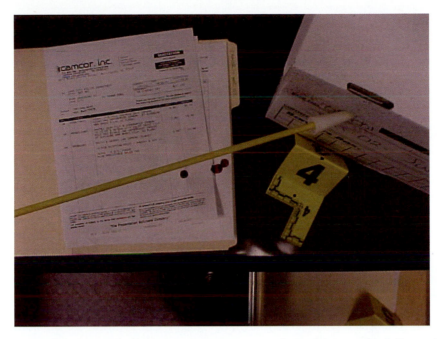

Figure 6.24   A combination of views of the trajectory, taken at right angles, allows the viewer to understand its relationship to the overall scene.

Figure 6.25   A photograph taken in the room looking back along the trajectory. This photograph in effect, demonstrates the "shooter's view."

Figure 6.26 Using a laser trajectory kit, photographs can capture the orientation of the trajectory as it extends into the room.

landmarks in the overall and evidence-establishing photographs. To properly employ the procedure, the crime scene technician must first be able to identify discrete patterns within the scene. Once the patterns are identified, each pattern is given a specific label (e.g., pattern 1, pattern 2). Because many patterns such as spatter, cast off, or arterial spurts are made up of a number of individual stains, within any given pattern there may be characteristics or individual stains of specific interest. Each of these is given an additional sublabel (e.g., pattern 1-a, pattern 1-b). These labels are easily created using adhesive notes and a bold marker. It is best if the labels used are readable from several feet away. Each of the labels is placed in the scene adjacent to the pattern or stain in question. Adhesive paper scales are then added for additional reference, oftentimes outlining an entire pattern or surface.

Once the labels are in place, the technician creates overall photographs of the various surfaces (e.g., walls and floors) that contain patterns. (See Figure 6.27.) It is important that, at the very minimum, the pattern labels (pattern 1, pattern 2) be readable in these overall photographs. This allows a viewer to see the overall scene and pattern relationships. The technician then creates an overall photograph of each individual pattern. (See Figure 6.28.) If subpattern labels were not clear in the surface overall photographs, the technician must ensure that all sublabels (pattern 1-a, pattern 1-b) are clear in the overall pattern photograph, or if the pattern is too big, take additional evidence-establishing photographs depicting portions of the pattern close enough to see these sublabel details. These photos allow the viewer to concentrate on a specific pattern. The technician then photographs the individual stains of interest within the pattern itself (pattern 1-a, pattern 1-b) using evidence close-up photographs. (See Figure 6.29.)

No photograph is without a label of some nature, and it is best if each overall and evidence-establishing photograph has a number of labels evident. This allows the viewer to always know orientation and location no matter what photograph they view. In effect, the labels and scales become the landmarks; they prevent the viewer from ever being lost in the scene. It should be evident that the addition of so many labels and scales results in

Figure 6.27 An example of the roadmapping technique. This is an overall photograph of a surface, depicting the orientation of patterns C, D, E, and J on the wall. The yellow scales are inserted to help show distances and heights.

Figure 6.28 An overall photograph of pattern D. In its full version, the small sublabels are readable in this photograph, but additional evidence-establishing photographs of pattern D would be helpful as well.

Figure 6.29 A close-up photograph of an individual stain of interest in pattern D.

significant alteration of the scene. Roadmapping is a highly intrusive procedure. For that reason, roadmapping is saved for the latter stages of the processing methodology.

No matter what a crime scene technician is trying to photograph, crime scene photography demands more of the technician than simply taking out a camera, pointing it in an arbitrary direction, and snapping a quick shot. The technician has to consider what is important, what s/he wants to illustrate, and how to best illustrate that information. With a little thought and using a combination of the three basic types of photographs discussed, a technician can effectively demonstrate almost any aspect of the scene.

The application of a basic photography methodology, which is consistently employed, will aid the crime scene technician by preventing mistakes of omission. A functional methodology includes the following procedures:

- Document the entire scene as soon as possible *in situ*, using overall photographs.
- Photograph all fragile items of evidence (e.g., footwear marks, bloodstain patterns on the body) as soon as possible, using both evidence-establishing and evidence close-up photographs.
- Document all known evidence items with evidence-establishing shots and evidence close-up shots. Use photo/evidence placards whenever possible to clearly differentiate the various items of evidence from one another.
- If items are discovered in the latter stages of the processing methodology (e.g., during second or third rechecks), ensure that appropriate photos are created. This may require creating additional overall photographs, even though the rest of the scene has already been altered.
- Create photographs that clearly demonstrate the result of examinations such as bloodstain pattern analysis or trajectory analysis. Recognize that these photos will show the scene in an altered condition. That alteration is unimportant; the photos

Crime Scene Photo Log

Case #: 02-01-0045   **Date:** January 13, 2002

Camera Used: Nikon F2a   **Time:** 1830-1940 Hrs

Film Type: ASA 400   **Scene:** 3567 Wayland Dr.

Photographer: SA Brown   **Film Roll #:** 1

Time	Photo #	Depicting	Distance	Remarks
1830	1	Overall of master bedroom from NE	13'	28 mm
1832	2	Overall of master bedroom from SE	12'	28 mm
1835	3	Overall of master bedroom from SW	15'	28 mm, from hallway
1837	4	Overall of master bedroom from NW	12'	28 mm
1840	5	Evidence establishing of shell casing	7'	Placard #1, 50 mm
1842	6	Evidence close-up of shell casing	6'	Placard #1, 55 mm macro

Figure 6.30   The crime scene photo log keeps track of each photograph taken and describes what it was intended to depict. The photo log can be as simple or detailed as desired. To be useful, it should include basic administrative data and, at the very minimum, identify the subject of the photo and the exposure number. Additional data such as the distance, time the photo was taken, and any remarks can certainly support the overall documentation effort, but they may not be needed or desired.

> are created to demonstrate something specific and are not intended to replace the photos shot before the scene was altered.
> - Always use a film roll reference card and a photo log. The film roll reference card is photographed as the first frame of each new roll. It identifies the basic information of what, when, and who produced the photos. A photo log keeps track of each photograph, ensuring that the purpose and subject matter of each photo is understood. See Figure 6.30 for an illustration of a crime scene photo log.

The primary purpose of the photographs is an investigative one. The photographs support the other scene documentation and graphically illustrate the condition of the scene as found. For that reason, there are no holds barred; the technician does not edit content because the scene is grotesque or disconcerting. Technicians will investigate crimes involving significant aspects of violence, sexual violence, and levels of inhumanity that are at times difficult to fathom. Crime scene photographs must capture this information. A supplemental purpose of photographs, however, is to illustrate the scene condition to the court. For a photograph to be admissible in court, it will likely have to withstand several tests. First and foremost, the question that will be asked is: "does the photograph accurately

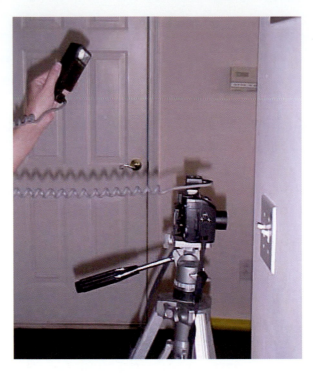

Figure 6.31 When taking evidence close-up photographs, the camera lens must be parallel to the plane of the evidence. In this case, the lens is placed parallel to the wall where a fingerprint is being photographed. At this range, if the flash were left attached to the camera, it would result in an overexposure. To remedy this, the flash is attached through a sync cord to the camera and held at a 45-degree angle some distance from the surface being photographed.

depict the scene?" If it does, the next issue becomes: "is the photograph generally free of distortion?" If the photograph is accurate and generally free of distortion, the issue becomes: "is the photograph material and relevant to some aspect of the case at hand?" Without compromising the primary purpose of taking the photographs, the technician can take certain steps to meet these legal requirements. These steps include:

- Know how to use the camera, so the focus and lighting of the resulting photographs are the best they can be.
- Do not introduce abnormal angles in the photographs unless there is no other way to get the picture. Crime scene photography is not fashion photography, where the cameraman dances about shooting any and all angles. The technician has to square the lens plane of the camera with the subject matter (Figure 6.31).
- Do not overuse the wide-angle lens (28-mm and under), since it introduces distortion.
- Choose the right lens for the right reason. Most crime scene photography work is accomplished with a 28-mm (overall photos), 50-mm, or 50-mm macro lens (evidence-establishing shots and evidence close-ups). A fish-eye or telephoto lens has limited application in normal crime scene photography.
- After capturing all relevant details, do not take grotesque or salacious photographs simply because they are sensational. Such photographs tend to incite juries. You cannot remove the violence (e.g., blood, gore, or sexual content) from overall photographs or those photographs created to depict the condition of the victim,

but the technician does not have to revel in it either. Deal with these scene aspects professionally and without introducing unnecessary sensationalism.

Basic Photography Issues

We have already identified the two main reasons why crime scene photography is poor. One reason was a failure to understand what crime scene photography is intended to do. The discussion of overall, evidence-establishing, and evidence close-up photographs dealt specifically with this issue. The second reason cited was a lack of experience in handling the camera and camera equipment. This text is certainly not a substitute for a good camera course, but it can highlight some basic camera-control aspects that will enhance the scene documentation product.

In order to produce quality crime scene photographs, the technician must control three basic aspects of the camera:

- Physical control
- Light
- Focus and depth of field

Good photography starts with a stable camera. Physical control of the camera is nothing more than stabilizing the camera while the shutter is released. Any movement of the camera as the film plane is exposed will result in a loss of clarity and focus in the resulting photograph. This is true for standard cameras as well as digital cameras. In the vast majority of crime scene photographs, a two handed grip by the technician is more than adequate for ensuring a stable camera. Operating a camera with a focal length of 55 mm and under, the technician should be able to control the camera at any shutter speed of 1/60th of a second or more. If the technician is using a lens with a focal length of greater than 100 mm, the minimum shutter speed for hand holds should be increased to 1/250th of a second.[2] If a situation requires the technician to decrease the shutter speed below these ranges or if the camera must be held in a difficult position, it may be best to place the camera on a tripod.

Light is everything in photography. Too much, and the photo is bleached out, resulting in loss of detail. Too little, and the picture is dark with loss of detail as well. The best advice in crime scene photography work is to use fill flash. No matter what the lighting conditions, a flash should be employed. Fill-flash techniques ensure consistent lighting across the spectrum of photographs produced at the scene. With the introduction of automatic cameras that have integral flash devices, the level of effort by the technician to match and use the flash has been significantly reduced. Many "smart" cameras sense lighting needs and adjust the level of the flash accordingly.

One problem that presents itself when creating close-up photographs is overexposure. Oftentimes, the camera lens will be situated inches away from the subject matter (e.g., when photographing fingerprints). A flash operated from its standard position on the camera will almost always produce an overexposure. The use of offset flash and oblique lighting in these situations will correct and eliminate overexposure and bleached-out photos. Although the camera lens is only a few inches from the subject, the flash is held at a 45-degree angle (obliquely to the subject) and at a greater distance (typically arm's length), as seen in Figure 6.31. Offset and oblique lighting will require a camera with a detachable flash and a sync cord, but these are a mainstay for crime scene work. In addition to using offset lighting, the technician can diffuse the light by attaching a commercial diffuser to the flash or by taping a piece of white cloth over the flash. Either technique cuts the power of the flash directed onto the surface, allowing on-camera flash even at a close range. Some flash systems have an adjustable flash head that rotates from a normal 90-degree position (flash facing directly forward) to a vertical position (flash head facing directly up). By changing the angle, light can be bounced off adjoining surfaces, which will effectively illuminate the picture and reduce overexposure. This will work effectively when shooting pictures at some distance (e.g., 12 in.), but at extreme close-up range, bounce lighting is not likely to eliminate the overexposure issue.

When working with a manual camera (one with an adjustable f-stop and shutter speed), the technician must recognize the correlation of f-stop in relation to light and the resulting depth of field. Depth of field relates to the focus of objects in front of and beyond the subject of the photo. If we focus the camera lens properly, our subject will always be in focus, but objects that are at a greater distance than the focus point may or may not be as clearly focused. The same is true of objects that appear in the foreground. The f-stop determines how wide the lens aperture opens, thereby controlling the amount of light the film is exposed to. The higher the f-stop number, the smaller the aperture, resulting in the introduction of less light. The more we can limit light for a given exposure, the greater the depth of field of the resulting photograph. When creating evidence close-up photographs, a short depth of field is generally not a problem. An expended casing or even a pistol have a very limited depth, if any part of the item is in focus, then for the most part all of the item will be in focus. Lowering the f-stop in order to introduce greater amounts of light in this situation will not hurt the resulting photo. In overall and evidence-establishing photographs, however, the technician wants greater depth of field. The underlying purpose of the photograph is to show an area; therefore the more items that are in clear focus, the better. The use of a low f-stop in this situation can impact negatively on the resulting photograph, as seen in Figure 6.32.

The focus of the subject of the photograph is determined singularly by the technician. Good focus begins with being practiced at using the camera and understanding how the focus system works. The best focus system for crime scene work is a split image. This focus system is typical in many single-lens-reflex (SLR) and digital cameras. To set the focus, the technician turns the lens focus ring, distorting the image in the viewfinder. The image "splits" into three parts, the top and bottom third of the focus circle remain aligned while the middle third moves out of alignment either right or left. By slowing turning the focus ring back, the middle portion of the image will come back in alignment with the bottom and top sections. When the three sections are aligned, the subject is in focus. Scales and rulers introduced in evidence close-up photos are effective aids in achieving a precise focus using a split-image system. By positioning the viewfinder over the straight thin lines of the ruler, the technician can clearly see when the best focus is achieved. The fact that these scales and rulers are made of high-contrast colors also works in the favor of the technician. This technique is particularly effective when focusing on small objects that lie close to or in the same plane as the ruler. Of course, the technician must also consider depth of field. If the scale is located on the floor and the subject matter extends up toward the camera lens any distance, it is possible to have those areas closest to the lens out of focus.

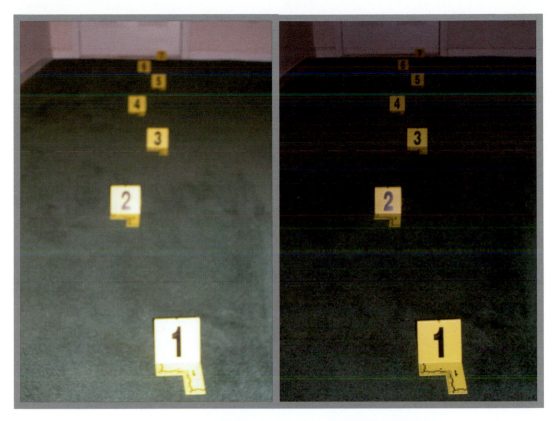

Aperture F 3.8
Focus set at Placard 1

Aperture F 8
Focus set at Placard 1

Figure 6.32 Depth of field is affected by the amount of light a lens allows into any exposure. The f-stop helps determine this. The smaller the f-stop, the more light the lens allows in; the larger the f-stop, the less light the lens allows in. The two photographs in the figure were exposed under the exact same conditions with the focus set at placard 1. On the left, with an f-stop of 3.8, the remaining placards are readable but out of focus. On the right, with an f-stop of 8, all of the placards are in clear focus.

Focus problems also arise in "smart" cameras, where sensors try to figure out where the actual focus should be. It may be necessary for the technician to turn off auto-focus features when shooting various photographs, particularly close-up photographs. Digital cameras present an additional focus problem. Often, digital cameras require sufficient light in order to find focus and register that an image is available. In low-light conditions, even where the human eye can see effectively, the camera may not register that any image is available. Arson scenes in particular can prove quite difficult. To overcome this problem, the technician can have another scene processor shine a flashlight on the point where the technician wishes to focus. Once a focus is achieved, the picture is taken. The light should remain on and stationary throughout the entire process, otherwise the camera may lose this focus point. This additional light will allow the camera to "see" enough to take the picture, while the use of fill flash from the camera will ensure a good-quality photograph. In nighttime and extreme low-light conditions, when shooting overall-type photographs, it may be impossible to achieve sufficient lighting with a single flash.

"Paint with light" is a flash technique that allows the crime scene technician to capture greater detail using multiple flashes in the same exposure. Oftentimes the technician is presented with an exterior crime scene at night in which evidence is scattered across a wide area. Basic photographs such as overall or evidence-establishing photographs are still required. Unfortunately, a single flash initiated at the camera's position may not carry across these areas. As a result, the photographs end up poorly illuminated. In paint with flash, the technician mounts the camera on a tripod. Once the camera is focused, the camera is placed on the "B" (bulb) setting. This setting keeps the aperture of the lens open so long as the shutter release is pushed. Using a shutter release cable, the technician can keep the shutter open even while away from the camera. After opening the shutter, the technician moves to various points on either side of the camera, manually initiating the flash in the direction of all of the evidence in the viewfinder. The combined illumination presented by multiple flashes provides a more detailed photograph. (See Figure 6.33.) In totally dark areas, the technician can even walk directly into the area contained in the viewfinder. This will allow the technician to initiate the flash from several angles on either side of the primary area, but at a position closer to the evidence than the camera. As long

A - Single automatic flash at the camera.

B - Multiple flashes while the camera was on the bulb setting

Figure 6.33 An exterior nighttime overall photograph. The darker photograph was exposed with a flash attached at the camera. The lighter photograph is the same scene at the same time. This photograph was exposed using the "paint with light" technique. The camera was set on a tripod and the shutter placed on the B (bulb) setting. Once open, three manual flashes were initiated, one on either side of the camera and scene and one at the camera. Note the differences in illumination.

as the technician keeps the flash in front of his/her body and pointed away from the camera, no ghost image of the technician is captured. Paint with light also works in low-light conditions such as periods at dawn or dusk, but in these cases the technician cannot step directly into the area captured by the viewfinder. The limited light present under low-light conditions offers just enough illumination that a ghost image of the technician may appear.

Video Photography

Video is a functional supplement to the crime scene photography effort. However, video footage (even digital video) is not a replacement for crime scene photography. Video is best used both as an initial effort by the technician and later in the processing when demonstrating the entire scene. Upon arrival at a scene, the crime scene technician should take the normal overall photographs of the scene, before any further alteration can occur. Once this is accomplished, the technician can utilize a video camera as well. Using a nonintrusive walk-through the technician captures as much of the scene as possible without disturbing anything. After all of the physical evidence has been identified and photo placards are in place, a second video effort is used to document the scene and the items of interest found. Video can be used at later stages in the processing methodology as well to explain specific aspects such as trajectory analysis or bloodstain pattern analysis.

There are a number of precautions to be considered when using a video camera. First and foremost, remember that the camera does not see or focus as effectively as the human eye. The technician can go into a room, pan it quickly by eye, and capture information. The camera cannot capture the same information in the same way. Routinely, video footage is filled with abrupt movements between points of interest or short periods where the camera is trained on an item of interest and then moved almost instantly. The photographer will zoom in and out on an item of interest, never stopping to show details, or the footage will contain dark images with little detail. Video camera movement must be thought out and deliberate. When panning from one point to another, move slowly. The cameraman should not start on one side of the room, pan to the opposite side and then pan back to the far side. Think out the sequence of points of interest and move methodically through the room. Once an area of interest is in the field of view and in focus, the technician should silently count out at least a 10-sec period before moving the camera to a new point of interest. Use of the zoom function should be limited. Treat zoom and wide-angle function the same as panning, making a deliberate effort to transition from one zoom angle to the next. Once a new view is accomplished, maintain the picture in a steady position for at least 10 sec. A camera strobe is a necessary piece of equipment when using video. Flashlights and the like will not suffice when trying to illuminate dark areas. Treat video photography the same as standard photography. Fill flash or, in this case, fill lighting is necessary to capture appropriate detail.

Another precaution when using video concerns the audio portion of the tape. For a number of reasons, the early video footage (e.g., documenting the scene on arrival) should be shot without audio. Off-color comments by others, wild theories, and the like can be captured and forever preserved. If narration is desired, the narrator should be confident of the information s/he offers, leaving out subjective comments. Anyone not directly involved in making the video should be removed from the scene so as not to capture unnecessary audio background. Narration is usually necessary when demonstrating trajectory or bloodstain pattern analysis. Once again, the narrator should think out what s/he intends to say rather than trying to shoot the video off the cuff.

Summary

Crime scene photography is not just a matter of point and shoot. Through improper photography techniques, the technician can produce identification and orientation problems and interject confusion for those viewing the photographs. Identification problems occur when viewers cannot tell from the photo where or what they are looking at. Orientation problems occur when it is impossible to determine up, down, right, or left in relation to the actual scene from the photograph. Confusion arises from both of these problems and from situations where the technician takes multiple photographs of similar items or of the scene in altered conditions. Any of these issues can impact on the ability of the photography to clearly represent the true condition of the scene as observed by the crime scene team.

Three basic photographs are used in crime scene work: the overall photograph, the evidence-establishing photograph, and the evidence close-up photograph. Although there may be other terms used when describing these three photograph types, the nature of what each photograph depicts is very forthright. Overall photographs depict the overall condition and orientation of the scene. They are usually taken from the corners of the room and overlap, allowing nearly every aspect of the scene to be observed. Evidence-establishing photographs capture specific items of evidence in the scene in relation to obvious landmarks (e.g., doors, large objects), allowing the viewer to understand exactly where the evidence item is in relation to the entire scene. Evidence close-up photographs show as much detail as possible of the evidence item itself. These photographs are often taken both with and without a scale of reference.

An effective way of documenting scene context in photographs is to use photo placards. These numbered or lettered placards make it easier for the viewer to identify where items of evidence may be in the scene. They can be useful in both overall and evidence-establishing shots.

To produce good-quality photographs, the technician must follow a standard documentation methodology and be able to effectively work whatever photographic equipment they have. This includes controlling the camera, light, and focus. The camera is controlled by holding it steady with two hands or by using a tripod when necessary. Light is controlled best by using fill-flash photography. No matter what the lighting conditions, the flash is used to reduce shadows and improve detail. Focus is a matter of understanding the specific camera that the technician is using and understanding the f-stop. To achieve greater depth of field for overall and evidence-establishing photographs, and thus better focus, the technician uses a smaller f-stop. In close-up photographs controlling depth of field is less of an issue.

Suggested Reading

Redsicker, D.R., *The Practical Methodology of Forensic Photography*, CRC Press, Boca Raton, FL, 2000.

Chapter Questions

1. What are the four key elements of crime scene documentation?
2. Describe how a photograph might create an identification problem.
3. Describe how a photograph might create a confusion problem.
4. What are the three basic photographs associated with crime scene photography?
5. What is the purpose of an overall photograph?
6. What is the purpose of an evidence-establishing photograph?
7. What are the minimum requirements to include in a crime scene photography log?
8. How does the f-stop affect the resulting photograph?
9. How can a crime scene technician prevent overexposure or bleaching out of close-up photographs when using fill-flash techniques?
10. Describe at least three critical mistakes that occur when using video cameras in the crime scene?

Notes

1. *Roadmapping* is a term first used by Toby Wolson, Miami Dade County Police, relating to capturing all pertinent aspects of bloodstain crime scenes. (Wolson, T., Bloodstain Pattern Documentation, presentation to the International Association of Bloodstain Pattern Analysts, Colorado Springs, CO, Sept. 26, 1992.)
2. Sirene, W., *Surveillance Photography Guides*, U.S. Dept. of Justice, Federal Bureau of Investigation, Washington, DC, 1979, p. 7.

Crime Scene Sketching and Mapping

7

In general conversation, crime scene sketching and crime scene mapping are often considered one and the same. Any difference would be a matter of semantics (e.g., a freehand drawing compared with a to-scale drawing), but for the purposes of this chapter, the text will draw a distinction between the two terms. Consider the sketch as an actual drawing of the scene. As one might imagine, there is a significant range in the quality of crime scene sketches. The sketch may be nothing more than a freehand drawing with no scale of reference, or it could be as intricate as a computer-generated to-scale document. To create a sketch, other than a simple freehand drawing, the technician goes through a process of measuring and fixing the items present in the scene. Crime scene mapping is this "process" of taking and documenting these measurements.

Whatever the quality of the crime scene sketch, it serves as a graphic document to show the layout, orientation, and interrelationships of the scene and the evidence. The sketch supports the photographs and notes and will ultimately complement the final report. Because it is a graphic document depicting pertinent portions of the scene, it allows the viewer to easily and quickly comprehend the interrelationships between the scene and the evidence. Scene sketches are also an important document for the investigator, as the crime scene sketch is quite helpful in subsequent analysis or reconstruction efforts. The crime scene map can help in physically reconstructing the entire scene or portions of the scene. As well, this technique of reconstructing the scene will often assist a jury in recognizing the spatial relationships and limitations present in the scene.

The level of effort directed at crime scene sketching and mapping varies widely. The primary factors in deciding how much effort to direct at a scene are the severity of the crime and the importance of the evidence interrelationships. In major crimes such as homicides, the scene sketch will be in depth, with significant crime scene mapping documentation. Such effort will allow for the creation of a to-scale sketch if required. In simple crimes, such as a business burglary, where the interrelationships of the evidence are less likely to be of importance, a rough freehand sketch may be all that is needed.

Essential Sketch Elements

The crime scene diagram prepared on scene is rarely a work of art (Figure 7.1). The concentration at the scene is on the measurements and evidence placement. Work of art

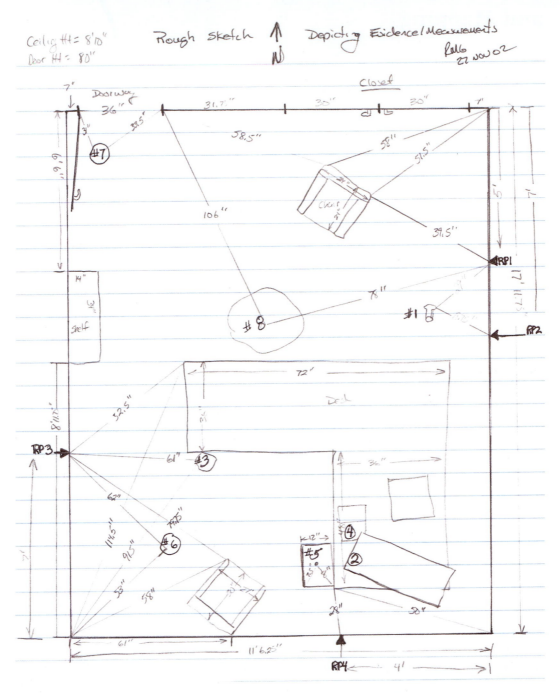

Figure 7.1 The rough sketch prepared on scene is rarely a work of art. This document generally lacks a heading, legend, or scale of reference, but it will include the layout of the area, significant articles and furniture, and specifics on evidence and measurements. Although lacking in aesthetic value, it must still be an accurate representation of the scene.

or not, this document should be graphically correct. General room layout and furniture placement should be consistent with the conditions found in the scene. From this initial document, the technician will usually create the formal crime scene sketch. The formal sketch, whether hand-drawn or computer-generated, has five basic elements. These are:

1. Heading
2. Diagram area
3. Legend
4. Title block
5. Scale and direction notations

The *heading* is a notation that indicates why the sketch was created. The technician may create a number of sketches, each with a specific purpose. Some examples include: the normal sketch depicting evidence and measurements, a sketch depicting a single evidential aspect such as bloodstains or bullet trajectories, or a sketch depicting placement of the actual scene in a larger area. Whatever the purpose of the sketch, the heading informs the viewer of the purpose.

The *diagram area* is the drawing itself. The diagram should graphically depict the scene and primary evidence. A significant problem in creating any diagram is clutter and the resulting confusion when too much information is included. When creating the formal crime scene sketch, the technician may decide to simplify the diagram. They do this by eliminating items that were noted and fixed during the scene examination but that are considered less important to the investigation. There is nothing wrong with simplifying a sketch so long as the essential character of the scene is not lost and the rough sketch created during the actual scene mapping is retained.

The *legend* tells the viewer what the various labels used in the diagram depict. Space in the diagram area of the sketch is always lacking. Lack of space forces the technician to place small circles and labels on the diagram, rather than attempting to draw shell casings, bloodstains, or whatever. The use of labels allows the technician to include more information without creating clutter or confusion, but each label must be defined in some fashion. It is best when the legend is included on the sketch, as this ensures a ready reference for the viewer. An important aspect of scene documentation is ensuring that the various elements of documentation complement and support each other. This is particularly true in relation to placards in the crime scene photographs and the labels used on the crime scene diagram. If the technician shoots a photograph depicting a shell casing with a placard labeled as "A," it creates confusion if the scene sketch arbitrarily uses a "1" to depict the same item. Whenever possible, ensure that there is consistency between the photographs and the sketch.

The *title block* of the sketch provides important information relevant to the location of the scene and the creator of the sketch. Different organizations may require different items of information, but this section typically includes the report number, the physical address of the scene, the name of the sketch creator, and the time and date when the sketch was created.

Finally, two annotations should be present on the sketch to identify the *orientation* of the sketch in relation to compass direction as well as to inform the viewer if there is some *scale of reference* used in creating the sketch. With regard to compass direction, it is often claimed that every sketch should be created with north facing the top of the page, but such an orientation is neither practical nor advisable in all situations. Rather, set the diagram area in the most effective orientation to depict the scene, and then simply identify where north is in relation to this orientation. The scale reference identifies whether a scale is used and what that scale is. A "not to scale" annotation is more than adequate for the typical freehand drawing. Computer-generated sketches usually report the scale automatically in the resulting legend.

Variations of View in Sketches

The typical crime scene sketch is presented as a bird's-eye view of the scene, as seen in Figure 7.2. Only horizontal surfaces are evident, and only evidence on such horizontal surfaces is included in the sketch. This type of sketch is clearly suited for the vast majority of crime scenes and provides the viewer with a more rounded and comprehensive understanding of the scene and evidence. But there are times when additional viewpoints are necessary as well. There are several variations of view for the crime scene sketch. These are:

- Cross-projection or exploded sketch
- Elevation sketch
- Three-dimensional sketch or view

A *cross-projection sketch or exploded sketch* combines the standard bird's-eye view of the horizontal surface of the room, while at the same time "laying down" a wall or walls in order to depict evidence that is present on these vertical surfaces. The cross-projection sketch allows the viewer to see the orientation and interrelationships of items of evidence on both the vertical and horizontal surfaces of the scene. It has been argued that to create a true "cross-projection sketch," the creator must lay down all walls, but arbitrary rules have no place in forensics. The sketch creator can lay down a single wall, multiple walls, or any combination that seems appropriate. This sketch technique is quite effective when dealing with walls that have bloodstain patterns or bullet holes in them. Figure 7.3 is an example of a cross-projection sketch.

An *elevation sketch* is drawn depicting a side view of some portion of the scene, typically an interior wall or similar vertical structure. Elevation sketches can be used to map and document evidence such as defects, stains, or other evidence on walls or other surfaces. The elevation sketch can also be used to draw an extended exterior scene, depicting in side view the orientation of various buildings and the like. This might be a functional approach when trying to depict a bullet trajectory. Figure 7.4 shows an elevation view.

The *three-dimensional sketch* or view offers an ability to present the crime scene information in a more realistic perspective. These techniques include everything from hand-drawn sketches to computer-created sketches and views. Creating quality hand-drawn three-dimensional sketches is an art form. Lacking such skills, a variety of software packages allow the scene mapping information to be used to create a virtual scene. Once created, a virtual camera can be positioned anywhere (within the limits of the program), allowing a semirealistic perspective of the scene from that position. Three-dimensional software allows us to put the jury in the scene and observe spatial relationships, limitations of sight caused by the scene layout, and other information that may ultimately be pertinent to claims by suspects and witnesses. Figure 7.5 is a scene photograph and virtual view of the same scene from a different position showing more of the pertinent spatial relationships.

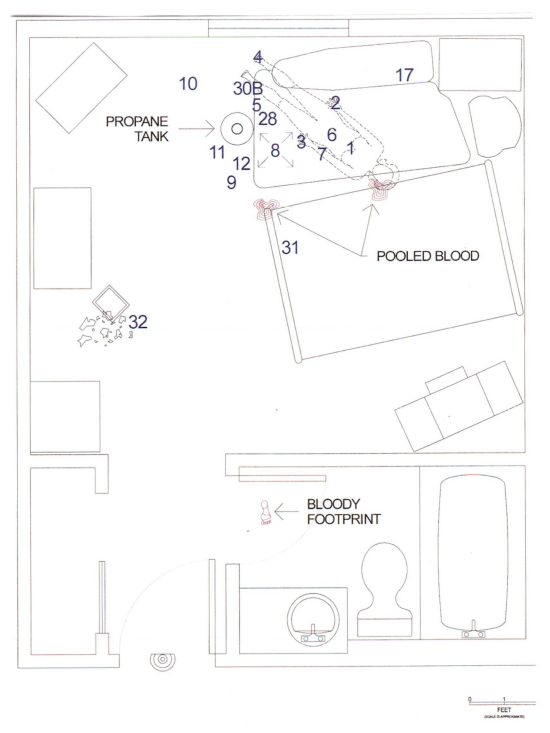

Figure 7.2 The typical crime scene sketch is that of a bird's-eye view. It looks down on the scene from above and effectively captures elements found on any horizontal plane (floors, tables, counters, etc.). (Courtesy of Ranger John A. Martin and the Texas Rangers. With permission.)

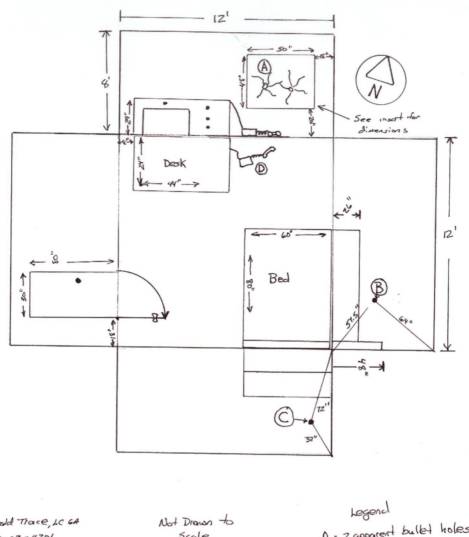

Figure 7.3 A cross-projection sketch or exploded view lays down vertical surfaces adjacent to the horizontal surface, allowing evidence on both to be displayed. This view helps the viewer to understand interrelationships between various articles.

A major concern in choosing software for such purposes is the utilities provided. A necessary component of the software is flexibility in changing and resizing furniture. Many software packages provide a "standard" furniture library that cannot be changed. These packages are too limiting to be of significant use in crime scene work. A second utility necessary is the ability to freely place the camera. The more freely and effectively the software allows for camera placement, the more functional the software is as a crime scene utility. Finally, the package must allow export of the "camera view" as a JPG ("j-peg") or bitmap file. This is important because the most effective mechanism of presenting these

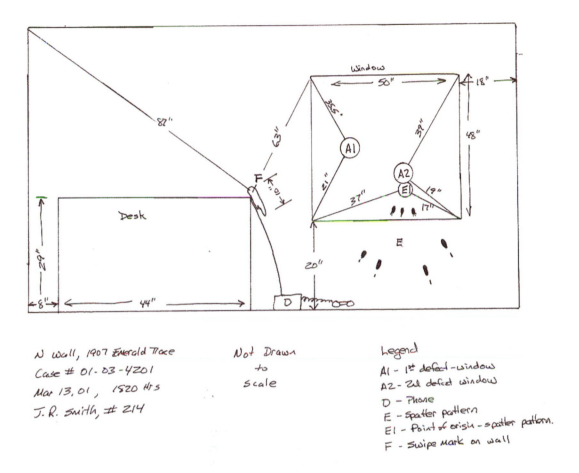

Figure 7.4 An elevation view in a crime scene sketch allows the technician to capture information relevant to vertical surfaces and the orientation of various vertical surfaces to one another.

views to a jury is not within the software itself, but rather in presentation software such as *PowerPoint.*[1] Unfortunately, most of the software manufacturers have failed to recognize police organizations as a viable customer, and thus the minor changes necessary to make these packages effective crime scene applications have not been made. On the other hand, some manufacturers took off-the-shelf software that sold for $30 to $40, added limited police-specific libraries, and then quadrupled the price of the package without bothering to make the additional changes necessary to round out the package as a crime scene tool. Simply put, the author has found no single software package that meets all of the crime scene investigation needs.

Methods for Crime Scene Mapping

In order to create an accurate scene sketch, there must be supporting documentation that defines the size of the scene and where in the scene various items were. Crime scene mapping is the process the technician uses to identify this information. In all but the most preliminary

Figure 7.5 Various forms of computer software can be helpful in sketching the crime scene. Virtual scenes based on the crime scene measurements can be prepared, and virtual cameras can be placed at specific points, thus allowing the technician to demonstrate spatial relationships that might not have been captured in the crime scene photography. In this instance, the inset crime scene photograph failed to demonstrate the space between the couch and wall. The virtual view allows the jury to see this aspect more clearly. The use of virtual methods demands accurate, detailed mapping by the crime scene technician.

rough sketch, the technician documents the size of the scene, elements within the scene (e.g., furniture and doors), and then "fixes" the evidence in some fashion. Fixing evidence allows the investigator to functionally place the item back in the scene with some level of accuracy. The specific method used to fix evidence is primarily a matter of habit as well as circumstance. As the severity of the crime increases, the likelihood increases that the scene and evidence interrelationships will become important at subsequent trial. In that situation, the more precise methods are employed. In a simpler crime, these scene relationships may not be as significant, and the less precise fixing methods may be more than adequate. The physical circumstance the technician finds at the scene (e.g., outdoors, indoors, no land-marks) also plays a role in choosing the crime scene mapping method. Some methods are more practical in certain circumstances. The most common mapping methods used are:

- Rectangular coordinates
- Triangulation
- Baseline coordinates
- Polar coordinates
- Triangulation or rectangular coordinates on a grid
- Triangulation on a baseline
- Total-station systems

Keep in mind that the overall sequence of the crime scene processing technique is still important. In standard processing practice, the scene is photographed *in situ* prior to initi-ating the sketch and crime scene mapping methods. The process of mapping the scene is itself intrusive, requiring the technician to move about the scene in order to take the various measurements. In practice, no matter which mapping method the technician uses, the tech-nician fixes all evidence first. Later, the technician measures walls, furniture, and other static items. This sequence prevents inadvertently moving an item of evidence before its position is fixed. As there are several different mapping methods that require discussion, it is appro-priate to take this latter task of detailing the general scene conditions (e.g., walls and doors) out of sequence and identify the general measurements required for the sketch and supporting notes. The technician should document the length, width, and heights of all walls, doors, windows, or openings and the specific location in the wall where such openings occur. Furniture items should be measured fully, identifying length, width, and height. Furniture is fixed using the same techniques used for evidence, unless an item is found to be flush against a wall. In that instance, a single measurement from a known point where the item is flush to a standard reference point on the same wall will accurately place the item in the scene.

Rectangular Coordinates

The rectangular-coordinate method is best suited for crime scenes with clear and specific boundaries (e.g., interior walls). It is well suited for interior crime scenes and is a fast and effective method, particularly when using a sonic, laser, or IR (infrared) measuring device. The technician fixes the evidence by measuring at right angles from the evidence to the surrounding walls and surfaces. Applying rectangular coordinates, the technician generally uses only two measurements from the center of mass to document each item of evidence. Thus this method is less precise than other techniques such as triangulation. Consider the pistol in Figure 7.6. The pistol is fixed in the scene by taking two measurements from the center of mass, to the south and west walls. Although this places the pistol at a specific

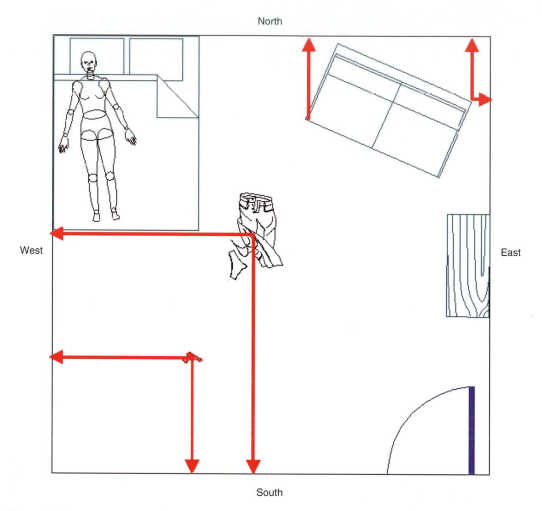

Figure 7.6 Rectangular coordinates used to document two specific articles of evidence, a pair of pants and a pistol. Rectangular coordinates require only two measurements from any item of evidence, but even with these measurements, the pistol can still be rotated 360 degrees, and thus it is not "fixed." Rectangular coordinates are effective, but they are not as precise as other techniques.

location, it does not "fix" the evidence, since the pistol can be rotated in that position in a full circle of 360 degrees. Although not typically done when using rectangular coordinates, nothing prevents the technician from taking two measurements from two different points on a regularly shaped object (e.g., two measurements from the butt and two measurements from the forward sight). Irregularly shaped objects are always treated the same in rectangular coordinates, requiring two measurements from the center of mass to a surrounding surface. For example, in Figure 7.6, the pants are placed in the scene by a measurement to the west and south wall. Furniture items in the scene are fixed in much the same way as other evidence. The love seat in the northwest corner can be placed by a measurement from the southwest base corner leg to the north wall and a measurement from the northeast base-corner leg to the north wall. Of course, it should be evident that movement east or west of this item is not limited by these measurements; therefore a third measurement to the east wall is necessary as well. So a minimum of three measurements in this instance fixes the love seat.

There are problems associated with the rectangular-coordinate method. The method is less precise than triangulation because it is based primarily on the use of only two measurements for any given article. Another problem associated with the method is that it can be difficult to measure accurately at right angles to walls that are 5 to 10 ft away. Nevertheless, rectangular coordinates are a functional and effective method so long as the technician recognizes the inherent level of imprecision. If the technician desires a "to-scale" drawing as a final product, this is not the best method to employ.

Triangulation

Triangulation is an effective method for fixing evidence. Triangulation's underlying rules are based on whether the item has a regular or irregular shape. Items that have a regular shape, which will not change with movement and contain specific identifiable points, are fixed using a minimum of four measurements. Examples of regularly shaped items include furniture, guns, or knives. In order to fix the item in the scene, the technician takes a total of four straight-line measurements from two distinct landmarks in the room to two distinct points on the article. Each pair of measurements in effect creates a triangle. Figure 7.7 shows the fixing of one end of a shell casing using two reference points along the wall.

Figure 7.7 Triangulation is a more precise method of fixing evidence than rectangular coordinates. As in the instance of the shell casing, a set of measurements from two distinct points (RP1 and RP2) to one end of the casing creates one triangle. A similar series of measurements from the opposite end of the shell casing would effectively set the casing in a very specific position.

Two more measurements from the opposite end of the casing would complete the triangulation process. Irregularly shaped items have asymmetric shapes with no specific identifiable points and also include items that will change shape when moved. Irregularly shaped objects are documented using two measurements from the center of mass of the item to two distinct landmarks, as well as a measurement of the overall width of the item. Examples of items with irregular shapes include blood pools, clothing, or a circular drinking glass that is upright. For example, the clothes in the center of the floor in Figure 7.6 could be placed down in the scene any number of times and never end up in the exact position they were found in. Thus two measurements from the center of mass to the nearest walls are more than effective at fixing them in the scene.

Typical landmarks used in triangulation are base corners of walls and doors. In crowded or cluttered spaces the technician may have to create reference points to eliminate landmark problems. To do this, the technician simply locates a ready reference point (RP) along a wall, identifies it with some marker (e.g., a post-it note), and then measures the distance of the reference point to a nearby base corner, as seen in Figure 7.8. This single measurement places the reference point, allowing it to be used like any other standard landmark.

In triangulation, regularly shaped articles end up with two "triangles" (four measurements), and irregularly shaped objects end up with one "triangle" (two measurements). These idealized triangles formed by the measurements can be seen in Figure 7.9. The gun

Figure 7.8 Additional reference points are established in the scene in a simple fashion. The reference point is placed along a wall or similar surface and marked so that it is recognized (using the yellow sticky note). A single measurement from a known point (the corner of the room) identifies where this RP is.

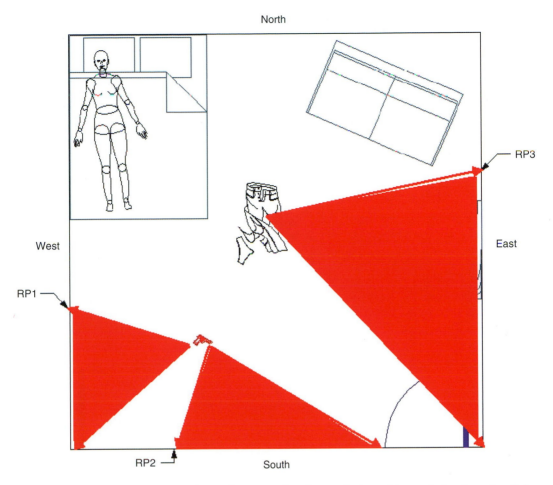

Figure 7.9 Example of triangulation being used to fix regularly and irregularly shaped articles. Regularly shaped items require two triangles (four measurements), and irregularly shaped articles require only one triangle (two measurements).

is measured from the heel of the grip to RP1 and the southwest base corner of the room, creating triangle one. The barrel tip is measured to RP2 and the southwest base corner of the doorway, creating triangle two. These four measurements fix this item exactly, with no movement or rotation possible. The clothing in the center of the scene, as an irregularly shaped item, is measured from the center of mass to RP3 and the southeast base corner of the room, creating a single triangle.

Furniture is treated the same as evidence when using triangulation, with the exception of items that are flush against walls. In Figure 7.10, the bed is flush against the north and west walls, thus measuring its dimensions alone sets and fixes it inside the room without further effort. The dresser on the east wall is flush against the wall, and the technician would measure its dimensions as well, but in order to fix it on the east wall, at least one measurement must be taken from a known landmark. A measurement from the southeast base corner of the dresser to the southeast base corner of the room effectively places it in the room. The love seat in the northeast corner presents a more difficult problem. It is freestanding in the room, not flush to any surface. Like any other item of evidence, four measurements from two points on the love seat to room landmarks are necessary to fix it

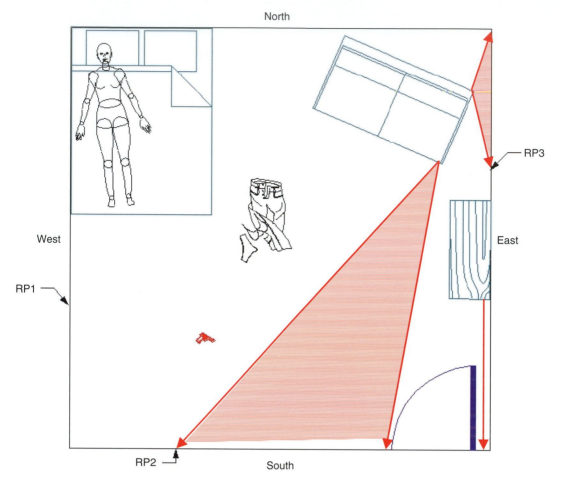

Figure 7.10 The same rules apply in triangulation for furniture items, unless an object is flush against a wall. The bookcase located flush along the east wall can be fixed by making a single measurement from the southeast base corner of the case to the southeast base corner of the room. The love seat, however, is not flush against a surface and is fixed using two triangles (four measurements).

in the scene. The measurements from the northeast base corner leg of the love seat to the northeast base corner of the room and to RP3 create the first triangle, while the measurement from the southeast base corner leg to RP2 and the southwest base corner of the door create the second triangle.

There is one caution when using triangulation techniques. The technician should not triangulate from items that are themselves fixed in the scene by triangulation. For instance in Figure 7.10, after fixing the love seat in the northeast corner of the room, the technician would not use the base corners of the love seat as landmarks for other items of evidence. The bed, on the other hand, could be utilized as a landmark without fear of introducing any error because it is flush against two walls.

The use of a standard form for documenting the measurements taken on scene will reduce and eliminate errors or omissions. Figure 7.11 is an example of a triangulation measurement log associated with the sketch in Figure 7.1.

Evidence Triangulation Measurement Log

Location: 5656 Tonesboro Rd Suite 3		Case#: 02-11-6310
Date: 26 NOV 02		Time: 1245 Hrs
Case Agent: R. M. Gardner		
Primary Datum set by: Point 1: N/A Point 2:		
Primary Datum Elevation (If necessary): N/A		

From	To	Distance	Remarks
Item # 1 40 cal spent casing			
— casing base	RP#1	29"	
— casing base	RP# 2	18.75"	
Item #3 Banci Holster			
— C/Mass of holster	SW base corner of the room.	91.5"	
— C/Mass of holster	RP# 3	61"	
Item #5 Bloodstain			
— C/Mass	SW corner of open drawer	7.5"	
— C/Mass	SE point where drawer/desk meet.	8"	
Item # 6 — Bloodstains			
— C/Mass	RP#3	62"	
— C/Mass	SW base corner of the room.	53"	
Desk			
— NW base corner E-W extension.	RP# 3	52.5"	
— Same point	SW base corner of the room.	114.5"	
— SW base corner N-S extension	RP#4	28"	
— Same point	SE base corner of the room	50"	
Shelf — flush to W wall			
— SW base corner	SW base corner of the room	8'11.75"	
— NW base corner	NW base corner of the room	6'6"	
Swivel Chair			
— SE edge in contact w/wall	SW base corner of the room	61"	
— NW base corner of leg	RP3	79.75"	
— same point	SW base corner of the room	58"	
Standard Chair in front of desk			
— NW base corner of leg	NE base corner of entry way	58.5"	
— Same point	NE base corner of the room	58"	
— NE base corner of leg	RP#1	39.5"	
— Same point	NE base corner of the room	51.5"	

Figure 7.11 Most of the basic measurements taken during the crime scene mapping are annotated directly on the rough sketch, but not all can be included. To supplement those measurements, it is appropriate to use an evidence measurement log. This is a triangulation measurement log that defines what item was fixed, where it was fixed to, and the resulting measurement. Not all of these data will make it to the final sketch, but the measurement log documents every measurement for future reference, such as when producing a to-scale drawing.

Baseline Coordinates

The baseline method of fixing evidence is very similar to the rectangular-coordinates process. Baseline is best suited for exterior scenes without evident landmarks, although it can also be used inside. Baseline begins with a datum point, a location from which the baseline will extend. In an exterior scene, the datum is set by triangulating it to a set of nearby landmarks. For instance, in Figure 7.12, the datum point is fixed by measuring from the southeast and northeast base corners of the nearby garage. Once the datum is set, the baseline is extended along a cardinal direction (north, south, east, or west) as far as necessary. The best method for baseline is to extend an actual tape measure, as seen in Figure 7.13. If this is not possible (e.g., when there is a need for an extended baseline), the baseline can be formed by a line or string, with reference points marked along the line.

Once the baseline is established, the technician measures the distance from each item (either from its center of mass or from identified points on the object) at a right angle to the baseline, as seen in Figure 7.14. This distance from the baseline is recorded. The technician then notes the distance along the baseline (the distance from the datum point) where the evidence measurement transects the baseline. These two measurements fix the evidence in relation to the baseline and datum. The use of a nonstretching fabric tape measure as the actual baseline, allows for easy identification of the distance from the datum point to the point where the line from the evidence crosses the baseline. If a string is used as the baseline, the technician must stretch a second tape measure from this transect point to the datum point to determine this distance. This requires additional effort and introduces additional error. As in the case with rectangular coordinates, it is important to square off the tape measure to the baseline, as seen in Figure 7.15. Infrared or laser measuring devices that have both a receiver and transmitter can be an effective tool when taking baseline measurements.

The outdoor scene in Figure 7.16 will serve to illustrate the differences using three additional exterior mapping techniques. This will allow the reader to compare the ultimate product of each technique. Figure 7.17 is an evidence measurement log created using the baseline method, while Figure 7.18 is the resulting crime scene sketch using the baseline method.

Polar Coordinates

The polar-coordinate method is an effective technique for mapping exterior scenes in which the evidence is significantly scattered over a relatively open area. Typical examples include aircraft crashes, scattered remains, or even bombing scenes, where bomb debris is widely distributed. The polar-coordinate method is not suited to situations where line of sight is limited by heavy woods or other obstacles.

Polar coordinates are based on surveying techniques. Using a sighting device, the technician measures two to three basic measurements (depending on need) from a known point to the evidence in question. These three measurements are the horizontal angle, the horizontal distance, and the difference in elevation (when recording elevation data). The sighting instrument used can be a surveyor's transit, a laser sighting device, or (in a worst case) a handheld compass.

Horizontal angle is measured as rotation of the sighting instrument from north in the horizontal plane, a measurement of 1 to 360 degrees. Horizontal distance is measured as the distance between the datum point and the evidence item. If the technician is not recording elevation data, horizontal distance is simple to record. The technician measures

Figure 7.12 When using mapping techniques such as baseline or grids, the datum point must be fixed in the overall scene in some fashion. Here, the datum point is tied to a nearby garage by use of triangulation. Because the datum point is a single point and not an object, two measurements will effectively fix this point in space.

Figure 7.13 When using the baseline technique, the most effective method is to extend a nonelastic tape measure as the actual baseline. Here, the technician sets the tape measure as a baseline, aligning it with a stake to keep it on a straight line with the datum point and at a consistent horizontal height. Using the tape measure as the baseline allows the technician to read the baseline measurement immediately without further effort.

Figure 7.14 Once the baseline is in place, items of evidence are measured at a right angle to the baseline using a second tape measure.

Figure 7.15 As shown in this photograph, it is important to ensure that the measurement from the evidence to the baseline is at a right angle by visually squaring the two tape measures. The position on the baseline (the white tape measure) and the measurement off the baseline (the yellow tape measure) creates a fixing coordinate for the evidence that is similar to that obtained using rectangular coordinates.

Figure 7.16 The various mapping methods create quite dissimilar sketches. This open field of evidence containing various evidence items marked by surveying flags will serve as an example to compare three methods: baseline, polar coordinates, and triangulation on a grid.

the straight-line distance from the datum point to the evidence using any acceptable measuring system (e.g., tape measure). If there is a need to record elevation data, horizontal distance must be a true horizontal distance, i.e., the distance must be measured along a true horizontal plumb. In this case, the use of a laser or IR measuring device is more appropriate. Lastly, elevation is measured as the difference in height from a benchmark (the datum point elevation) and the evidence. Elevation data are not always necessary, and the technician must decide in advance whether to record this information. Elevation is recorded by aiming an optical or laser instrument (using a horizontal line of sight) at an elevation rod held in place at the evidence item. Before recording elevation, the technician must accomplish two additional steps. First, s/he determines the difference between the datum point elevation and the sighting instrument (the height of the instrument above the datum point). This distance is subtracted from the elevation reading to establish the actual elevation difference between the datum point and the evidence. Second, the technician must properly place the sighting device in the scene, ensuring that the sighting device is at a higher elevation than any evidence items. Failure to accomplish this last task will make it impossible to gather elevation data.

As with every other exterior mapping method, the polar-coordinate method starts with setting a datum point. The datum point can be set by use of a GPS device, triangulation to evident landmarks in the area, or (in a worst case) by physical location using a metal

Evidence Baseline Measurement Log

Location: Open field S of 5535 N. Parkway, Lake City GA	Case#: 02-11-5731
Date: 25 NOV 02	Time: 1220 Hrs
Case Agent: R. M. Gardner	
Primary Datum set by: Point 1: 48'2" to SE base corner of garage. Point 2: 141'5.5" to NE base corner of garage.	
Baseline Orientation: N-S 25' base.	

Evidence # or Description	Distance Along Baseline	Distance off Baseline	Direction From Baseline
A - 40 caliber Glock Pistol	21'	59"	W
B - Expended 40 cal. casing.	16'5"	60"	W
C - Expended 40 cal. casing.	11'9"	26.25"	W
D - Expended 40 cal. casing.	11'11"	64"	W
E - Nokia Cell Phone	16'	19'8"	W

Figure 7.17 An example of a baseline measurement log for the field of evidence shown in Figure 7.16. Note that each item of evidence is fixed with two measurements, the same as when using rectangular coordinates. In this case, the technician obtains a measurement from the evidence to the baseline (at a right angle) and a measurement from that point along the baseline to the datum point.

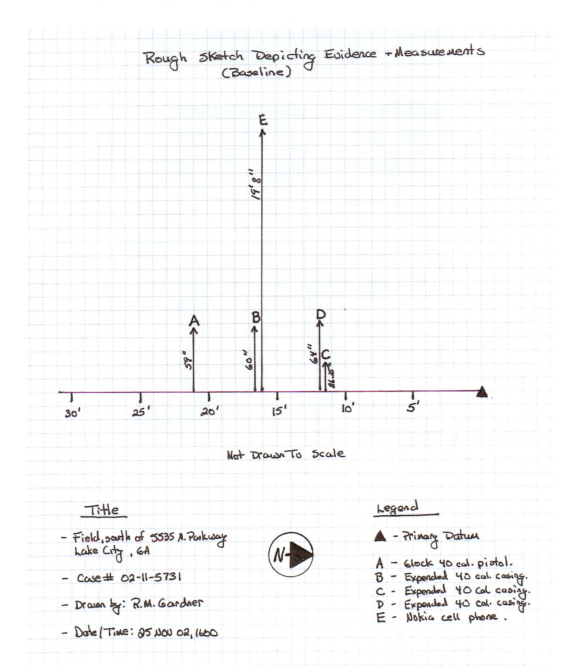

Figure 7.18 An example of a crime scene sketch prepared using the baseline method. The five items of evidence from the field of evidence in Figure 7.16 are mapped.

pipe or rebar. For instance in Figure 7.19, the officer sets the datum point using a short piece of rebar. Lacking any other method of precisely placing the datum point, once the scene mapping is complete, the rebar is driven into the ground. This will allow the technician to return at any later date and locate its position using a metal detector. When polar coordinates are used, the datum point should be set in a position from which the majority of known evidence items can be seen. In a widely distributed evidence field, it may be

Figure 7.19 Polar coordinates begin with setting a datum point. Whatever sighting device is used, the datum point is at the ground level directly beneath it. As in this example, a piece of metal rebar is used to mark the datum point. Once the sighting tripod is in place, the technician uses a laser device or a plumb line to ensure that the rebar is directly beneath the point of rotation of the sighting device.

necessary to place the datum point in the center of the field. This allows a full circle of sightings to be used, rather than a narrow band of degrees.

Once the datum point is in place, the sighting device is placed over it and centered. Centering can be done with a plumb line or a laser, as seen in Figure 7.19. Centering the sighting device ensures that it is rotating from a position directly over the actual datum point, which is at ground level where the rebar was staked. Once centered, the tripod should be securely positioned so that any inadvertent jarring or movement will not upset its position. Once this is complete, the technician rechecks the centering. An alternative method is to reverse the sequence of placing the datum point and tripod. Because the position of the datum point is arbitrary, it really does not matter where the datum point ends up. Therefore, it is often easier to securely set the sighting instrument tripod first. Once the tripod is in place, the rebar can be then placed using the laser or plumb to identify the centered position beneath the device. Either sequence is effective.

If the technician is measuring elevation as part of the data set, the datum point must be placed in a position at a higher elevation than the surrounding evidence. In this case, the technician must also measure and record the distance between the height of the transit or laser sighting device and the ground beneath (since the actual datum point is at ground

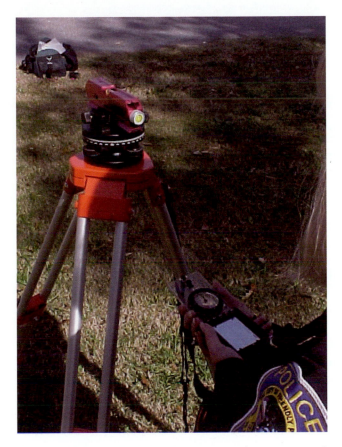

Figure 7.20 In polar coordinates, a sighting device is used to measure the angular direction of the evidence from the datum point. For this measurement to be accurate, the sighting device must be aligned with magnetic north. The technician uses a compass to align the barrel of the sighting device after the tripod and datum point are set.

level). This distance is subtracted from any elevation readings that are ultimately recorded for evidence.

Once centering is complete, the sighting mechanism must be aligned with magnetic north, as seen in Figure 7.20. The transit or laser has a 1-to-360-degree scale with a sighting mark that rotates independently of the sighting device. The sighting mark and 1/360 are aligned while the instrument is aligned with magnetic north; once this is done, the sighting-mark ring is locked down. From that point on, any rotation of the sighting device rotates the sighting mark on the degree scale in relation to north, as seen in Figure 7.21. Use caution when setting the sighting mark. For ease of reading this scale, it is usually manufactured with an offset. The sighting mark actually aligns at either the right or left of the sighting device rather than directly beneath the barrel of the sighting device. This offset allows the technician to look down at the side and see the reading, rather than trying to look under the barrel of the sighting device. A failure to recognize and set up the instrument with this offset will result in inaccurate readings. It is imperative that the technician know the instrument and set it up properly. The final adjustment to the sighting mechanism is to level the transit or laser sight using bubble levels on the device.

Once the sighting device is set and centered, mapping of the scene can begin. The technician has a coworker stand in position at the evidence item, placing an elevation rod

Figure 7.21 Depending upon the sighting device used in polar coordinates, a sighting mark will be present somewhere on the rotating portion of the device. Once the device is aligned with the evidence, this mark will align with an angular scale on the base of the device. In this case, the azimuth or angle to the evidence is 259 degrees.

at the base of the evidence item, as seen in Figure 7.22. If available, a rod level should be used to prevent holding the sighting rod at an odd angle. When using a surveyor's transit, alignment of the sighting device and the sighting rod is evident through the optical lens of the transit. With a laser device, alignment is evident when the laser dot appears on the sighting rod. When the device is aligned, the technician notes the position of the sight mark in degrees on the scale. Once the direction from the datum point is established, the technician measures the distance from the datum point to the evidence. This distance can be measured using a tape measure, as seen in Figure 7.23, or with a laser or infrared measuring device. When measuring elevation data, the latter method is preferred. These measurements establish a specific vector (direction and distance) from the datum point to the evidence, fixing it in the scene. If the technician is collecting elevation data, the point where the transit or laser aligns on the vertical scale of the sighting rod indicates the elevation off the datum point, as seen in Figure 7.24. This measurement is annotated as well. This measurement, minus the distance measured between the sighting device and the datum point (the instrument height), identifies the elevation of the evidence relative to the datum point.

Because line of sight is an important aspect of polar coordinates, there may be occasions where multiple datum points will be necessary to map a scene. This is particularly true

Figure 7.22 To find the correct azimuth, an assistant stands at the evidence item and places a sighting rod at the base of it. The technician then aligns the optical or laser sighting device on the sighting rod.

Figure 7.23 Once an azimuth is determined, the horizontal distance from the datum point to the evidence item is measured with either a tape measure or laser measuring device.

Figure 7.24 In some instances, elevation data are required when using polar coordinates. Elevation is determined by aligning the optical device and reading where the device aligns with the sighting rod or, as in this case, by using a laser device. To calculate elevation data, the user must know the vertical distance between the sighting device and the datum point. In this case, the point where the laser appears on the elevation rod is 4 ft, 2 in. above the evidence. The vertical distance between the datum point and the sighting device is subtracted from this 4 ft, 2 in. to place the item in relation to the datum point.

when trees or other obstacles prevent direct line of sight from a single datum point to all evidence. In such instances, the technician can set a second or third datum point at alternative positions that eliminate the line-of-sight issues. There are no limitations on the number of datum points the technician can use. When using multiple datum points, however, it is preferable to keep a separate measurement log for each and not combine data from multiple points on the same log. All of the information can certainly be plotted on the same sketch, but mixing datum information on the log can lead to confusion or error.

The resulting documentation using the polar-coordinate method is somewhat different than that created by baseline or triangulation techniques. Figure 7.25 is the evidence measurement log created using polar coordinates, while Figure 7.26 is the resulting sketch.

Triangulation or Rectangular Coordinates on a Grid

In some instances, it may be necessary to create a grid system to map the evidence accurately. Grids are effective for large-scale scenes where there are multiple teams actively mapping an area with no significant landmarks or in small-scale scenes such as gravesites.

Evidence Measurement Log – Polar Coordinates

Location:	Open field S of 5535 N Parkway, Lake City GA	Case#:	02-11-5731
Date:	25 NOU 02	Time:	1220 Hrs
Case Agent:	B.M. Gardner		
Primary Datum set by:	Point 1: 78' 3" to SE base corner of garage. Point 2: 147' 10" to NE base corner of garage.		
Instrument Elevation :	4' 6"	Oriented : Ⓝ S E W	
Instrument:	Tracer Laser Level		

	Evidence/Description	Heading from Datum	Distance to Datum	Evidence Elevation
1	A - 40 Cal Glock Pistol	244°	40' 10"	4'2"
2	B Expended 40 cal casing	258°	39' 1.5"	4'2°
3	C Expended 40 Cal casing	260°	35' 4"	4'25"
4	D Expended 40 cal casing	266°	38'5"	4'5"
5	E Nokia cell phone	260°	54' 8"	3' 11.5"
6				
7				
8				
9				
10				
11				
12				
13				
14				
15				
16				
17				
18				
19				
20				
21				
22				
23				
24				
25				

Figure 7.25 An example of a polar-coordinate measurement log for the field of evidence shown in Figure 7.16.

In large-scale scenes, such as those involving scattered remains, triangulation may be the most appropriate method to employ with the grid. The grid is created and identified though the use of stakes, which in effect become the triangulation landmarks. Although the technician can lay out barrier tape to identify the sides of the grid squares, in larger scenes the tape becomes a hindrance to movement. In smaller scenes such as gravesites, rectangular coordinates are often the preferred method for documenting measurements to the grid. The entire grid must be laid out, as in archeology techniques, or a rigid grid is overlaid onto the site.

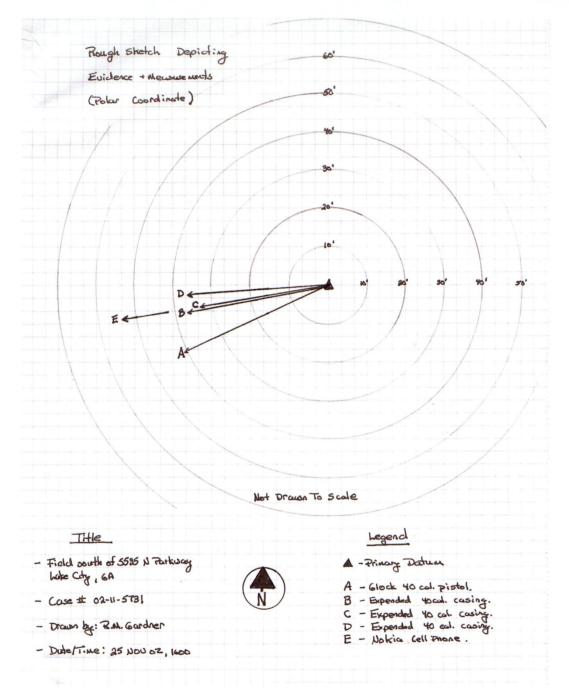

Rough Sketch Depicting
Evidence + Measurements
(Polar Coordinate)

Not Drawn To Scale

Title

- Field south of 5585 N Parkway
  Lake City, GA
- Case # 02-11-5731
- Drawn by: R.M. Gardner
- Date/Time: 25 NOV 02, 1600

Legend

▲ - Primary Datum

A - Glock 40 cal. pistol.
B - Expended 40cal. casing.
C - Expended 40 cal. casing.
D - Expended 40 cal. casing.
E - Nokia Cell Phone.

Figure 7.26 An example of a crime scene sketch prepared using the polar-coordinate method.

Creating the grid is the most time-consuming aspect of using the grid technique. The most effective method for setting up the grid is to follow standard Cartesian coordinates, using only positive numbers. To accomplish this, the datum point is set in the lower left corner of the grid, as seen in Figure 7.27. The left border of the grid becomes the positive Y-axis, and the lower border of the grid becomes the positive X-axis. In this fashion, the known field of evidence is contained in the upper right quadrant of the coordinate system.

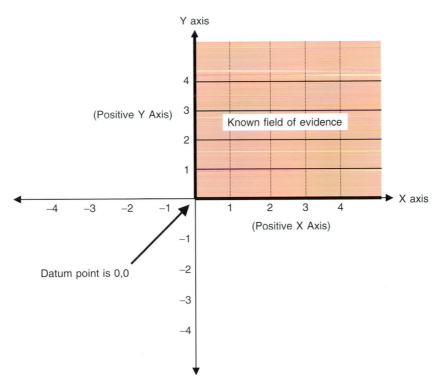

Figure 7.27 Grid systems require setting a datum point and establishing, at a minimum, positive X- and Y-axes. The datum point is set in the lower left corner of the grid (point 0,0). Whatever the size of the grid, the upper right quadrant should encompass the known field of evidence. If for any reason evidence were later found outside of this area, the grid could be expanded using standard Cartesian coordinates to include any item found in any relationship to the original grid.

If, at some point in the processing, evidence is discovered outside of this area, the grid can be extended in any direction, and the evidence can be accurately and effectively added to the sketch.

As with previous mapping methods, the process begins by setting the datum point (in Cartesian coordinates the datum point is 0,0). Additionally the technician must decide in advance the size for each grid (e.g., placing each stake 10 ft from the next). The size of each grid is typically dependant upon the overall area involved and how distributed the evidence is. From the datum point, the technician extends a primary baseline of the grid to the right for whatever distance is required. This creates the lower two corners of the grid (the X-axis). Once these corners are staked, the technician sets a second baseline at a right angle to the first (the Y-axis), extending it out from the datum point the same distance as the primary baseline. This is best accomplished using a compass or transit to ensure that the two lines are at right angles to each other. These two lines establish three outer corners of the grid. Before proceeding further, the technician checks the square of the grid by measuring across the grid and applying the 3-4-5 rule.[2] From a point three units from the grid corner on one axis, to a point four units from the same corner on the adjacent axis, the distance between the two points is five units. So if the grid stakes are set 10 ft apart, from a point 30 ft up the Y-axis to a point 40 ft along the X-axis the distance is 50 ft, as seen in Figure 7.28. Verifying this measurement allows the technician to be confident

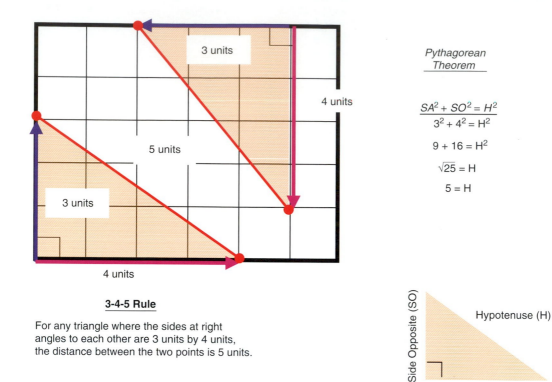

Pythagorean
Theorem

$$SA^2 + SO^2 = H^2$$
$$3^2 + 4^2 = H^2$$
$$9 + 16 = H^2$$
$$\sqrt{25} = H$$
$$5 = H$$

3-4-5 Rule

For any triangle where the sides at right
angles to each other are 3 units by 4 units,
the distance between the two points is 5 units.

Side Opposite (SO)

Hypotenuse (H)

Side Adjacent (SA)

Figure 7.28 Squaring the grid. After creating X- and Y-axes for the grid, it is important to ensure that the two lines are at right angles to one another. The most effective way to square the grid is to apply the Pythagorean Theorem or a simplified version known as the 3-4-5 rule. The interval of the grid junctures is always the same along each axis (e.g., every subgrid square is 10 × 10 ft). Based on this rule, the distance between any point three intervals (30 ft) along one axis to a point four intervals (40 ft) along an adjoining axis will be equal to five intervals (50 ft). This relationship is true anywhere in the grid configuration, and a quick measurement between any two points will verify that portion of the grid as square.

that the sides are aligned properly at right angles to the datum point. Once this check is made, the fourth corner can be staked, and it too is checked using the same technique.

The technician measures and places stakes along the baseline at whatever interval was chosen for the grid. The technician repeats this process for the opposite side of the grid. The entire process is then repeated for the remaining two sides, resulting in all four exterior sides of the grid being staked at the appropriate interval. Use of a string or laser will help keep the stakes on opposite sides of the grid in alignment. Once the outer limits of the grid are in place, rows of interior stakes are placed across the grid. The technician uses the exterior sides to ensure alignment of these interior stakes. At any point in the process, the technician can check an individual interior grid to ensure that it is square by using the method described in Figure 7.28.

Once all stakes are in place, the stakes should be physically marked, identifying each uniquely within the Cartesian coordinate system (e.g., stake 0,5, stake 10,10). Once the grid is in place and marked, the technician triangulates the evidence to the surrounding stakes, as seen in Figure 7.29. Figure 7.30 is a simplified grid/triangulation measurement log, and Figure 7.31 is the resulting sketch.

Figure 7.29 Once the grid is in place, the technician measures from the various grid junctures to the evidence. The mapping method used can be rectangular coordinates or, as in this case, triangulation.

Rectangular coordinates can be used in a grid system as well. This method is employed in gravesite excavation, where evidence is measured at right angles to the grid side. In these small localized areas, rectangular coordinates are an effective and precise method. For ease of plotting and recognizing where in the overall grid the evidence is, each intersection becomes a subdatum point that identifies a specific interior grid. In Figure 7.32, the intersection of 5,5 would be a subdatum point identifying the grid defined by the stakes 5,5, 10,5, 10,5 and 10,10. The technician would first identify the grid (e.g., grid 5,5) and then the corresponding rectangular coordinates for the evidence using the X and Y position (e.g., measurements off the Line 5,5 – 10,5 and the Line 5,5 – 5,10) for that particular grid. In print, this all might seem somewhat confusing, but in practice the technique is efficient and effective.

Triangulation on a Baseline

In situations involving exterior crime scenes where the field of evidence is not too widely scattered, but where there are no adequate landmarks, the technician can apply a combination of baseline and triangulation, as seen in Figure 7.33. The baseline is created in a standard fashion across the field of evidence, although in this instance the use of a tape measure as the baseline is not necessary. Instead of taking specific measurements on the baseline at right angles, reference points are marked at various positions on the baseline (e.g., every 10 ft). Evidence is then triangulated to these reference points. The baseline and reference points become the landmarks, and triangulation is used to fix the evidence as accurately as possible. If sufficient landmarks are present, both ends of the baseline should be triangulated in the scene, rather than just the datum point.

Evidence Triangulation Measurement Log

Location: Open field S of SS35 N. Parkway Lake City GA		Case#: 02-11-5731
Date: 25 NOV 02		Time: 1220 Hrs
Case Agent: R.M. Gardner		
Primary Datum set by: 0,0	Point 1: 63'5" to SE base corner of garage. Point 2: 155'3" to NE base corner of garage.	
Primary Datum Elevation (If necessary):		

From	To	Distance	Remarks
Front sight of Glock - A	0,5	37.75"	
" "	0,10	67.5"	
Base of the clip of Glock - A	5,0	16.5" → 1'6.5"	
" "	5,5	15.5"	
Base of casing - B	5,0	70.25"	
" "	10,0	64.75"	
Base of casing - C	10,5	45.5"	
" "	15,5	44.5"	
Base of casing - D	10,10	61"	
" "	15,10	65.25"	
C/Mass of Nokia Phone E	5,15	63"	
" "	10,15	56"	

5' Grid   X 0,0 – 15,0 oriented S-N , Y 0,0 – 15,0 oriented E-W

Figure 7.30 An example of an evidence measurement log for the field of evidence found in Figure 7.16 using triangulation on a grid. Note that each stake in the grid has a distinct identify (e.g., stake 0,10 is zero intervals along the X-axis and ten intervals along the Y-axis).

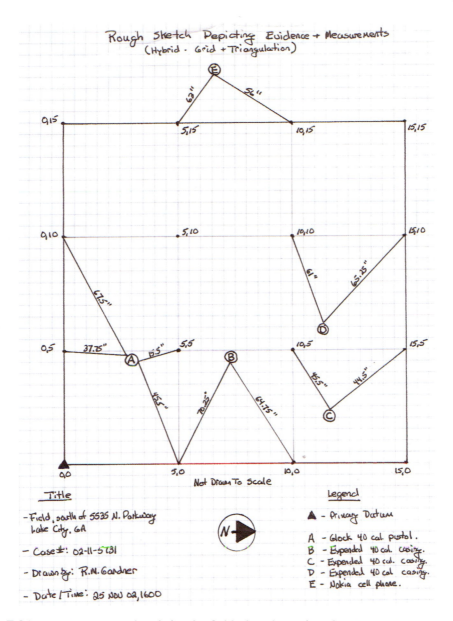

Figure 7.31 A crime scene sketch for the field of evidence found in Figure 7.16 created using triangulation on a grid. Compare the differences between Figure 7.18, Figure 7.26, and this figure. All present the same information in different fashions.

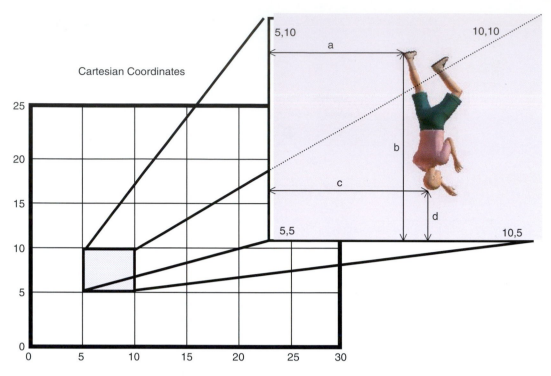

Figure 7.32 The use of rectangular coordinates in a grid system. This method is most effective when excavating gravesites and other localized areas. The measurements are made from the evidence to the nearest interior grid side and not to the exterior of the overall grid. The interior grid in effect becomes a sub-datum point. Oftentimes, to aid in making these measurements, a fixed grid (constructed of wood or PVC pipe) is placed over the area, rather than running strings between the stakes of the grid.

Total-Station Mapping

Total stations are automated surveying systems that use methods very similar to polar coordinates. A total station combines automated transits, lasers, and computer technology. This allows the technician to capture and download data from the scene into computer-aided drafting (CAD) software, creating accurate scaled drawings, as seen in Figure 7.34. Total-station systems found their first foothold in forensics in traffic accident investigation, allowing accident investigators to quickly and accurately document extensive scenes involving debris, vehicles, skid marks, and the like. The systems ultimately made their way into the hands of homicide investigators and have been used extensively in exterior scenes (Figure 7.35). Eventually, these systems were also successfully used in interior homicide scenes.

In a manner similar to polar coordinates, total stations create an accurate survey developed from three basic measurements taken from a known datum point: horizontal angle, vertical angle, and slope distance. The accuracy of the total-station survey is based on the system's ability to measure distance and angle. A total-station system can measure angles to a precision of 0.0013888 degrees and distances to within a few millimeters, depending upon the nature of the internal electronic distance meter (EDM).[3] Interestingly enough, the internal survey that a total station creates requires no reference to magnetic north. Once properly leveled in the scene, alignment of the total station to magnetic north is an unnecessary step and one that is not recommended.[4] The reasoning behind this is

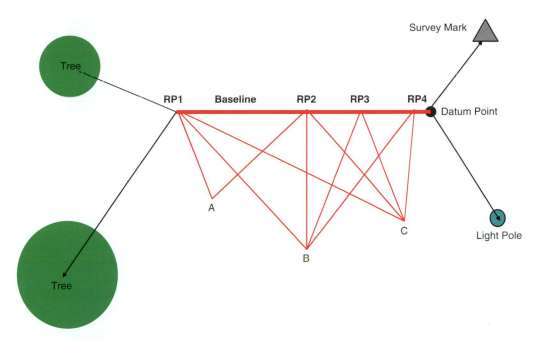

Figure 7.33 Triangulation on a baseline. In exterior scenes that lack specific landmarks, an effective method is to place a baseline in the scene and establish a number of reference points (RPs) along the baseline. The evidence is then triangulated to the RPs. As with any baseline, the datum point must be fixed in the scene (triangulated to the survey mark and the light pole). If possible, the end point of the baseline should be fixed as well (triangulated to the two trees, with each tree marked with a metal forestry seal).

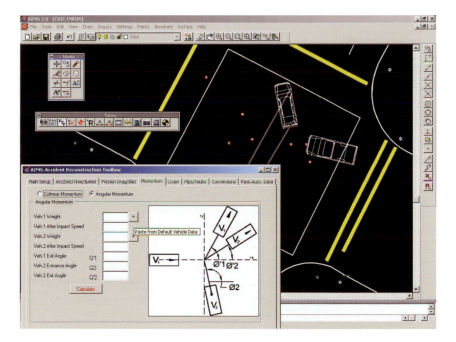

Figure 7.34 Total-station systems combine methods similar to polar coordinates with computer technology to produce very accurate crime scene sketches. (Photograph courtesy of Nikon, Inc. With permission.)

Figure 7.35 Use of a total-station system in an exterior crime scene. Although total stations suffer the same problem as polar coordinates (the need for a line of sight between the instrument and the evidence), total stations allow the investigator to quickly establish multiple datum points. Even in an area with numerous trees, the system can be moved to accommodate line of site while keeping all of the datum points tied to one another. (Photograph courtesy of Roy Heim and the Tulsa Police Department. With permission.)

the accuracy of the total station. Given that the instrument cannot be aligned using a magnetic compass to the same level of accuracy that the total station can measure an angle, surveying techniques suggest simply assigning a convenient north. The internal survey created is still accurate because the total station is set in the scene by sighting on several known landmarks.

The sighting device of a total station is aimed at a laser reflector, which is positioned by the evidence in a similar fashion as the elevation rod used in polar coordinates. The system identifies the horizontal angle in the same way as polar coordinates, but with a greater level of accuracy. Vertical angle is measured as the angle up or down from a vertical plumb from the device to the reflector. Unlike the leveled line-of-sight devices used in polar coordinates, the relative elevation of the total station (higher or lower) to the evidence is not a matter of concern. Lastly, the total station measures the slope distance as the distance between the device and the reflector. This measurement is made by the EDM, an internal infrared or laser measuring device. Using trigonometric relationships, the computer can calculate the horizontal distance (described in polar coordinates) using the vertical angle and slope distance, as seen in Figure 7.36. Because these systems are true surveying devices, they are far more functional than any other method of mapping, particularly when operating on difficult terrain.

Functionally, any point in the scene can be accurately measured, and that information is recorded quickly by a total station. This efficiency allows the technician to take readings from a variety of points on neighboring landmarks, roads, trees, or whatever, which allows

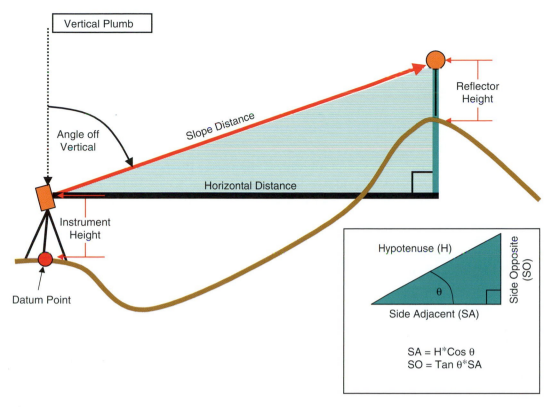

Figure 7.36 Total stations work on similar measurements as the polar-coordinate method, but the technology enables the system to read a sighting to evidence located either below or above its position. The sighting device measures the slope distance and the vertical angle. Using trigonometric relationships, the total station combines both of these known measurements to determine the true horizontal distance to the object. Elevation is captured in a similar fashion as polar coordinates. The system takes into account the instrument height and the reflector height, and then determines the relative elevation of the evidence to the datum point.

more detail to be incorporated into the survey. If multiple datum points are necessary, the system is moved and the datum points are tied to one another through a technique known as a "back sight." To create a back sight, the reflector rod is positioned at the new datum point and a reading is taken to this new point from the total station's original position. The machine is then moved and leveled at the new position, and a reading is taken with a reflector held at the previous datum point. The back sight helps ensure that the internal survey is accurate.

Total-station systems do present several limiting considerations. First, they are expensive. Second, the learning curve to properly employ them in the field is a little more extensive than any of the other crime scene mapping methods. They are also prone to a variety of errors. These errors can be eliminated with proper use, but that demands an experienced operator. As with any equipment, the crime scene is not the place to learn how to use a total station. The most significant error issue involved in the total station's use is movement or jostling of the machine once leveled at a datum point. Remember, the total station is measuring distance to the millimeter and angles to 1/1000th of a degree. Once the total station is placed in the scene, any rough handling can lead to minor error. Although the chaotic conditions of the crime scene have diminished significantly by the time any crime scene mapping is employed, experienced operators have found it prudent to assign someone to guard the total station once it is placed at a datum point.[5] Another consideration is environmental conditions that affect visibility (e.g., fog or smoke), as they can also impact the total-station survey. Nevertheless, total stations represent a significant tool for the future of crime scene mapping.

Summary

The crime scene sketch serves to graphically demonstrate the position and interrelationships of the various items of evidence within the physical scene. When combined with photographs and notes, the sketch provides a greater understanding of the scene. This document is of value to the investigators for developing and checking investigative theories, but it can also assist the jury in recognizing the various interrelationships within the scene.

The effort directed at crime scene mapping and sketching by the technician is very much a product of the severity of the crime and how important the various interrelationships of the scene are to any investigative questions that may exist. In simple crimes such as burglaries, the more basic methods may be effective at detailing these interrelationships. In more significant cases such as homicides, the techniques employed should "fix" the evidence as precisely as possible in the scene. No matter which method is employed, a crime scene sketch has five basic elements: heading, diagram area, legend, title block, and scale and direction notations.

The vast majority of crime scene sketches are produced in a bird's-eye view, i.e., the view is from above looking down. From this point of view, all horizontal surfaces are easily demonstrated. Additional variations of view, such as the cross-projection sketch or the elevation sketch, allow the technician to more effectively demonstrate evidence present on vertical surfaces.

The methods used for crime scene mapping include rectangular coordinates, where the technician takes two measurements from the evidence at right angles to the surrounding surfaces. Although rectangular coordinates effectively place evidence in the scene, they are not the most precise method for fixing evidence. Another method of fixing evidence is baseline coordinates. In this method, a baseline is extended out along a cardinal direction, and a measurement is made from the evidence at a right angle to the baseline. The most effective method of fixing evidence is triangulation. In the triangulation technique, two to four measurements are made from two distinct points on the evidence to distinct landmarks in the scene. The number of measurements is a function of whether the item is regularly shaped or irregularly shaped. Regularly shaped items require four measurements, while irregular items require two measurements. Polar coordinates use a sighting device to establish an azimuth reading from a known point to the evidence. This is combined with a linear measurement between the two points, effectively fixing the item in the scene. Total-station systems capture crime scene data using similar methods as polar coordinates, but they do so using computerized sighting devices. These data are used to produce computer-generated crime scene sketches. In certain instances, particularly in exterior scenes and gravesites, it is necessary to combine methods, such as (1) triangulation or rectangular coordinates on a grid or (2) triangulation on a baseline.

Suggested Reading

Hochrein, M.J., *Crime Scene Mapping*, Federal Bureau of Investigation, St. Louis, MO, 2002.

Chapter Questions

1. What is the primary purpose of the crime scene sketch?
2. What are the five essential elements of the crime scene sketch?
3. What are two variations in creating a sketch that will effectively allow the crime scene technician to document evidence on vertical objects?
4. In rectangular coordinates, how are fixing measurements made to surrounding walls?
5. Give an example and describe fixing a regularly shaped object with triangulation.
6. In what circumstance is baseline mapping most effective?
7. What two additional steps are required when using polar coordinates to map a scene in which elevation data are required?
8. In what situation are rectangular coordinates on a grid particularly effective?
9. In what situation would triangulation on a baseline be effective?
10. Why is it unnecessary to orient a total station to true north?

Notes

1. *PowerPoint* is a registered trademark of Microsoft Corp.
2. Skinner, M. and Lazenby, R.A., *Found! Human Remains*, Archeology Press, Simon Fraser University, Burnby, British Columbia, 1983, p. 19.
3. Cruikshank, K.M., Use of the Total Station: Introduction and Basic Techniques, Portland State University, OR, n.d.
4. Cruikshank, K.M., Use of the Sokkia Set 4Bii Electronic Total Stations, Portland State University, OR, 1997.
5. Meaux, C., Harris County Sheriff's Department, verbal discussion, Feb. 2003.

Narrative Descriptions: Crime Scene Notes and Reports

8

As discussed in Chapter 6, crime scene documentation consists of four key elements: photographs, sketches, and the narrative descriptions found in both notes and reports. This chapter outlines the nature of the narrative documentation.

The crime scene technician has the purpose and mission of objectively identifying the nature of events that occurred at a scene. If the technician is to accurately document the condition of the scene in as pristine a condition as possible, it is imperative that narrative scene descriptions be:

- Detailed, with all pertinent facts and conditions documented
- Accurate, with few inferences or subjective evaluations included
- Understandable, i.e., logical and organized

Keep in mind that while creating the narrative description, rarely does the technician have any idea of the issues and alibis that may be in contention at trial. So the narrative must be completed in the hope of answering any and all questions that may ultimately be posed by the investigation or trial. Any given observation may be the critical detail that will support or refute some claim regarding what happened on scene. Besides answering investigative issues, there is another simple fact that the crime scene technician can be assured of: the report narratives are the primary document that outsiders will use to judge the overall competency of the investigation. The narrative report is viewed by counsel and other investigators, and portions often are read to the jury. Media can and will access this document as well. The narrative need not be a prize-winning piece of writing, but the professionalism of the technician will be judged based upon its content.

Investigative Notes

Investigative notes are a staple of any crime scene examination. The crime scene technician's notes should begin with notification of the crime, identify specific actions upon arrival, and provide a clear and detailed record of all observations and actions taken while in the scene. Descriptions of techniques employed, areas where the techniques were employed, and the results of such techniques are all appropriate for inclusion in the notes. This is particularly important when a method meets with negative results.

When an investigative technique is employed with positive results, additional effort in the way of photographs, annotations to the crime scene sketch, and specific mention in the crime scene report are used to document that result. For example, the recovery of a latent print or chemical enhancement of a bloody footwear mark will merit specific mention in the crime scene report. Positive effort always leads to descriptive documentation in the final report; the technician found evidence and wants others to know what was found and where s/he found it. A negative result, however, causes the technician to move on to additional areas or attempt some other technique. Technicians rarely report all of the places where investigative effort met with negative results while fingerprinting or using some other investigative process. Similarly, technicians often do not comment on situations in which they observe no evidence, such as rooms that are undisturbed. Unfortunately, lawyers have a way of making much ado about nothing with regard to such negative results. They often make claims of inappropriate effort or improper procedures on the part of police, using this claim as a basis to let the jury know that the police "lost the crucial exculpatory evidence." Granted, in some instances a failure to act by the crime scene investigator will result in the loss of evidence, but far too often this claim is nothing more than rhetoric used to confuse the jury. Therefore, it is important that the technician comment in some fashion on efforts that fail as well as making observations on conditions that are otherwise unremarkable. In the formal crime scene report, negative efforts may get nothing more than a sentence or two. For example, a simple statement such as "examination of the west wall failed to locate any latent fingerprints" clearly makes the point that effort was expended but met with no result. Whenever possible, the technician's notes should explain what methods were employed and specifically where they were employed. If challenged in court, the notes provide documentation that will effectively eliminate wild and unsubstantiated claims by counsel.

Other areas of specific interest in the technician's notes include actions recorded during the initial observation and during the overall observation steps defined in Chapter 4. All notes should accurately reflect action and effort, but when describing the scene in these two steps it is imperative that the notes be detailed and concise. Synopsized paragraphs with generalized information serve little, if any, function at a later date when trying to answer specific questions. Detailed narrative descriptions, however, will often assist the investigator in evaluating some point that may not be clear from a photograph or sketch. The following is an example of the detail that might be appropriate given what can be observed in Figure 8.1.

Describing the Victim

There is a white male present in a prone position on the east side of the floor approximately 15 ft from the south end of the hallway. The victim appears to be in his mid-30s, short in stature, with brown hair. The victim is lying in the hallway with his head oriented to the north, legs oriented to the south. The victim's left hand is outstretched to the west, palm down. The right arm is bent at the elbow, with the right forearm directly adjacent the east wall. The hand is positioned palm down. The victim's feet are spread slightly, with both feet facing to the east. The victim's head is on the left side, facing east as well. The victim is wearing a pair of dark blue in color pants, a light gray in color T-shirt with a multicolored emblem on the back top third of the T-shirt. On the left shoulder (west side) of the T-shirt there is an evident defect in the shirt. The defect is circular in nature with slightly

Figure 8.1 An overall photograph of a body in a crime scene. The narrative description supporting this photograph cannot be simply: "There is a body on the floor, with a revolver 2 ft to the north." Narratives are used to supplement photographs, answering details the investigator can see while there on scene, details that may not be evident from the photograph alone.

abraded edges and surrounded by what appears to be a saturation of blood. There is no evidence of stippling or powder burns in or around the defect. The saturation stain extends in a generally circular shape around the defect for approximately 5 cm in all directions. There are no other injuries, bloodstains or exudates noted. Approximately 5 ft to the north of the victim's head there is a .38-caliber, $2^1/_2$-in.-barreled revolver. The revolver is oriented with the barrel pointing to the northwest, and the base of the grip oriented to the south. There are what appear to be four unexpended bullets in the cylinder and one expended bullet that is directly beneath the hammer.

Including all of this detail might seem unnecessary, particularly given that complete photographic coverage of the scene will be forthcoming as another product of the crime scene processing. But any of these details could be important in trying to understand what did or did not happen. Often small details that are present in the notes allow the investigator to verify some detail that is only suggested by a photograph. Once again, the notes in conjunction with the sketch and photographs are used to corroborate and support each other. Using the detail in the written notes, the crime scene technician will ultimately pull out salient facts and observations for inclusion in the formal crime scene report. Crime scene notes may never be used for anything other than this purpose, but the bottom line is that all of the details of what the technician observed are still documented. If any question arises at some future date, the notes may be functional in answering the issue. Far too often, the author encounters crime scene documentation in significant scenes (e.g., murder scenes) that is both incomplete and worthless for answering these critical questions. Whether this is an organizational training failure, a lack of leadership, or individual incompetence, it is unacceptable by any standard. The professionalism of the crime scene technician and the organization will ultimately be judged by peers and the criminal justice system alike based upon the documentation effort.

Case Example: Professionalism Demonstrated through Work Product

Figure 8.2 represents the total scene documentation produced by a major metropolitan detective bureau, including the "crime scene sketch" in a robbery homicide crime scene. The organization involved is not a five-man police department, but rather an organization with a dedicated homicide division serving a city with a population of more than 1 million. This "documentation" was backed up by a whopping total of seven crime scene photographs. Figure 8.3 represents a single page of notes from a single investigator at a homicide scene. The supporting notes of this investigator alone included an additional 23 pages of documented effort of similar detail and quality. The overall crime scene documentation included over 250 photographs and multiple to-scale crime scene sketches.

In evaluating the professionalism of the organization that produced Figure 8.2, one might quickly assume mere incompetence of the detective. But the example demonstrates far more than incompetence. This organization clearly lacks leadership. This is a homicide scene, and the death of a human being in this organization rates an entire page. In this organization, the detectives have become nothing more than garbage collectors. One must either believe that the chief of police has no concept of the quality of effort expended by his/her detectives or simply does not care. The chief of detectives and whatever supervisory investigative staff that exists in the chain of command has absolutely no excuse. As they are paid to supervise the investigations, either they are not doing their jobs, or they have made the decision to accept such mediocre effort.

In contrast, Figure 8.3 demonstrates obvious concern on the part of the individual investigator as well as an organizational mindset that places value on quality and professionalism. This is an organization where standards are set and individuals are held accountable to those standards. Organizations of this nature build pride and competence in their investigative personnel.

After comparing the quality of work product in Figure 8.2 and Figure 8.3, every crime scene technician must ask him- or herself a simple question: which work product would I prefer to have my name associated with? Pride, professionalism, duty, no matter what motivates the technician, something must drive the technician to meet his or her obligations to some acceptable standard. There simply is no excuse for failing in this endeavor. To prevent that point from being misused — and specifically for the sake of any attorney reading this passage — the author would reiterate that rarely will good crime scene documentation be without error or omission. It is impossible to capture every nuance in the crime scene or realize the importance of every small detail. No one expects the crime

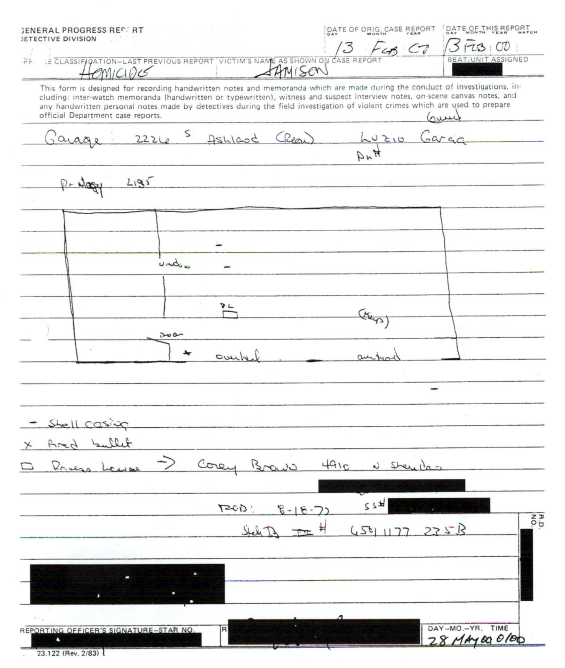

Figure 8.2 This single page represents the totality of investigative effort by a crime scene investigator (notes, sketch, and crime scene report) at a homicide scene. This document fails to discuss bloodstains present in the scene and other evidence. The scene was more than a four-sided box, yet this documentation fails to provide any clue as to the character or condition of this scene. This is more than incompetence; this is laziness and fails on every level to meet the basic duties expected of a crime scene technician.

scene technician to be perfect. The technician's standard is not "zero defects," but neither is it "zero effort" as demonstrated in Figure 8.2. There are a lot of different levels of competence demonstrated every day in crime scene work, but honest competent effort is readily recognized. The crime scene notes will tell the tale. Either the technician was

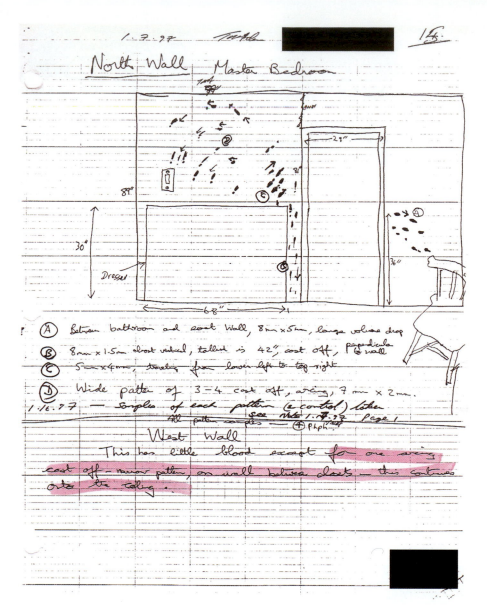

Figure 8.3 This figure represents a single page of detailed notes taken from 23 pages of notes prepared by one crime scene investigator at a homicide scene. This type of crime scene documentation is accurate, detailed, and clearly shows the competence and professionalism of the writer.

competent and actively pursued his or her role and duty at the scene, or the technician was merely a garbage collector.

Although it should not be necessary, the retention of crime scene notes is an area of concern requiring comment. Notes are the investigator's best evidence. Notes usually hold far more specific detail than the formal crime scene report, and more importantly, they are a contemporaneous record. Although they may not be works of art nor completely error free, notes tend to be more accurate as to the true conditions observed. The final report will be neatly printed and spell-checked, but never doubt that errors can creep into a final report. Typical mistakes include compass directions that become mixed up, or numbers related to lengths, or heights that are subsequently transposed during dictation or final typing. That is not to say that similar errors will not be found in the technician's notes, but because the notes are contemporaneous, they are far less likely to hold these transposition and typographical errors. For this reason alone, once the final report is written, notes do not become redundant or unnecessary. They cannot be disposed of. The crime scene technician's notes should become an integral part of the case file and maintained for as long as the formal case file.

Crime Scene Reports

Ultimately, the technician must combine all of the salient facts, observations, actions, and effort into a functional organized report for inclusion in the investigative report. Once again, there is no one right way to format the crime scene report, particularly given the variety of investigative report formats that exist from agency to agency. But whatever the report format used, the technician must ensure that the crime scene report is not:

- A cursory discussion of the central theme items found in the scene (e.g., the body, the gun) and nothing more
- A rambling discourse on why the suspect "had to" have committed the crime
- A description of only the evidence that fits a particular hypothesis

The difficulty of creating a crime scene report for any complex scene is in maintaining some level of organization that allows all pertinent aspects to be discussed and yet does not end up rambling on and on. The technician must pull the salient facts from his or her notes and observation, as not every single detail can be included, while still attending to the important aspects that will allow the reader to understand the scene. The most effective way of doing this is to organize the crime scene report into sections that deal with specific issues. This format works effectively whether the crime scene report is a stand-alone document or whether it is simply a supplemental report filed by the technician. A suggested format for these sections would include:

- Introduction
- Characteristics of the scene
- Conditions of the scene
- Environmental conditions
- Factors pertinent to entry and exit
- Scene documentation
- Collection of physical evidence
- Search for latent prints
- Additional examinations

Introduction Section

The introduction is intended to identify who worked the scene examination, where the scene was, the time and date of the examination, and a short explanation regarding the reason for the scene examination. An example of the introductory section might include the following:

Example: Introduction

Between 1400 and 2335 Hrs, 10 Jan. 2002, Detectives G. Smith and R. Hanson conducted an examination of a reported death scene located in Apartment 3A, 4657 Jonesboro Road, Lake City, GA. The following conditions, observations and actions were noted.

Characteristics of the Scene

The "characteristics of the scene" section is intended to provide a general description of the scene (e.g., building, room, or area) and associated features of the scene such as doors, windows, openings, and geographical features of exterior scenes and their relationship to the surrounding area. Furniture, appliances, and other standard artifacts that would be present in the scene day to day are described in some detail as well. This section describes stable and static conditions at the scene. Some examples for a "characteristics of the scene" section include the following:

Example: Characteristics of the Scene — Exterior Scene

The rape scene is located on the northernmost section of the LC Center, a small business strip mall. Smith's Laundry is the last business located on the northern side of the one-story strip mall. All businesses are contained in a single building. From the northwest corner of the laundry, the building extends at least 150 ft to the south. A sidewalk, 4 ft in width, runs along the north side of the building from the northwest corner of the laundry, 60 ft to the east. At this point the building extends to the south then east again, creating a small corner. A chain-link fence begins at this corner and extends east to the rear of the strip mall; the fence effectively encloses and eliminates access to this rear area. To the immediate north of the building is a small parking area, which is bordered by a landscaped barrier that rises at least 10 ft in elevation to the parkway. Lighting on the north side of the street is minimal, and the rear area where the dumpster is located is dark. The view of passing traffic on the parkway is significantly obscured by a number of pine trees that line the roadway. The sidewalks are of concrete construction, while the parking area is asphalt.

Example: Characteristics of the Scene — Interior Scene

5396 Lakeland Road is a single-story cinderblock business, one part of a larger strip mall operation. The business is set up as a karaoke bar. The main business entrance is located on the west side of the building; the entire west wall consists of tinted pane glass. There are two employee/service entrances located at the rear (east side) of the building. The southernmost service entrance on the east side of the building was the apparent point of entry. This door consists of a heavy metal door, with a single in-door locking mechanism. Mounted on the inside of the door there is an additional sliding-bar mechanism. This entrance leads through a small tiled foyer, into the primary business. The main floor plan is set up with multiple small tables and chairs (15 tables), a number of video machines, and a small service counter. The main floor is tiled. The service counter is located in the northeast corner of the main floor. The counter is set in an L-shape, extending off the east wall, with the L opening to the north wall. On the customer side of the counter, the height of the counter is approximately 5 ft. On the service side of the counter, the height is approximately 4 ft. On the section of the service counter extending from the east wall, there is a single cash register. There are a number of additional items present on the counter to include a receipt book, a notebook, and misc. items. Adjacent the east wall is a sound system/amplifier. An entryway to the immediate east of the service counter leads into additional storage and service areas. There is a single wood-frame door located to the immediate north of the service counter; this door is closed and locked.

Example: Characteristics of the Scene — Interior Scene

The apartment is a ground-floor, two-bedroom apartment. There is one entryway leading from the north side of the building into the living room and one entryway leading from the north side of the building into the kitchen. A screened-in sitting porch is present on the west side of the building, with no entrance/exit way from the porch itself to the exterior. The sitting porch and living room are connected through a double sliding glass door. The living room connects to a small hallway and dining area, which is to the immediate south of the kitchen. The hallway extends south approximately 20 ft, with two bedrooms on the west side and a bathroom on the east side. The master bedroom is located at the far southwest side of the apartment, and contains a single queen bed, a standard dresser and one night table. There is a large window in the west wall, with curtains in place. The smaller bedroom has two twin beds in it, a chest of drawers and one small night table. It has a single window with small venetian blinds, closed and in place. The kitchen, where the victim is located, is oriented with cabinetry and sinks on the east side, with a washer and dryer located at the far northeast side. There is a cabinet and stove combination on the northwest side and a refrigerator in the southwest corner. A small window is present in this area that looks out on the front porch.

Conditions of the Scene

The "conditions of the scene" is a section intended to identify the specific conditions that are pertinent to the investigation. This includes identifying the cleanliness, level of disarray, descriptions of items of evidence (including transient evidence, e.g., odors), and other pertinent aspects. Rooms or areas that are undisturbed or lack specific items of evidence should be commented on in some fashion (e.g., the kitchen was found to be unremarkable). The "conditions of the scene" section, in any significant case, can become extensive. Oftentimes, the most effective method of describing the conditions is to break this section into subsections, dealing with each subset room or area. Whenever possible, do not include subjective factors and inferences formed from the scene condition in this section. Try to report the conditions objectively without inference. This can be very difficult to accomplish, particularly when describing circumstances involving negative evidence, i.e., situations in which something that the technician would expect to be present is not.

Example: Condition of the Scene — Exterior Scene

The sidewalk leading from the front of the strip mall along the north side of the building is unremarkable. There is a large pile of pine needles 44 ft east of the northwest corner of the sidewalk, which extends into the parking area at least 7 ft. The pine needles are undisturbed. Alongside the chain-link fence is an area of mud and debris and another pile of pine needles. Examination of the entire area fails to show any recent disturbance. A check after completing the scene examination determined that simply walking in this area caused evident footwear marks. At the end of the fence line, the building orientation creates another corner. Adjacent this location is a dumpster, set approximately 5 ft east of the building. Once again the area is muddy, with another pine needle collection created as a result of runoff. The only disturbances in the mud are those caused by the movement of one wheel of the dumpster. The total movement evident is only 2 or 3 in., and it is unclear if this is recent. Between the building and dumpster are two pieces of paper. One is a local newspaper, dated 19 Jan. 2000; the other is an 8×10-in. folded piece of paper. Beyond being water-logged, neither paper has been stepped on, muddied or damaged. Beyond the dumpster, the parking lot extends eastward to the very rear of the strip mall grounds. There are substantial amounts of red clay present, which is situated in the most direct line of departure for anyone leaving the area to the rear. There are no footwear marks or disturbances present with the exception of large tire marks, that appear to be a commercial sized vehicle. These marks do not appear fresh. This rear alleyway behind the strip mall extends to the south to North Jones Drive, but a locked chain barrier prevents entry or exit of vehicles on the south side. Beyond those items described, there was nothing else remarkable noted.

Example: Condition of the Scene — Interior Scene

The service entryway on the east side of the building was standing open, with evident pry marks caused by a two-pronged instrument. The overall blade width of this instrument appears to be in excess of $1^1/_2$ in. The metal screws holding the sliding bar on the inside surface of the door have been forced from the metal frame door, allowing the bar to disengage. Examination of the tiled floor of the foyer fails to locate any evident dust prints.

The main café is unremarkable, with the exception of a missing cash drawer from the cash register. There were no evident pry marks present on the opening to the register. Approximately $24 in U.S. currency is located in the rear of the cash register cash drawer opening, suggesting that some item was inserted in an attempt to open the drawer. Although the position of the cash register on the counter indicates it was displaced and moved in some fashion, other items on the counter show little evidence of displacement or movement.

Examination of the main room located three dust prints of possible significance. One was located on the tile floor of the main room (Placard 2), leading to the foyer and the point of forced entry. This shoe mark was a complete tread, possibly of a heavy running shoe or boot. The orientation of the mark was with the toes pointed to the southeast. An additional mark was located on the main floor (Placard 3). This mark was a tennis shoe style tread. The toes were oriented facing south. A third dust print was located behind the counter facing the south (Placard 5) but failed to produce a lift of any value. A fourth dust mark was evident on the wood door, to the immediate north of the service counter (Placard 4). This door was later identified as additional storage and the location of the video tape recorder for the surveillance system. This print was similar to the tread design observed behind the counter. No other items appeared to have been damaged, and there was no immediate evidence to suggest that the internal doors had been jimmied in any fashion.

It should be noted that the alarm system was active and operational. However, motion detectors in the building are set to only activate when there is motion in or around the west wall (the main entrance). While conducting scene processing, these motion detectors did not activate until the main doors were approached.

Example: Condition of the Scene — Interior Scene Involving a Body

The living room was unremarkable, with no signs of evident disturbance. The dining room was unremarkable as well; there was a pair of men's shorts and a shirt draped across a small wooden stool, located in the northeast corner of the dining area. The master bedroom was unremarkable. The bed was made and no bedclothes were evident on the floor. The smaller bedroom was unremarkable, with both beds made and no apparent clothing out. The bathroom was clean, unremarkable, with no evident wet linen, or toiletry items out. In the southeast counter area of the kitchen there was a cup of coffee, which was approximately 2/3 full, a spoon was sitting adjacent the cup. Alongside this area was a small religious type book, opened to page 64/65. The annotations in the book were apparently messages for the day. The book was open to the appropriate time frame (Sunday 7/15). The sink was cluttered, but no dirty dishes were present, nor evidence in the immediate area of any meals being prepared. The stove had a single clean aluminum pot on it, but this item was empty and not on a burner. Neither the burners nor the stove were on. There was a telephone located on the south wall, on the east side of the kitchen. The phone was on the hook. There was a small plastic bag with garbage present on the top of the dryer. With the exception of the victim's presence, the kitchen is unremarkable with no sign of disturbance.

An elderly black male was lying on the kitchen floor. He was wearing a white T-shirt and a white pair of briefs. His head was oriented to the north, with his feet extending back to the south. His position was immediately north of the counter that held the cup of coffee. The man's right arm was bent at the elbow, almost parallel with the upper arm. This arm was lying adjacent the right side of the body, against the dryer and cabinet. The left arm was beneath the body, bent at an approximately 45-degree angle. There were no evident injuries noted on the posterior side of the individual and no defects in the clothing. There was no incontinence noted, other than minor urine discoloration in the briefs. Although not significant in volume, a brown and red exudate was evident to the east side of the individual's face. Rigor was set in the lower and upper extremities. No evident livor was noted. Upon turning the individual over, a 45-mm laceration/abrasion was noted over the right eyebrow colocated with a large knot. The injury is linear and lies relatively horizontal with the eyebrow. There are no injuries evident on the knees or elbows, and no other injuries or defects are noted on the body and clothing.

Environmental Conditions

The "environmental conditions" section reports on any weather or scene conditions noted at the time of the investigation. If a known time frame exists for the event or crime, this is a good place to identify any known weather conditions that existed during that time frame (e.g., type of precipitation, amounts, and temperature ranges). The evident impact of the existing conditions on the scene should be noted as well (e.g., rain washing away bloody areas, wet shoe prints drying on asphalt).

Example: Environmental Conditions — Exterior Scene

On arrival the roadway and entire scene was wet, with light to medium rain falling as the scene was processed. The rain had been steady for some hours prior to the reported event. The rain did not impact on the characteristics of the scene, but made movement across the muddied areas impossible without leaving some evidence.

Example: Environmental Conditions — Interior Scene

A light rain fell over the previous two days. As a result the sidewalk leading to the apartment was noted to have standing water present. At the time of scene examination external temperatures were in the 50s. The apartment thermostat was set at 82 degrees and the heater was on. The air inside the apartment was noted to be hot and dry.

Factors Pertinent to Entry and Exit

The "factors pertinent to entry and exit" section is intended to deal with both known and possible avenues of approach and departure from the scene. First and foremost, the technician should identify the objective characteristics of the entry/exit. However, some level of inference is also necessary in evaluating the likelihood that a given approach was or was not used.

Example: Factors Pertinent to Entry and Exit

The victim placed the suspect in the scene as having approached from the east or rear of the strip mall. It would nearly be impossible for anyone exiting this area on foot to pass without running across multiple locations of mud and debris. Any vehicle located at the rear would have to exit via the north side, adjacent the laundry. As previously noted, there is no evidence to suggest such an entry or exit.

Example: Factors Pertinent to Entry and Exit

There was no forced entry evident. The lock on the garage door was intact when fire units arrived. The window in the east wall was determined to have been devoid of any pane material, prior to the fire. Galvanized steel beams that are still in place, however, prevented access by a person, but objects could easily be introduced through this opening.

Scene Documentation

The "scene documentation" section is intended to describe the basic efforts taken to photograph and sketch the scene. The technician can describe the equipment used, the nature of the documentation created (e.g., a rough sketch, detailed total-station sketch), and if considered necessary for immediate reference, details about which photo placards relate to which items of evidence.

Example: Scene Documentation

Photographs were exposed of the general area using a Nikon F2A camera, employing both a 50-mm lens and a 55-mm macro lens, with 400 ASA color film. A rough scene sketch was prepared detailing the general characteristics and measurements.

In the photographs, placards were placed at four locations depicting the following:

Placard 1: Large pile of pine straw adjacent the north sidewalk, undisturbed
Placard 2: Smaller pine straw pile adjacent the fence line, undisturbed
Placard 3: Pine straw collected from runoff at the corner of the building, undisturbed
Placard 4: Location of the two papers, between the dumpster and building

Collection of Physical Evidence

The "collection of physical evidence" section can be used in a variety of ways depending upon custom, SOP (standard operating procedure), and the nature of other evidence-collection documents that the organization utilizes. If custom or SOP demand creating a consolidated written log of all evidence collected at the scene (which many organizations use), then there is no purpose in recreating that information in the report (Figure 8.4). In that instance, a short description of major items of evidence that the technician feels are important can be included. This will provide an immediate reference to the report reader, without having to refer to the evidence log. If the organization does not use a consolidated evidence log, then a description of what was seized and where it was found is a very functional inclusion to this section of the report.

Search for Latent Fingerprints

Since fingerprints are a standard item of interest at nearly any scene, a section of the crime scene report is directed at fingerprinting efforts. This section should identify the areas

EVIDENCE RECORD AND WORKSHEET

Date _____ Offense _____ Search Warrant # _____ Case # _____

Location of Premises Searched _____

Item No.	Object	Location	Gathered By	Time
#2	Boxer shorts Blue Polka Dot Jockey Size 30	Washing Machine		1105
#3	Boxer shorts Stafford Size 30 Light Teal	Washing Machine		1105
#4	Boxer shorts Stafford Size 33 Light Blue	Washing Machine		1105
#5	Washing machine agitator	downstairs washing Mach.		1111
#6	Toilet tank lid cover	downstairs bath - toilet		1255
#7	toilet mat	downstairs bath - toilet area		"
#8	Washing machine drain hose	from washing machine		"
#9	Fluid (water)	from drain hose - washing machine		1355
#10	Fluid	from "J" shaped drain hose connector	Hixson	1358
#11	Sheet w/stain	from bed in office/bedroom	"	1700
#12	Sheet	" " " " "	"	
#13	Mattress cover	" " " " "	"	
#14	Pillow	" " " "	"	
#15	Pillow	" " " "	"	
#16	Pillow	" " " "	"	
#17	2 Mattress covers	" " " "	"	
#18	1 Comforter	" " " "	"	1715

Figure 8.4 A crime scene evidence log is often used in lieu of other documents to show where all items of evidence were located in the scene and to identify who collected the items. When such a document is used, it is rarely necessary to repeat this information in the narrative report.

where fingerprinting was attempted, where it succeeded, and the nature of the prints recovered (e.g., partial latent prints, palm prints, footprints).

Example: Search for Latent Fingerprints

A brush-and-powder examination was made of the door and door frame. The interior handle of the apartment was superglued and then dusted. Several partial latent prints were recovered here. The coffee table in the living room was examined under ALS, using fluorescent powder, resulting in the recovery of three more partial latent prints and one partial palm print.

Additional Examinations

Once these standard sections are dealt with, the remaining format of the crime scene report is open to describe any additional evaluations or examinations, dependent upon the specifics of the crime and the efforts directed at the scene. Sections or descriptions that might be included are:

- Evident fire patterns and fire-flow evaluations at fire scenes
- Trajectory analysis in shooting scenes
- Bloodstain pattern analysis in violent scenes
- Electrostatic lifter examination for footwear
- Specialized chemical enhancements (e.g., luminol, amido-black, or fluorescein enhancements) and their results

General Considerations

Reporting investigative conclusions is one of the more difficult aspects of the crime scene report. Conclusions are for the most part a function of a crime scene analysis, which is dealt with in depth in Chapter 12. Whatever the nature of the report format utilized by an organization, it is best to try and keep a clear distinction between those parts of the report that define objective observations and actions (processing) and any conclusions drawn from those observations and actions (analysis).

Remember also that the crime scene report is a post-scene product, created as a result of effort and observations made on scene and from the detail found in contemporaneous notes, photographs, or sketches. It is not possible for the technician to include every single act and observation accomplished at the scene, nor is it necessary. But considerable thought by the technician is important to prevent arbitrarily rejecting for inclusion in the final report any information and observations that perhaps do not support a particular hypothesis or that in some fashion may be exculpatory. Objectivity is the critical component of any final crime scene report. It is also important that the technician review the final document thoroughly. Details of directions, measurements, and orientation are often inadvertently skewed in the final document. Typographical errors in this type of information can affect the substantive information contained in the report.

Finally, remember always that although the technician has a responsibility and duty to accurately report the details found in the scene, that detail will often come back to haunt him or her. Counsel on both sides will effectively try to misrepresent the crime scene report and findings using that detail. Trials are anything but pure searches for truth. Counsel (prosecution and defense) will actively seek to present the technician's information out of context if they feel it serves their purpose. Unfortunately, there is no easy answer for this dilemma. One cannot ignore the duty to factually report information. Thus the often-encountered answer presented by jaded investigators of "report as little as possible" is not appropriate. One-page documents without detail serve no function in answering the questions the court will expect answered. Never doubt that the technician will be held accountable for whatever he or she writes.

Summary

Crime scene documentation in the form of narrative descriptions is produced at two distinct periods. The first includes all of the crime scene notes taken contemporaneously while conducting investigative efforts on scene. The second includes the crime scene report, which consolidates and synopsizes the relevant details that the crime scene technician thinks are important. Both narratives must be detailed, accurate, and understandable. Short, synopsized narratives that speak to only central theme items in the scene will serve little function in supporting other crime scene documentation or in resolving specific investigative issues that may develop months or even years later.

Crime scene notes should document all of the investigative effort. This is particularly important when a technique is employed on scene but achieves negative results. Since no evidence was located, rarely will this information be listed in any other crime scene document. A mention in the notes will prevent attorneys from misrepresenting what was or was not present in these areas.

The format of crime scene reports is very much a matter of custom and SOP. Whatever the format, it is best to break the report into functional paragraphs that deal with specific issues and aspects of the scene. This format should include a description of the static conditions of the scene, its current condition, environmental aspects, a discussion of entry and exit points, and any specific techniques employed to recover physical evidence. Whatever the level of effort spent in writing a narrative description of the crime scene, the technician can be assured that everyone will judge his or her professional competence and the quality of the investigation based on this document.

Suggested Reading

Bevel, T. and Gardner, R., *Bloodstain Pattern Analysis: with an Introduction to Crime Scene Reconstruction*, 2nd ed., Chap. 9 and 10, CRC Press, Boca Raton, FL, 2001.

Geberth, V.J., *Practical Homicide Investigation*, 3rd ed., Chap. 4 and 22, CRC Press, Boca Raton, FL, 1997.

Chapter Questions

1. Name the three general attributes that all crime scene report narrative descriptions should have.
2. Why is it important to document investigative efforts that fail to produce evidence?
3. Why must the crime scene technician retain crime scene notes even after the crime scene report is completed?
4. What type of information is described in the "characteristics of the scene" section of the crime scene report?
5. What type of information is described in the "conditions of the scene" section of the crime scene report?
6. Why is some level of inference allowable in the "factors pertinent to entry and exit" section of the crime scene report?

Basic Skills for Scene Processing

9

Every crime scene represents an individual challenge. Each has its own unique problems and its own unique issues, and the scene technician must meet these with a mixture of skill and knowledge, all the while employing a healthy dose of flexibility. Beyond these unique challenges, within almost every crime scene, the technician will encounter basic evidence-recovery issues. The skills needed to meet and resolve these problems include using light technology, recovering fingerprints, and casting a wide variety of impressions.

Applying Light Technology

Clean white light is the most important tool the crime scene technician uses in any crime scene. Light allows the technician to see, which allows the technician to identify evidence. If evidence is not seen, then it is not collected; missed evidence serves no function in defining the nature of the event being investigated. So the most basic consideration of light (as detailed in Chapter 5) is ensuring the presence of sufficient illumination on scene in order to conduct a thorough search. The full spectrum of light, however, serves a far more important role at the scene than ever before. Alternative light sources (ALSs) allow the crime scene technician to employ a variety of narrow wavelengths of the light spectrum in an effort to identify, visualize, and document a variety of different types of physical evidence. As Houseman and Maloney wrote, "As forensic investigators, limiting ourselves to evidence which is only visible under the visible light spectrum would be like refusing to allow a criminalist to use a microscope in a trace evidence examination."[1] In order to understand the full application of an ALS at the crime scene, it is necessary to look into the nature of light and basic theories of radiant energy.

The nature of the most basic properties of light and radiant energy continues to elude modern science. Visible light is simply that portion of the electromagnetic spectrum that we humans visualize as colors. Light has properties consistent with particles (photons) and properties consistent with waves. To date, physics has yet to define a consolidated theory of this very complex phenomenon. Despite its dual nature, all radiant energy is measured by the length of its wave (from peak to peak), and this quality is measured in nanometers (1 billionth of a meter). Thus the radiant-energy spectrum we visualize as color includes violet (400 nm) through red (700 nm).

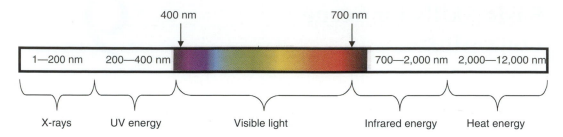

Figure 9.1 The full range of the light and radiant-energy spectrum includes gamma and X rays up to heat-energy and radio waves. Visible light is only a small portion of this spectrum, ranging from 400 to 700 nm.

However, the spectrum of visible light is just a small part of a much broader band of radiant energy, which includes everything from gamma rays to radio waves (Figure 9.1). The radiant-energy spectrum starts with gamma and X rays (1 to 200 nm) and includes the phenomena we feel as heat (12,000 nm). An interesting feature of these radiant-energy waves is that the lower the wavelength, the greater is the energy level. The greater the energy level, the greater the penetration the wave has on an object. A classic example of the power of this penetrating wave is the X ray. X rays, with their very short wavelengths, penetrate soft tissues more effectively than they do the more dense bone structures. As a result, by capturing the X rays that pass through the tissue on an X-ray film, medical professionals can observe and visualize denser objects (bones, bullets, and other foreign bodies) and damage, such as bone fractures (Figure 9.2). The X rays' behavior as a penetrating wave provides a rather significant utility in forensic science.

When light energy encounters an object, it can act on the object in four basic ways. The energy will be reflected, absorbed, transmitted, or converted (or any combination of the four). Reflected light defines the color of any object we visualize; for instance, blood absorbs all light rays except that of red. The red wavelengths are reflected back, and we visualize them as the color red. White represents a reflection of all wavelengths, while the color black is the absorption of all wavelengths. In between these two points, we see a vast array of wavelength combinations that allow us to distinguish about 250 different shades of color. Transmission of light relates back to its penetrating power; light energy can pass through an object. In terms of visible light, the object involved plays a significant role in whether light is transmitted or not (e.g., an object that has translucent or transparent properties is a good transmitter of light). The final behavior of light — conversion — is of significant concern to the scene technician. Light energy can be converted from one wavelength to another, creating the condition known as luminescence. This luminescence occurs as both fluorescence, which happens so long as the object is exposed to an active energy source (e.g., the continued presence of an ALS), and phosphorescence, in which the object continues to give off light in the converted wavelength even after removal of the energy source.[2] It is in the conversion of light energy where the ALS finds its widest use at the crime scene. Items that would otherwise be difficult (if not impossible) to see undergo fluorescence when exposed to varying wavelengths of light energy, thus allowing the evidence to be visualized, photographed, and collected.

To understand conversion as it utilized at the crime scene, remember that radiant energy acts as both a wave and a particle. When an object is exposed to a radiant energy (e.g., an ALS), some of that energy (specific energy wavelengths) is reflected back, giving

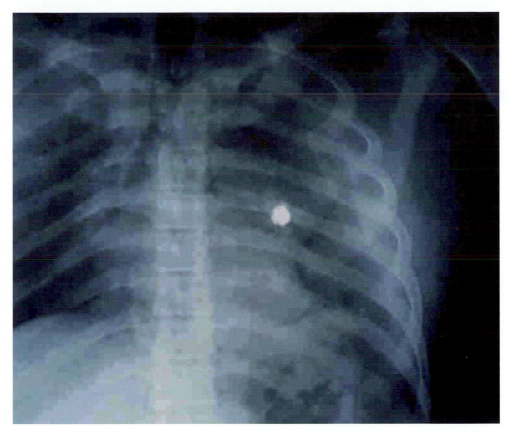

Figure 9.2   The penetrating power of radiant energy has been applied in medical imaging for a number of years. This technology has been an integral part of forensic work, as seen in this radiograph, which demonstrates the presence of a projectile in a corpse.

the object color. At the same time, some of that energy is absorbed. The absorption of light energy as photons excites existing electrons in the object. As these excited electrons stabilize and fall back to a normal energy state, they release the extra energy once again as light. But this release is at a much lower state of energy than the original energy wavelength. See Figure 9.3.

An ALS allows the crime scene technician to create light energy of a specific wavelength. Then, by employing an appropriate barrier filter for the eyes or the camera lens, the technician eliminates the original wavelength, leaving only the converted light energy from the object to be observed. Through the barrier filter, the technician will observe the fluorescence. As it happens, many objects of significant concern to the crime scene technician fluoresce brightly, including biological fluids like semen and spittle, and trace evidence such as a variety of fibers.

Converting the visible light spectrum in this fashion is certainly an important aspect of using light in the crime scene, but the full spectrum of radiant energy utilized in forensics is far greater than one might imagine, and its usefulness certainly predates the advent of lasers and other high-capacity ALS. As mentioned previously, medical imaging in the form of X rays (1 to 200 nm) has been a standard feature in forensic medicine for some years. Predating the development of the "blue light" or ALS was the Wood's lamp or miner's

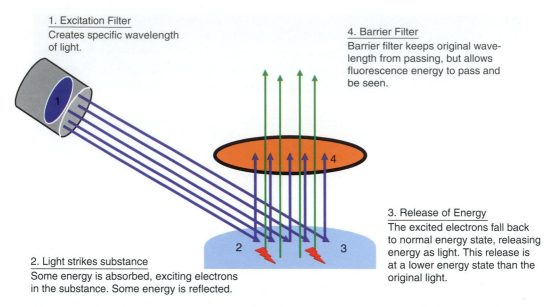

1. Excitation Filter
Creates specific wavelength
of light.

4. Barrier Filter
Barrier filter keeps original wavelength from passing, but allows
fluorescence energy to pass and
be seen.

3. Release of Energy
The excited electrons fall back
to normal energy state, releasing
energy as light. This release is
at a lower energy state than the
original light.

2. Light strikes substance
Some energy is absorbed, exciting electrons
in the substance. Some energy is reflected.

Figure 9.3 Conversion of light is an important technique in forensic work. An ALS produces a specific wavelength of light, part of which is reflected and part of which is absorbed. The absorbed energy excites electrons in the substance, and when these electrons fall back to a normal state, the excess energy is released as light but at a different wavelength. A barrier filter allows the original wavelength to be eliminated, while the remaining fluorescence is left to be observed by the technician.

light, an ultraviolet (UV, 200 to 400 nm) light source that was used extensively in searching out stains in scenes or recognizing alterations of documents as early as the 1940s. Additionally, infrared light sources were once quite popular in surveillance photography, allowing photographs to be exposed in complete darkness using an infrared flash without the subject ever realizing a photo had been taken. Today, the spectrum involved in forensics includes everything from X rays to heat energy.

Depending upon need and circumstance, light technology can be used in a variety of applications in any crime scene. The following is a discussion of the applicable wavelengths and their crime scene function.

Shortwave Ultraviolet Light (180 to 254 nm)

Shortwave UV (UVB/C) light is used in a relatively new application known as reflected-UV imaging systems (RUVIS). In a nutshell, RUVIS technology allows the visualization of latent prints before dusting. Under enhanced UV light, untreated latent fingerprints are evident to the technician. RUVIS systems are not associated with traditional ALS systems and are sold as separate kits. When using RUVIS, the technician is equipped with both a standard shortwave UV light source and a handheld video viewer. The viewer combines video with technologies developed in night-vision optical devices to enhance the UV image. As a result, without any other processing, latent prints in the scene are detectable to the technician through the video viewer. RUVIS technology is also effective at enhancing cyanoacrylate or "superglue" latent prints. Current systems are said to be difficult to work because the user has to manipulate two hardware features (the light source and viewer), and although the manufacturer suggests ease of use, practitioners indicate that the systems are not yet at the point-and-look stage. These systems are also expensive, but the cost will come down as this technology advances. This technique has significant potential in the crime scene search and could well revolutionize our approach to fingerprinting scenes.

Handheld UVB/C lights arc available for a variety of purposes in the crime lab, but they have limited function at the crime scene. The technician should use these devices with caution. UVB/C energy penetrates human skin and can cause disruption in the form of UV burns, which are similar to sunburns. Additionally, UV eye protection is necessary when employing a UV light source.

Longwave Ultraviolet Light (365 to 415 nm)

Longwave UV (UVA) has a myriad of applications in the crime scene. One effective use of UVA light is as a quick check of possible bloodstains. A bloodstain exposed to UV light absorbs all light of that bandwidth, reflecting nothing back. Thus the stain will appear black under UVA. Although not a conclusive test for blood, it is an effective presumptive test and can often eliminate the unnecessary collection of stains that appear to be blood but are actually from some other source. This property is also effective for providing sufficient contrast of bloodstains that are found on red- or violet-colored objects. Such stains often fade into the background so well that it is impossible to photograph them. UVA often provides sufficient contrast between the background and stain to allow the stains to be visualized in a photograph, as seen in Figure 9.4.

UVA is also an effective tool for visualizing biological stains such as semen, spittle, or saliva. These stains will fluoresce a lime green color when observed with UVA, even without

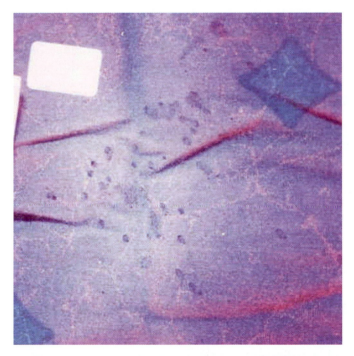

Figure 9.4 Bloodstains on a dark purple background. Under normal light, these stains are difficult to see and nearly impossible to photograph. A UVA light source causes the stains to absorb all light and appear black, while the background cloth lightens and reflects the light. The end result is sufficient contrast that allows the stains to be photographed.

a barrier filter. As a precaution, the scene technician should wear UV goggles when employing a UVA light.

Near-UV and Violet Light (415 to 485 nm)

Near-UV and violet light serve a variety of functions in the crime scene. At 450 nm, this wavelength — when combined with a yellow barrier filter — can be effective in searching for and visualizing bite marks and bruises on human skin. Wavelengths between 455 and 485 nm are used to visualize fluorescein reactions with latent blood. The barrier filter employed in this method is typically the yellow filter, but an orange filter can be effective as well, particularly when using the higher wavelength. The use of fluorescein is described in detail in Chapter 10. At 455 nm, biological fluids are easily observed in combination with an orange barrier filter. At 485 nm, latent fingerprints developed in ninhydrin can be visualized using a yellow barrier filter.

Crime Scene Search with Blue Light (485 to 530 nm)

Depending upon the particular light source involved, many crime scene search (CSS) filters employ a broad passband filter encompassing from between 390 and 520 nm. This is especially true for a typical "blue light" source. Most ALS systems also have a CSS setting, but these are often a more discrete wavelength. In combination with an orange barrier filter, either will cause any number of biological fluids, fibers, or hairs to fluoresce (Figure 9.5). If engaging in a general fiber search, the technician should consider using a wide range of wavelengths, as no one wavelength will affect every single dye encountered. In searching for hairs, remember also that red and blond hairs tend to fluoresce, while darker hairs do not. Oblique white light may be the most effective method for locating dark hairs. Wavelengths of 525 to 530 nm, in combination with an orange barrier filter, are also excellent for developing and visualizing latent fingerprints with fluorescent powders.

Orange–Red (570 to 700 nm)

The orange and red wavelengths are effective for viewing inks on items present in the scene as well as questioned documents at the crime lab. Wavelengths of 570 to 700 nm may also assist in visualizing subcutaneous bruising. A red barrier filter is used at these higher wavelengths.

Infrared (700 to 2000 nm)

Infrared wavelengths are most often employed in questioned document examinations at the crime lab. Beyond the 570- to 700-nm wavelengths of orange and red, infrared has little direct application to crime scene processing.

Heat Energy and Thermal Imaging (12,000 nm)

Thermal imaging is a very fluid and changing technology. Thermal-imaging devices are routinely employed in police air operations (e.g., forward-looking infrared radar [FLIR]) because they allow police officers to see in total darkness. More recently, thermal-imaging devices have been used to identify travelers with raised temperatures as a means of preventing the spread of infectious disease. Heat energy as a crime scene application is a

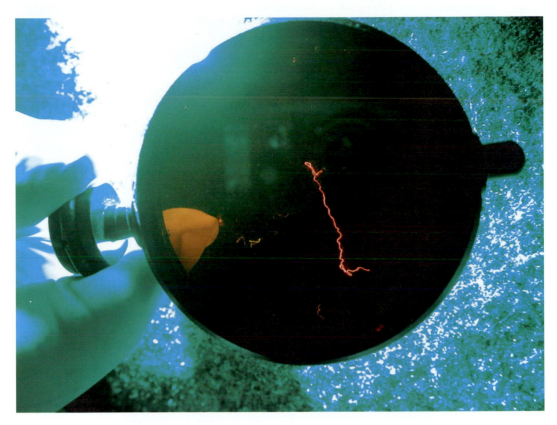

Figure 9.5 A small fiber fluorescing brightly in the presence of an ALS light source and orange barrier filter. This fluorescence allows the crime scene technician to more readily observe these small trace items of evidence. (Figure courtesy of Special Agent [Ret.] Don Hayden. With permission.)

relative newcomer. Thermal imaging has been used effectively to locate decomposing bodies and to find hot spots in fire scenes. This technology is now available to law enforcement in the form of a portable, handheld, battery-operated device that is used to distinguish between recent and older tire marks in serious accident scenes. In terms of our typical crime scene application, the question is just how quickly this technology will advance. Figure 9.6 is a video capture by a handheld thermal-imaging device showing a 10-min-old hand print on a wall. Despite the time lapse, the thermal imager is able to "see" the temperature differences between the wall and the radiant energy left by the hand. Imagine the utility of what future devices might do. Both RUVIS and thermal-imaging technology have the potential to make locating fingerprints and trace DNA (deoxyribonucleic acid) a focused effort, compared with the general search techniques we now utilize.

Choosing an Alternative Light Source

There are a number of variations of ALS technology available to the crime scene technician. In most departments, the decision of whether or not to use ALS is mostly a function of budget. Never doubt that some form of ALS is necessary for conducting a valid crime scene search, particularly in serious crimes against persons (e.g., rapes, aggravated assaults, and

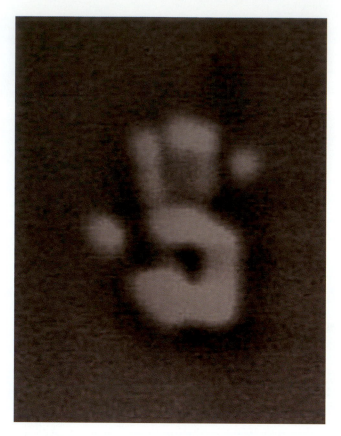

Figure 9.6 Thermal imaging offers promise for the future of forensic work. This photograph shows a hand print observed on a wall using a handheld thermal-imaging device. The hand was placed on the wall for 30 sec, and this image was taken 10 min later. The residual heat of the hand is still evident, even in this first-generation device. If the technology advances, imagine the possibilities for searching crime scenes for fingerprint evidence. Thermal-imaging devices are currently used to search for decomposing corpses, grow houses (marijuana), and other heat-related signatures.

homicides). Unfortunately, not every department can afford to outfit its crime scene team with a fully functional ALS. In deciding which type of light source to purchase, the technician must consider how the device will be used, the capabilities of the device, and budget constraints.

At the low end of the equipment spectrum, an organization may choose to buy a simple UVA or CSS light (e.g., a blue light). As discussed previously, UVA lights are available as a stand-alone product. CSS lights run the gamut from small LED (light-emitting diode) penlights, to quartz-halogen flashlights outfitted with a broadband excitation filter, to even larger handheld lights with similarly broad excitation filters. The cost of these devices can run anywhere from $50 for the small penlights to several hundred dollars for the more sophisticated devices. However, these devices suffer from one primary limitation: they offer only a single wavelength for use in basic crime scene searches. They are rarely effective for providing clean, color-corrected white light for a general scene search, and they provide no flexibility when additional wavelengths are needed for other specialized applications.

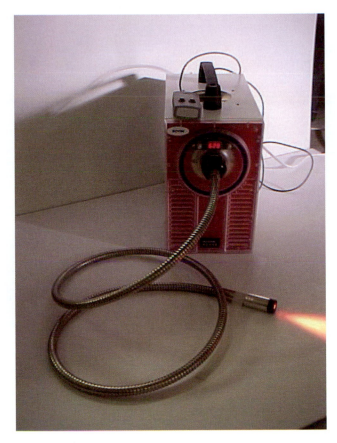

Figure 9.7 A fully functional ALS device. An LED displays the current wavelength of light, which is controlled by the operator using a small remote control. The light wand consists of a liquid light guide. The cost of these fully functional devices is restrictive for small departments.

A fully functional ALS system and its cousin, often referred to as a forensic light source (FLS), offer a wider variety of wavelengths while also serving as a source of white light. With a fully functional ALS, the technician simply dials up a specific wavelength or rotates through a variety of preset filters attached to the ALS light wand (Figure 9.7). A fully functional ALS is also capable of directing clean white light in hard-to-search areas, or it can be used to illuminate items of evidence during detailed examinations. Note, however, that there is some mid-ground between the ALS and FLS. Another alternative is a handheld high-watt light source that can accommodate optional filters for use in various applications (Figure 9.8).

The cost of an ALS starts at $8,000 and can reach as high as $16,000. The FLS system — a hybrid light source that lies somewhere between the ALS and the typical blue light — attempts to provide utility to the technician without the associated costs. FLS systems sell much cheaper, starting at about $3,000, but for good reason. The output bulb of an ALS is typically a xenon or metal-halide lamp, emitting 300 to 400 watts, while an FLS is typically powered by a quartz-halogen bulb capable of no more than 250 watts. These quartz-halogen devices put out significantly lower lumens than their high-end cousins, and in terms of delivering clean color-corrected white light, the halogen lamp is simply not as efficient. Nevertheless, the FLS offers utility and a wide assortment of selective wavelengths that are capable of dealing with most crime scene applications.

Figure 9.8 A handheld ALS used to illuminate fluorescent fingerprint powder. This unit comes with several filters that can be exchanged in the unit for specific purposes. Although such units do not provide the flexibility of a fully functional ALS, they do offer greater capability than a simple "blue light."

Recovering Fingerprints

The ability to lift fingerprints is a basic skill necessary to process a crime scene. At the same time, fingerprinting is also very much an art form. Anyone can throw powder around a scene, but not everyone can routinely or effectively recover usable latent fingerprints. With a little practice, however, technicians can master the basic techniques and learn to recover fingerprints from most of the surfaces they are likely to encounter.

Although the underpinnings of the fingerprint discipline are stable and unchanging, the technology of fingerprinting is constantly advancing. With each new forensic journal publication, one can be sure to find a new method or variation of a fingerprinting method. The majority of these new techniques are directed at chemical enhancement of prints at the crime lab, resolving issues where the conditions (e.g., background color/contrast or surface texture) make it nearly impossible to recover usable latent prints with standard techniques. Because the technology is in constant change, this book cannot serve to illuminate each and every technique available. What the text will concentrate on are basic on-scene techniques that the crime scene technician should master. Before describing these techniques, it is important to explain what conditions drive the choice of technique.

Fingerprinting almost always begins as a search. Occasionally, visible latent or patent fingerprints are evident to the naked eye, particularly when using oblique lighting as a search tool. When presented with a visible latent print, the print is photographed like other evidence prior to any further examination or enhancement. In most cases, however, the crime scene technician must make a conscious decision of where to search for latent fingerprints.

Where the crime scene technician looks for fingerprints is not an arbitrary decision. Lawyers have been heard to argue in court, "Isn't it true that glass surfaces are an excellent medium for recovering fingerprints, officer?... So why didn't you examine the television screen, or the mirror in the back bedroom?" This simpleton mindset that we should look for fingerprints on the "best surfaces" is so logically flawed that one must question the intelligence of any lawyer willing to stand up and actually present it. The technician does not wander aimlessly through the scene looking for smooth nonporous surfaces just because such surfaces tend to produce better results. The crime scene technician focuses the search for fingerprints in those areas where the suspect is likely to have interacted. Given the context of the scene and the nature of the crime being investigated, the areas of specific consideration will include points of entry, points of exit, and any appropriate surfaces in and around the area where the actual crime was committed. Consideration is also given to the nature of the object and how one would typically touch or manipulate the item. For example, when adjusting a rear view mirror, one typically places several fingers on the back side of the mirror and very often places an opposing thumb on the front mirror surface.

Simple logic and an eye for detail will serve the crime scene technician immensely in this endeavor. It is rarely appropriate to cover every single wall and surface in a crime scene with powder. Prior to initiating the search, the technician should consider (just as s/he did in the initial assessment) what actions must have been taken to accomplish the crime. Were lights turned on? Were appliances or phones used in the scene? What rooms were involved in the crime? Is there evidence to suggest a struggle on a floor, in which the suspect may have touched the floor itself? The answer to any one of these questions can impact the technician's decision of where to search for fingerprint evidence. There is never a simple answer to the question: "What is an appropriate surface?" The answer is always scene and context driven. Because any number of surfaces may be present in a scene, and because any one of these surfaces may hold critical evidence, the technician must be prepared to deal with a variety of surface characteristics.

Surface Characteristics

Surface characteristics define the fingerprinting methods employed on scene. The nature of the surface to be printed and its current condition decide which techniques the technician can or should employ. The basic types of surfaces encountered are:

- Porous surfaces: paper, cardboard, untreated wood
- Nonporous smooth surfaces: varnished and painted surfaces, plastic surfaces, glass
- Nonporous rough surfaces: vinyl, leather, textured countertops, and other textured surfaces
- Special conditions: anomalies such as human skin, adhesive tapes, and blood prints

The next major consideration is whether the surface is wet or dry, which will also impact on the methods utilized. Finally, another significant concern is whether the item is collectable (e.g., either small enough to be collected or of a nature that it can be cut out for collection) and whether the agency involved has crime laboratory support. The crime scene is typically the worst place to fingerprint, simply because conditions (e.g., lighting, location, humidity) are never ideal. Thus if an object can be collected, it is often best to

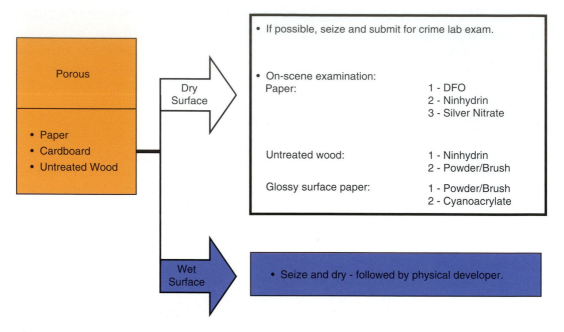

Figure 9.9   Fingerprint guide for porous surfaces. Typical porous surfaces include paper, cardboard, and untreated woods. Techniques are displayed in relative order as to their use and effectiveness. As in the case of untreated wood, ninhydrin is the best method to use followed by powder-and-brush technique.

seize it and submit the item for processing at a laboratory, where additional systems such as lasers and chemical treatment techniques are available. If the technician is dealing with a homicide, this type of lab support is usually present. In less severe crimes (e.g., burglaries, robberies), which are important and can be solved through fingerprint evidence, lab support may not be available. In these instances, the technician becomes responsible for deciding what can be done on scene or at the evidence processing room and for conducting such processing. Since any surface condition can be found at any crime scene, it is imperative that the technician be competent in dealing with any condition.

Porous Surfaces

Items such as paper products, cardboard, or untreated woods are the mainstay of porous surfaces encountered in the crime scene. See Figure 9.9. If the item can be seized and dealt with under more controlled conditions, that is always the best course of action. For on-scene examination of dry paper, the best treatment is with 1,8-diazafluorenone (DFO), followed by ninhydrin, and then followed by silver nitrate. Latent prints on wood often respond best to ninhydrin but also react well to standard powder-and-brush techniques. Latent prints on glossy paper products are developed with either powder and brush or by using cyanoacrylate fuming, followed by powder-and-brush techniques. Wet porous surfaces should be dried and then treated with physical developer.

Nonporous Smooth Surfaces

Items such as painted or finished surfaces, a majority of plastic surfaces, and glass or Plexiglas surfaces are the primary items in the nonporous smooth category. See Figure

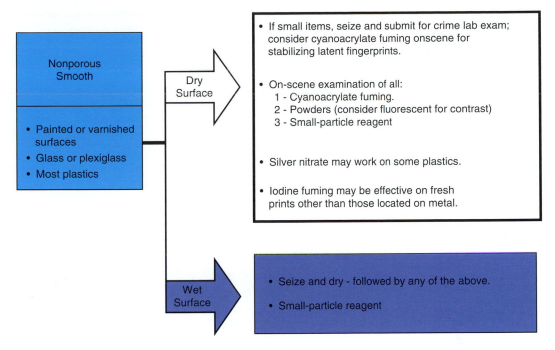

Figure 9.10   Fingerprint guide for nonporous smooth surfaces.

9.10. As in all cases, if the object is small enough to be seized, it is usually best to seize and process the evidence under more controlled conditions. An alternative is to fume the objects on scene, stabilizing the prints to prevent inadvertent destruction during movement to a lab or evidence processing facility. The primary methods employed under these conditions are to cyanoacrylate-fume first, followed by powder-and-brush techniques. Fluorescent powders in use with an ALS are effective when dealing with difficult surfaces that do not provide sufficient background contrast. Small-particle reagent (SPR) is also an effective technique under these conditions, even when the surface is not wet. Additional techniques include silver nitrate, which may be useful when dealing with plastics, or iodine fuming, which can be effective when dealing with fresh latent prints. If these surfaces are wet, the technician has two alternatives: (1) seize the item and allow it to dry, followed by use of any of the described methods, or (2) apply SPR while the surface is still wet.

Nonporous Rough Surfaces

Items such as vinyl, leather, or textured surfaces represent a problem for both developing and lifting latent fingerprints. Developing prints on textured surfaces requires a deft touch. The basic techniques for rough nonporous surfaces are the same as for smooth nonporous, which include cyanoacrylate fuming followed by powder and brush. See Figure 9.11. Quite often, latent prints will be developed on such surfaces, only to be lost when lifting is attempted. As a result, a number of specialized lifting tapes and materials have been developed for dealing with these surfaces. These include applying silicone-based casting material over the latent, the use of specially manufactured textured-surface fingerprint tapes and casting gels, which act in a similar fashion to silicone, creating a rubberized backing to which the latent adheres. If these surfaces are wet, they should be dried and then developed using powder-and-brush techniques.

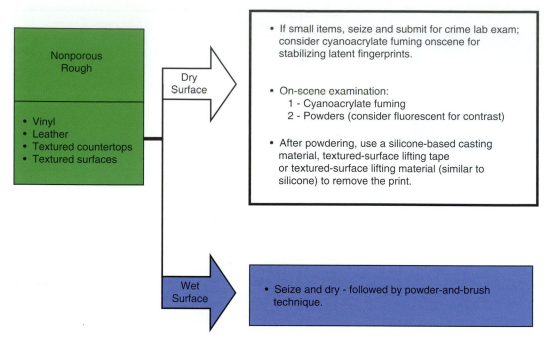

Figure 9.11   Fingerprint guide for nonporous rough surfaces.

Special Surfaces or Conditions

Some surfaces and conditions defy general classification due to their peculiarities and demand special consideration. This includes surfaces such as human skin, the adhesive sides of tapes, rough polystyrene surfaces, and situations involving bloody prints.

Human skin is a difficult but functional surface for the development of latent prints. Alive or dead, human skin can be processed with a variety of techniques from the simplest, such as magnetic powder and brush, to the more involved techniques such as iodine fuming with silver plates. See Figure 9.12. Processing human skin is certainly appropriate in close-in killings (e.g., strangulation) or in any situation in which it is believed the body has been manipulated in some fashion. In rapes or assaults involving live victims, the technique is also worthy of effort, presuming that the incident is reported in a timely fashion. When processing dead bodies, the most effective technique is the adding-machine-paper process, described later in the chapter. Damp skin does not negatively affect this particular process. Cyanoacrylate fuming is also an effective technique, but moisture (most bodies are processed after refrigeration) will negatively impact the results. Simple dusting of the skin using magnetic powder is another effective method (Figure 9.13), but it too suffers from moisture issues. Iodine fuming is quite effective on human skin, but lifting of the iodine-enhanced prints on skin requires the use of a silver plate. On live victims, neither cyanoacrylate nor iodine fuming are appropriate, in which case the technician should revert to the adding-machine-paper technique.

Adhesive tapes are routinely encountered in robberies, rapes, and homicides. One of the most effective techniques for dealing with the adhesive side of tape is the crystal violet, alcohol, and water process. This technique is discussed in detail later in the chapter. Additionally, a number of manufacturers have developed sticky-side powders that allow dusting of the adhesives. See Figure 9.14. A problem encountered when dealing with an adhesive tape is that the portions of tape manipulated by the suspect are often turned over, balled up, or

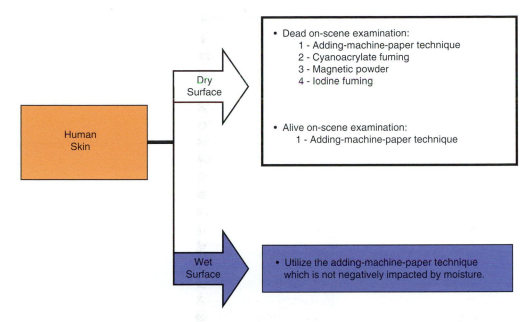

Figure 9.12   Fingerprint guide for human skin.

Figure 9.13   A magnetic powder-and-brush technique applied to the skin of a corpse with a positive result. Although the probability of obtaining latent prints is low, skin can and will hold fingerprints with identifiable ridge detail.

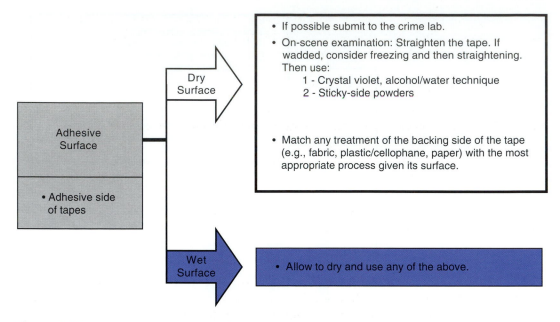

Figure 9.14 Fingerprint guide for adhesive tape.

otherwise wadded into an unusable mass. One method for freeing the tape from itself without damaging any latent prints is to freeze the tape and attempt to straighten it once frozen.

Bloody prints in the scene require a level of expertise and practice in the use of a variety of chemicals. Methods that are effective include development with amido-black, leuco-crystal violet, and alcohol-based fluorescein. Patent bloody prints can be photographed and lifted in their natural condition or dusted with powder and lifted. See Figure 9.15.

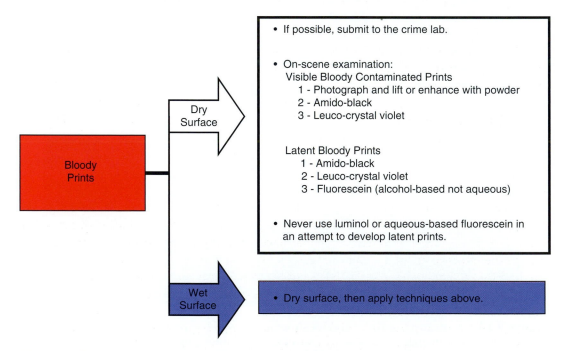

Figure 9.15 Fingerprint guide for bloody fingerprints.

Polystyrene materials such as packing foam or Styrofoam cups present a difficult surface as well. In these instances, cyanoacrylate fuming or the use of small-particle reagent are the most likely techniques to produce results.

On-Scene Fingerprinting Techniques

Through experience, the crime scene technician will learn many of the techniques described above. There are, however, three basic techniques that each technician should be familiar with and have practiced prior to processing any significant scene. These methods include basic powder techniques (standard and magnetic), superglue fuming, and use of small-particle reagent (SPR). Additionally, the technician should be experienced in recovering prints from human skin using the adding-machine-paper technique and in the use of crystal violet solutions on adhesive tape. Finally, the technician should recognize methods of recovering latent prints when confronted with fire scenes.

Basic Powder Techniques

Powder and brush remains the mainstay method by which fingerprints are recovered from nonporous items in the scene, but powder techniques are not as simple as they look and demand more than throwing powder about in a sporadic fashion. The loss of fingerprint evidence at the crime scene can be attributed to two issues related to brush-and-powder techniques. These include overpowdering a latent print and applying too much pressure when dusting the print. Latent prints are not particularly stable and are easily damaged. Dusting a print demands a light touch on the part of the technician as well as choosing the proper brush for the appropriate step. Standard fingerprint brushes come in a variety of configurations. The fiberglass brush is the typical brush used when searching a surface. Additional brushes include the camel-hair brush, feather brush, and other specialty brushes. These brushes are used most often to clean up and bring out detail once a latent print is located; however, the camel-hair brush was and remains an effective initial search brush particularly when dealing with small, irregular surfaces.

After choosing the search brush, the brush is prepared by spinning it in the hand, as seen in Figure 9.16. This action flairs the bristles in the head, which often become compacted in their storage tubes. The choice of powder color by the technician is of some significance. Always choose a color that provides contrast to the surface in question. If the technician is unsure about contrast, it is best to apply a test print to the surface involved in an area that is not considered important. Failure to use a good contrasting powder may result in the technician not seeing the latent print as the powder first begins to adhere. This can result in overpowdering or excessive brushing and lead to destroying the print before it is even recognized. As a solution to the contrast issue, bichromatic powders are available that, in effect, provide contrast under nearly any condition. These types of powders are dual-colored powders that provide contrast on light or dark surfaces. When examining a number of different colored surfaces in a single area, this type of powder will reduce the effort of changing color for each new surface encountered. Another functional method for enhancing contrast is the use of fluorescent powders. These powders are used in a standard fashion, but they are viewed and photographed under an ALS (Figure 9.17). Fluorescent powders are particularly useful on multicolored surfaces, where consistent contrast under normal lighting is impossible. An important reminder when using a powder-and-brush technique is not to mix powders on a single brush. Once a brush is used for a light or dark powder, it should not be used for any other color powder.

Figure 9.16 Preparing a fiberglass fingerprint brush for use. The technician spins the brush in the hand, which flairs the bristles and expands the brush head. After extended storage, the bristles of a fingerprint brush will often stick together. This technique will correct that condition.

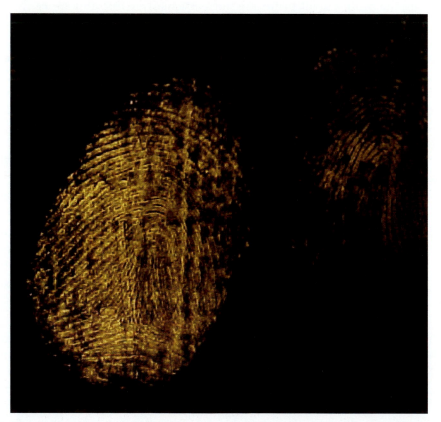

Figure 9.17 In addition to standard fingerprint powders, the technician can use fluorescent powders, which when viewed or photographed under an ALS will provide good contrast.

Figure 9.18 Powder is applied to the brush by dipping the brush in a small amount of powder held in a fold of paper. Dipping the brush directly into the powder container results in the transfer of contaminants and moisture, which can ultimately affect the quality of the powder.

No matter which brush or powder is utilized (excluding magnetic powders), the most classic mistake observed in fingerprinting technique is to insert the brush directly into the powder container. This action leads to damaging the bristles, often leaves contaminants (including moisture) in the powder, and invariably leaves too much powder on the brush itself. The more effective technique is to place a small amount of powder in a fold of clean paper and powder the brush by lightly stroking it in the powder, as seen in Figure 9.18. Once powdered, the brush is lightly tapped or spun to remove excess powder. Then, using light circular strokes, the technician examines the area in question. Once a partial latent appears, the technician concentrates on the area in question with an even lighter stroke, reducing the circular action. Excess powder should be removed from the print to enhance detail in both the photograph and the lift. Although with experience the technician can certainly develop a latent print using only a fiberglass brush, enhancing the print is best accomplished with a finer bristled brush. The camel-hair brush or marabou feather brush are particularly effective at this stage of the examination, as they reduce the friction and decrease the probability of damaging ridge detail.

The use of magnetic powder and a magnetic "brush" is not significantly different from that of the standard brush-and-powder technique. Magnetic powders include small metallic shavings that cling to the magnet in the magnetic "brush." In effect, the technician is moving suspended powder across the surface, rather than brushing the surface with a powdered brush. As there are no bristles involved, it is less likely that the technician will damage ridge detail when applying the powder. Damage is still possible, particularly if the technician uses too much powder. A positive impact of the magnetic brush is its ability to effectively remove excess powder from a surface.

Once a latent print is developed, it should be photographed in place. Even under the best of circumstances, it is always possible to damage or destroy detail of a print through a lifting technique. Photography captures detail and ensures that some record of the print is available. Choosing which lifter to use for the latent print requires a second consideration of contrast. The technician must find a lifting medium and color that ensures that the powdered print will be visible once it is lifted. Lifting tapes and lifters come in a variety of forms. The typical forms include lifting tape (available on rolls in varying widths), hinge lifters, rubber or gel lifters, and precut lifting tape. Hinge lifters and rubber lifters come with their own backing (e.g., white, black, or transparent); lifting tapes require some type of backing medium. This backing sheet can be as simple as using a 3 × 5-in. card or as formal as commercially printed latent cards that allow the technician to annotate each print with detailed data on where and by whom it was recovered. Rubber lifters are designed primarily for use in situations where the surface involved is curved or irregular (e.g., a doorknob). The rubber lifter is pliable, allowing it to bend on application with the curve of the surface, which reduces distorting the latent.

To lift the latent print, the technician exposes the adhesive side of the rubber lifter or hinge lifter, or pulls out an appropriate length of lifting tape, and then carefully applies one edge to the surface involved, just beyond the latent print. With a smooth and steady motion, the technician rolls a finger across the remaining tape or lifter, gently forcing it in place over the latent print. Once attached, additional pressure is applied to the lifter in order to eliminate air bubbles and ensure a consistent collection of the powder. The next step of the process is to remove the lifter or tape from the surface in a smooth and steady action. Hesitation or irregular motion while removing the lifter will result in lines that run across the adhesive surface. Although these lines will not always harm the print, they can make it more difficult to see latent detail in areas where the line crosses the recovered print. Once removed from the surface, a protective cover is applied to the lifter to protect the latent print. In the case of a rubber lifter or hinge lifter, the adhesive section is smoothly pressed against the opposite side of the lifter. Lifting tape is applied to an appropriate backing.

Latent prints developed on rough or irregular surfaces present a significant difficulty. Using standard lifters (e.g., hinge and tape lifts), the latent is often recovered in a fragmented condition or with too much background detail from the surface, effectively making it impossible to see the detail of the latent. Rough-surface lifting tapes are available for this condition as well as a variety of silicone compounds. Both reduce this effect and increase the probability of recovering a functional latent print. Silicone lifting material is also an effective response when presented with a surface that is not firm enough to apply pressure to a standard lifter or lifting tape, and in cases where the shape of the surface is so irregular that even a rubber lifter is unlikely to bend sufficiently to prevent distortion of the latent (Figure 9.19).

Superglue Fuming

Cyanoacrylate or "superglue" fuming is a technique developed in the late 1970s by the Japanese. The fumes of the superglue react with the latent print, hardening and stabilizing the print. In the lab, the fumed print can be dyed using rhodamine 6G, Androx, or basic yellow dyes, which allow visualization and photography of significant detail in the minu-

Figure 9.20 A makeshift superglue fuming chamber created from PVC pipe and plastic. The superglue is applied to the small metallic container at the bottom of the chamber. The article to be fumed is suspended in the chamber so the fumes can get to every surface. (Figure courtesy of Special Agent [Ret.] Don Hayden. With permission.)

in question all affect the time it takes to develop a latent print. Given all these variables, the fuming is controlled by placing a test print in the chamber or area being fumed. This is effectively accomplished by using a small piece of tin foil on which a test print is applied. The foil is suspended in the chamber or isolation area and monitored. As the fumes react with the latent print, a visible white deposit becomes evident. A classic mistake in fuming is to allow the reaction to continue until the print is clearly visible. At this point, the print is overfumed, which can mar detail in the minutiae. The reaction should be halted when the test print first begins to appear. The technician then checks the actual surfaces in question to determine their condition. If additional fuming is needed, the process is continued. If not, the process is complete, and collection of the prints is effected. A latent print developed at the scene with superglue can be photographed and collected using a powder-and-brush technique or submitted to the lab for processing by fluorescent dyes. A significant benefit for superglue fuming lies in the number of tries the technician can make in lifting the print. In standard brush-and-powder development, it may be possible to repower and make a second lift of a latent print, but nothing guarantees that a second lift will be possible. With superglue, a latent can be lifted and repowdered any number of times without reducing the quality of the third- or fourth-generation lift.

Small-Particle Reagent

Small-particle reagent (SPR) was developed as a method to recover latent prints on wet surfaces. SPR consists primarily of molybdenum disulfide suspended in a water solution. The suspended particles react with and attach to the fats found in the latent print. To develop the print, SPR is sprayed over the surface a number of times, each time allowing the liquid to drain off. Once a print begins to develop, the technician continues the spraying until sufficient contrast is achieved (Figure 9.21). The surface is then allowed to dry. If necessary, the surface can be gently washed with water to remove excess SPR. Once again, the surface is allowed to dry, after which the latent print is photographed and lifted using a standard lifter (Figure 9.22). SPR is now manufactured in light, dark, and a fluorescent spray.

Although originally intended for wet surfaces, SPR is effective on almost any nonporous surface and is said to be effective in situations involving oily windows, oxidized metals, galvanized surfaces, or salt-water-sprayed areas.[3]

Figure 9.21   Small-particle reagent (SPR) was designed for use on wet surfaces. Small particles suspended in the liquid react with the fats of the print and bind to them. The SPR is sprayed onto the surface a number of times until the print becomes visible. Here it is applied to the exterior of a vehicle with condensation. As with any fingerprint method, an appropriate contrasting color is required. SPR comes in both black and white, and in this instance black SPR is used against the white paint. (Figure courtesy of Special Agent [Ret.] Don Hayden. With permission.)

Figure 9.22 SPR-developed prints are recovered using standard lifting techniques. The SPR is allowed to dry completely, photographed, and then lifted with lifting tape or a hinge lifter. (Figure courtesy of Special Agent [Ret.] Don Hayden. With permission.)

Using these three methods (powder and brush, superglue fuming, and SPR), the crime scene technician can functionally deal with the vast majority of scene-specific surfaces encountered. Nonporous surfaces may require additional chemical treatments such as DFO, ninhydrin, or silver nitrate, but these advanced techniques are best applied at the crime lab and can be learned in time. Two advanced techniques necessary to round out the technician's skills include the adding-machine-paper technique and the crystal violet technique; these two methods are intended, respectively, for recovering latent prints from human skin and adhesive tape.

Adding-Machine-Paper Technique for Human Skin

The origin of this particular technique is unknown, but the method was developed and fine-tuned by a number of the FBI's Evidence Response Team units, who now employ it in the field with outstanding results. The method involves the use of adding-machine paper rolls, along with a variety of powders. The adding-machine paper is quite porous, and when in contact with the oils of a latent fingerprint, it readily absorbs them. A significant advantage of the method is that it will still work effectively when the body is slightly wet with condensation. Rarely will the ME (medical examiner) or coroner allow manipulation of the body prior to their initial evaluation, and thus the remains are almost always sent to the morgue and refrigerated before any attempt at fingerprinting is allowed. This invariably results in condensation on the body. In this process, condensation actually helps

Figure 9.23 The adding-machine-paper technique for recovering latent prints from human skin requires minimal equipment. Any standard roll of adding-machine paper can be utilized; additionally, the technician requires tape, a pen, magnetic powder, and a brush. The magnetic powder used should be very fine.

the fingerprinting process rather than hindering it. The necessary components, illustrated in Figure 9.23, are nothing more than a roll of adding-machine paper, a magnetic brush with a fine powder, and a pencil or pen.

The most effective technique for conducting this method is to roll the paper with gentle pressure onto the area of the body in question. This is best accomplished by placing the roll of paper on a pencil or dowel, which the technician uses to manipulate and guide the roll onto the skin, as seen in Figure 9.24. An assistant holds the loose end of the paper to ensure that it does not become a hindrance to the technician and to prevent it from being contaminated. After rolling the area in question and tearing off the length from the roll, the technician marks the tape identifying specific landmarks (e.g., right outside wrist, right elbow). Marking eliminates losing the relative orientation on the body of any subsequently recovered prints.

After completing the roll and removing the length of paper, the technician then tapes the paper contact-side up in a box or container. Using a fine fingerprint powder, the technician lightly powders the contact side of the paper, as shown in Figure 9.25 and Figure 9.26. Experimentation using a variety of powders will likely identify a number of functional

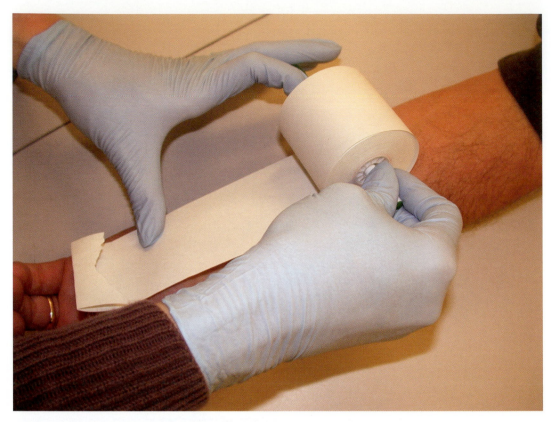

Figure 9.24 The adding-machine paper is slowly rolled out along the area of the skin the technician wishes to check. Only a small amount of pressure is required in this effort. It is often helpful to have an assistant hold the end of the paper, so that the end does not roll up and interfere with the forward edge.

Figure 9.25 Once the rolling is complete, the paper is taped into place on a flat surface with the contact side facing up. Magnetic powder is applied in a normal fashion, but using very light strokes.

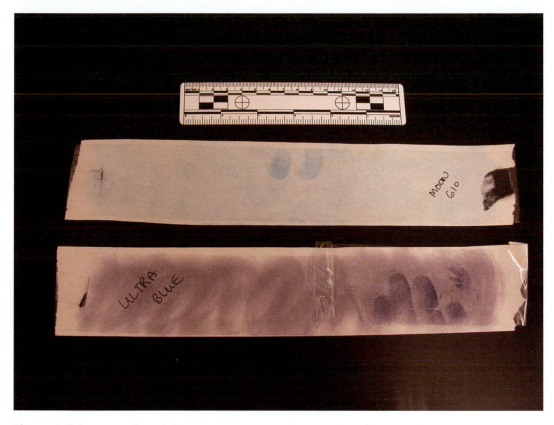

Figure 9.26 Examples of fingerprints recovered using the adding-machine-paper technique. Using this technique, prints have been recovered from both live and dead victims.

powders. Two proven powders for this technique are Moonglo and Midnight Blu, produced by DOJES.[4] The specific type of adding-machine paper used, however, has yet to be identified as a factor in obtaining results.

Prior to releasing the body at the scene, it is important to ask attendants (e.g., ME investigators or EMS personnel) to try not to handle areas such as the forearms, wrists, or ankles, particularly if there is some belief that the subject manipulated the body at the scene. These areas often hold recoverable prints. In considering how to apply this narrow width of paper, the technician must also consider where one expects to locate latent prints. For example, if dealing with a manual strangulation, it is wiser to apply the paper to the neck in a vertical orientation to the body rather than along the horizontal or lengthwise plane. In a vertical orientation, the technician is more likely to recover multiple digits in their proper orientation on a single sheet, where a lengthwise orientation would more than likely result in recovery of a single digit, or portions of multiple digits. This latter situation would require realignment of the various recovered paper lengths in order to capture the full context of the latent prints and their overall orientation.[5]

Crystal Violet Solution for Adhesive Tape

A long-standing method of recovering latent fingerprints from the adhesive side of tape is the use of a solution of alcohol and crystal violet dye. This technique is easy to accomplish and produces outstanding results. To use this method, the technician creates a stock solution

Figure 9.27 A fingerprint developed on the adhesive side of transparent tape using the crystal violet method.

by mixing approximately 1.5 g of crystal violet powder in 100 ml of ethyl alcohol. From this solution, the technician adds 2 ml per 100 ml of water to create a working solution. Depending upon the size of the tape involved, the quantity of working solution may have to be adjusted in order to fully immerse the tape. The tape is dipped or immersed in the working solution for a period of 30 sec to a minute, after which it is immediately held under cold running tap water. The crystal violet dye will react with any latent prints present, producing a blue or violet coloration that usually provides good contrast (Figure 9.27). If sufficient contrast is not achieved after the first washing, the entire process can be repeated.

Fingerprints in Fire Scenes

Suspicious fire scenes represent a rather significant anomaly to the crime scene technician, at least in terms of the search and recovery of fingerprint evidence. In confined-space fires (e.g., interior-room fires), a hot gas layer will develop at the ceiling level. The depth of this hot gas layer grows with time and can extend into the lower regions of the room. Temperatures in the hot gas layer often reach between 900 and 1100°F before the room achieves flashover (a combustion event involving the gases in the hot gas layer). At the same time, heavy black smoke envelops the room, descending in advance of the hot gas layer. As a result of these events, in the aftermath of the fire, nearly every surface in the room has been exposed to significant heat and soot. The well-meaning crime scene technicians arrive at the fire scene and, seeing the physical destruction of typical fingerprint surfaces of interest (e.g., walls and doors) as well as the presence of heavy soot on those items remaining, simply throw their hands in the air and give up. Believing that fingerprints will not be present, they put forth little if any effort in seeking fingerprints. This belief, however, is unsupported by fact, as fire scenes often hold outstanding fingerprint evidence that is nearly indestructible.

As early as 1957, U.S. Army Crime Laboratory fingerprint examiners were working with a technique of fingerprint development involving fire and soot. The camphor technique involved exposing hard-to-print surfaces to a gentle flame created by burning camphor, after which the soot was dusted off with a feather duster, thus exposing the print. If necessary, the item was gently washed to better remove the soot. It was evident to the fingerprint examiners that heat seemed to bake the print in place as well as react with the soot to create a pigmentation that made the latent print visible.[6] Whatever the actual mechanism, the end result was stable visible prints. Based on the camphor development process, John Thorton and Buster Emmons of the Houston Arson Bureau subsequently began examining fire scenes with a more critical eye to fingerprint recovery, and they developed a methodology for recovering latent prints in the fire scene. The technique requires good lighting and involves examining metal and glass surfaces found in the scene. After initial evaluation of such surfaces, if no latent prints are noted, excess soot is removed from the item by gently washing it in tap water. The item is then reexamined, since the latent prints stabilized by heat often become visible only after washing. Whether located before or after washing, these latent prints may still contain a significant level of attached soot. This soot can be further cleaned by the use of fingerprint lifters. In effect, excess soot is removed from the latent with lifting tape, enhancing the visible ridge detail.[7] Remember that the print itself is baked in place and quite stable, so washing and lifting have a negligible impact in harming any ridge detail. Once cleaned, the print is photographed for subsequent examination. In some instances, items may have been exposed to heat but not significant soot. Under these circumstances, the heat still stabilizes the latent print, but enhancement using powder-and-brush technique may be necessary to bring out ridge detail. Items of specific interest in the fire scene include suspected accelerant cans and the surviving entry and exit surfaces which may be present in the form of pane glass (broken or unbroken). This method is effective on almost any smooth nonporous surfaces found in the fire scene, particularly glass and metal surfaces.

Casting Impression Evidence

Impression evidence presents itself in the crime scene in a number of forms. Tool marks, footwear or barefoot impressions, tire marks, and even bite marks routinely appear as evidence and require collection. Beyond documentation by close-up photography, casting is the primary mechanism of recovering impression evidence. The term *impression*, however, at least in forensics, can be deceiving. Impression evidence includes both three-dimensional depressions, such as those found when a shoe leaves a mark in soft dirt, and two-dimensional marks, such as those found where a dirty shoe leaves a mark on a solid substrate. Although these two-dimensional marks are not true impressions, casting techniques are an effective means of recovery. The primary methods of recovering impression evidence that the technician should master are the use of rubberized casting compounds (e.g., silicone and rubber compounds for tool marks), the electrostatic lifting device (ESLD), plaster and dental-stone casting of both two- and three-dimensional impressions, and the use of gelatin and other adhesive lifters.

As was the case in latent print recovery, the crime scene technician considers a number of factors when deciding which method to use to recover an impression. What is the nature of the surface? Impressions can occur on dirt, hard floors, metals, paper, carpets, skin, or even food. The condition of that surface may force an issue in collection. Is the surface wet, dry, or does it hold contaminants? There are no absolute rules in deciding what method to employ, but different methods have specific limitations that may force one method over another.

Before any attempt to recover impression evidence, the impression should be photographed in place. Impression evidence is difficult to photograph properly and can be very challenging when dealing with dust prints. The first step of impression photography is to ensure that the camera is squared to the impression. This means matching the film plane to the plane on which the impression is located. This basic technique of squaring the lens to the subject is always important in evidence photography, but it is crucial in impression-evidence photography. When shooting the evidence close-up photographs, the camera should be tripod-mounted, and a scale of reference should be inserted alongside the impression. The camera is then lowered to include as much detail as possible from the impression while keeping the entire impression of concern in the viewfinder. The technician should take multiple photographs using the fill-flash technique. At least four photographs are taken with the flash held at a 45-degree angle to the impression. The flash is moved for each photograph, from the right side of the impression to the left side, to the top and to the bottom. This combination of oblique lighting, as well as directing the light from different angles, often enhances detail of interest to the shoe or tool mark examiner. Dust prints are extremely difficult to photograph, often requiring the technician to lower the ambient light and forcing the use of a high-intensity white light with a focused beam. An ALS is an effective tool in this instance.

Rubber Casting Compounds

A number of commercial rubber casting compounds are available from various forensic suppliers. It is important to understand that these commercial products offer a capability far and above the casting capability of any over-the-counter silicone products available in a hardware store. Forensic casting compounds have been designed to capture microscopic details of tool-mark impressions for the tool-mark examiner. These products are expensive, but when recovering tool-mark evidence, there is no substitute. These products are effective for tool marks, plastic prints (e.g., a fingerprint in wax or putty), and although not the most economical solution, they can also be used to recover dusted latent prints on curved surfaces. Rubberized casting compounds are most effective when used on hard substrates such as metals, wood, bone, or plastic. They are not effective in situations such as recovering bite marks from human skin or for casting dirt impressions.

The casting compounds come in two containers, one with the base material and the other with a curing compound. Following the specific instructions for mixing, the crime scene technician blends together a sufficient quantity of material to fully cover the impression in question. See Figure 9.28. A critical aspect of preparation is thoroughly mixing the base and the curing catalyst. Ensure a complete mixture of the compound before applying it to the impression. A failure to create an even mix will result in portions of the base material failing to set, or it will cause the compound to set too fast. Never rush the mixing.

The mixed compound is then pressed into the impression, ensuring that air pockets are filled (Figure 9.29). The compound is left to stand for a sufficient drying period (typically 12 to 15 min) and then removed (Figure 9.30). Just because the technician finds the exterior of the compound dry to the touch does not guarantee that the material in the impression (obviously the area of interest to the technician) is dry. Do not rush removal.

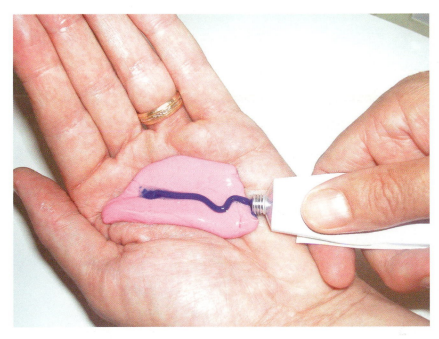

Figure 9.28   Specialized rubber casting material for tool marks. The material comes with both a base (the pink putty) and a catalyst (the extruded blue line). The two must be mixed thoroughly if the material is to set properly. The most effective method of mixing the materials is to work both together vigorously in the hands until an even color is achieved with no streaks.

Figure 9.29   Once mixed, the rubber casting material is pressed into the tool mark. The technician must ensure that the casting material is forced into the entire mark and that no air bubbles are formed. Although not always necessary, in this instance a small dam of modeling clay was placed beneath the tool mark to keep the casting compound in place while it sets.

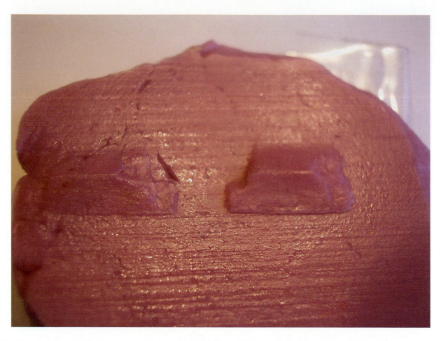

Figure 9.30   The resulting cast from Figure 9.29. General features of the impression tool mark (two prongs) are evident. Even the background surface of the wood (the linear striations on the flat surface) is captured by the casting material.

It is far better to let the cast sit awhile than to remove it too soon. A good practice is to cast the impressions, continue on with some other aspect of scene processing, and then return to recover them later.

Electrostatic Lifting Devices

Electrostatic lifting devices (ESLD) were developed in Japan in the 1970s. They found their way to England and Europe in the early 1980s and then began appearing in the U.S. Today they are a common tool of the crime scene technician. The ESLD works on a very simple concept: opposite charges attract. In the scene, the various surfaces hold a positive charge, while the particles of dust deposited are negatively charged. The ESLD is used to create a more-concentrated charge, delivering up to 15,000 V to a lifting medium. The medium is usually a Mylar-like film that resembles a space blanket. This greater charge in the film attracts the dust and dirt particles, transferring them from the weakly charged scene surface onto the lifting film. Once transferred, the residual charges (positive and negative) keep the dust print in place.

The ESLD can be used on almost any surface, including floors, walls, doors, and other hard surfaces as well as clothing, carpets, or even paper. It can be used effectively to recover impressions from either vertical or horizontal surfaces. Typical applications in the crime scene are floors, doors, and walls. Use of the ESLD requires certain safety precautions, however. First and foremost, the ESLD is used on dry surfaces only. Second, it is important to understand that the charging wand or charging device will create a significant charge in volts, but not in amps. It can produce a nasty shock, but it will not hurt you. The ESLD charge dissipates quickly, but contact with either the lifting material, the grounding plates, or the charging wand while the ESLD is in use may result in an unwanted surprise.

Figure 9.31 Oblique lighting is the most effective method of visualizing possible dust prints. The light source (e.g., an ALS or flashlight) is held at a very sharp low angle to the surface being checked. (Figure courtesy of Special Agent [Ret.] Don Hayden. With permission.)

The use of the ESLD on hard surfaces begins with a search of the scene. The technician looks for dust impressions using oblique lighting. Both the observer and the light source need to be low to the surface in question, as seen in Figure 9.31. The technician searches an area or entire floor (depending upon the size), marks or identifies in some fashion any areas in question (e.g., chalking the perimeter of a disturbance), and then attempts a lift of that area. During the visual search, dust prints may appear as a disturbed area on the floor, so the technician should not overlook an area simply because s/he cannot see specific tread or pattern designs. On carpet, a specific pattern may or may not be evident during the visual search. Carpet situations usually involve a systematic lifting attempt of all areas in primary walk paths or other areas of interest based on the scene context. In the case of paper or clothing, there may be no impression evident during the visual examination, although in these cases it is common to see some form of residual dust or dirt.

Once an area is identified for examination, the technician cleans and inspects the film lifter. Mylar film is reusable and is easily cleaned with a lint-free towel. The lifting material usually comes in rolls that can be cut to any size. A practical method of handling the material is to cut shoe-sized pieces in advance and mount them to a cardboard border (2 to 3 in. in width, encircling the entire Mylar sheet). The cardboard is superglued to the top (shiny) side of the Mylar sheet and keeps it from wrinkling in transit. The border also helps in laying the sheet flat at the scene. Whether using precut pieces or pulling a sheet directly from the roll, the technician chooses a lifter that will cover the entire area in question. The lifting film is laid with its dark side down on the surface as flat as possible. The film is then charged. In some systems, this means touching a charging wand to the film as seen in Figure 9.32; in others, the device is placed on the film, where electrical leads make direct contact.

Most systems employ a grounding plate or wand that is laid adjacent to the area being examined. Particularly in situations involving vertical surfaces, the technician may have to tape the plate or wand in place or otherwise be creative when positioning the grounding plate as the manufacturer describes. Once the ground device is in place, the charge is applied, and the film is rolled flat to remove excess air bubbles. The most effective rolling instrument is a clean fingerprint ink-pad roller. If a roller is not available, air bubbles can be smoothed out of the film using a plastic spatula, a piece of cardboard, or any other nonmetallic object with a flat surface. As the charge is applied, the technician will note a crackling sound, accompanied by the film being drawn into the surface. This is an indication that the device is working correctly. The film is charged for a period of seconds. Then the device is turned off, and the charge is allowed to dissipate. If for some reason the film fails to be drawn to the surface in question, the technician should continue the charge and increase its intensity. Once the examination is complete and the device turned off, the charge will dissipate in 5 to 10 sec. The technician then lifts the film and examines it under oblique lighting (Figure 9.33). If any impressions of evidentiary value are noted, the film is secured, marked, and retained like any other item of evidence.

After recovery, the lifting film is best stored flat in a box. Clean pizza boxes are an excellent container for lifting films. A single lifting film is taped shiny-side down inside the box; this leaves the surface containing the impression facing up. When the pizza box is closed, the surface containing the impression is secure and will not rub against any other surfaces.

Plaster and Dental-Stone Casting Techniques

When presented with three-dimensional impression evidence such as tire and shoe marks in soil, an effective method of recovery is to cast the impression using either plaster of Paris or dental stone (Figure 9.34). Given an option, dental stone is the preferred medium, because it sets harder, is more forgiving of error during mixing, and tends to recover more detail than standard plaster. Additionally, when casting three-dimensional impressions, dental stone does not always require a form mold to contain the casting material. Dental-stone casting is also an effective technique for recovering

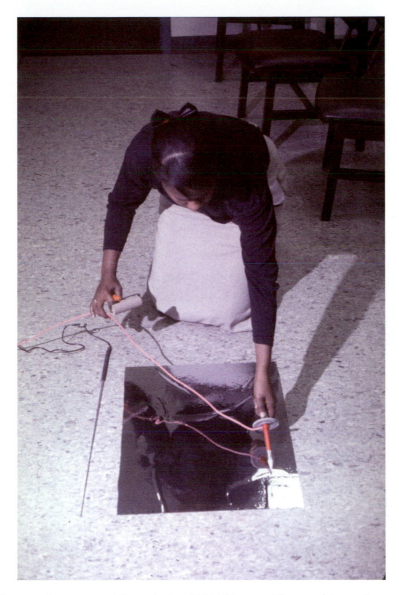

Figure 9.32 An electrostatic lifting device (ESLD) in use. The wand is used to apply a charge to the lifting film. The roller is used by the technician to roll out air pockets. The silver rod adjacent to the film is a grounding device.

two-dimensional impressions such as water- or liquid-tracked shoe marks on asphalt or other surfaces.

The text will continue to refer to dental stone as the lifting medium, since this is the preferred method. The methods employed for plaster of Paris are the same as dental stone, with the exceptions that greater care in recovery is necessary when using plaster, and a form is almost always required in order to obtain a sufficient depth of plaster material. This depth is needed to add strength to the finished plaster cast.

The first step in casting a three-dimensional impression is to prepare the impression. Obvious loose debris that accumulated in the impression subsequent to its creation can

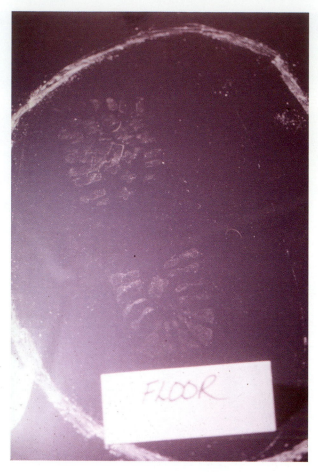

Figure 9.33   The resulting lift using an electrostatic lifting device. The white ring around the lift is chalk, used by the technician to outline the nearly invisible print when it was discovered using oblique lighting.

be removed with tweezers. Debris that is an integral part of the impression (e.g., matted-down leaves) or debris extending out of the impression (e.g., a twig or small root) should always be left in place. Any attempt to remove such debris can easily damage or destroy the impression. This is particularly true of small twigs or items sticking out of the impression. Because these items are buried, the technician has no way of knowing how far they extend or how large they are. Don't worry about trying to have a "clean" cast, since these items of debris rarely alter the quality of the cast.

Impressions made in extremely loose soil, powders, or sand may benefit from treatment by a fixative. Commercial fixatives are available from various forensic suppliers, but any aerosol shellac spray (e.g., a clear shellac paint or hairspray) is effective. These fixatives should be applied with great care, as direct spraying will destroy the impression. The intent of the spray is to harden the impression just enough to help it survive the pouring of the dental stone. The spray should be directed above the impression, allowing it to settle onto the material. Overspraying is likely to result in damaging the impression as well, since this can fill in the minutiae of interest to the lab examiner. Beyond hardening impressions in powders or extremely soft soil, fixatives serve no specific function. They were once used

Figure 9.34   A cast of a shoe mark made with dental stone.

as a release agent to prevent soil from clinging to the cast, but with the current use of dental stone, this function is unnecessary. Dental stone sets hard enough that subsequent cleaning of the cast by the shoe-mark examiner does not damage detail.

Forms are used in casting to contain the casting medium. They can be made of expandable metal sleeves or fashioned from wide tape, heavy gauge paper, or cardboard. Although the use of a form is not a necessary evil when using dental stone, the form is still functional for making the cast symmetrical. The technician will encounter occasions when the form is required. Two prime examples are where the impression is on a slope or when casting submerged impressions. In these cases, the form contains the dental stone and prevents it from flowing down the slope or from dispersing into the standing water. If a form is used, it is extended around the impression, ensuring that an ample buffer exists from the sides of the form to the edges of the impression. If the technician finds the impression on a relatively flat area, then no form is necessary. The dental stone is simply poured into and around the impression, creating a pancakelike mass.

After preparing the impression, the technician prepares the dental stone. Dental stone can be mixed in containers of just about any nature. The most effective method for transporting, mixing, and pouring the stone is the use of large resealable zip-lock–style plastic bags. It is best to premeasure the dental stone to a specific weight to ease mixing at the scene. Authors such as Bodziak suggest preparing 2-lb bags (approximately 4 cups of material), which is mixed with approximately 12 oz water.[8] Measuring the prescribed amount of water is simple, as there are rarely circumstances when a soda can or similar 12-oz drink can is not available. Initially, the water is added in bulk, approximately $1/_2$ to 2/3 of the required volume. The bag is then sealed and manipulated by hand until the dental stone is thoroughly mixed. As needed, the remaining water is added until the consistency is that of a thick pancake batter. Remember that the material must flow; if it must be squeezed from the bag, the mixture is too thick and will result in a poor cast. On the other hand, if the mixture is too thin, although it will flow easily into the impression, it will either take hours to cure or perhaps never cure. Thin-mixture casts, even in dental stone, tend to be structurally weak and prone to breakage.

Once mixed, the zip-lock bag is lowered to the level of the casting surface and slowly poured into an area adjacent to the impression that does not contain detail. The technician allows the material to flow out from this point and slowly cover the remaining area of the impression. One does not pour from a height or pour the material across the impression like syrup on pancakes. The impact of casting material falling from a height can ruin impression detail. Pouring the material over the exposed impression also tends to cause damage to detail. Whether a form is used or not, the technician ensures that a sufficient volume of casting material is poured into the impression so that the entire impression is covered to a depth of at least $1/_2$ in. Baffling the flow of the casting material into the form or slowly spreading the material with a spatula are acceptable methods as well. The latter may be necessary if it becomes evident that the casting material has already begun to set after the technician begins pouring. At this point, it is too late to remove the material, at least not without destroying the evidence. If the set is not too advanced, the technician can carefully manipulate the material into position. In this circumstance, Bodziak also suggests using a stick or a finger to manipulate the material "vibrating it back and forth on the surface," which helps the material settle into place in the impression.[9]

After pouring, the material is allowed to set. The time required is variable, depending upon how thick the mixture was and the ambient temperature. A time span of 20 to 30 min is a good rule of thumb for most situations. During the set, the cast can be marked in a number of ways. One method is to insert a paper clip halfway into one end of the cast, allowing it to set with the material. Afterward, the exposed clip provides a method of attaching a standard evidence tag. Another solution is to use tags with strings (either evidence tags or blank paper tags). The strings of the tag are submerged into the material before it sets, and the tag can then be annotated after recovery. Of course, the cast itself can be marked, either with a Sharpie (after it is recovered) or by etching the material before it sets completely. As discussed with rubber casting material, the technician should never rush recovery. The exterior of the cast may appear set, but the interior may not be. There are a number of additional aspects of evidence recovery that go along with casting that can be attended to during the curing period. This includes recovering soil samples from the vicinity for subsequent trace-evidence examination. These soil samples should come from the immediate area of the cast and include soil to a similar depth as the impression. Soil samples are best collected and secured in clean plastic film canisters.

Although dental stone sets very hard and is not easily damaged, the technician should still use care in recovering the cast. Oftentimes, the cast must be levered out of the ground, and too much pressure applied too quickly can result in the cast breaking. The cast should air dry for an extended period prior to any attempt to ship or examine it. Cleaning the cast is not recommended. Submit the cast as it is, and allow the lab examiners to determine what process they will use to clean excess dirt from the cast.

There are occasions when the technician may encounter submerged impressions. These may consist of impressions in shallow standing water, impressions that have been filled up with water, or impressions made in mud at the bottom of a body of water. Dental-stone casting is possible in any one of these three situations. When confronted with an impression under a significant body of water, the most effective method to follow is to utilize a form and place it around the impression. If possible, build a channeling form around the

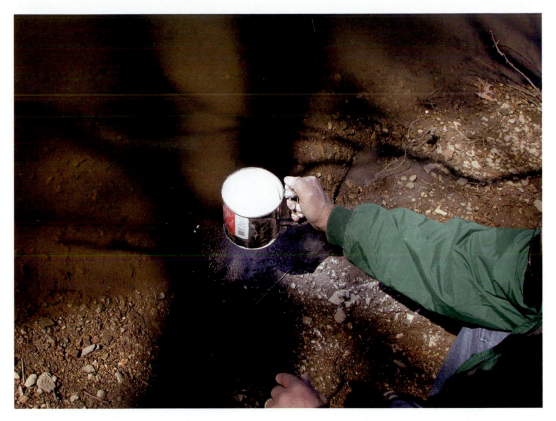

Figure 9.35 Casting a footwear mark containing standing water. When presented with a mark that has standing water in it, the technician slowly sifts dental stone into the water rather than using wet-mixed dental stone. (Figure courtesy of Special Agent [Ret.] Don Hayden. With permission.)

impression that reaches above the water line. Slowly direct the mixed dental stone into the form by allowing it to sink to the bottom through the water. The technician should be prepared to mix a large quantity of dental stone in order to achieve any result. In situations where the impression is filled with water, the technician can sift dental stone slowly into the standing water, as seen in Figure 9.35. When the water becomes viscous, a form is added around the impression, and the process is continued until a thorough mixture is achieved. The form will prevent additional water from seeping in and allow the mixture to set, as seen in Figure 9.36.

An additional consideration for using dental stone to cast three-dimensional prints is casting snow prints. A commercial (wax based) forensic product is available that is sprayed into the snow print prior to casting. The wax provides structure to the snow impression and prevents damage from heat. Casting materials, including dental stone, produce a significant level of heat when curing, enough to melt the details present in the snow print. Having employed the wax in Alaska for several years, the author found it useful, but also troublesome. The wax comes in the form of an aerosol spray. If left in a crime scene vehicle for extended periods or exposed to the elements at the crime scene for too long, the spray cans would often fail. The cans should not be left in vehicles overnight and should be kept in a warm area (the interior of the passenger compartment with the heater on) until just before use in the scene. Bill Gifford, now retired from the Anchorage Police Department,

Figure 9.36 Casting a footwear mark containing standing water. Once the majority of the standing water is absorbed and the mixture becomes viscous, a form is added, and additional dental stone is added. (Figure courtesy of Special Agent [Ret.] Don Hayden. With permission.)

suggests using standard dental-stone techniques with an added step. The dental stone is cooled in the snow before it is poured. Setting the mix to the side and allowing it to cool in the snow and ambient air will significantly reduce any melting effect caused by the curing of the dental stone.[10,11]

Dental-stone techniques are useful not only for casting three-dimensional impressions, but also when trying to recover two-dimensional impression evidence. This technique is very successful when casting wet prints on hard surfaces, including concrete. These can be marks caused by moisture on the shoes or some other contaminant (Figure 9.37). To capture such prints, the technician uses magnetic powder to cover the wet print (Figure 9.38). Once powdered, a form is taped in place around the impression, as seen in Figure 9.39. Taping the outside edges of the form in place is an important step. Since the form cannot be depressed into the hard floor, taping effectively contains the mixture and prevents leakage. Oftentimes, a seal breaker is necessary to remove the casts from the surface. The dental stone will adhere to the floor, making it difficult to remove. An effective seal breaker is to place a piece of doubled-over tape on the floor, beneath the top edge of the form. The tape should extend to either side, allowing the technician to grasp the tape easily. Be sure to place the tape in such a fashion that it does not overlay any of the impression. After the cast cures, the technician grabs the tape and leverages up on it as a means of removing the cast from the surface. Figure 9.40 is an example of a two-dimensional print recovered with dental stone.

Figure 9.37 Wet footwear marks on a hard surface. Wet footwear marks can occur on hard surfaces such as concrete, but they are readily lost due to evaporation. These marks can also be lifted with dental stone. (Figure courtesy of Special Agent [Ret.] Don Hayden. With permission.)

Figure 9.38 Wet footwear marks on a hard surface. After evaluating the wet prints, the technician lightly dusts the most detailed wet prints with magnetic powder. (Figure courtesy of Special Agent [Ret.] Don Hayden. With permission.)

Figure 9.39 Wet footwear marks on a hard surface. Using tape or paper, a form is created and taped into place around the dusted wet print. Dental stone is added to the form in a normal fashion and allowed to set. (Figure courtesy of Special Agent [Ret.] Don Hayden. With permission.)

Figure 9.40 A wet print recovered using dental stone. (Figure courtesy of Special Agent [Ret.] Don Hayden. With permission.)

Gelatin and Other Adhesive Lifters

Gelatin and adhesive lifters are among the most effective tools for collecting two-dimensional impression evidence from a variety of surfaces. Gelatin lifters — a gelatinous substance on a pliable substrate — can be used on almost any surface, including porous surfaces like paper. Adhesive and rubber lifters are limited to recoveries from nonporous smooth surfaces like floors. Adhesive lifters are akin to a large fingerprint-lifting tape, with a little more rigidity. Rubber lifters are nothing more than large, rubber, fingerprint lifters. Two-dimensional prints, such as wet prints on smooth surfaces, can be dusted with magnetic powder, as described in the section on dental stone, and lifted with these lifters. Latent shoe marks caused by the rubber of the shoe sole can also be dusted to enhance detail and then lifted with lifters. Visible dust prints respond effectively to gelatin lifters, and when the technician is presented with dirt, oil, or grease prints, this may be the only functional recovery method possible.

Of the three lifters, gelatin lifters are more functional than their predecessors (the adhesive and rubber lifters), but that function comes with a price. Gelatin lifters cost quite a bit more and are also prone to damage due to extremes in temperature. Based on cost alone, gelatin lifters should be maintained exactly as the manufacturer suggests until actual use.

Whether using a gelatin, rubber, or adhesive lifter, the technician removes the clear cover from the adhesive backing of the lifter and — bending the adhesive section of the lifter in the middle — places the lifter into position on the impression. The lifter is slowly lowered into place from the middle, using caution to prevent unwanted air bubbles or creases of any sort (Figure 9.41). After laying the lifter in place, the technician rolls it with a fingerprint ink-pad roller, as seen in Figure 9.42. An alternative method for use with the gelatin lifter is to place one end in contact with the surface and slowly roll the remaining lifter into place. After application, the lifter is raised with a steady motion from one end (Figure 9.43). The technician should not attempt to lift the adhesive from both ends. Equally important, the technician should not stop or hesitate halfway through the lift. As with fingerprint lifters, either action can damage the lifter or the detail captured on the lift. Once removed, the technician places the lifter on a solid substrate and replaces the clear plastic cover, smoothing out any air bubbles.

Summary

Three basic techniques the crime scene technician should understand and be prepared to employ in processing a crime scene include the use of an ALS system, fingerprinting a variety of different surfaces, and casting impression evidence.

The ALS is useful in a wide variety of functions at the crime scene. Critical aspects of the ALS include its use as a search tool for biological fluids, fibers, and hairs. A broadband filter (390 to 520 nm) is the typical filter employed in a standard blue light. This filter, in combination with a longwave UV light (365 to 415 nm), can be helpful when looking for biological evidence such as sperm, spittle, and urine. The dyes used in various fibers are all quite different, so the crime scene technician must employ a wide range of narrowband wavelengths to search for fiber evidence. When searching for hairs, red and blond hairs may fluoresce, but dark hairs generally will not. Dark hairs are best found using clean white light directed at an oblique angle to the surface being searched. Near-UV wavelengths

Figure 9.41 Two-dimensional prints on hard surfaces can be collected using gelatin and rubber lifters. Here, the technician lowers the lifter in place, bowing both ends. Contact is made in the center, and the lifter is slowly smoothed into place from this point. (Figure courtesy of Special Agent [Ret.] Don Hayden. With permission.)

(415 to 485 nm) as well as orange–red wavelengths of 570 to 700 nm can be effective for visualizing bruises and bite marks on human skin.

On-scene fingerprinting techniques include basic powder-and-brush methods, the use of superglue fuming to stabilize latent prints, the use of small-particle reagent to recover prints from wet surfaces, and a host of other techniques. The decision of which technique to use in recovering latent fingerprints is very much a matter of what kind of surface the latent print is located on. The various techniques are based on surface characteristics, which include porous, nonporous smooth, and nonporous rough. It is important for the technician to realize that the on-scene techniques represent only a small portion of the methods available for fingerprint recovery. The crime lab can recover fingerprint evidence in situations where no on-scene technique would work. This demands that the technician assess the importance of the surface and the likelihood that on-scene techniques will work. It is often better to seize and send items to the lab for analysis rather than risk losing the fingerprint on scene. Fingerprints can also be recovered from a number of difficult surfaces, including the adhesive side of tape, from human skin, and from surfaces exposed to heat and soot. The most effective method for recovering prints from adhesive tape is the use

Figure 9.42 Once the lifter is in place, the technician rolls out any air bubbles using a fingerprint roller. (Figure courtesy of Special Agent [Ret.] Don Hayden. With permission.)

of crystal violet. The most effective method for recovering latent prints from human skin is the adding-machine-paper technique. Neither technique requires significant supplies, and both are easily mastered for on-scene efforts. Fire scene evidence might appear on first glance to be a poor medium for fingerprints. Despite appearances, fire scene evidence can be examined visually for latent prints. If none are located, the soot is carefully washed off the object with running water. Very often, latent prints on these objects stabilize and are made visible by the effects of both heat and soot during the fire.

Impression evidence occurs in the crime scene as tool marks, bite marks, footwear marks, and tire marks. It is collected using three basic methods at the crime scene. It can be cast using rubber or plaster-based materials; it can be recovered using an electrostatic lifting device; or it can be recovered using large rubber or gelatin lifters. No matter what technique is chosen, quality crime scene photographs of the impression evidence are required as well. Minutiae of interest to the impression evidence examiner are not always captured by the various recovery techniques, and photographs may provide better evidence on which to conduct an examination.

Casting of tool marks is accomplished using silicone-based casting material. When presented with tool-mark evidence, it is best to collect the tool mark as well and submit both the mark and the cast to the crime lab. Three-dimensional impression evidence such as tire and footwear marks in soft surfaces (e.g., dirt) is collected using plaster-based casting material. Dental stone is the most effective plaster material to use based on its strength.

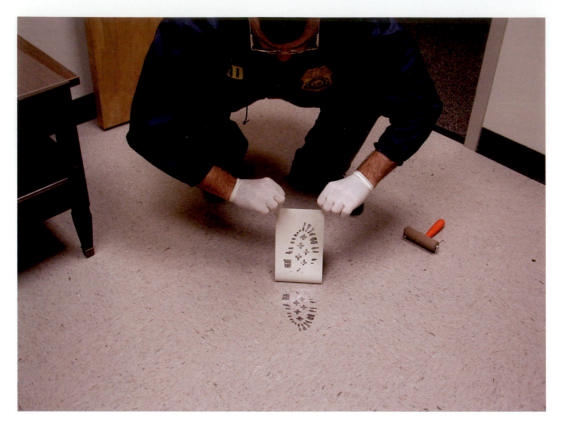

Figure 9.43 When removing the lifter, the technician starts at one end and, using a single and steady motion, removes the lifter off the surface. A protective transparent cover is then placed on top to protect the recovered mark. (Figure courtesy of Special Agent [Ret.] Don Hayden. With permission.)

Two-dimensional marks such as wet prints on concrete can be cast with dental stone as well. The mark is first dusted with magnetic powder, and then dental stone is poured over the top. Other two-dimensional prints such as marks on floors and other hard surfaces can be recovered using large rubber or gelatin lifting sheets. Dust prints on floors, paper, carpets, and clothing can be recovered using an electrostatic lifting device.

Suggested Reading

Bodziak, W.J., *Footwear Impression Evidence*, CRC Press, Boca Raton, FL, 1995.

Police Scientific Development Branch, *Fingerprint Development Handbook*, Home Office Policing and Crime Reduction Group, Heanor Gate Printing Ltd., Derbyshire, U.K., 2000.

Chapter Questions

1. Explain how the conversion of light is utilized as a search tool in the crime scene.
2. Fingerprinting technique is based on the surface being examined. Identify and provide an example of the four basic surface types.

3. Identify the purpose of fluorescent fingerprint powder and provide an example of when it is used.
4. What is the primary reason for using the superglue-fuming technique?
5. What are the steps used to locate fingerprint evidence in fire scene evidence?
6. What are the steps used to photograph an impression prior to casting it?
7. Under what conditions is the electrostatic lifting device used?
8. Under what conditions and for what purpose would a fixative spray be used when casting impression evidence?
9. What are the steps used to cast an impression with dental stone when the impression contains standing water?
10. What is the primary distinction between conditions where a gelatin lifter can be used as compared with adhesive or rubber lifters?

Notes

1. Housman, D.G. and Maloney, M.S., Forensic Light Sources, a paper and presentation to the Association of Crime Scene Reconstruction, Kansas City, MO, 1999.
2. Ibid., p. 6.
3. Sirchie Fingerprint Laboratories Criminal Investigative Tools Catalog, Sirchie Fingerprint Laboratories, Youngsville, NC, 2000, p. 80.
4. Moonglo and Midnight Blu are trademark names of DOJES, Inc., Ocoee, FL.
5. Nielson, L., SA FBI ERT, verbal conversation, Oakland, CA, Jan. 2003.
6. Corr, J.J., The Use of Flame in the Development of Latent Prints, unpublished paper, Jan. 1957.
7. Thorton, J.E. and Emmons, B.W., Development of Latent Prints in Arson Cases, n.d., pp. 1–7.
8. Bodziak, W.J., *Footwear Impression Evidence*, CRC Press, Boca Raton, FL, 1995, p. 83.
9. Ibid., p. 84.
10. Gifford, W., verbal communication, Oct. 2002.
11. Gifford, W., Casting footwear and tire tracks, *The Scene (Assoc. Crime Scene Reconstruction)*, 10, p. 8, 2003.

Advanced Techniques for Scene Processing

10

Beyond the basic techniques described in Chapter 9, there are a number of advanced techniques that are equally important to the crime scene technician. This chapter considers two specific techniques: bloodstain pattern analysis and bullet trajectory analysis. Often when presented with situations involving evidence of this type, specialists will be brought in to assist in the processing. A specialist, however, is not always available. Therefore, at a minimum, the technician must understand and properly document this type of evidence so that a subsequent analysis can be conducted. Though somewhat advanced, these evaluations are typical of many violent crime scenes, and it is in the best interest of the crime scene technician to develop skills in both areas.

Bloodstain Pattern Analysis

The consideration of the bloodstains at the crime scene can provide important information to the crime scene technician. The discipline of bloodstain pattern analysis considers the location, shape, size, distribution, and other physical characteristics of bloodstains in the scene, and from this derives information regarding the nature of the event that created the pattern. Thus bloodstain patterns tell us "what" happened. This information, when combined with the information derived from any deoxyribonucleic acid (DNA) analysis, may allow an investigator to corroborate or refute specific investigative theories as well as subsequent statements offered by suspects, victims, and witnesses. Although the crime scene technician may not be trained in depth in bloodstain pattern analysis, it is imperative that s/he be able to recognize critical classifications of stains and know how to properly document scenes.

The methodology employed in bloodstain pattern analysis is relatively simple. The technician:

- Becomes familiar with the entire scene
- Identifies the discrete patterns among the various bloodstained surfaces
- Categorizes these patterns based on the established taxonomy of bloodstain pattern analysis
- Evaluates aspects of directionality and motion in the stain or pattern
- Evaluates interrelationships among stains, patterns, and other evidence

- Evaluates angles of impact, points of convergence, and areas of origin (if necessary)
- Evaluates viable source events to explain the pattern (based on all of the above)

A primary aspect of bloodstain pattern analysis is to categorize the various bloodstain patterns into the established taxonomy. This determination alone effectively limits the possible source events that may have created the pattern. For example, by defining a pattern on a suspect's clothes as spatter, the pattern cannot be explained by mere contact with a bloody body. Before discussing these categories, it is important to realize that beyond defining this underlying event, an in-depth analysis of each pattern may provide the investigator with specific information relating to where the associated event occurred, what items were involved in the event, and the relative position of people and objects at the time of the event.

Directionality and Impact Angle

An examination of the individual stains within any pattern will likely establish the direction the droplets were traveling at the moment they struck a surface. This is referred to as the directionality of the stain. This determination is based on the collapse of the fluid droplet; the resulting long axis of the stain; and the creation of small scallops, tails, and satellite stains that appear on or around the stain. In elliptically shaped stains, these scallops and satellites will appear on the side opposite the source of the stain. In the more spherically shaped stains, the scallops and tails will appear in a heavier concentration on the side opposite the source. See Figure 10.1. By considering the directionality of a number of stains

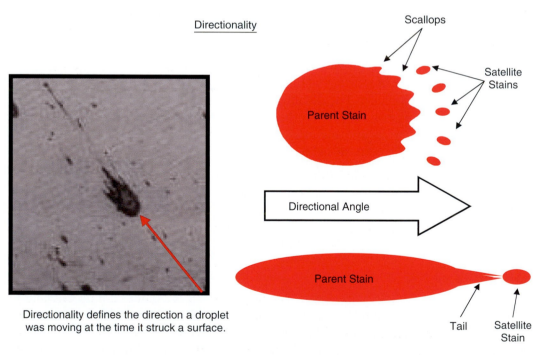

Directionality defines the direction a droplet was moving at the time it struck a surface.

Figure 10.1 Directionality of a bloodstain is defined by both the long axis of the stain and the presence of scallops, tails, and satellite spatter. These small characteristics appear in a greater concentration on the side opposite where the droplet first struck the surface. The directionality of the stain in the inset photo is upward and to the left. The origin of the stain then must be somewhere along a line aligned with this directional angle, but extended in an opposite direction.

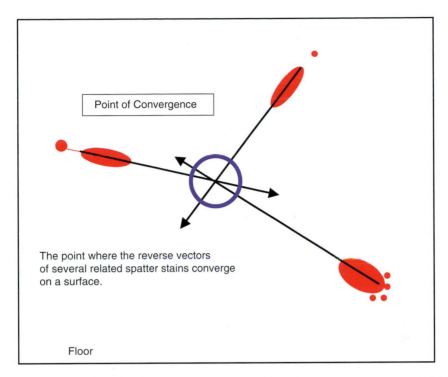

Point of Convergence

The point where the reverse vectors
of several related spatter stains converge
on a surface.

Floor

Figure 10.2 By visualizing a line aligned with the directional angle and extended back into the scene for a number of related spatters, a point of convergence will form where the lines cross each other on a surface (e.g., a floor). The area of origin for the pattern would be located in three-dimensional space above the convergence point.

in a pattern, the technician can visualize the general area from which the droplets originated. The reverse vectors defined by the individual stains' directionality will (if the stains are related) converge in the scene. This convergence is a two-dimensional area referred to as the pattern's convergence point, as seen in Figure 10.2.

Given a suitable stain and surface, the crime scene technician can also establish the approximate angle at which a droplet struck a surface. This is defined as the impact angle of the stain. A droplet of liquid in flight is a sphere. As a result, any measurement of the diameter of the droplet will be equal. Refer to Figure 10.3. As the droplet collides with a target, a right triangle can be visualized. It is formed by the diameter of the droplet, the path of the droplet, and the area on the target where the droplet first touches and then terminates its movement (triangle abc in Figure 10.3). The internal angle of lines acb in this triangle is the angle of impact (the same as angle *i* in Figure 10.3). If we transpose the triangle and compare it to the bloodstain, it is clear that there is an analogy and relationship between the two, as seen in Figure 10.4. The major axis of the bloodstain is analogous to the hypotenuse of the triangle (line bc), and the minor axis of the bloodstain is analogous to the side opposite (line ab). Using the trigonometric relationship sine (SIN) and the two known measurements from the bloodstain, the technician can solve for the unknown angle (angle *i*), as seen in Figure 10.5. As confusing as all of this might sound, the act of determining the angle of impact is quite simple. The technician simply measures the long and short axis of the stain. This measurement does not include any portion of the tail, scallops, or satellite spatter. The technician then divides the short axis by the long axis, which will always result in a number of 1 or less. Using a scientific calculator, the technician

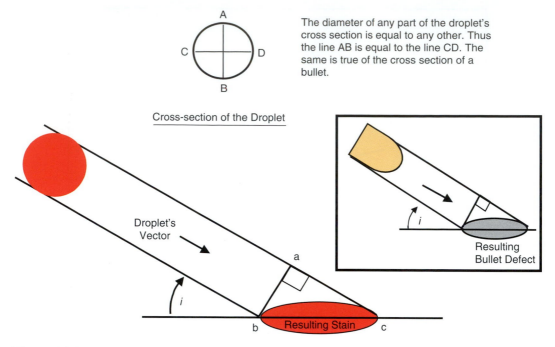

Figure 10.3   The vector a droplet is following combined with the surface it impacts creates a right triangle (abc). By drawing certain relationships between the stain and this right triangle, the technician can identify the angle of impact (angle *i*). These relationships are true of defects created by bullets as well.

then determines the inverse SIN of this number, which is the angle of impact. See Figure 10.6. This same relationship is true of defects created by bullets, which will be discussed later in the chapter. The impact angle for any given stain can also be approximated by simple examination of the shape of the stain. The more circular-shaped stains indicate impact angles between 70 and 90 degrees. Bear claw-shaped stains usually indicate an impact angle between 40 and 60 degrees. Long, elliptically shaped stains indicate acute angle impacts of 30 degrees and less. See Figure 10.7.

Having defined directionality and the angle of impact for a number of stains in a spatter pattern, the analyst may be able to identify the area of origin. Area of origin is the approximate position in three-dimensional space where the event occurred. See Figure 10.8. Information derived from directionality, point of convergence, and an area-of-origin analysis can assist the crime scene technician in understanding the direction and origin of the event that created the pattern and can effectively place individuals in the scene at discrete moments in time during the crime.

Categorizing Bloodstain Patterns

A significant part of bloodstain pattern analysis is evaluating the physical characteristics of a pattern and, based on those characteristics, making a classification of the stain or pattern. Bloodstain pattern analysis has established classifications of stains, also known as a taxonomy of stains. The underlying basis of this taxonomy is the creation event. By defining a pattern as belonging to a certain classification, the analyst defines and limits the possible ways in which the pattern came to be. It is important to remember, however, that

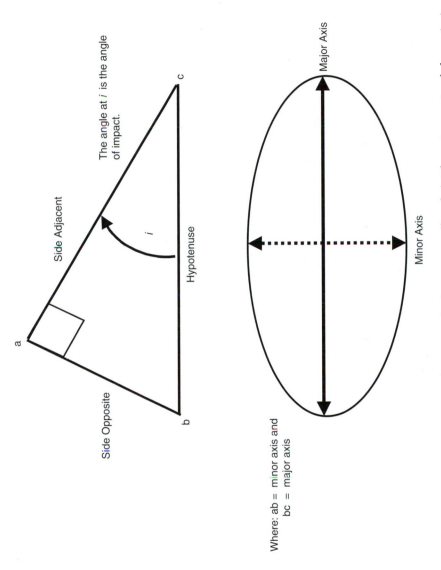

Figure 10.4 The long axis of the stain or defect is analogous to the hypotenuse (line bc). The minor axis of the stain is analogous to the "side opposite" portion of the triangle (line ab). A measurement of the stain's width and length provides two known values that allow the technician to solve for the unknown angle (angle *i*).

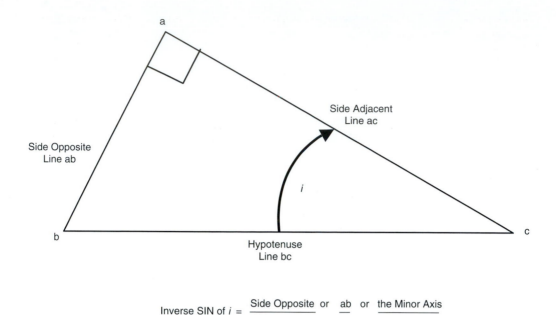

$$\text{Inverse SIN of } i = \frac{\text{Side Opposite}}{\text{Hypotenuse}} \text{ or } \frac{\text{ab}}{\text{bc}} \text{ or } \frac{\text{the Minor Axis}}{\text{the Major Axis}}$$

Figure 10.5 The formula used to define the impact angle is based on the trigonometric function of SIN. The inverse SIN of the angle at i is equal to the minor axis divided by the major axis.

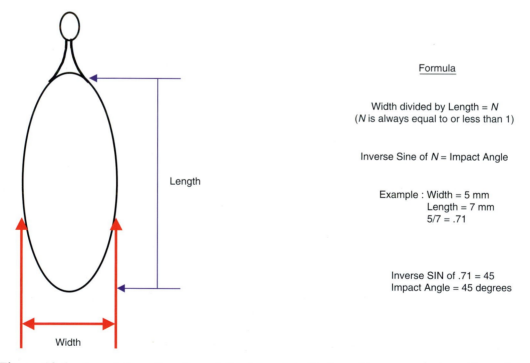

Figure 10.6 A verbal explanation of the impact angle formula may seem complicated. In practice, however, it requires a simple division of two numbers and the conversion of that number using a scientific calculator. The width of the stain divided by the length will result in a number equal to 1 or less. The inverse SIN of this number is the impact angle.

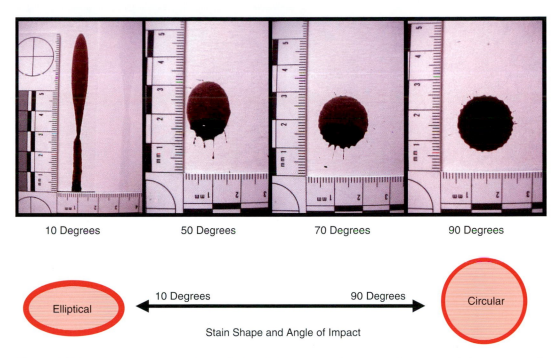

Figure 10.7 There is an empirical relationship between the shape of a stain and the associated impact angle. The more elliptical the shape, the more acute is the angle. The more circular the shape, the more likely it is that the droplet struck at a 90-degree angle.

no matter how specific the categorization, bloodstain pattern evidence is almost always class-characteristic evidence. It may be possible to identify the general class of event that created a stain (e.g., an impact to a blood mass), but it is usually impossible (based on the bloodstain alone) to identify a stain to a specific event excluding all others (e.g., this pattern was created by a blow from a λ-lb hammer and not by a blow from a rock). This nuance in the limitation of bloodstain pattern analysis is not always understood by novices and frequently leads to inappropriate conclusions.

Bloodstain patterns are grouped into two basic categories: passive stains and dynamic patterns. Passive stains result from an action other than a directed force to a blood mass. Examples of passive events include dripping blood, contact by bloody objects, and similar events. Passive stains can be further categorized as contact patterns, blood clots, drip patterns, drip trails, and blood pools or flows.

Blood clots may assist the technician in defining the passage of time since bloodshed and the discovery of the scene. By considering the directionality of a blood trail — a series of individual stains dripping from an object — the investigator may recognize the movement of parties or objects in the scene (Figure 10.9). Drip patterns occur when an object dripping blood is stationary for a period of time. The resulting drip creates a small blood pool as well as a number of small random satellite droplets (sometimes in the hundreds) surrounding the blood pool (Figure 10.10). Although very simple patterns, blood pools and blood flows help the technician in establishing the movement and position of individuals bleeding in the scene. Blood flows will always obey gravity; therefore, the presence of abnormal blood flows may indicate movement by the victim before death and or disturbance of the scene by the subject or parties who arrived afterward.

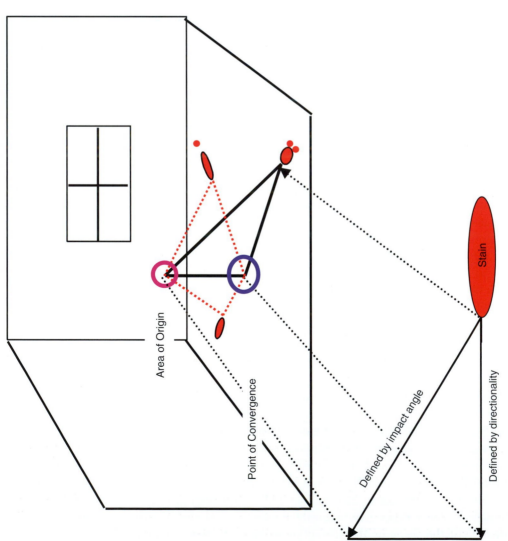

Figure 10.8 By considering the directionality and impact angles of several related spatter stains, the technician can establish an area of origin for the pattern.

Figure 10.9 A drip trail is a series of related drops falling from an individual or object. Directionality of the individual stains may define the direction the individual was moving at the time. At the top center, there is an associated drip pattern and a single drop that has been disturbed by a wipe. The drip pattern indicates the object was stationary for a moment. The condition of the disturbed drop indicates the disturbance quickly followed the deposition of the drops.

A variety of contact stains are included in the passive category. These occur when blood is transferred from one object to another through some form of contact. The variations of contact stains include pattern transfers, wipes, swipes, and saturation stains.

A pattern transfer occurs when an object wet with blood contacts another surface such as cloth or clothing articles, leaving a recognizable pattern. Typical pattern transfers include hand or footprints (Figure 10.11) and patterns of bloodied knife blades or blunt-force weapons. Rarely will a pattern transfer be examined and "identified" to a single specific object, but such patterns will assist the investigator in recognizing the nature and characteristics of weapons used in an assault and, more importantly, define where these objects were during the incident.

Wipe patterns (Figure 10.12) occur when a preexisting stain is disturbed by another object. Through analysis of a wipe pattern, the analyst can obviously establish the sequence of the two events and, usually, the direction of motion of the disturbance. Oftentimes the relative time between the deposition of the original stain and its subsequent disturbance can be estimated. This latter information can be significant when considering the presence of a suspect's shoe marks or hand prints in a scene, particularly if there is a claim that the suspect merely discovered the crime some time afterward.

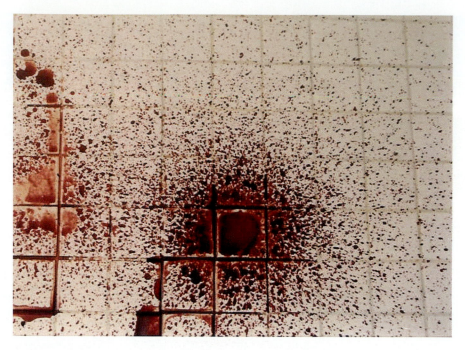

Figure 10.10 A drip pattern. Drip patterns consist of a number of random stains surrounding a central pool or stain. These patterns can mimic spatter, but the orientation of the small stains is different. In spatter, the stains radiate out on related directional angles. Drip pattern satellite stains are randomly oriented on the surface.

Swipe marks (Figure 10.13) occur when a bloody object makes contact through some form of lateral motion with an unstained object. As with the wipe pattern, the direction of the motion is often evident in a swipe pattern.

Saturation stains occur when blood is drawn into clothing, cloth, or permeable items. Saturation stains rarely provide the technician specific investigative information and often mar or destroy other blood patterns of interest.

Dynamic patterns are created by forceful events, where fluid blood is projected out from a source under some force or compression. Dynamic bloodstain patterns include spatter, castoff patterns, arterial patterns, splashes, and spines.

Spatter occurs when a blood mass is broken up into droplets. Blood, like all fluids, is incompressible, and the force of an impact will cause the blood to break up into small droplets, which are projected out from the origin onto surrounding objects and surfaces. Spatter patterns are patterns involving a number of small individual stains that radiate out from a central location. The individual size of the spatter stains may range greatly from small submillimeter stains up to larger 4- to 5-mm stains. The number of stains present in the pattern may be a few to literally thousands, as seen in Figure 10.14. Spatter patterns occur primarily as impact spatter, where a blood source is compressed by an impact of some nature (e.g., gunshot or blunt trauma). Spatter can also occur as a result of the breathing of a victim. If blood is present in an airway, exhalation by the victim will break the blood into small droplets, which are forced out of the airway. This type of spatter is referred to as expiratory spatter. Detailed analysis of a spatter pattern may result in defining an area of origin for the event, which, if successful, will limit the possible positions in the scene from which the event could have occurred.

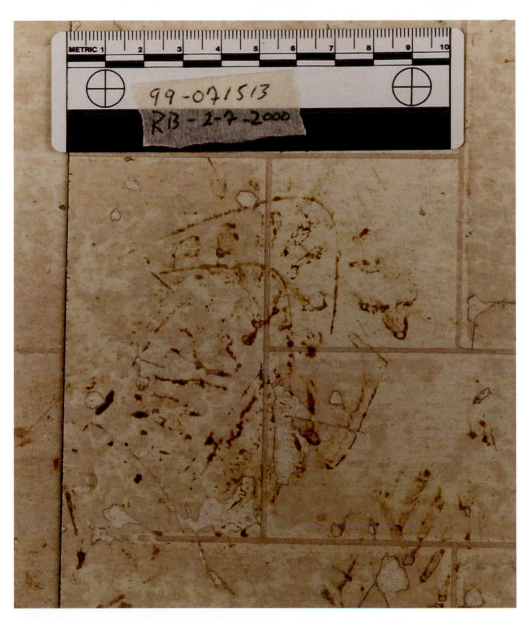

Figure 10.11 A pattern transfer. A bloody shoe in contact with a floor left a repetitive pattern transfer. In most instances, bloodstain patterns provide only class characteristics, but in this instance, the resulting bloodstain offers the forensic footwear examiner the opportunity to individualize this evidence to a specific shoe.

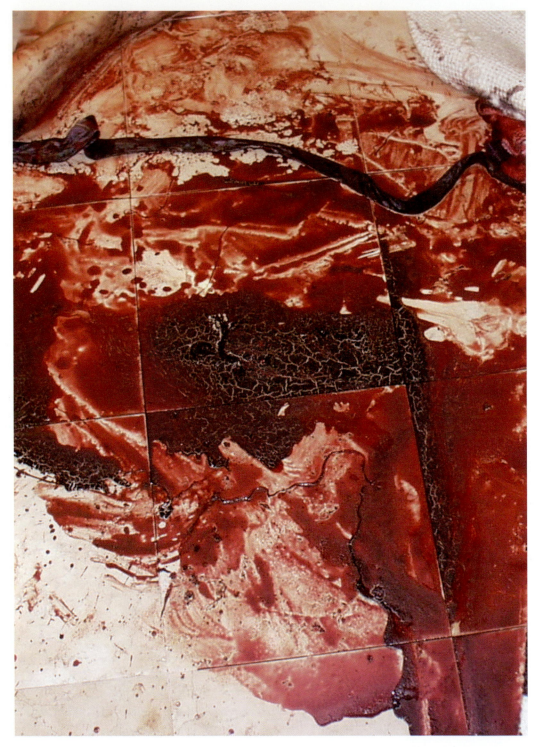

Figure 10.12 Numerous wipe patterns in a pool of blood. A wipe is a disturbance of a preexisting bloodstain. Sequence of action and direction of the wipe are all characteristics that can be determined.

Figure 10.13 A swipe mark on a tub. Swipes are produced when a bloodied object comes in contact with another surface with associated lateral motion. A significantly bloodied object was in contact with the upper surface of the bathtub and was moved into the tub.

Castoff patterns (Figure 10.15) occur when an object is bloodied and then moved or swung with some force. Blood is flung from the object by inertia at various points along the arc of the swing, resulting in a series of individual stains oriented on a surrounding surface in a typically linear orientation. Castoff patterns occur most often as a result of the swinging of weapons and other bloodied objects during an altercation, but may also result from offensive or defensive actions of victims or suspects whose appendages are bloodied. Castoff patterns appear as a series of individual stains that are oriented in a linear or curvilinear pattern on a surrounding wall, ceiling, or surface. Castoff patterns assist the technician in understanding the orientation and position of the item being swung and assist in determining the minimum number of swings of the associated item.

Arterial patterns (Figure 10.16) result from blood in volume that is projected into a scene under pressure from an artery or the heart. Depending upon the wound, they may appear as distinct patterns, known as arterial spurts, or large-volume patterns known as arterial gushes. Arterial patterns may include large-volume elliptical stains as well as patterns that rise and fall in waves on various scene surfaces. By considering the orientation of an arterial pattern to the scene, the investigator may be able to define movement of the victim following breaching of the artery.

Splash patterns occur when a volume of blood is projected into the scene with minimal force. They most often appear as large-volume patterns with large droplets surrounding the main stain. Splash patterns are not typical of crime scenes, although they often occur in suicides involving head wounds inflicted in upright victims. Splash patterns may also be present in staged crime scenes.

There are a number of additional patterns of interest that are generally categorized as miscellaneous patterns. The two most common are fly spots and void patterns. Fly spot

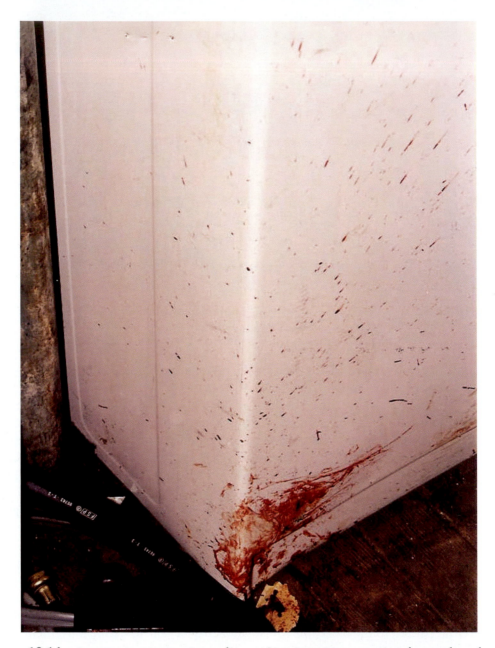

Figure 10.14   A spatter pattern on an appliance. Spatter patterns consist of a number of small stains that radiate out from a central point. They result from forceful impacts to a blood source. The directional angles of the individual spatter stains will lead back to a point of convergence on the surface. In this instance, the event occurred at the front left corner of the appliance. Spatter was ejected up and outward from this point on to the various surfaces.

Figure 10.15 A castoff pattern. Castoff patterns are created when a bloodied object is swung in some fashion. Droplets of blood detach from the object at varying points along the swing. The resulting pattern consists of a series of stains oriented in a linear or curvilinear formation. Directionality of the individual stains in the pattern identifies the direction of the swing. Pattern F is a very linear castoff pattern initiating in the upper center of the picture and extending down to a point near the No. 9. The pattern to the right is a spatter pattern.

Figure 10.16 An arterial pattern. These patterns can appear in varying orientations. They often involve large elliptical stains or a large volume of smaller stains, as are evident on the doorway. The stains will present a linear or curvilinear orientation that may appear as a wave that rises and falls on the surface. Arterial patterns result when an artery or the heart is breached by injury. The pressure variations of the circulatory system project the blood out of the breach, creating the wavy patterns. (Photograph courtesy of Special Agent [Ret.] Steve Chancellor. With permission.)

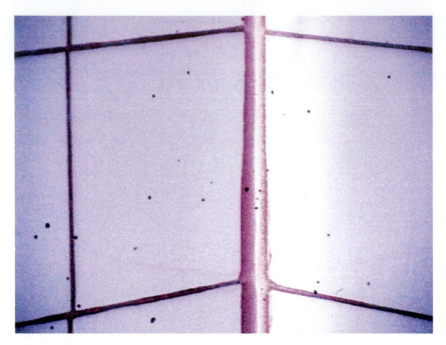

Figure 10.17 Fly spots on tile. Fly spots occur when flies feed on a blood source and either track the blood or regurgitate blood back in the scene. The patterns often mimic spatter patterns. (Photograph courtesy of Detective Mike McGuffey, Covington Police Department. With permission.)

patterns (Figure 10.17) occur as a result of fly activity in a scene. The movement of flies can track blood from a body or blood source and deposit it on surrounding walls and surfaces. Flies also regurgitate blood onto these surfaces. The resulting patterns may mimic spatter patterns, appearing as a number of small circular stains. In some instances, they may also mimic directional spatter. Void patterns occur when a secondary object is present between a bloodstain event and a nearby surface. Voids appear most often in spatter events, where hundreds of small droplets are forced into the scene and onto the surrounding surfaces. The secondary object may prevent many of the small spatter stains from reaching a nearby wall or surface, resulting in an area devoid of any blood but surrounded by spatter. Void patterns assist the technician in understanding the relative position of items at the time of the event. The technician must always be cautious and not presume that the natural end of a pattern is associated with a void.

The major effort of bloodstain pattern analysis is to identify the discrete patterns present in the scene and to categorize each. Once categorized, theories regarding the creation or presence of a stain pattern at a specific location within the scene can be considered in light of this information. As with most forensic disciplines, proper application of bloodstain pattern analysis will certainly negate possible theories, but it may not limit the theories to only one.

Documenting Bloodstain Patterns

If the technician is not trained in bloodstain pattern analysis and a trained analyst is unavailable to visit the scene, it is imperative that the crime scene technicians obtain complete documentation of the stains and stain patterns. For this reason, recognizing discrete patterns within the overall scene is a critical skill for every crime scene technician. After recognizing the discrete patterns, each pattern must be documented with overall photographs of that pattern alone as well as detailed close-up photographs of pattern or selected individual stains within the pattern. Close-up detail is a critical factor in bloodstain pattern photography. Photographs taken of millimeter-sized stains from several feet away are unlikely to allow for any type of analysis and are, for the most part, a waste of effort. Investigators must ensure that good close-up photographs are included in any bloodstain photography. The technique of roadmapping, which was explained in Chapter 6 and demonstrated in Figure 6.27 through Figure 6.29, is the most effective way to document bloodstained scenes.

Obtaining serology and DNA samples from each pattern is important as well, even if there is only one victim associated with the scene. Sampling of each pattern ensures that the pattern can be identified back to a specific source. In violent confrontations, nothing precludes an assailant from being the source of a bloodstain pattern, so the technician should never assume that all bloodstain patterns are the victim's. This is particularly true in situations involving edged weapons, where it is quite common to see self-wounding of the assailant. A final consideration in bloodstain pattern documentation is to accurately place the pattern in the scene. Although the crime scene photographs will assist in this process, detailed measurements of the location, size, as well as descriptions of the overall orientation of the patterns are necessary. The creation of additional sketches that detail location and orientation of stain patterns will be helpful.

Presumptive Tests for Bloodstains

The technician may occasionally find small reddish-brown stains that are not easily identifiable as blood; this could be due to the age of the stain or the visual reference. Rather than arbitrarily proceeding with processing and collection, the technician may wish to increase his or her confidence level in the nature of the stain. Presumptive field tests for blood provide a simple mechanism of accomplishing this, but it is imperative to understand that they are merely presumptive for the presence of blood and, with one exception, are certainly not specific for human blood. Nevertheless, these presumptive tests provide a convenient first indication.

Two of the primary field tests for the presumptive presence of blood are phenolphthalein and leucomalachite green. Either test can be purchased in kit form from a variety of forensic suppliers or mixed in bulk by an organization's lab. Kits are the more effective tool for crime scene application, as they can be stored without refrigeration in standard crime scene equipment.

These tests are based on an oxidation–reduction reaction of the chemicals that occurs in the presence of heme, a component of hemoglobin, which is the primary oxygen carrier found in red blood cells. A primary concern of these chemicals is that they also react with other substances, so a positive reaction is not conclusive evidence for the presence of blood. However, combining the visual characteristics of a stain with a positive presumptive test should lead to increased confidence on scene, which will ultimately be backed up by more conclusive testing at the crime lab.

Phenolphthalein consists of three basic solutions. The phenolphthalein solution itself, ethanol, and hydrogen peroxide as an oxidizer. The first step is to sample the suspect stain

Figure 10.18   Odd pigmented stains or old stains may not appear to be blood. The presumptive blood test gives the crime scene technician a greater level of confidence that the stain is indeed blood. To conduct a presumptive test, the technician samples the stain with the corner of a clean filter paper or a clean swab. The solutions of the presumptive test are then applied in sequence to the paper or the swab.

by taking the corner of a folded filter paper or a clean cotton swab and lightly rubbing the surface of the stain, as seen in Figure 10.18. If the stain is particularly old, the technician can moisten the filter paper or swab first with a drop of the ethanol. The area of the filter paper placed in contact with the stain is moistened with one drop of ethanol and then one drop of phenolphthalein reagent. No color reaction should occur. Any pink color reaction that occurs within the several seconds of the second step and prior to applying the oxidizer (hydrogen peroxide) would indicate a false positive test. After ensuring there is no false positive, a drop of hydrogen peroxide is applied. An immediate pink color reaction should occur in the presence of blood (Figure 10.19). A control swab or filter paper that is placed in contact with an area that is clearly unstained is treated in the same manner. No color reaction should be evident on the control. The control serves to ensure that there are no contaminants present that might create a false positive. The same basic procedures are utilized with the leucomalachite green test, which yields a green color reaction rather than pink for a positive test.

Figure 9.19 When confronted with very irregular or curved surfaces, latent prints can be lifted using silicone material such as that used to recover tool marks. This technique will often recover a better lift than the use of a rubber lifter. Note, however, the small air pocket in the middle of the print. The technician always attempts to prevent such bubbles, as they result in the loss of minutiae.

tiae. Because lab dyes were involved, these techniques were originally considered a "lab" process; in fact, the author can recall several dressing downs received from lab personnel for using the superglue technique on scene. By the early 1980s, however, the technique was a standard on-scene process, as it allowed the crime scene technician to effectively stabilize latent prints. Once fumed, the latent print is not susceptible to damage in transit and can be dusted or lifted a number of times.

Fuming is appropriate in situations involving rough or smooth nonporous surfaces and in the case of dead bodies. It is also an effective method for dealing with polystyrene products. To fume an article, the technician isolates the item in question. On scene, this can be done by simply taping a plastic bag around the area to be examined or by using collapsible fuming tents or chambers (Figure 9.20). Interiors of vehicles can be isolated and effectively fumed by simply closing the windows. The superglue is placed within the isolation area, and without further effort, the chemical reaction and fuming will begin. Heat and humidity enhance and speed the fuming process, so a light (e.g., a work light) or coffee-cup warmer are often employed as a heat source to speed the development of the prints. The actual superglue is applied through a variety of means. Liquid superglue can be placed on a small piece of foil (e.g., a metallic muffin wrapper or the cut-out top of a soda can), or the technician can use commercial superglue packs. These packs are opened when needed and simply placed inside the isolation area. Superglue packs reduce the problems of handling or spilling liquid glue. When dealing with large areas, fuming guns are also available, which employ an internal heat source and superglue cartridges.

A critical consideration in superglue fuming is not to overfume the latent print. Temperature, humidity, the amount of glue used, as well as the ability to isolate the area

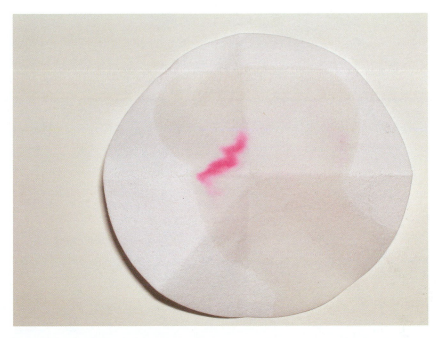

Figure 10.19 Phenolphthalein results in a pink color response in the presence of blood. This photograph demonstrates a positive presumptive test. It must be followed by a verification of DNA or human blood at the crime lab.

Forensic suppliers provide both the phenolphthalein and leucomalachite tests as disposable single-test individual kits. These kits are just as effective as the solution stocks and require the technician to sample the stain and then break a series of self-contained glass vials in the order indicated. A positive test results in the appropriate color reaction. The decision to use either the self-contained tests or stock solutions is generally a matter of convenience and whether a supporting lab is available to order and resupply the stock solutions.

As well as trying to verify the presence of blood, the technician may need to enhance both latent and patent bloodstains present in the scene. Patent bloodstains, those visible to the eye, may be difficult to discern as a result of a lack of contrast in the background substrate. Latent blood may exist in the scene for any number of reasons; these include light smearing of bloody objects or clean-up attempts by suspects. The primary methods for enhancing latent or slightly visible bloodstain are based on the use of luminol, fluorescein, amido-black, and leuco-crystal violet (LCV).

These reagents are available from forensic suppliers in kit form, eliminating the difficulty in locating and mixing the solutions in bulk. Similar to the presumptive tests, when applied to a surface, luminol reacts in the presence of heme by producing a chemiluminescence that has a blue–green coloration. As an oxidation reaction, luminol reacts to a number of items and products found in any household. These include certain metals, vegetable peroxidase, and cleaning chemicals such as bleach. Amido-black and LCV are both protein stains, reacting to proteins present in the blood.

Luminol Enhancement of Latent Bloodstains

The luminol solution is a combination of distilled water, luminol (3-aminophthalhydrazide), sodium perborate, and sodium carbonate. When prepared from bulk, the respec-

Figure 10.20 A positive response of luminol in the presence of latent blood. The color reaction is blue–green, develops gradually, and will remain active for several minutes. In this instance, there was a latent blood source wiped against this clothing. Luminol reactions must be photographed in the dark.

tive ratio for the mixture is 100 ml of distilled water, 0.1 g of luminol, 0.7 g of sodium perborate, and 0.5 g of sodium carbonate. Using commercially prepared kits is the simplest and most effective method for the crime scene technician, eliminating the need to procure, then mix, and store the chemicals. In kit form, two dry chemical mixtures are added to approximately 8 oz of water. The solution is mixed thoroughly and then strained through filter paper to create the final working solution. Filtering is necessary to remove undissolved particles that can clog the spray head. Once sprayed onto the suspected area, a blue–green chemiluminescence reaction occurs (Figure 10.20). This color reaction can only be observed by darkening the area and removing any ambient light.

Luminol reacts to any number of substances with a false positive reaction. Bathrooms routinely present a possibility for a false positive result. This includes both sinks and toilets. Figure 10.21 is a photograph of a sink, cleaned with a typical bathroom product prior to the introduction of luminol. There is a distinct color response. Toilets often respond as well, particularly if they contain a bowl deodorizer, such as those that are deposited in the water reservoir. False-positive color reactions present distinct differences from a positive color reaction. These differences are manifest in three areas: color, duration, and intensity. A positive color reaction for blood is typically a blue–green color. In terms of intensity and duration, a positive response to blood will initiate in a matter of several seconds after application and remain active for several minutes. A typical false positive response to cleaning solutions (e.g., bleach) is an immediate and intense reaction (almost a flash of

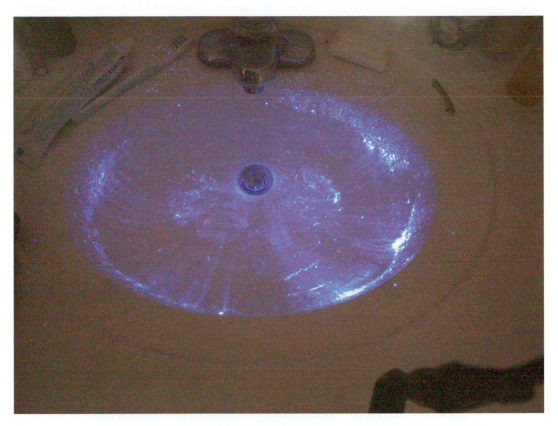

Figure 10.21 A luminol response in a sink. This is not a positive response to blood, but a reaction to a bleach-based cleaning product. The color is lime green to white; it developed instantly, and such reactions often lead to the observation of a number of small flashes (which cannot be photographed). These responses are often misrepresented as a positive response.

light) that dies out quickly. The initial color response in these circumstances is often a light green to white, rather than a blue–green. Toilets, on the other hand, often present a long-duration blue–violet color response.

Luminol reactions are somewhat difficult to photograph, because they require a darkened area. As with many of the techniques discussed in this book, photographing luminol reactions should be practiced prior to attempting it in an actual crime scene. When using a standard film camera (SLR or large-format camera), the technician should begin with an extended shutter duration of up to 3 to 5 min. To eliminate camera motion, the camera must be mounted on a tripod and shutter held open with a lock-down shutter-release cable. Toward the end of the exposure and prior to closing the shutter, the technician should direct a small flashlight onto surrounding surfaces in both a bounce-lighting and paint-with-light effect. This effort should be brief and not directed at the area where the primary color reaction was noted. The beam of the flashlight is bounced or deflected off the ceiling or walls near the luminol reaction. This allows both the color reaction and the surrounding scene details to be captured on film. When using a digital camera (one with a bulb setting), exposure durations of 20 sec to 1 min are usually adequate. Digital cameras do not require absolute darkness while taking the picture and significantly reduce the necessity of using paint-with-light techniques.

Fluorescein Enhancement of Latent Bloodstains

Fluorescein also reacts to the heme in blood, but the response is observed only under an alternative light source (ALS). In the presence of blood, the solution will fluoresce green–blue when viewed with an ALS set between 455 and 485 nm. The most effective barrier filter is a yellow filter, although an orange filter will work as well.

The fluorescein solution is a combination of distilled water, sodium hydroxide, fluorescein, and zinc. It too is available in commercial kits or can be bought in bulk and mixed as needed. To prepare the solution, the technician combines and vigorously mixes 25 ml of distilled water with 0.25 g of fluorescein and 0.5 g of zinc. The mixture will produce a gray solution. This solution is allowed to settle for 15 min, ultimately leaving a light-green-colored, clear solution at the top. The technician draws this clear solution off with a pipette for dilution in distilled water. This diluted solution is the working stock. The mixing ratio of the working stock varies, but a 1:100 ratio is a good starting point.

The working solution is sprayed onto the suspect area; this is followed by a light misting of 3% hydrogen peroxide over the same area. The area is then viewed with illumination from an ALS at a wavelength between 455 and 485 nm and using a yellow barrier filter. The reaction can be photographed using a barrier filter as well (Figure 10.22).

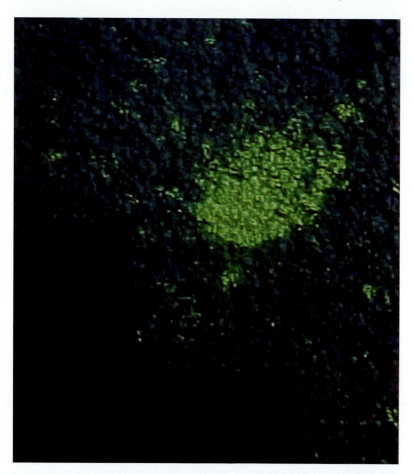

Figure 10.22 A pattern transfer in latent blood on a carpet as viewed with fluorescein. The crime scene technician must observe and photograph the fluorescein reaction with an alternative light source (ALS) set between 455 and 485 nm and a yellow barrier filter.

The spraying mechanisms used for either luminol or fluorescein include: clean household bottle sprayers, commercial chemical sprayers, and air-brush sprayers. In choosing a sprayer, the only true consideration is volume and quality of the spray. The finer the spray produced, the more effective is the reaction. A fine spray is far more important when using fluorescein, but a poor sprayer will also adversely affect luminol. Cheap bottle sprayers often do not make the best application method, particularly when directed to vertical surfaces. The heavy spray results in runs that alter and mar the area being enhanced. When using fluorescein, a thickening agent (Ketrol) can be dissolved with the working solution to prevent flows and dripping on vertical surfaces. The thickener is added slowly to the working solution before being sprayed on the surface.

Amido-Black Enhancement of Latent Bloodstains

Protein-stain-enhancement techniques are functional crime scene techniques as well. These include water-based amido-black and leuco-crystal violet. Water-based amido should only be used on static surfaces in the crime scene and not on evidence items. Water-based techniques will not fix the blood and can interfere with subsequent analysis. Obviously, any surface being enhanced should be sampled for serology/DNA prior to application of the enhancement technique. Specific areas that react to the chemical enhancement can subsequently be sampled as well, providing both pre- and post-samples for serology and DNA analysis. Both of the protein techniques are available in kit form for ease of mixing and storage. These techniques are particularly effective for developing bloody footwear marks on a variety of scene surfaces, including floors and carpet.

Water-based amido-black is a solution mixed and sprayed onto a surface. The ingredients are 500 ml of distilled water, 20 g of 5-sulfosalicyclic acid, 3 g of amido-black, 3 g of sodium carbonate, 50 ml of formic acid, 50 ml of glacial acetic acid, and 12.5 ml of Kodak Photo Flo 600 solution. This solution is diluted in one liter of distilled water. Although ready for use once it is mixed, the solution works best if prepared several days in advance. The diluted working solution is sprayed onto a surface. The reaction takes between 30 sec and 3 min. If necessary, the area can be rinsed with tap water.[1] Amido-black results in an enhancement that is blue–black in color (Figure 10.23).

Bullet Trajectory Analysis

Given our society's infatuation with firearms, it is not surprising that a significant number of violent crime scenes involve guns. As a result, understanding ballistic evidence becomes significant not only for the purpose of properly processing the scene, but also in analyzing and understanding the scene. At every shooting scene, the technician seeks a variety of different types of ballistic evidence that may help to define where, in what order, and under what circumstances a given firearm was utilized.

To understand all that ballistics evidence can define, the technician must consider three separate areas, and the resulting information from each must be incorporated into the ballistic analysis. Ballistics is broken down into three areas of study:

1. Internal or interior ballistics
2. Terminal ballistics
3. External or exterior ballistics

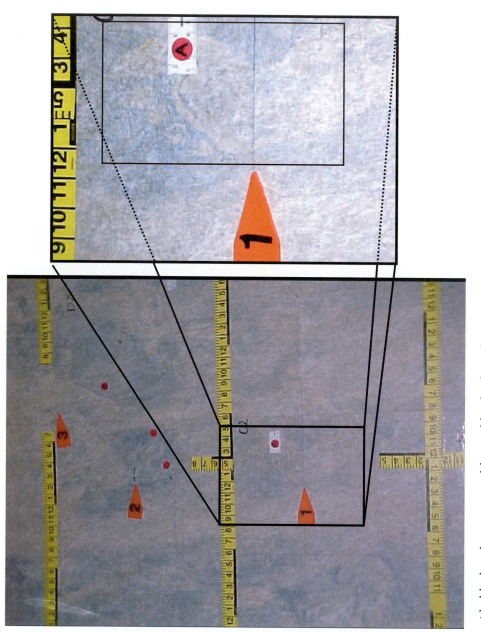

Figure 10.23 Amido-black enhancement of latent blood. The subject mopped this floor clean following a multiple murder. This resulted in smearing latent blood across the entire surface. While it was still wet, the subject walked barefoot on the surface. This resulted in a negative mark (an area lacking blood). In most instances, the amido-black enhancement results in a positive mark, where the mark itself is blue.

By combining information from each area of ballistics, it may be possible to limit the position(s) of victims or perpetrators at the moment that a given firearm was discharged. Each area of study is accomplished by a different group of individuals, but ultimately all of the information must be consolidated in order to make sense of it. These groups include:

- *Forensic firearms examiners* are the people who deal with internal ballistics. As explained in Chapter 2, this is the study and examination of the firearm itself, which also includes ejection patterns, gunshot residue deposition, and other related aspects. Although most firearms examiners are trained and capable of performing external ballistics, few in practice have the opportunity to visit crime scenes as a result of workload.
- *Crime scene technicians* are the group usually responsible for conducting external ballistics. This area of ballistics considers the path and trajectory of the bullet after leaving the weapon to its final impact. External ballistics is based primarily on evaluation of bullet defects in the scene.
- *Forensic pathologists* deal with terminal ballistics. This is the consideration of the effect of the bullet on a human target and includes defining the path of the bullet through the victim.

Internal Ballistics

Forensic firearm examinations entail significant issues. When presented with a weapon, the examiner first considers the condition and functionality of the weapon in question. Next, the examiner looks at a variety of class and individual marks that allow association and identification of bullets, casings, and weapons to one another. Beyond identifying weapons and comparing bullets and casings to weapons, there are three additional areas of ballistics the forensic firearm examiner considers that may assist in reconstructing the shooting incident.

The first is the evaluation of ejection patterns. For the most part, common semiautomatic and automatic weapons encountered in criminal investigations eject right and slightly backward. But the specific pattern of ejection created by a given weapon may be of interest, particularly when considering the location of a cluster of casings in the scene. Ejection-pattern studies call for repetitive firing of the weapon from a known position and consideration of where the casings fall. Individual casing position in the crime scene, however, is a matter of a number of variables. A single casing's position does little to define the position of a weapon when fired. At best, it may support or refute a particular position and nothing more.

The second area of study by the firearm examiner is the evaluation of both gunshot residue patterns and shotgun shot patterns. By considering the location and size of either type of pattern, whether it is on skin, cloth, or some other target surface in the scene, the examiner can often make a range-to-target determination. These conclusions usually require the specific weapon and ammunition used in the event, from which the examiner will conduct a number of test firings at known distances. The examiner then compares the known-distance patterns to the questioned pattern from the scene or victim.

A third area of consideration is the examination of bullets and bullet fragments for trace evidence and damage. This visual examination may provide specific information regarding what items a bullet or bullet fragment came in contact with along its trajectory.

The firearms examiner looks for evidence of three types of characteristics on the bullet or bullet fragment:

1. Layering of trace evidence, indicative of sequence of targets struck
2. Damage to the projectile, indicative of the type of target the bullet struck
3. Deformation of the projectile, indicative of the angle of impact[2]

Terminal Ballistics

The forensic pathologist considers the effect of projectiles on the body and will provide valuable information that may assist in limiting the position of the victim at the time of wounding. The pathologist describes all injuries, including bullet wounds, in the "evidence of injury" section of the autopsy report.

An important aspect that the pathologist will address when describing bullet wounds is the range of the wound. This description defines the distance from the muzzle to the wound at the time of firing. The pathologist determines this based on the characteristics present in the wound, including burning in or around the wound, soot deposits, and the presence of stippling. Stippling or tattooing is the embedding of unburned and partially burned gunpowder residues in the skin. Based upon the examination, the typical categories of muzzle ranges the pathologist will describe are:

- *Close contact or hard contact:* the muzzle is in direct contact with the skin or pressed into the skin.
- *Loose contact:* the muzzle is in extremely close proximity to the skin, but at the moment of firing, a gap is created between the two.
- *Near contact:* the muzzle is not more than 5 in. from the skin.
- *Intermediate range:* the muzzle is between 5 and 40 in. Intermediate-range gunshot wounds are deduced from the presence of stippling around the wound. Different types of powders travel and embed at different distances, resulting in an ability to define the wound as intermediate.
- *Indeterminate range:* this determination means that no conclusion can be drawn on muzzle distance. This determination is found in situations where there are no markings except for the bullet defect. In the past, many pathologists would define this wound as "distant," suggesting a distance in excess of 40 in. Most pathologists now use *indeterminate* to describe distant wounds, simply because there is always a possibility that a secondary target, unknown to the pathologist or investigator, that may have taken the flash, soot, and stippling effects.

Another critical consideration the pathologist will address is whether a defect is an entrance or exit wound. A projectile may enter the body and not exit (creating a penetrating wound), enter the body and exit (creating a perforating wound), graze the body or travel parallel to its surface (creating a grazing wound or tangential wound), or enter and exit the body a number of times. As a result, there may be any number of bullet defects. Based on the characteristics of each defect, the pathologist can define a generalized description of the path of fire (e.g., front to back, left to right). In the instance of multiple wounds from a single bullet, such information will often define a very specific position of the victim's body at the moment of that wounding.

When describing a wound path, the pathologist typically defines what organs or structures the projectile passed through and then states its generalized course through the body (e.g., left to right, front to back, and slightly downward). In the latter description, what the pathologist describes is the path in terms of a standard anatomical standing position. Such descriptions do not, in and of themselves, define the orientation of the shooter to the victim in the scene, since either individual can bend, twist, or rotate on various anatomical axes at the time of the shot.

External Ballistics

External ballistics considers the trajectory of the bullet after leaving the weapon. The information derived is dependent upon the scene and the targets involved. If a bullet strikes various targets within a scene, the evidence left by those strikes can be informative. The location of these items, the shape of the resulting defect, and the interrelationships of this evidence may allow for some level of understanding as to where the weapon was fired from and where the victim was at the time of the firing.

In the shooting scene, the technician may be presented with any number of defects. Some result from penetrations or perforations of walls, doors, or other structures; some result from deflections or tangential shots in which the bullet strikes a surface and glances off. In addition to actual bullet defects, there may be defects that mimic or appear to be related to bullet impacts. In circumstances involving penetrating or perforating impacts, visible bullet fragments and/or complete bullets will often verify that the defect is a bullet impact. When dealing with defects associated with glancing or tangential impacts, however, it is unlikely that visible fragments will be present to aid in this verification. In either circumstance, chemical tests can aid in verifying the defect as a bullet impact.

Bullet Defect Verification

Over time, most technicians will observe and evaluate a number of bullet defects, including glancing impacts. This visual evaluation will leave the technician with some level of confidence that a defect is associated with a bullet and not some other action. Figure 10.24 shows a bullet defect. To increase this confidence and to deal with defects for which the technician has no confidence, chemical tests are available to help verify the presence of copper and lead, the two primary components of bullets. Lead is deposited on scene surfaces from two distinct actions. The first is from friction of the bullet with a target surface, resulting in the deposit of metallic lead. A second source of lead is ionized lead, associated with the gaseous discharge of the primer materials. This deposit may occur as a result of a muzzle in close proximity to a scene surface.[3] These gunshot residues are examined at a crime lab using the scanning electron microscope (SEM). The presence of metallic lead in a suspected defect is evaluated on scene using the sodium rhodizonate test.

To conduct the test, the technician requires three working solutions. The first is a 10 to 15% solution of glacial acetic acid. Using a piece of filter paper at least twice the size of the evident defect, the technician moistens the paper with the acetic acid. The paper is then pressed against the suspect defect. If metallic lead is present in the defect, the solution will cause a transfer of lead acetate onto the filter paper, with no evident visual change. The filter paper is then sprayed with a working solution of sodium rhodizonate. The working solution is prepared by adding approximately 4 g to 100 ml of water. The ratio of water to sodium rhodizonate is not critical; while on scene, the technician can simply

Figure 10.24   A bullet defect. Typical defects have regular margins that are circular to elliptical in shape. Often, a small abrasion ring is evident on the margin of the defect. With experience, most bullet defects are evident based on visual reference alone.

add a small amount of sodium rhodizonate to the water until the solution is similar in appearance to a strong tea.[4] This solution is then sprayed onto the filter paper. In the presence of metallic lead, the filter paper treated with sodium rhodizonate will immediately turn a bright scarlet color. If available, a final confirmatory test can be accomplished by spraying the filter paper with a 5% solution of hydrochloric acid (HCl). This will result in the previous scarlet color turning blue–violet.

Copper is deposited in the scene defect as a result of friction from the impact of jacketed or semijacketed bullets. The chemical test using dithio oximide (DTO) will verify the presence of metallic copper. The metallic copper test uses a base solution of 10% ammonia on the filter paper, which is applied to the defect. This results in a transfer of copper to the paper. The paper is then treated by spraying a solution of DTO onto the suspect area. As with the lead test, a positive test is evident in a color reaction (green).

Simple and effective tests for either copper or lead are available. These commercially available tests are named Plumbtesmo (the lead test) and Cuperotesmo (the copper test).[5] Both tests come as small pretreated filter papers that are moistened with distilled water and then pressed against the defect. Each gives a color positive reaction (reddish violet) in the presence of their respective metal. The only limiting factor of the commercially prepared tests is the size of the filter paper. The precut papers are usually too small to capture all of the lead or copper wipe/splash surrounding the defect.

Metal wipe and splash occur from the friction of the bullet in contact with the surface. This surrounding evidence will often aid in understanding the direction of travel as the bullet struck the target. Using either rhodizonate or the DTO test, the filter paper is cut to extend out from the defect at least an inch or two in either direction. If present, these small splashes of molten lead or copper will be visualized by the chemical process. The splashes will show evident directionality, radiating away from the defect in the direction the bullet was traveling.

Defining the Bullet Impact Angle Based on Defect Shape

Having examined a defect by visual means and validated a defect through either the presence of a bullet, bullet fragments, or by means of a copper or lead test, the technician is left to consider in what direction and at what angle the bullet struck the target. There is an empirical relationship between the shape of the bullet defect and the angle of the bullet's impact into the target. This relationship was first observed and validated in terms of blood droplets impacting targets,[6] but the relationship is based on the nature of the defect caused when an object with a circular cross section (an object that is either cylindrical or spherical) strikes a target. Bullets, unless tumbling or deformed by prior impacts, present this circular cross section.

Bullet defects resulting from nontumbling impacts will tend to be circular to elliptical in shape. Just as in the case of bloodstain shapes, a defect that presents a circular shape indicates an impact at close to 90 degrees to the target plane. As the angle of impact becomes more tangential, this shape changes to an ellipse. By examining the ellipse and measuring the long and short axes of the defect, the resulting measurements can be applied to the same trigonometric formula that was used to define a bloodstain's angle of impact. This formula is:

$$\text{Minor axis divided by the major axis} = N$$

The inverse SIN of N is equal to the approximate impact angle.

Unlike drops of blood, bullet defects do not always present clean, precise margins. When striking metal or other substrates, the leading edge of the defect will often present a clean margin, while the far edge will present a rough appearance. Lacking a complete ellipse to measure, the technician can use a method of ellipse matching to increase the accuracy of defining the impact angle. Ellipse matching was first applied to bloodstain pattern analysis. Charlie Green of the Colorado Springs Police Department suggested the technique as early as 1989, and it was later utilized by Dr. Alfred Carter as the underlying method employed in his bloodstain pattern software, Backtrack Images.[7] This technique was subsequently directed to evaluating bullet impacts by the Royal Canadian Mounted Police with success. Studies to date indicate that it increases the accuracy of the bullet defect evaluation.[8] Simply put, the technician completes the ellipse indicated by the leading edge of the impact and then uses this visualized ellipse in determining the length of the major and minor axes. The technique is illustrated in Figure 10.25.

To aid in understanding these relationships, refer back to Figure 10.3 through Figure 10.5. A relationship is evident between the defect and a right triangle created by the bullet path and the target. By analogy, the major axis of the defect is the same as the hypotenuse of the right triangle, and the minor axis is the same as the side opposite. Using the trigonometric relationships evident in all right triangles, the side opposite divided by the hypotenuse is equal to the inverse sine of the internal angle (the angle of impact into the target). As with bloodstains, all that is required of the technician is the ability to measure the length and width of the defect and employ a scientific calculator. With practice, this technique is quickly applied at the scene.

Using this method, the computed angles are sufficiently accurate to provide important information regarding the event, but they do not provide a precise angle of impact. In some instances, they may be of limited value, depending upon the surface on which they

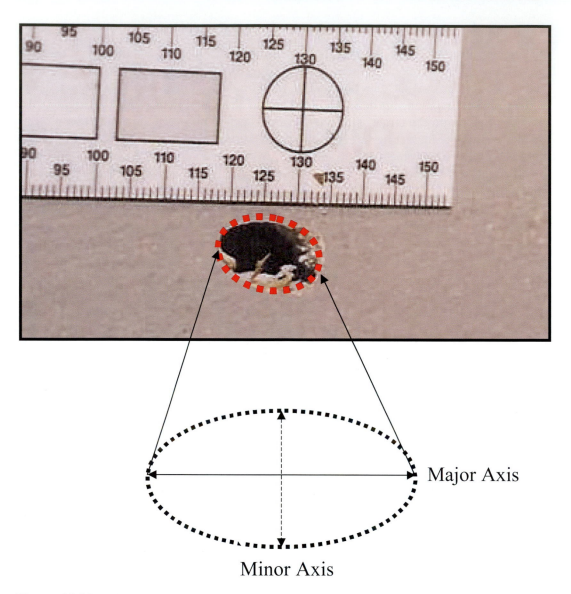

Figure 10.25 The same relationship exists between the bullet defect and its impact angle as was evident in the shape of a bloodstain. Bullet defects, however, do not always produce an easily measured defect. The technique of overlaying an ellipse and matching it to the well-formed sections of the defect was developed by the RCMP to assist in identifying the angle of impact. Once matched, the technician measures the ellipse rather than the defect.

are found or the characteristics of the defect's margins. This is particularly true when considering defects in human skin. Maloney et al. found that computed impact angles of defects in a substrate similar to the human body had deviations as high as ±20 degrees.[9]

Direction of Fire

The next significant concern for the technician is to recognize in which direction the bullet was traveling. The technician starts with morphology of the bullet hole. What is the shape of the defect? What characteristics are evident? As with entry and exit wounds in humans,

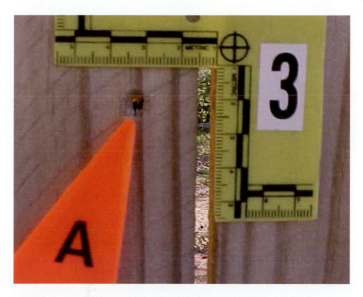

Figure 10.26   An entry defect in soft pine. The margins are regular and demonstrate a small circumferential abrasion ring as well as a light gray wipe mark. Depending on the substrate involved, the size of the defect may or may not match the diameter of the bullet.

bullet defects in other substrates share certain basic characteristics. Entry defects tend to present an appearance of a cleanly punched hole. Additionally, they often demonstrate bullet wipe as well as an inward beveled circumferential ring around the defect. Figure 10.26 is an entry defect in soft pine. The defect presents a regularly shaped margin with a slightly noticeable beveled edge all around the lip of the defect. Exit defects, on the other hand, tend to be more irregular. They may demonstrate a coning effect on the exit side or demonstrate material that is pushed away from the defect. Figure 10.27 is the associated exit for the entry hole shown in Figure 10.26. Note the more irregular shape of the defect,

Figure 10.27   The corresponding exit bullet defect from Figure 10.26. The margin is irregular, and there is evidence of material that was pushed out of the defect.

Figure 10.28 Bullet defects in windshield glass present a more distinct problem for locating the entry and exit. Both sides will produce a coning effect. These two exterior-side defects in a windshield are quite similar to the interior side defects shown in Figure 10.29. Note the abrupt edge of the cone around the inner white section of the defect.

the cone of wood that was punched out, and the slight evidence of wood material pushed away from the fence.

Bullet impacts into windshields with safety glass present even more difficulty. Modern windshields are typically two individual pieces of glass fused together with a plastic laminate between them. Entry and exit defects will present a similar appearance. Figure 10.28 is the exterior surface of a windshield with three entry bullet defects. Figure 10.29 shows the interior surface and the exit defects of impacts 2 and 3. On first examination, both sides of the defect demonstrate what appears to be a coning effect. By touch and visual examination, the entry side of windshield glass will demonstrate an abrupt edge, while the exit side will have a sloping edge (a cone). Additionally, the displacement of glass and the projectile through the plastic laminate will leave distinct evidence of the direction of travel. Figure 10.30 is a close-up view of the windshield and shows the laminate displaced upward in the photo (inward), verifying the direction of travel as from outside the car to the interior. In plate-glass windows, the coning effect in the exit side of the defect will be far more distinct. The exit side of the defect will have an evident sloping edge that is difficult to mistake (Figure 10.31).

Use of Trajectory Rods and Lasers to Demonstrate Bullet Flight Paths

Given a penetrating or perforating bullet defect in the scene, one effective method of establishing the trajectory of the bullet is through the use of trajectory rods. These rods can be self-manufactured or purchased in kits. Commercial kits are available from a variety of

Figure 10.29   Interior-side bullet defects. The cone surrounding the white inner section is more distinct and, if felt, a slope will be evident. This is different from the abrupt edge in Figure 10.28.

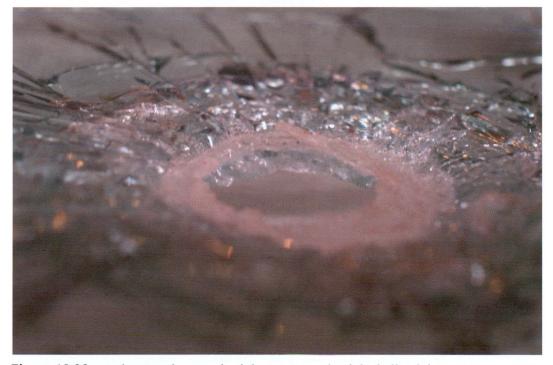

Figure 10.30   A close-up photograph of the interior side of the bullet defects in Figure 10.28 and Figure 10.29. Note the upward beveling of the plastic laminate between the two layers of glass. Small, but observable characteristics such as this may assist the crime scene technician in verifying entry side from exit.

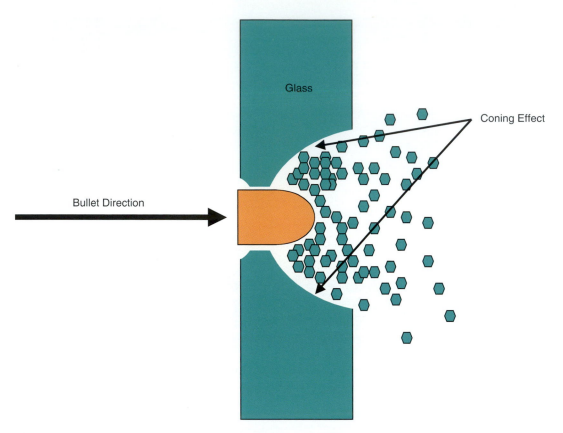

Figure 10.31 The coning effect on the exit side of plate glass is always quite evident. It results from the bullet crushing and forcing the particles out on the far side of the glass.

forensic suppliers and tend to be the best method, as they include hole-centering guides and use nonwarping metal rods. Self-manufactured trajectory kits often involve the use of wooden dowels. Although wooden dowels will certainly function in a pinch, the dowels often have minor warps that will throw off any trajectory determination. Long-term storage of these dowels will almost certainly lead to warping. Additionally, the failure to employ a centering guide, as will be described, will reduce the accuracy of the trajectory determination.

Typical contents of the trajectory kit include: metal trajectory rods, hole-centering guides, a metal mounting plate used to attach the rods to a tripod, an angle finder, and a trajectory laser, as seen in Figure 10.32. Trajectory rods are available in two sizes, a standard size that is adequate for defects caused by calibers greater than .32 and a smaller diameter rod for defects caused by smaller projectiles such as a .22-caliber bullet. These smaller rods require more caution in use, as their small diameter makes them prone to accidental warping. A rigid rod holder is important for protecting the rods both in storage and during transit.

When presented with a perforating or deeply penetrating defect in walls, doors, furniture, and other objects, the technician carefully inserts a rod into the defect, being sure not to force the rod in any way. Note that in Figure 10.33, without a centering guide the trajectory rod slips to the bottom of the defect. On the opposite side of the wall, the rod will tend to lay against the upper edge of the defect as it balances itself on its center of gravity. This raw positioning can affect the ultimate angle of the rod by as much as 5 to 8 degrees. Centering guides eliminate this error. The guide is placed on the rod, with the

Figure 10.32 A trajectory rod kit. Components include the trajectory rods, an angle finder, white plastic centering guides, base plates for mounting trajectory rods on tripods, and trajectory lasers. The technician can evaluate and demonstrate trajectories over a short distance with the rods. The laser allows evaluation of trajectories extended out to distant points.

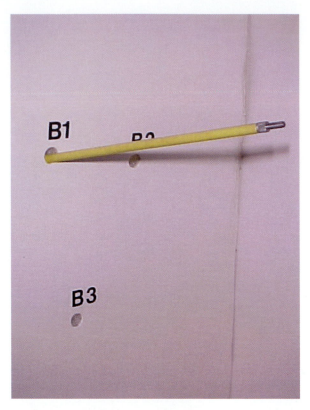

Figure 10.33 Insertion of a trajectory rod in a bullet defect before the addition of a centering guide. The rod is inserted in or through the defect. Rods without a guide will not center properly in the hole. This can throw off the resulting trajectory by several degrees.

narrow end facing the defect. It is then guided into the defect without forcing it. The technician feeds a small rubber grommet onto the rod to hold the centering guide in place, eliminating any subsequent slipping of the guide on the rod. If the hole perforates the surface (e.g., in the case of walls or doors), a second centering guide is fed onto the rod as it extends out of the far side of the wall, as seen in Figure 10.34. The two centering guides ensure that the rod lays parallel with the defect. Once in place, the angle is measured with the angle finder, as seen in Figure 10.35.

In many instances, the rod will provide ample visualization of the basic angle and direction of the trajectory, but the use of a laser will more effectively define the trajectory in relationship to the overall scene. This is particularly true if the bullet traveled a significant distance before impacting the surface. The trajectory laser is attached to the trajectory rod as shown in Figure 10.36. The laser beam itself is not evident unless it strikes a surface. In daylight, the use of a small white placard is helpful in tracking the path of the laser from the defect through the scene and for photographing that path (Figure 10.37). At night or in darkness, photographic fog is also available, but the fog can be difficult to work with, as any air current will diffuse the fog cloud. Even with barriers or in a calm exterior scene, it can be difficult to create a fog of sufficient density to photograph the entire path. The most effective technique is to place the camera on the bulb setting (a 1-min bulb duration is usually sufficient) and fog the laser beam as the camera shutter remains open (Figure 10.38). In a darkened or even slightly darkened interior scene, fog is easier to work with.

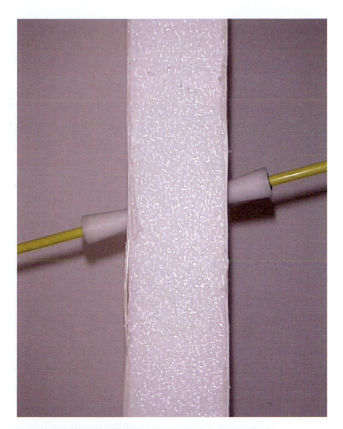

Figure 10.34 A trajectory rod inserted properly in a perforating defect with centering guides. The guides should be used in cases involving both penetrating and perforating defects.

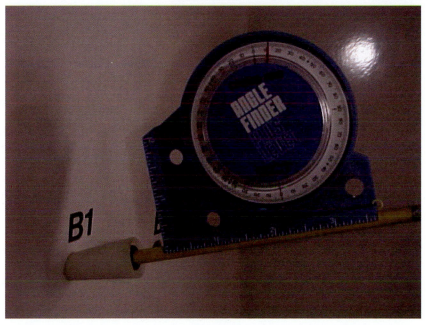

Figure 10.35 An angle finder allows the technician to read the impact angle. This is a 12-degree downward angle relative to the ground plane. The angle is 78 degrees if evaluated relative to the target surface (e.g., the wall). When describing impact angles of defects, it is important to clearly differentiate what relationship the angle describes.

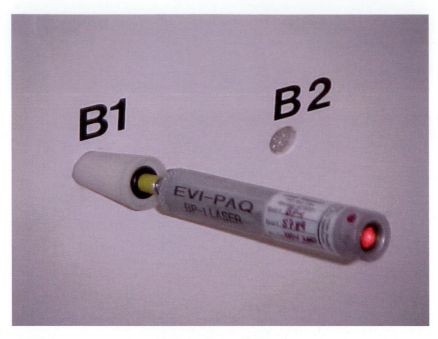

Figure 10.36   A trajectory laser attached to a trajectory rod. This allows the trajectory to be extended out to distant surfaces or to show relationships between corresponding defects.

Figure 10.37   A small white placard is helpful when following the laser line in a scene. Unless the laser strikes a surface it cannot be seen. The technician centers the laser dot on the placard and then, by slowly moving the placard, follows the laser along the flight path. This is particularly effective in bright outdoor scenes.

Figure 10.38 Laser fog is a great way to demonstrate a laser trajectory. The fog is commercially available. When sprayed into the scene, the particles remain airborne and the laser reflects off them. Laser fog is difficult to work with when there are active air currents, such as in exterior scenes. This photograph was taken on the bulb setting (1 min), during which the technician stepped into the frame and sprayed both ends of the laser line. In an interior scene, the fog will usually remain long enough to photograph without the need for respraying.

By setting the camera on bulb (using a shutter exposure between 8 sec and 1 min), both the laser beam and sufficient scene detail can be captured.

Given a penetrating defect, but no deep channel to feed a trajectory rod into (e.g., often seen in foam-core doors), the rod and centering guide are placed in the entry defect as deeply as possible. The trajectory rod itself is supported by a tripod, as illustrated in Figure 10.39. Tripod support of the rod also works when dealing with a defect that is obliterated or removed for some reason. This method demands a photograph of the defect prior to it having been damaged. The technician must establish the defect's original size and orientation in the scene and must also have information that accurately places it back into the scene at the appropriate height and distance from known landmarks. At the scene, a trajectory rod is attached to a tripod. The trajectory rod is then positioned with the tip at the appropriate height on the surface where the defect was originally found. Keeping the tip in place, the tripod is adjusted accordingly by the technician so that the impact angle and directional angle indicated by the photograph match the rod's position.

There are several concerns when using trajectory kits and evaluating trajectories. These include considering the distance between the weapon and the impact, ensuring that the bullet is not tumbling, and objectively demonstrating the evident trajectory. In terms of distance traveled, a bullet fired from a short-barrel weapon will follow a straight-line path for some distance before any evident parabolic arc occurs as a result of air

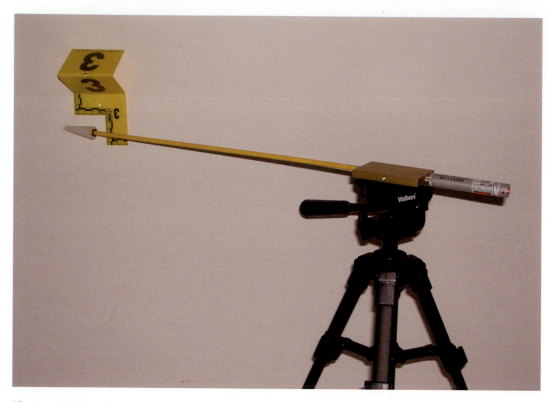

Figure 10.39 The trajectory kit can be used even when there is no deep defect to insert the rod into. The rods are attached to a tripod using the mounting plate, and the tripod and rod are brought into alignment at the defect. This method is effective for evaluating possible trajectories from photos and sketches.

resistance and gravity. If evaluating bullet paths less than 30 m, the assumption that the bullet is traveling in a straight line path is acceptable. Beyond that distance, it is best to contact a forensic firearms examiner for advice as to the nature of any given weapon and bullet combination. In shots involving greater distance, all is not lost. Software programs such as *External Ballistics 4.0* provide a mechanism for evaluating the possible trajectories presented by such shots (Figure 10.40). The limitation of these software programs is that they require significant data up front, information that may not be available based upon the scene or investigation.

The technician should always give consideration to the possibility of intermediate impacts of the bullet on targets prior to their terminus impact. If a bullet strikes an intermediate target and begins to tumble, straight-line flight paths may not be a valid assumption. Tumbling bullets, however, create irregular defects that are easily recognized in the scene.

When using methods other than a rod or laser to demonstrate a flight path, the technician should use caution. For example, stretching string along the flight path can demonstrate the path to some extent. The problem with this method is that it is always difficult to align the string to the angle indicated by the defect. Minor errors in alignment over any distance will lead to significant variation from the actual flight path. If a significant distance is involved in the flight path, it is difficult if not impossible to stretch the string tightly enough to eliminate sag across its entire length. Both of these errors and their

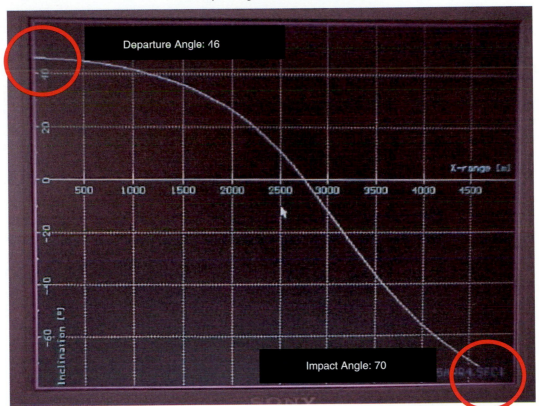

Figure 10.40 In circumstances involving extended trajectories where the bullet is clearly following a parabolic flight path, software programs can to some extent assist in defining the variables of the trajectory. In this screen capture, the software shows the departure angle and maximum range of a specific round, based on a number of variables and its impact angle.

resulting variation, if present, are enough to make the demonstration of little or no use to the jury. In a worst case, this variation may even invalidate the conclusion indicated by the demonstration.

How accurately does trajectory analysis (in and of itself) define or eliminate possible orientations between a shooter and the target? The answer is highly dependent upon the case circumstances and is also affected by the many limitations discussed in the text. The most likely scenarios include:

- A single penetrating bullet defect in a victim. In this instance, terminal ballistics will define or at least suggest the general path of the bullet. The shape of the defect may suggest or corroborate the impact angle at the point it struck the body. However, lacking any way to functionally place the weapon in the scene — and given the fact that the body can bend, twist, and move to almost any position imaginable — there is no objective method of eliminating the majority of possible orientations between the shooter and victim.
- Multiple bullet-wound defects in the body or clothing caused by a single projectile. In this circumstance, the alignment of the corresponding defects will at least define

the orientation of the associated body parts at the moment of wounding (Figure 10.41). So long as the required orientation is retained, the remainder of the body can still be moved, rolled, and oriented in any number of ways. A circumstance of this nature will help eliminate possibilities, but it may not narrow the field sufficiently to assist the investigator significantly.

- A single bullet defect on a solid substrate without sufficient penetration for inserting a trajectory rod, or cases where there is a tangential shot that leaves an elliptical defect but no penetration. In this instance, calculating the impact angle using the mathematical method will provide a parameter of possible flight paths. Using the ellipse-matching method, the calculated impact angle is likely to be within ±2 to 3 degrees. This circumstance will certainly limit the possible flight path of the bullet.

- A single bullet defect that penetrates or perforates a solid substrate, allowing deep insertion of the trajectory rod. In this instance, the indicated flight path is very accurate, particularly if there is a perforating defect and two centering guides can be employed on the trajectory rod. This circumstance will clearly limit the possible position of the shooter.

- Single or multiple bullet defects (corresponding defects) in solid substrates and an associated perforating or penetrating wound defect to the victim. In this instance, it may be possible to place both the shooter and the victim in a distinct orientation at the moment of wounding.

Trajectory Analysis Documentation

As with bloodstain pattern analysis, the shooting scene requires extra documentation effort on the part of the crime scene technician. Just as small bloodstains will appear quite similar, photographs of bullet defects in similar substrates will be almost indistinguishable from one another. Close-up photography of bullet defects without supporting evidence-establishing shots will result in an inability to reorient the defect to the scene. These scenes demand complete photography as well as detailed crime scene sketches (overhead and elevation views).

When taking photographs of bullet defects, it is imperative that each defect be distinguishable from any other. Numbering the defects is the most effective way to do this, with accompanying evidence-establishing shots that clearly demonstrate where in the scene the defect is. Corresponding defects that perforate doors and other objects can be given an alphanumeric designation (e.g., defect 3A for the entry and defect 3B for the exit). Evidence close-up photographs should include a scale of reference and an annotation as to magnetic north or which direction is up. Such annotation is essential for anyone trying to verify or establish the directional angle of the defect. The methods previously described for photographing impression evidence are essential here as well. The technician must take care to square the film plane of the camera to the surface of the defect and avoid interjecting odd angles. In addition, the technician will find that oblique lighting is often necessary to bring out the three-dimensional detail of these marks. Tangential defects or deflections on surfaces should be photographed with a scale of reference (at least 6 in. of adhesive ruled tape) that is oriented to the long axis of the defect. This aids the viewer in recognizing the directional angle of the impact.[10]

In terms of sketches and notes, the specific location of a defect on any given surface must be recorded. This location should be reported as a complete X, Y, and Z position.

Figure 10.41 When available, information from all three areas of ballistic study must be considered together in order to narrow the possibilities of a given trajectory. Here three corresponding defects in a T-shirt, combined with a known trajectory of the bullet through the body, allow for a specific orientation of the upper arm and body at the moment of the shot. This effectively limits the possibilities, since any attempt to lower or raise the arm or to move it forward would force the three defects out of the alignment indicated by the path of the bullet through the body.

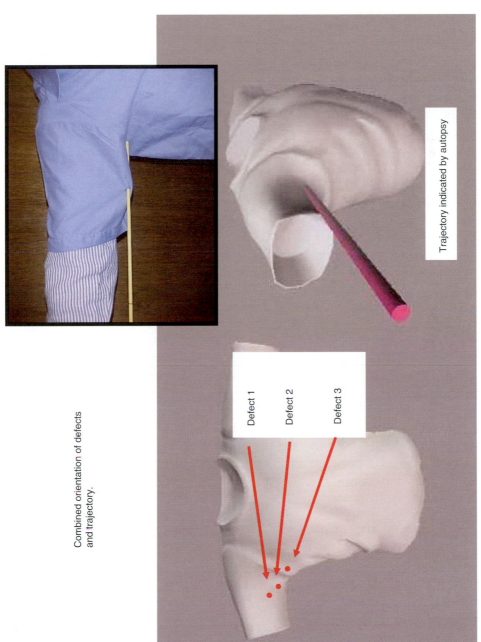

Trajectory indicated by autopsy

Defect 1
Defect 2
Defect 3

Combined orientation of defects and trajectory.

Without this information, it is impossible to conduct a subsequent evaluation of the shooting scene, should this be needed. Sketches should clearly distinguish perforating defects from deflections or penetrations. Terminal defects that hold bullets or fragments should be marked, and the nature of the recovered bullet (complete, fragment, jacket, etc.) should be detailed in the notes. After recovery by the technician, all casings, bullets, and bullet fragments must be uniquely identified by specifically documenting where each was recovered. The technician cannot simply throw these items into a single bag. By doing so, the technician will lose valuable scene context regarding which weapon was being fired from which position.

Summary

Bloodstain pattern analysis is directed at evaluating the bloodstain patterns found in the scene in an effort to categorize them into an established taxonomy. This categorization is based on the nature of the creation event. The technician considers a number of physical characteristics of the stain and patterns, including but not limited to shape, volume, dispersion, and orientation. From this evaluation, the technician can effectively define how the stain was created. The primary categories for bloodstains are passive and dynamic, with a multitude of subcategories. Bloodstain patterns effectively establish what happened in a scene, rather than who. Based on bloodstain pattern analysis, it is possible to determine the nature of the events that occurred in the scene, the general area where those events occurred, and the relative positions of people and objects at discrete moments in time.

After categorizing a stain or pattern, the technician evaluates the pattern and other indications of motion to determine in which direction the individual droplets were traveling at the time of impact. Directionality is defined by the long axis of the individual stain and the presence of scallops, tails, and small satellite spatter. After determining the long axis, the technician determines where the scallops, spines, and satellite spatter are located. The concentration of these characteristics will be found on the far edge of the long axis.

In addition to evaluating directionality, the technician can apply a simple mathematical formula to determine the impact angle of the individual stains. This information, when combined with directionality, will suggest the area of origin of the event. By visual reference alone, the technician can estimate the approximate angle of impact. Long elliptical stains generally indicate an impact angle of 10 to 30 degrees. Bear claw-shaped stains suggest impacts between 40 and 60 degrees. Circular stains suggest impact angles between 70 and 90 degrees.

Even if the technician does not conduct a complete analysis, it is imperative that the technician be able to recognize discrete patterns within the scene. The primary patterns of interest include spatter, arterial or projected patterns, castoff stains, contact pattern transfers, wipes, swipes, flows, drip patterns, and drip trails.

There are a variety of presumptive blood tests that can be used on scene. These include phenolphthalein and leucomalachite green. These tests provide the crime scene technician with a greater level of confidence when presented with an aged bloodstain or stains that do not appear normal. Chemical enhancement of latent blood using luminol and fluorescein allows the technician to visualize latent bloodstain patterns that are either too light to see or have been washed up in some fashion. Luminol requires darkness to view the results, while fluorescein requires an alternative light source to visualize.

Trajectory analysis (ballistics) is based on three different areas of study: internal ballistics (conducted by the forensic firearms examiner), terminal ballistics (conducted by the forensic pathologist), and external ballistics (typically conducted by the crime scene technician). The information provided by all three areas of study must be combined to gain an objective understanding of how and where a weapon may have been fired in the scene.

External ballistics — typically the responsibility of the crime scene technician — is primarily a function of evaluating bullet defects at the scene. The first consideration is to recognize a bullet defect. Defects can penetrate, perforate, or deflect off an object. The resulting defects can appear quite similar or distinctly dissimilar. When presented with a suspect bullet defect (a defect whose origin is unknown), the technician uses chemical tests to identify the presence of lead or copper, the two primary constituents of a projectile.

After verifying the presence of a bullet defect, the technician must examine it for directionality and impact angle. Both indications will suggest or define the probable path of the bullet prior to striking the target. The shape of a bullet defect, much like the shape of a bloodstain, indicates the angle of impact. Trajectory-rod kits allow the technician to demonstrate these flight paths and to identify corresponding defects (defects created in multiple objects by a single bullet).

The information derived from a trajectory analysis is very much dependent upon the number and type of bullet defects available. In instances where there is nothing more than a defect in the victim, the resulting analysis will not significantly limit the possible flight paths or orientations of the shooter and victim. On the other hand, when there are multiple corresponding defects that perforate and penetrate a number of surfaces, the analysis will likely establish and significantly limit the orientation and position of the shooter and victim.

Bloodstain pattern analysis and trajectory analysis both require significant documentation effort for court purposes and for any outside experts who might be called in to assist. Proficiency in these advanced techniques requires study and practice on the part of the crime scene technician. Because both types of evidence are routinely encountered in a variety of crime scenes, the crime scene technician should strive to become proficient at both.

Suggested Reading

Bevel, T. and Gardner, R., *Bloodstain Pattern Analysis: with an Introduction to Crime Scene Reconstruction*, 2nd ed., CRC Press, Boca Raton, FL, 2001.

Garrison, D., *Practical Shooting Scene Investigation*, Universal Publishers/uPublish.com, USA, 2003.

Chapter Questions

1. Describe the basic steps used to conduct a bloodstain pattern analysis.
2. What are the two primary categories of the bloodstain pattern taxonomy, and what distinguishes one from the other?
3. What is the general rule regarding the relationship of a bloodstain's shape and impact angle?
4. What is meant by stain directionality, and how is it determined?
5. How are point of convergence and area of origin used to evaluate a spatter pattern?
6. What are the three key elements considered when viewing and evaluating a luminol reaction?

7. What are the three areas of study that make up ballistics?
8. What are three ways the crime scene technician might verify that a defect is associated to a bullet impact?
9. How effective are angle-of-impact determinations for bullet holes in solid substrates? How effective are they for bullet defects in human skin?
10. Why is effective documentation of both bloodstain patterns and bullet defects so important?

Notes

1. Herzig, W., verbal communication, Sep. 2003.
2. Moran, B., Shooting Incident Reconstruction, presentation to the Association of Crime Scene Reconstruction, Las Vegas, NV, Oct. 2001.
3. Bartsch, M.R. et al., An update on the use of the sodium rhodizonate test for the detection of lead originating from firearms discharges, *J. Forensic Sci.*, 46, 1049, 1996.
4. Jason, A., Was This Caused by a Bullet? Detecting the Presence of Lead, presentation to the Association of Crime Scene Reconstruction, Oklahoma City, OK, Oct. 1997.
5. Cuprotesmo and Plumbtesmo are registered trademark names of the Macherey-Nagel Co., Duren, Germany.
6. Balthazard, V. et al., Etude ges Gouttes de Sang Projecte, paper presented at XXII Congress de Medicine Legale, Paris, France, June 1939.
7. Backtrack Images is a registered trademark name of Forensic Computing of Ottawa, Ottawa, Canada.
8. Barr, D., Impact Angle Determinations, presentation to the Association of Crime Scene Reconstruction, Atlanta, GA, Oct. 2000.
9. Maloney, M. et al., unpublished research, 1999.
10. Garrison, D.H., *Practical Shooting Scene Investigation*, Universal Press, Parkland, FL, p. 25.

Special Scene Considerations $\huge 11$

No matter what level of skill a crime scene technician possesses, there are always scenes — fire scenes, scattered or buried remains, landfill body recoveries — that present special difficulties. Such scenes are typically complex, requiring significant technical and physical resources to manage and evaluate properly. A complete understanding of the complexities involved in each of these scenes is beyond the scope of a single chapter in a book. What this chapter provides is some basic information that may help in preparing the crime scene technician for the rigors and requirements of special scenes.

Fire Scenes

Fire scenes are one of the most complex and difficult scenes to work. The difficulties of the fire scene lie in the conditions found at the scene and the difficulty in objectively evaluating fire signs in an effort to understand fire flow and origin. Scene conditions include the fire damage itself, the resulting creation of unstable structures, the presence of significant debris covering evidence, and the fact that burned surfaces are black and do not reflect light effectively.

The National Fire Protection Association's *Guide for Fire and Explosion Investigations* sums up the process of fire investigation well, stating: "A fire or explosion investigation is a complex endeavor involving both art and science. The compilation of factual data, as well as an analysis of those facts, should be accomplished objectively and truthfully…. With few exceptions, the proper methodology for a fire or explosion investigation is to first establish the origin(s) and then investigate the cause."[1] The NFPA correctly argues that this complex crime scene analysis is properly done through the use of scientific method.

The phrase "origin and cause" drives every fire investigation. Only by identifying and evaluating all fire signs is it possible to understand fire flow. Without an understanding of fire flow, it is often difficult to identify the origin of the fire. With no known origin identified, the ability to establish what caused the fire is difficult as well. Even in the best of circumstances, a fire investigation is often a negative corpus case, in which the investigator must rule out accidental and natural causes for the fire. In order to do this, one must understand what the fire is doing and why. So searching for, locating, and documenting signs of fire flow are critical aspects of fire scene investigation.

On first look, fire scenes are at best chaotic. Not only has the fire damaged the scene, firefighting efforts disturb and destroy evidence as well. As discussed in previous chapters, identifying who may have altered the scene is an important function of the crime scene investigation. In the fire scene, this action is a bit more complex. During fire suppression operations, the firefighters may force entry into buildings, vent areas by breaking out windows, tear down walls, or move objects such as furniture. Subsequent to fire suppression, firefighters then engage in a technique known as "overhaul." During this process, they search for hot spots that might flare up, and if located, they eliminate the hot spot. Overhaul is an extremely destructive process, where walls or ceilings are often torn into and debris moved or removed from the scene. It is imperative that the crime scene technician coordinate with fire authorities to obtain an understanding of how and where the fire was fought and what actions were taken during overhaul. This may help explain anomalies presented by debris in odd positions in the scene. It can also help in locating evidence that may have been thrown from the building or moved within the building. The crime scene investigator should obtain a copy of the fire suppression report prepared by the firefighters for inclusion in the fire investigation report.

A short section in a single chapter is nowhere near the space necessary to effectively teach fire investigation. Detailed discussions of fire science and fire scene investigation are available from a number of sources, including three works listed in the "Suggested Reading" section at the end of this chapter: *Practical Fire and Arson Investigation*, by Redsicker and O'Conner; *Kirk's Fire Investigation*, by DeHaan; and an absolute "must have" reference by the National Fire Protection Association, NFPA 921, *Guide for Fire and Explosion Investigations*. For purposes of this discussion, suffice it to say that a fire is a living, breathing phenomenon. In order to exist, a fire requires heat, fuel, oxygen, and an uninhibited chemical chain reaction between the three. For example, simply placing a burning match on a log is not enough to sustain fire. In its infancy, fire is an endothermic reaction. It requires sustained heat to actually break down the fuel source (the log) into gas and vapors that burn, a process known as pyrolysis. Fuel, heat, and oxygen are present, but the short-lived heat source of the match does not have the ability to break down the mass of the log into its chemical constituents. Fire is achieved only when there is a sustained interaction between the pyrolyzed fuel and the heat and oxygen. Fire becomes exothermic once this uninhibited chain reaction begins, producing self-sustaining heat. Together, these four fire ingredients are known as the fire tetrahedron. The investigator's purpose at the fire scene is to understand this complex relationship and determine how the fire moved through the scene.

As amazingly complex as fire science is, structure fires follow generally predictable behaviors. Fire tends to flow up and outward from a source in a three-dimensional pattern. Fire flow can change direction, however, moving toward an oxygen source or with a fuel source. Upon encountering a horizontal obstruction (e.g., a ceiling), fire will flow laterally across the obstruction. In a confined space such as a room, fire develops in very regular fashion. Initially, a hot gas layer develops at the upper layer of the confined space. Over time, this gas layer will expand downward, marring and charring anything above the hot gas boundary. Linear charring around the entire room will demonstrate just how far the hot gas layer extended down. If the fire is not suppressed, when the temperature in a confined space reaches 1100°F, the phenomenon known as flashover will occur. In flashover, nearly any ignitable surface in the room will begin burning. Thus even items below the hot gas layer and not directly exposed to flame will suddenly ignite and help propagate the fire.

Figure 11.1 An example of a V pattern on the door. Flames will propagate in a three-dimensional pattern, which rises and expands outward. The top right-hand corner of the door was exposed to the flame, scorching and burning the surface. The fire flowed out the door and into the ceiling. V patterns help define fire flow.

Fire Patterns

All of these predictable behaviors of fire leave both blatant and subtle effects in the scene, referred to as fire patterns. Fire patterns show the progress of the fire, demonstrate the nature of the fuels involved, and help to locate and isolate the actual origin of the fire. They are, as the NFPA says, "the visible and measurable physical effects" on the material in the scene.[2] They may manifest themselves in any number of ways, including demarcations on a surface, such as the classic V pattern caused by a flame rising on a wall (Figure 11.1). Fire signs may also present themselves as a surface effect, such as bubbling of paint on a wall, a "clean burn pattern," or the directional melting of glass in a light bulb (Figure 11.2). Fire signs are also evident as damage patterns, where the level of damage present in one area is contrasted with another in an effort to determine which was exposed to the

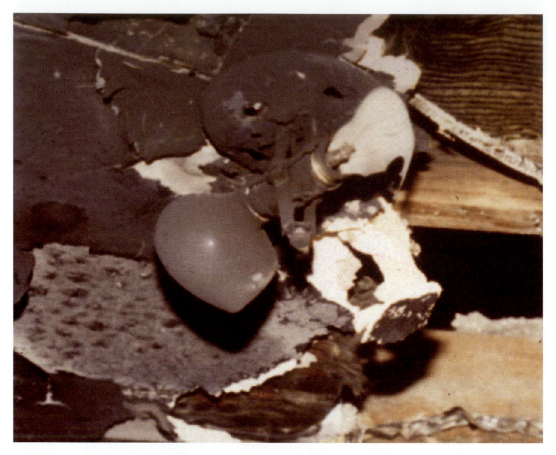

Figure 11.2 This light bulb was exposed to an approaching heat source and melted in a directional fashion. Plastic and glass objects will often melt on the side from where the flames approach, giving a strong indication of fire flow in that area. The heat source in the photo approached from the right lower corner.

fire longer. The most common fire signs found in the fire scene include char patterns, smoke and soot patterns, and damage patterns.

Char patterns usually result from direct flame involvement. This includes deep charring in joists or studs as well as more subtle char from heat convection or radiation that limits itself to the exterior surface of materials (e.g., paints or veneers) in the scene. Char patterns and char depth analysis can often demonstrate the relative time of burn for a surface as well as indicate the direction of the fire movement (Figure 11.3).

Smoke and soot patterns result from the outflow of fire products. These patterns include the smoke associated with the hot-gas-layer pattern, which will be evident on the vertical surfaces in a confined space, or smoke and burn plumes on surfaces indicating where a fire vented itself (Figure 11.4). Smoke and soot patterns help the investigator to recognize the development and flow of the fire. The nature of the soot found deposited in the scene, even the color of smoke and flame during the actual fire, can provide clues regarding the nature of the fuel source burning.

Damage patterns can be evident on a single object or extend across an entire room. As an object is subjected to flame and heat from the fire, the exposed surfaces are damaged. The damage may be charring, melting, or soot deposits. Surfaces on the object that are

Figure 11.3   A hallway exposed to a significant fire. The variations in the depth of char in the supporting wall studs at different points along the hallway allow some interpretation of the relative time these areas were exposed to the flames. The deeper the char depth, the longer is the period of burn. Char-depth patterns are always considered in a macro fashion, looking at large areas. In a small localized area, a number of variables might produce different char depths.

Figure 11.4 A room initially isolated from the main fire. The horizontal demarcation on the walls and door indicates how far down the hot gas layer descended. The fire ultimately broke through the wall into the room.

not directly exposed to the fire receive less damage. If these objects remain unmoved in the scene, they will provide specific indicators as to fire flow. Glass and plastic objects often have very distinct damage patterns, melting in the direction of the approaching heat source. Additionally, there may be spalling patterns in concrete foundations, "crazing" of glass, ghosting patterns, and the consideration of melting point of various articles and materials. The nature and variety of fire patterns are anything but limited.

The primary problem associated with searching for fire patterns is the level of damage present in the fire scene. Soot, smoke, and debris develop over the course of the fire and may mar, destroy, or cover fire patterns of interest. Granted, damage or fire patterns on vertical surfaces may be very apparent, but patterns on floors and other horizontal surfaces can be covered by heaps of burned and partially burned debris (Figure 11.5 and Figure 11.6). Fire investigation is a dirty job. In order to find many patterns, the investigator must remove the debris. But this is not as easy as just shoveling out everything on top of the floor, since evidence may exist within the debris itself (Figure 11.7 and Figure 11.8). Much as in the archeology techniques used for gravesite recovery, the fire investigator must search the debris layer by layer to establish what is where.

Vertical surface patterns such as V patterns on the wall will typically suggest areas of specific concern on the floor. Floors are always of particular note, since the fire investigator is looking for indications of low burn. Points of origin for the fire are often found in proximity to low burn patterns, which of course demands significant excavation of the floor and debris. It is important to note that the mere presence of multiple locations of low burn in the scene does not identify the fire as arson. This condition may result from the presence of accelerants, or it can occur as a natural part of fire flow. A classic instance

Figure 11.5 A bedroom closet in a suspicious house fire. The contents of the closet have burned and now exist as debris, covering the floor and lower surfaces. Without excavation, it is impossible to understand fire flow in this area.

Figure 11.6 The closet from Figure 11.5 after excavation. With floor and lower wall surfaces exposed, there is significant evidence of low burn in the area that was not evident before the excavation.

Figure 11.7 Debris on the floor of the closet. In fire scenes, everything looks the same. This makes it difficult to recognize evidence. Something is evident on the floor in the debris, but what is it? Figure 11.8 answers the question. Fire scene excavation is conducted layer by layer, so that items of importance are not missed.

Figure 11.8 The same item from Figure 11.7, when turned over, is revealed to be a fireplace lighter. Its proximity to the low burn in the closet is significant. The cause of the fire was subsequently determined to be children playing with this lighter in the closet. Excavation prevents items such as this from being missed.

of multiple natural low burn patterns results from drop-down debris (e.g., drapes). These articles are present in the hot gas layer, and after igniting, they fall to the floor or other lower surfaces, creating additional points from which the fire will propagate. In order to fully understand the nature of the fire flow and the reason behind low burn, it is not uncommon that an entire floor will have to be cleared.

Problems Associated with Fire Scenes

Fire scenes are a dangerous place to work for a variety of reasons. A critical consideration at the fire scene is structural stability. Floors and walls may be weakened and can easily collapse while the fire investigator is working the scene. Collapse becomes an even greater hazard during excavation efforts. The local fire marshal is an important resource to help ensure the team's safety. Other hazards exist in the scene such as exposed metal, nails, and other objects. Inhalation hazards are also a problem. During any action other than a simple walk-through, significant levels of dust are disturbed, which the unprotected investigator is bound to inhale. To reduce these hazards, each team member should be equipped with good solid boots, heavy pants, and long-sleeve shirts, as well as gloves and particle masks.

Lighting is another problem associated with the fire scene. Electricity is often disrupted by the fire, and all of the scene surfaces are blackened, reflecting little light. The lack of reflected light produces a situation where there is little difference between highlight detail and shadow detail. This makes it difficult to see, search, or navigate the scene. Work lights, as discussed in Chapter 5, are necessary to ensure complete processing of the fire scene.

The light and reflectivity issue of the fire scene is a particular problem when taking photographs. Quality fire scene photographs are difficult to achieve. When using a standard 35-mm camera, it is a good practice to bracket exposures. The investigator should take the metered exposure indicated by the camera; the investigator then opens the f-stop one to two stops taking the same photograph. As a result the investigator ends up with two to three photographs of the same area, but at different exposures. Digital cameras give immediate feedback and allow the investigator to correct any problems on the spot. Low-end digital cameras, however, do not work effectively in fire scenes. They are often unable to find a focus point, and the pictures are both out of focus and underexposed. In this instance, it is imperative to return to a standard film camera to supplement the digital photographs.

Fire Scene Methodology

The specific methodology for dealing with a fire scene is not that much different from any other crime scene, with the noted exceptions of the dangers involved and the concentration on fire signs. The technician must assess the scene, determine its extent, and then in an orderly fashion begin processing the scene.

Assessment begins on the exterior of the building, where fire-flow patterns may be well defined. The exterior perspective will also help the technician in understanding the full extent of the fire damage (e.g., smoke venting through roofs and attics that would otherwise not be evident from the inside). If possible, view the scene from an elevated position to better understand fire patterns or damage that may be on the roof.

In the assessment and observation phase, it is best to work from the least damaged areas to the more heavily damaged areas. This will give the technician a better understanding of the condition of the scene prior to the fire and will make it easier to understand what the technician is observing when confronted with the chaos of a heavily damaged room. Remember that a primary goal of the investigation is to understand how the fire moved through the scene and thereby locate the point or points of origin. Once located, the investigation shifts focus and seeks to understand what caused the fire. With that in mind, there are two rules of thumb in fire investigation. The first rule is that the area exhibiting the most damage was exposed to the fire for the longest time; therefore, it is more likely to contain the point of origin. This is nothing more than a guideline, however, and any number of factors can prove it invalid. A second rule of thumb is to seek out any indication of low burn. Throughout assessment, the technician looks for indications of fire flowing from low points to higher points. These areas require significant examination and often demand excavation in order to understand their relationship to the overall fire flow.

After the assessment, observation, and initial documentation phases are completed, the examination is best conducted by evaluating specific fire patterns independently of other patterns and evidence (e.g., in a step-by-step evaluation, looking at the burn patterns, then the smoke patterns, then at char depth, etc.). If the scene involves a large area, it may be necessary to break the larger area down into zones and then apply the step-by-step process to each. No one fire sign will tell the entire story, but all of them must be taken into account. Excavation of floors or rooms will be necessary in order to see low-lying fire patterns. Areas excavated should be thoroughly photographed before the excavation and throughout the process.

There are a number of helpful resources available to the investigator faced with a significant fire scene. These include the local fire marshal, fire department fire investigators, as well as a variety of investigators from the federal agencies. When presented with a complex fire or a fire death, it is imperative to include these individuals on the investigative team. Use caution, however, when employing such individuals. Arson certification, state or otherwise, indicates nothing more than the fact that an individual is trained to a specific level. It in no way ensures the quality of the resulting product. Two case examples will illustrate the point well.

Case Example 1: Arson in Spite of the Facts

At the scene depicted in Figure 11.4, a state-certified fire department arson investigator arrived on scene early in the morning immediately following the fire. He remained for a total of 15 min before declaring the scene "arson" due to low burn. He returned the following day to actually process the scene, although he failed to excavate important areas involving the low burn. Ultimately, his conclusion was that the "suspect" had poured a trailer of kerosene from the living room of the mobile home, down the hallway into a back bedroom, and onto the unconscious victim. The suspect then returned to the living room, igniting the blaze and leaving from there. The hallway depicted in Figure 11.9 shows an area on which the kerosene was allegedly poured. The door to the back bedroom in which the victim was found is depicted in Figure 11.4. Note the lack of any burning on the last 3 ft of linoleum leading into the bedroom from the hallway. Also note the lack of burnt linoleum in the bedroom. Of particular note, there is a consistent hot-gas-layer pattern present, indicating that the door of the bedroom was shut. In Figure 11.4, it is clear that the fire burned through the adjoining walls to enter this bedroom. Beyond the fire pattern issues, there were no less than two contradictions to the "arson" investigator's theory. The first was that the "suspect" claimed to have exited through the back bedroom window, injuring himself in the process. Bloodstains supporting this claim were evident on the exterior wall of the mobile home below the broken window, and the suspect had significant lacerations caused by climbing through the glass. The second contradiction was the presence of a hand print outlined by smoke and soot, outstretched on the wall immediately above where the victim's arm was found. This print clearly showed that the victim was conscious as the fire was burning and depositing soot and smoke on the wall.

Case Example 2: Test Your Hypothesis

In this instance, the investigator was an ex-ATF (Alcohol, Tobacco and Firearms) agent who, one would hope, was significantly trained in arson and fire scene investigation. The case was a grisly quadruple murder in which the victims were disrobed, raped, and shot before the scene was set afire. Of interest in the case, a confession was obtained detailing certain aspects of setting the fire. In trying to make sense of these details, the prosecuting attorney first sought the insight of an MD (medical doctor) whose specialty was burns. The MD was alleged to have commented to the prosecuting attorney that the burns present on the victims were indicative of a fire burning directly on their skin. This information was presented to the ex-ATF agent, and he was asked to comment. His conclusions fell in line with the prosecutor's input, and the theory presented at trial was that the suspects piled flammable items on top of the four victims' bodies, poured lighter fluid over the

Figure 11.9 A hallway in a fire scene. The arson investigator's theory was that the suspect poured kerosene from the living room, across this surface, and into the bedroom behind the door at the top of the picture. The kerosene was lit and resulted in the fire. The immediate problem with the theory is that there is no burn on the linoleum several feet before the door. Moreover, as Figure 11.4 indicates, there is no surface burn on the floor of the bedroom, and the bedroom door was closed during the fire. Theories of how and why the fire occurred must not contradict the physical evidence.

items, and then set them ablaze. This fire led to adjoining surfaces and ultimately involved the entire room, including the ceiling. Of interest at the scene, the ceiling received significant damage, and ceiling tiles fell on top of the victims as they lay in the scene.

Upon cursory examination, the state's theory tended to make sense. However, upon close examination of the fire scene, certain exceptions to the theory were quite evident. First and foremost, once the ceiling tiles were removed from the bodies, there was no debris on top of the bodies. The second problem was that the bodies beneath the ceiling tiles were, for the most part, undamaged — certainly nothing in line with the belief that a fire had been burning directly on them. The doctor, when called to trial, stated that he had never told the prosecutor that the fire burned directly on the bodies and had certainly never written anything of that nature in his report. In this instance, the "arson" investigator seemed to have fallen into the trap of accepting the prosecutor's pet theory without challenging it. Additionally, he accepted the verbal conclusion of a doctor from a lawyer, a dangerous act in and of itself, without ever verifying the information. There is no question that the investigator failed to challenge his own theory, as scientific method demands, by comparing his conclusions with the excavated condition of the bodies. But that was not the only problem; the investigator also made multiple claims unsupported by the scene. He told the jury that a hot-gas-layer pattern on a wall and door juncture was in fact a V pattern of flames rising up the wall from the fire on the bodies. This pattern extended down the wall to a point about 5 ft off the ground, which would logically demand that the pile of burning debris was at least several feet high and burning so intensely that it reached out across the large gap of space between the bodies and the wall. Of course a hot-gas-layer pattern develops throughout a room. In this scene, all one had to do was look at the other two door and wall junctures to see the exact same pattern the investigator claimed was a V pattern. See Figure 11.10.

In the scene, immediately to the south of the bodies, there was debris on the floor consistent with the items described in the confession as well as fire patterns rising from the floor level. The overall fire flow was more than apparent and explained nearly every aspect of the fire scene. Thus, the manner in which the fire was set did not in and of itself negate the guilt of the individual. But guilty or not, that is certainly no excuse for presenting false and misleading information to a jury, simply to bolster the overall theory of the crime and make it fit a confession.

The author has always taken note of the difference between "arson" investigators and fire scene investigators. Fire investigators show up at a scene, take the necessary steps to evaluate and collect their data, and then allow the data to define the conclusion. The former show up, call the scene an arson, and then search for anything that will support their conclusions without considering any alternative hypothesis. They also tend to rationalize away any data that gets in the way of their theory. Just as a death investigator treats every body as a homicide until proven otherwise, there is nothing wrong with the fire investigator treating every fire scene as an arson. That mindset ensures that every facet of the investigation is pursued until proven unnecessary. The distinction is that "treating" the scene as an arson does not require wild and unsupported claims of arson. As with any investigation, the scene must speak for itself, and it cannot speak clearly until it is understood.

In fire investigations, as with all investigations, the crime scene technician must collect the data before coming to conclusions. Otherwise, the technician is likely to ignore important data at the scene and simply seek information to support theory. It is the author's experience that the ability to be an objective investigator is less a function of training and more a function of personal ethics. Although certification and proficiency testing help build objectivity in the investigator, no level of certification or proficiency testing will eliminate the possibility of subjective interpretations. Be very cautious of individuals, no matter what their credentials, who arrive on scene and arbitrarily put their final conclusion before their analysis.

Figure 11.10 An alleged V pattern on a door. An expert claimed a flame was rising on this door, resulting in the pattern. The problem is that the burn is linear across the door, and there is no burn beneath it. The pattern is nothing more than the hot-gas-layer pattern. The surrounding wood burned faster than the flame-retardant gypsum in the wall. By merely looking at the other door/wall junctures in the room, the nature of the fire pattern became evident.

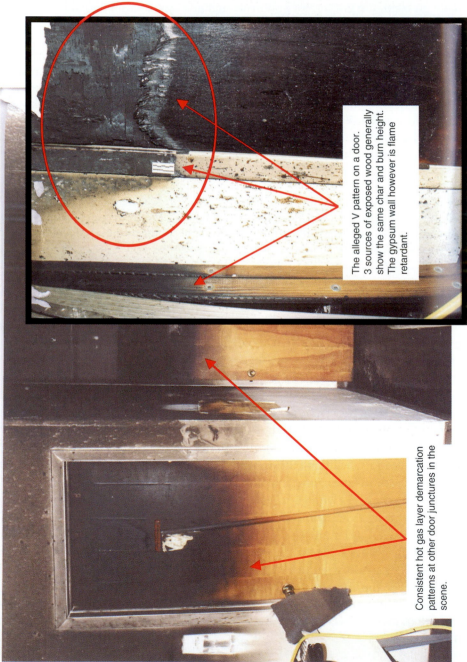

The alleged V pattern on a door. 3 sources of exposed wood generally show the same char and burn height. The gypsum wall however is flame retardant.

Consistent hot gas layer demarcation patterns at other door junctures in the scene.

Landfill Recoveries

It is not uncommon to encounter cases involving bodies that have been disposed of in a landfill. The dumping of a body into a landfill creates significant issues for the investigative team. Rarely can a search be mounted without some intelligence regarding when and where the body was dumped. Any ad hoc search is likely to produce no results and exhaust vast amounts of investigative resources.

Functional landfill search and recoveries are possible. But not every case will present a set of circumstances that make a landfill search a viable possibility. When the right circumstances present themselves, the experiences of organizations like the San Jose Police Department and Detective Sergeant Bruce Wiley provide a simple functional technique to apply in such scenes. Success presumes a situation in which the investigative team is looking for a body dumped from a specific location on a specific date (e.g., as when presented with a confession, where the suspect identifies the dumpster and date when the body was disposed of). Another condition necessary for any successful recovery is a managed waste site.

Managed waste sites are not just dump-and-run operations. It is not uncommon for the managed waste company to have extensive records reflecting truck routes, truck identification, when specific trucks came in, where they dumped their load, and at what time they dumped their load. Even lacking such specificity, managed dumps typically use a technique known as an engineered compacted landfill. In effect, the waste site is broken down into cells. On a recurring basis (often daily), trash is dumped at a specific location. A trash cell may be as large as 100 to 150 square ft. After dumping the trash from the trucks, this area is compacted by large heavy-equipment compactors. Each cell is subsequently covered with clean dirt, generally a 1-ft compacted layer. Each new cell is thus separated from the previous cell by this buffer of dirt, creating what Bruce Wiley refers to as a "layer cake" effect.[3] The waste company's records should make it possible to quickly distinguish and identify a cell's location and its date of creation. These records give focus to what would otherwise be a "needle in a haystack" search.

Problems Associated with Landfill Recoveries

There are, of course, significant associated problems when dealing with a landfill recovery. The three primary issues are the compacting of the body and evidence, the heat generated by the landfill, and the various hazards present in the landfill.

Compacting both in the truck and at the landfill will result in significant damage to the body and to associated evidence. Compacting begins when the trash is dumped from the dumpster into a truck. Repeated compacting in the truck over the course of a trash route creates a mixing-bowl effect. Associated artifacts (e.g., clothing, personal effects, or coverings) are often separated from the body itself. Once dumped at the landfill, large compactors weighing in excess of 100,000 lb are used to compact the trash cell. The end result is that the body may be mangled, with organs lost or bones broken, making it difficult to define specific homicidal injuries and preventing the recovery of associated evidence. See Figure 11.11.

Landfills produce significant heat, which is generated by the decomposing trash. Temperatures often reach in excess of 170 degrees. This heat will create difficult environmental conditions for anyone involved in the search. Besides heat, there are a variety of hazards present in the landfill. Despite regulations preventing the disposal of toxic or biohazardous

Figure 11.11 The corpse of a murder victim after being exposed in a landfill. The action of the trash truck, compaction at the landfill, and the nature of items the body is disposed with result in significant postmortem injuries as well as the loss of associated articles and evidence. (Photograph courtesy of Bruce Wiley, San Jose Police Department. With permission.)

materials, never doubt that such items are present. Anything the investigator can imagine will be found in the trash. Even normal trash articles such as broken glass, sharp metal, or decomposing waste present hazards and create possible injury mechanisms.

To deal with all of these hazards, personal safety equipment is necessary for anyone working in the landfill search. This equipment includes safety boots, high-risk latex gloves, eye protection, Tyvek sleeves, rain pants, and particle masks. Hard hats may be necessary as well, not only to prevent accidental injury from moving trash around, but also as a precaution against items dropped by scavenger birds that routinely appear once trash is exposed. Safety vests should be required, since heavy equipment (backhoes and bulldozers) will be operating in and around the teams. A variety of sturdy hand tools are necessary for the search teams, the most important tool being a three-prong cultivator rake. This tool has been found to be effective when raking through compacted trash.

Landfill Recovery Methodology

The specific technique to apply in a managed landfill is to first identify the appropriate cell or cells in consultation with the landfill operator. Once this is done, the landfill operator must remove cells that were deposited on top of the cell(s) in question (Figure 11.12).

Figure 11.12 The inset picture shows the scene in an engineered, compacted landfill prior to removing the additional trash cells that were deposited over the cell of interest. The larger picture shows the same scene after removal of the additional cells that were deposited over the top. Removing overlaying cells and locating a specific cell is not a trivial matter. (Photograph courtesy of Bruce Wiley, San Jose Police Department. With permission.)

Figure 11.13 A backhoe is used at the far end of the cell to remove one shovelful of trash at a time. The observers watch the shovel and the pit. If any items of interest are noted, they call a halt to operations. (Photograph courtesy of Bruce Wiley, San Jose Police Department. With permission.)

Once the cell is exposed, the services of a backhoe and bulldozer are needed throughout the operation.

Human resources are an obvious concern. The technique described here requires both observation and rake teams. Each observation team requires two individuals. Each search/rake team requires at least four to five individuals. In order to make any progress, a minimum of three search/rake teams must operate simultaneously. To field a functional group, total human resources will easily exceed 25 to 30 individuals.

The backhoe is placed into operation at the far end of the slope for the cell in question and begins digging downward (Figure 11.13). An observation team is placed at the slope where the backhoe is operating. One member is responsible for watching the hole where the shovel is digging. The other member is responsible for watching the shovel as it is removed from the hole. Using this method, should the body be visible to either, operations can be halted immediately without further damaging any evidence.

Directly behind the slope where the backhoe is working, a large flat area is required. Each shovelful of trash removed by the backhoe is dumped and spread as evenly as possible with the shovel blade (Figure 11.14). Rake teams then search through this single shovelful of trash. Dumping more than a single shovelful in one location will result in the team being overwhelmed quickly. It is possible, however, to run multiple rake teams simultaneously, each working a single pile. When the teams have completed their examination and nothing is found, the area is bulldozed clean and the process repeated.

The backhoe works from the far end of the cell, along its exposed slope, moving backward. The bulldozer is generally employed on the portion of the cell as yet unexposed,

Figure 11.14 As each shovelful of trash is removed, it is deposited on a flat area behind the backhoe. Using hand tools, the teams search through the debris. Once the trash has been searched and nothing found, a bulldozer scrapes this area clean to make way for the next shovelful of trash removed from the pit. (Photograph courtesy of Bruce Wiley, San Jose Police Department. With permission.)

pushing the searched trash off the cell into a designated area (Figure 11.15). This is a long, tiring, and difficult job, so it is appropriate to keep one team resting in reserve. Teams are routinely cycled through a rest period, allowing each group to recoup and recover.

Cadaver dogs can assist in the search process, but there are clear limitations. The various hazards present in the trash will affect the dogs as well. Methane pockets in particular may represent a significant hazard for the dogs. The amount of decomposing trash (e.g., meat, fecal matter in diapers) will tend to create distractions for the dogs. If possible, dogs should be employed only in the early morning. Landfills are likely to overwhelm the dog's senses, so do not expect outstanding results from even the best-trained dog.

Despite the large size of the typical trash cell (e.g., 100 ft × 100 ft × 30 in. in depth) created in an engineered landfill, the cell is still a discreet area when compared with the entire landfill. Thus it can be searched effectively in a matter of days using the described technique. If, however, additional cells are involved, the task becomes more daunting, costly, and time consuming. Unfortunately, the various technologies used to search for buried remains (e.g., gravesites), such as magnetometers and ground-penetrating radar, will not work in the landfill, even as a means of narrowing the scope of the search. The entire area is a debris field, and the high-technology tools will not be able to see through this chaotic distribution. There may be situations in which it is not feasible to attempt a search, and there are no rules that will absolutely define whether such a search is feasible.

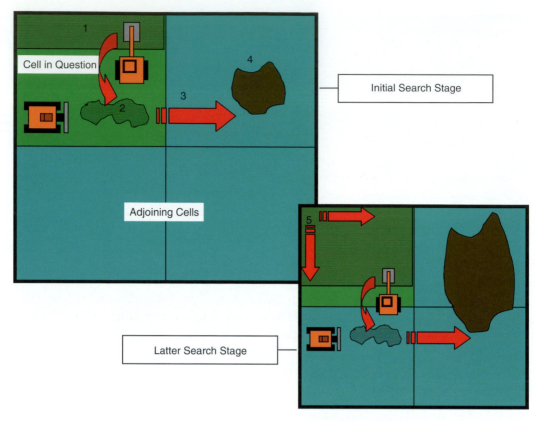

Figure 11.15 The sequence of events for searching a compacted trash cell. (1) The backhoe removes a shovelful of trash from the pit. (2) The trash is deposited on a flat area behind the backhoe, where searchers examine it. (3) Once examined, a bulldozer moves the trash off the cell in question. (4) The searched trash is pushed to a holding point where it will not interfere with operations. (5) The backhoe works the pit along the front edge, working backward until the entire cell has been cleared.

The investigative team will have to make a case for the search based on a number of factors, including the known intelligence; the level of cooperation demonstrated by the waste management company; and the physical, human, and monetary resources available. This is not a task to be undertaken lightly or started on a whim.

Buried and Scattered Remains

Any homicide scene demands significant effort on the part of the crime scene team. Bodies that have either been buried or exposed to the environment for an extended period create additional issues. When a relatively fresh body is found outside, it is certainly possible that items associated with the body and the crime may have been dispersed. But this dispersal is at the surface, and standard crime scene search techniques are more than sufficient to locate any evidence. Evidence items associated with buried bodies or bodies that decompose on the surface over an extended period tend to be widely dispersed in the surrounding soil and vegetation. This demands the application of archeological techniques in an effort to locate and document the evidence and its scene context.

Buried Bodies

Cases involving buried bodies generally occur in one of two basic varieties. The police will either be presented with a grave (e.g., someone stumbles upon a foot extending out of a shallow grave), or they will be seeking a grave, based upon some form of intelligence (e.g., looking for additional bodies in and around a dump site of a serial murderer). A study of 788 reported homicides involving burial of the victim's remains found that 55% were located only when a witness to the actual disposal or the subject divulged the location of the clandestine grave.[4] Lacking such information, searching for a clandestine grave is a demanding task, requiring skills well beyond the typical investigator's ability. The "forensic backhoe" technique routinely demonstrated on the nightly news is not the appropriate response. As was evident in the landfill situation, the backhoe is the only viable method of moving compacted trash. But arbitrarily digging up a backyard in hopes of stumbling upon a grave is crude and ineffective. Even if the backhoe operator stumbles onto a body, the technique is likely to destroy significant amounts of evidence. Lacking intelligence that directs the search to a very specific and discrete location, the best advice for the investigative team is to seek professional help in the form of organizations such as NecroSearch International. This group is a nonprofit organization that assists law enforcement agencies in locating clandestine graves. NecroSearch developed out of the research effort known as Project Pig. This collaborative research effort was conducted over a number of years at the Highland Ranch in Douglas County, CO. It involved the application of diverse disciplines and technologies such as botany, thermal imaging, geophysics, archeology, entomology, geology, and aerial photography in an effort to detect clandestine gravesites through nonintrusive means.[5]

If the search for a grave involves a discrete location (e.g., a yard or cellar), visual techniques as well as technology can help in locating the grave without introducing significantly intrusive methods. Depending upon a number of factors (e.g., the length of time the body has been buried, the type of soil the body is buried in), the grave may exhibit any number of appearances, including disturbed soil, a grave mound, or even soil compaction. Vegetation around the immediate grave is likely to have been disturbed by activity, therefore it may be absent from the grave or in a state of regrowth that is visually dissimilar to the surrounding vegetation.

Nonintrusive technologies that may help locate the grave in a discrete area include the use of magnetometers, ground-penetrating radar, and infrared thermography. Magnetometers detect anomalies in the surface's magnetic field. They will quickly recognize metallic objects (e.g., weapons) but are also useful in recognizing a grave. The displacement of soil, such as encountered when a grave is dug and filled, results in a "remnant magnetization" that the magnetometer can detect.[6] Ground-penetrating radar (GPR) is another effective technique. GPR sends a low-frequency signal into the ground that is returned in different ways after encountering different conditions.[7] The GPR produces what could best be described as a cluttered display, but anomalies such as displaced soil or bodies are often evident to the operator. Infrared thermography works due to a difference between the surrounding heat signature of the soil and that present at the gravesite. Initial theories involving infrared thermography held that the grave would produce a higher heat signature than the surrounding ground due to decomposition. Through experimentation, the opposite was actually proven correct. Graves create a dead space that produces a lower heat signature than the surrounding ground, and the technology can often recognize this heat differential.[8] A final nonintrusive technique for locating a grave is the use of a trained cadaver dog.

Intrusive techniques for locating graves include the use of probes and vapor monitors. Vapor monitors are used to detect decomposition gases. A primary gas produced by decomposition of any nature (e.g., human, animal, or plant) is methane. Various devices can be used to detect these vapors, including hydrocarbon detectors utilized by the fire department. Vapor detectors are best employed when the temperature is greater than 45°F, and these are typically used in conjunction with a probing technique.[9]

Probes are used to detect differences in the compaction of regular soil and disturbed soil. The probes are made of 3/8-in. stainless steel and are generally 40 in. in length. A handle of some nature is affixed to one end, allowing the user to insert the rod into the ground and apply pressure. Individuals outfitted with a probe can be placed on line and follow a standard line-search pattern, or each searcher can be given an area that is searched using a strip or grid technique. In either situation, the probe is inserted every 10 to 15 in. in a horizontal pattern directly in front of the searcher, a pattern that was developed from avalanche search techniques. In effect, a probe is made directly in front of the searcher's left foot, one halfway between the feet, and one directly in front of the right foot. Using a line of searchers, everyone steps forward after the probe, one normal step, and repeats the probing.

The probe is inserted into the soil, and any differences noted are brought to the attention of the team leader. Once an anomaly is located, additional probing may help narrow down the grave outline. The use of a methane detector can also corroborate the find prior to expending any effort digging. It is important that probing teams practice prior to the search to get a feel for how compact the ground conditions are. This becomes a standard they will compare each probe to. The protocol used by the probe team should begin with a line of searchers working across the suspected area or anomaly. The line works across the area and then reforms to cross the same area at a 90-degree angle. If the probe penetrates an area to a greater depth based on the same level of effort, that may suggest an underlying soil disturbance. All areas of interest are flagged for further evaluation. Areas of greater compaction are of interest as well. These may occur in situations where the grave is capped by branches or rock, creating a "hard spot."[10]

Once a gravesite has been detected or is suspected, excavation of this focal area is required. But the grave, although the focus of the investigation, is not the end-all of possible evidence present at the scene. Upon initial discovery, the team must document the overall surface context in and around the suspected grave before it is destroyed. As with every crime scene, the technician considers paths in and out of the area and the possibility of deposited or discarded evidence along any paths. Specific effort is directed at looking for any associated evidence (e.g., tools, tire marks, or items discarded) in the immediate area. A grid is then established over the area, including datum points for elevation readings. The grave is a three-dimensional artifact, and the elevation aspects must be documented. All surface artifacts are mapped to the datum point and collected. The use of a rigid grid is an effective technique for gravesite examination. A PVC or wooden grid is placed over the grave, and all measurements are made in relation to the grid. Once the grid is leveled and secured, it provides a stable landmark for making all two- and three-dimensional measurements. This method has also been used effectively in situations involving surface finds, if the majority of the remains are localized in one area.

The surface of the site is examined with a metal detector, and any hits are flagged. Once surface debris is removed, these areas can be excavated independently. Loose debris (leaves, twigs, and the like) are removed by hand from the respective grids and examined for any potential evidentiary value. The technician should use caution when doing this so that scene context is not lost (e.g., disturbing a set of twigs fashioned in a cross over the grave) and to ensure that underlying items of evidence are not disturbed. All natural loose debris is removed until the mound is exposed. The ground level is then reexamined for any objects or items of evidence, which are documented, mapped, and collected using standard procedures. Ground plants are then removed by cutting them at the surface (Figure 11.16). The same precaution with regard to removing plants exists as when casting an impression; plants are never pulled or uprooted. In most instances, plants are cut at the ground level, but if a root system is needed by the forensic botanist, the investigator may have to carefully excavate the plant as the exhumation proceeds. Coordination with a forensic botanist (like those employed by NecroSearch International) will provide specific guidance on what samples of plants to retain as evidence.

Screens are used to examine all litter, debris, or soil removed from the site. This will preclude missing small items such as bullets, teeth, small bones, and other artifacts. Fill soil and debris should always be managed in such a fashion that the context of where the soil originated is not lost. This allows the technician to reassociate any artifacts discovered during the screening to a general origin (depth and grid) in the grave. Experts in the field generally suggest a two-level screening effort. The first screen is made up of $^{1}/_{4}$-in. mesh, while the second is made up of 1/16-in. mesh.[11] Double-screening will make it more likely that small objects such as hairs, fibers or shot pellets are located and recovered.

Actual excavation of the site is undertaken in levels. General archeological protocol dictates that the excavation proceed in arbitrary levels following the surface contour until an evident stratum is located (man-made or natural). This new stratum is exposed in its entirety and then mapped. Once excavated and mapped, the process continues for each newly discovered stratum. Thus the dig proceeds along layers. The primary tools required for excavating include trowels and brushes. In archeology, sites are generally excavated along established balks, which are vertical boundaries that help the archeologist recognize the various vertical levels and maintain order in the dig. In gravesite excavation, balks are uncommon and unnecessary, as the grave itself will have specific limits. The grave usually represents an artifact created during a single episode with distinct edges. The grave is always excavated to the physical extent of this initial disruption. As digging proceeds, it will not be difficult for the technician to reach down into the grave and excavate so long as the grave is shallow. In deeper graves, it may be necessary to create a dig trench alongside the grave. This trench is excavated in such a fashion that those excavating can be positioned at a depth lower than the surface without having to stand inside the grave. The dig trench is only created when necessary. If used, the trench is always higher than the last exposed surface of the grave. This precludes the dig trench from disturbing evidence associated with the grave side (e.g., tool marks) and also prevents any incursion into the grave itself.

Stratification is a basic concept of archeology that is applicable to gravesite excavation. Each obvious layer or significant artifact encountered is removed in the reverse order of its deposition. Identifying and documenting this stratification provides the investigator with significant scene context regarding the specific actions taken during the creation and subsequent filling of the grave. As the technician digs down, s/he looks for any change in soil, for debris, or for the presence of artifacts. When an identifiable stratum is observed, the site is exposed to that level and fully documented in an effort to understand why it is there. Simply shoveling the fill soil from the grave will disrupt the stratification, and all of

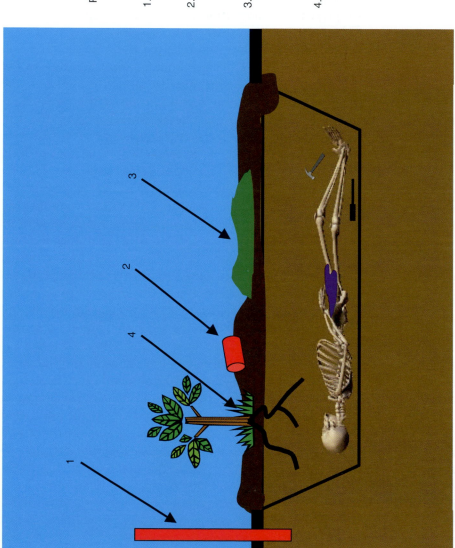

Preparing the Site for
Excavation

1. Set datum and grid.

2. Locate and map
all surface artifacts.

3. Remove all surface
debris by hand (e.g.,
leaves, loose twigs).

4. Cut growing plants
close to the surface.

Figure 11.16 Preparing a gravesite for excavation involves more than just digging a hole. (1) The technician must set a datum point and grid. Graves are three-dimensional artifacts, so elevation is an important aspect as well. (2) All surface artifacts must be located and mapped to the grid. (3) All loose debris is removed until the grave outline and mound are evident. (4) Growing plants are never pulled out, as their root system may extend into the grave. They are either cut close to the surface or excavated in order to recover the root system for botanical study.

this sequencing evidence will be lost. To preclude this, dirt is removed in no more than 2-in. layers. If a thinner stratum is encountered (e.g., a 1-in. layer of gravel), then less soil is removed when working through that stratum. This prevents the digging effort from disturbing the underlying cadaver or any evidence that may be deposited deeper in the fill. Once excavation of the fill is started, the tools used by the technician are the trowel and brush. The trowel is used to carefully slice or scrape fill dirt from the excavation rather than "digging" it out. The technician uses the brush to carefully remove loose fill on the layer being examined. Shop vacuums are an effective tool as well. Although never used to excavate the fill dirt, the vacuum can be used to remove loose fill dirt that has fallen into the excavation, much as a surgeon uses suction to remove excess blood. All vacuumed dirt is screened.[12] As the grave sides are exposed, they should be excavated carefully. The technician specifically looks for evidence of tool or footwear marks present on the grave sides. Any marks noted are documented and collected using casting techniques before disrupting the grave further.

New artifacts, as they become visible, are carefully exposed, documented, and mapped to the overlying grid. This includes measuring the objects' elevation in relation to the grid datum point. Lacking other methods (e.g., total stations or the use of a rigid grid and stadia poles), elevation data are easily measured using a string, string level, and plumb. A leveled string is stretched from a datum elevation mark, across the excavation, and over the artifact in question. The string level is centered on the string and ensures that it is level across its entire length with the datum elevation. Once the string is in place, the technician lowers a plumb and tape measure from the string to the artifact, measuring and recording this distance.

Following standard archeological practice, the dig is kept "in phase," where all identifiable aspects of a given layer are exposed before proceeding to the next.[13] See Figure 11.17 and Figure 11.18. Given the small surface area involved in a grave, this is usually an easy undertaking.

Special Agent Michael Hochrein, a noted author and lecturer on buried body recoveries, makes the comment that a sharp trowel is a necessity. The technicians should keep a file on hand to maintain the trowel edge, as this allows the digger to effectively cut layers from the soil and to distinguish different layers as they are encountered. Used with care, postmortem trauma by the excavator is usually avoided. As the body is exposed, Hochrein suggests using devices such as plastic-coated utensils or bamboo sticks.[14] In the early stages of excavation, small flat-bladed shovels may be effective as a method of scraping discrete layers from the surface, following the original surface contour. Once the grave's outline is discovered, however, the shovel is abandoned, and the trowel becomes the primary excavation tool. Good trowel and excavation techniques cannot be taught; they are more a matter of experience. Unfortunately for the crime scene technician, this is a technique not often encountered, so it should be engaged in carefully.

Upon initial exposure of the body, there is a tendency to forget concepts such as stratification and keeping the dig "in phase." There may be a desire to expose the cadaver quickly. The technician should maintain elevation control (layered removal of soil), slowly exposing the body and collecting any associated artifacts that are found. A significant number of photographs should be exposed, documenting each step of exposure and condition of the body. Once the body is completely exposed, its position is documented in relation to the grid, and any associated articles found on or beside it are documented, mapped, and collected. The body is then removed, and excavation continues until the technician reaches the base of the pit.

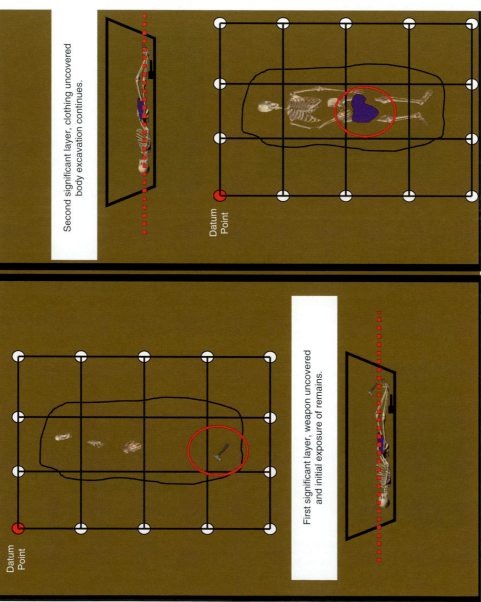

Figure 11.17 Excavation of the grave is undertaken in layers in order to capture the stratification of the grave. Fill dirt is removed in no more than 2-in. layers across the entire surface until a stratum or artifact is located. In the figure, two distinct strata are located, a layer holding the hammer and a layer holding the clothing. Each is exposed slowly and documented before moving to the next layer. Portions of the remains may appear early in the excavation, but the layered approach is not abandoned.

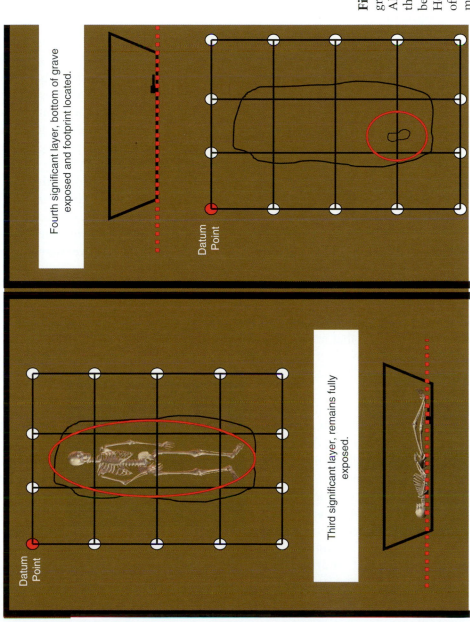

Figure 11.18 The end-all of the grave excavation is not the body. Although it is a primary layer, once the body is removed, the grave must be excavated to the bottom of the pit. Here additional evidence in the form of bullets, artifacts, and shoe and tool marks are all possible.

Removal of the body is not the end-all of the grave excavation. The bottom of the gravesite has the potential to hold important evidence. Tools used to dig the grave may have left marks on the edges or bottom; individuals standing in the grave while digging it may have left shoe marks; or objects may have been thrown into the grave before depositing the body. The technician should not rush the removal of the body from the grave, since the presence of the body on top of these marks may protect them from fill or compaction, particularly in recent burials. Haphazard disturbance of the grave at this point, or rough handling while removing the remains, can result in the destruction of such evidence.

As with arson, buried bodies demand a level of expertise that cannot be explained in such a short section of a single chapter. There are a variety of references available to the crime scene technician that effectively demonstrate and teach this subject in depth.[15,16,17]

Scattered Remains

Scattered or skeletonized remains also appear in two basic types. The find is either localized (e.g., the skeleton or badly decomposed body is found relatively complete at a single location), or it is widely dispersed over a large area. Any combination of dispersal patterns are possible resulting from dispersal by animals, erosion, or flooding. Each scene is examined in the same fashion, but widely dispersed remains will prove more difficult to map. Compared with grave recoveries, however, scattered remains are somewhat easier to examine and document, but the process is not as simple as just walking about and picking up bones.

Dispersal of a cadaver can result from homicidal actions, but it is very likely a function of animal activity. If the remains were left exposed for an extended period, the skeleton and associated artifacts can be dispersed over a wide area. Upon initial discovery, the first step is to verify the remains as human. Presented with a single bone, it is difficult for the layperson to be confident that it is in fact of human origin. Decomposing bear paws, in particular, have an amazing visual similarity to the human hand. A forensic pathologist will assist the investigator in this aspect.

Once the remains are verified as human, a grid is established over the primary find location. The size and scope of the grid is dependent upon the amount of surface scatter. The use of a line search is effective when dealing with scattered remains, particularly when confronted with remains that are dispersed over a large area. During the search, obvious remains are flagged when observed. As with a buried body, the immediate surface surrounding the remains is checked with a metal detector. Any hits or artifacts are flagged and examined in detail later.

After documenting the surface context and all obvious remains, the area immediately surrounding the remains is cleaned and exposed using the same techniques described for the grave. All surface debris and plants are removed. Specific care should be used when plants are noted growing in or around the bones and other material. The condition of the plants should be documented and photographed and the plants recovered as evidence. Growth through remains or objects can provide important details regarding the length of time the body has been present at the site. All items encountered are documented, mapped, and collected using standard crime scene procedures. Once this task is completed, all areas directly surrounding any remains should be troweled to a depth of at least 2 in. and all of the removed soil screened for artifacts.

Mapping of either graves or scattered remains can be a difficult challenge. The use of a total-station system is very effective when presented with scenes of this nature, particu-

Figure 11.19 Throughout the search effort for scattered remains, it is important to use some method of tracking what items have been found. Here, the skeleton is reconfigured on a Tyvek suit on scene to assist in visualizing what bones have yet to be recovered. (Photograph courtesy of Roy Heim, Tulsa Police Department. With permission.)

larly scattered remains. Lacking a total station, the crime scene technician can use the techniques of rectangular coordinates on a grid or triangulation on a grid (both described in Chapter 7) to effectively document the scene. Graves will always require an elevation-view sketch to properly demonstrate the relative depths and interrelationships of artifacts and layers discovered during the excavation.

An associated problem in recovering scattered remains is cataloging the find, in other words, knowing when all of the bones have been located. Without some form of on-scene demonstrative aid, it can be difficult to know what is left to be sought or to recognize when all of the primary bones have been discovered. Archeologists often employ a skeletal diagram, marking each bone off the diagram when located. This can be accomplished at the crime scene using a standard skeletal diagram available from most pathologists. Another simple and effective method is to lay the skeleton out in proper configuration at the scene (Figure 11.19). This allows searchers to visualize and focus on those portions of the skeleton still missing. The only caution when using this latter method is to ensure that each bone is properly tagged before it is placed into its orientation. This prevents contextual information (e.g., where the bone was found) from being lost. This technique should not be used when the bones are wrapped, contained, or buried in some fashion, as both trace and contextual information will be lost.

Entomological Evidence Associated with Bodies

Entomology is the study of insects. Forensic entomologists use the various insects found in, on, and around dead bodies in an effort to establish the postmortem interval. In situations involving buried bodies or decomposed surface remains, insect activity is quite common, but forensic entomology is not limited to only gravesites and scattered remains. It can be used in any death case where time of death is uncertain due to decomposition and there is insect activity.

The types of insects found around the grave or decomposing remain may include species attracted specifically to the carrion (e.g., flies), predator species that feed on the former (e.g., beetles), and omnivorous species attracted to any kind of food source (ants and wasps).

In the initial stages of decomposition (death to +2 days), several species of blowflies will be attracted to the body. The adult flies lay their eggs on the corpse, which subsequently hatch and grow through four larval stages. During this period, the larvae feed on the remains. After their final postfeeding stage, the larvae change to pupae. Adult flies later emerge from the pupae, starting the cycle over. As the body decomposes, putrefaction odors draw more flies as well as additional species of insects, including beetles. Using the apparent life stages of flies present on the corpse, the quantity of those species, and the succession and presence of additional species, it is possible for the forensic entomologist to estimate the postmortem interval.[18]

In order to accomplish this task, specific information and specimens must be obtained by the crime scene team. It is best if the forensic entomologist is called to the scene to collect the specimens and observe them *in situ*, but that is not often possible. Otherwise, specimens must be collected of each evident stage of insect (e.g., pupae, maggots, adult flies). One half of the specimens are preserved, while the remaining specimens are kept alive in order to allow them to mature. Collection should occur immediately upon discovery, as adult flies and beetles will relocate quickly once the body is disturbed.

Larvae are the easiest to locate and collect. Fly larvae can be collected with forceps or by using a moistened modelers' paint brush. Live samples should be placed in a container with moisture and a food source (e.g., a piece of liver and moistened paper towel) to prevent cannibalism. The recommended number of larvae to collect ranges significantly from source to source. A minimum of 20 to 30 live larvae are usually sufficient unless the technician is specifically asked to collect more. The preserved sample should be of a similar quantity. Adult flies and wasps must be caught using a net. Pupae are usually found in drier environments, away from the maggot mass, to prevent predation. They can be found in clothing and surrounding soil. Beetles are often located in the soil beneath the corpse. All are collected in both live and preserved states.

Preserved specimens are placed in vials of ethyl or isopropyl alcohol. Live specimens require moisture and air but also demand careful sealing. Adult flies can emerge from the pupae at any time. Each sample is annotated as to the nature of the specimen when collected (e.g., larva, pupa, or adult), where it was collected, and the time and date of collection. Additionally, the estimated number, size, and temperature of the larval mass should be noted. The specific location on the corpse of each mass should be noted as well (e.g., wound sites or natural openings). Soil samples from a variety of areas, including beneath the corpse and at distances of approximately 3 ft around the corpse, should be collected and placed in small containers. The technician marks each container with identifying data describing where it came from.

Elements of the scene important to the forensic entomologist include whether the area is shaded or sunlit, how much light it gets over the course of a day, the nature of the foliage (e.g., wooded, grassy), the weather conditions (including soil and air temperatures), and the condition of the body (e.g., buried, partially buried, clothed). The technician should note all of this information in the documentation, as well as the general description of all evident insects and an estimate of the number present. This information is recorded in the same manner as standard crime scene information. The forensic entomologist may provide the crime scene technician a death-scene-study form that details all pertinent data they require. In that instance, the form is completed and returned with the specimens.

The best advice for the crime scene team is to locate a forensic entomologist in advance of any need. The investigative agency can then coordinate the specific data and the nature of specimens that the supporting entomologist will require. This preemptive effort will spare the team from expending effort on scene, only to learn later that they failed to collect the requisite information for that particular scientist.

Summary

Fire scenes represent a significant difficulty not only because of the complexity of the scene, but also as a result of the damage caused by the fire. This can create conditions that are both difficult to work and dangerous to work in. An investigation of a suspicious fire is also known as an origin-and-cause investigation. The first step of the effort is to examine the various fire patterns in an attempt to locate the origin of the fire.

Fire patterns allow the investigator to read the fire flow through the scene. These fire patterns include char patterns, smoke and soot patterns, and damage patterns. Each pattern is of importance, and together they may indicate or suggest the point of origin. Inherent in this search is the fire investigator's continual efforts to identify points of low burn. Although a low burn in and of itself does not prove arson, points of origin are most often encountered at these locations.

When searching through the fire scene, the best methodology is to begin on the outside of the structure, move into the least damaged areas of the structure, and then move on to the most damaged areas. In areas that are significantly damaged, it may be necessary to conduct excavation of the debris in order to expose fire patterns on floors and other surfaces. Excavation is carried out in a layer-to-layer process so that evidence in the debris itself is not lost. A critical consideration of the crime scene technician is in understanding what fire-suppression activities occurred within the scene. Fire suppression can effectively damage and destroy the scene context and mislead the crime scene technician.

Landfill recoveries present significant obstacles. Lacking some level of intelligence regarding when and where the body was disposed, it may be impossible to mount a landfill recovery. If a location and date of disposal is known and the landfill operates as a "managed waste site," it is possible to isolate and search specific cells of compacted trash for remains. The process requires heavy machinery, a number of searchers, and can take several days. Landfills represent significant hazards, so additional protective clothing and search tools are necessary when conducting such searches. Even when the remains are found, the nature of the landfill (frequent compaction by heavy equipment) will reduce the value of the evidence remaining with the body. Landfill recoveries are not a task to be entered into lightly or on a whim.

Buried bodies and scattered remains require a significant level of preparation as well. Finding a grave is a task in and of itself. Appropriate techniques include both nonintrusive and intrusive means. Nonintrusive methods include magnetometers, ground-penetrating radar, infrared thermography, and the use of cadaver dogs. Intrusive techniques include probing the ground for anomalies and testing for vapors such as methane. The use of heavy equipment such as a backhoe is not an appropriate search method. These means destroy evidence and scene context, presuming of course that they are able to locate the grave in the first place.

The excavation of a grave is accomplished using archeological techniques that document the stratification of the gravesite and thus capture any associated scene context. Graves are not simply dug up with a shovel; they are excavated in layers following an established methodology. Excavation tools include the trowel and brush, where discrete layers of dirt are removed from the entire grave surface slowly and methodically. As objects are encountered, they are mapped in the scene, including their elevation in the grave. Any fill dirt recovered from the grave is screened in order to locate small artifacts. Once the body is uncovered and removed, the grave excavation is not complete. The floor of the grave as well as the sides may also hold important evidence, such as shoe marks or tool marks.

Scattered remains are a little easier to work with than buried bodies. Remains can be scattered through a number of mechanisms, including animal activity, erosion, and flooding. Line searches are an effective means to search for scattered remains. Once located, all remains and artifacts are mapped in the scene and recovered. The ground beneath the remains is removed and screened to a depth of at least 2 in. in an effort to locate small artifacts.

In both buried and scattered-remains cases, entomology evidence can be useful in establishing the interval of death. Insects such as flies, beetles, wasps, and ants will invade the area, seeking a food source. By considering both the life stages of insects present and the quantity of insects, the forensic entomologist may be able to limit the interval of death significantly.

Suggested Reading

National Fire Protection Association, *Guide for Fire and Explosion Investigations,* NFPA 921, NFPA, Quincy, MA, 1998.

Barker, P., *Techniques of Archeological Excavation*, Universe Books, New York, 1982.

DeHaan, J., *Kirk's Fire Investigation*, Prentice Hall, Upper Saddle River, NJ, 1997.

Haglund, W. and Sorg, M., Eds., *Forensic Taphonomy: the Post Mortem Fate of Human Remains,* CRC Press, Boca Raton, FL, 2002.

Redsicker, D. and O'Conner, J., *Practical Fire and Arson Investigation,* CRC Press, Boca Raton, FL, 1996.

Chapter Questions

1. What is meant by "origin and cause" when discussing fire scene investigation?
2. In what ways will firefighting activity affect the fire scene investigation?
3. What are the basic types of fire scene patterns encountered?
4. What are some of the problems associated with investigating fire scenes?
5. What is a "managed waste site," and why is it so important to a successful landfill recovery?
6. What conditions and circumstances negatively affect the recovery of evidence in a landfill recovery?

7. Why is the use of a "forensic backhoe" an inappropriate means for searching for a clandestine grave?

8. What is meant by stratification of the grave, and why is "keeping the dig in phase" so important to recovering scene context?

9. When dealing with scattered remains, how and why might plants be of some significance in the scene?

10. Describe the basic methods required when collecting insects for entomological study.

Notes

1. National Fire Protection Association, *Guide for Fire and Explosion Investigations*, NFPA 921, NFPA, Quincy, MA, 1998, pp. 921–929.

2. Ibid., pp. 921–924.

3. Wiley, B., Gloria Bonilla: A Tragic Success Story, presentation to the Association of Crime Scene Reconstruction, Denver, CO, Oct. 2002.

4. Hochrein, M.J. et al., The Buried Body Cases Content Analysis Project: Patterns in Buried Body Investigations, paper presented at 51st annual meeting of the American Academy of Forensic Sciences, Orlando, FL, Feb. 1999.

5. Le Cochon Connection: Search Methods and Techniques for Locating Clandestine Graves, a presentation by the Rocky Mountain Division of the International Association for Identification, Aurora, CO, May 1989.

6. Davenport, C.G., *Geophysical Surveying: a Handbook for Criminal Investigators*, self-published, Lakewood, CO, 1997, p. 13.

7. Ibid., p. 43.

8. Weil, G. and Graf, R.J., *Infrared Thermographic Detection of Buried Grave Sites*, EnTech Engineering, St Louis, MO, 1997.

9. McLaughlin, J.E. et al., *The Detection of Buried Bodies*, Andermac, Yuba City, CA, n.d., p. 24.

10. Hochrein, M., personal communication, Aug. 2003.

11. Ibid.

12. Ibid.

13. Barker, P., *Techniques of Archeological Excavation*, Universe Books, New York, 1982, p. 80.

14. Hockrein, M., personal communication, Apr. 2003.

15. Dirkmaat, D.C. and Adovasio, J.M., The Role of Archeology in the Recovery and Interpretation of Human Remains from an Outdoor Setting, in *Forensic Taphonomy: the Post Mortem Fate of Human Remains*, Haglund, W. and Sorg, M., Eds., CRC Press, Boca Raton, FL, 1996, pp. 39–64.

16. Morse, D., Duncan, J., and Stoutmire, J., *Handbook of Forensic Archeology and Anthropology*, Florida State University Foundation, Tallahassee, 1983.

17. Hochrein, M.J., An Autopsy of the Grave: Recognizing, Collecting and Preserving Geotaphonomic Evidence, in *Advances in Forensic Taphonomy: Method, Theory and Archeological Perspectives*, Haglund, W. and Sorg, M., Eds., CRC Press, Boca Raton, FL, 2002, pp. 45–70.

18. Kondratieff, B., Forensic Entomology, presentation to the Rocky Mountain Division of the International Association for Identification, Aurora, CO, May 1989.

The Role of Crime Scene
Analysis and Reconstruction

12

The recurring analogy between a jigsaw puzzle and the crime scene investigation is an effective one. Every action taken by the technician at the scene is done with the specific purpose of capturing data. In effect, the technician captures pieces of the crime scene puzzle in the hope that it might help the investigator understand the true nature of the events that transpired. The problem for the scene investigator is that there are only so many pieces available. Granted that these pieces may be rich in information, but they simply cannot fill in every part of the crime scene puzzle. Thus the crime scene investigator cannot afford to arbitrarily discard or ignore any single piece. In some fashion, each piece must be considered against the whole in an effort to understand what it defines about the event. This analysis is the final step of crime scene processing.

Analysis is accomplished in two distinct venues. The first venue of analysis is that of the crime laboratory. Items recovered at the scene are examined by forensic scientists using the various forensic disciplines described in Chapter 2. Given the limits of the technology, the scientists and technicians deduce what they can from each item. This analysis produces a vast array of refined forensic data that are both discrete and specific: this is Mary's fingerprint; that DNA (deoxyribonucleic acid) is not from the suspect; this glass was broken from the outside. An interesting aspect of this analysis is that the scientist works within a narrow discipline and does not correlate the results in relation to other forensic results. In many instances, this narrow analysis is more than enough for the court. The discrete data provided by the forensic scientist may solve the investigative or judicial questions posed. For example, given a rape charge in which the suspect claims no association or contact with the victim, the presence of the suspect's DNA in a sperm sample recovered from the victim will effectively help a jury to decide guilt or innocence.

More often than not, simply having a wealth of discrete data fails to resolve the difficult questions posed by a crime. The specifics of what occurred, in what order those events occurred, and claims of mitigation are all concerns of the jury. The jury gets all the data and is left to figure it out, guided by lawyers, as if the lawyers were somehow objective. Unfortunately, possession of data does not imply understanding. One can possess all the facts in the world, but unless you can correlate those facts in a logical and appropriate fashion, their true meaning will remain elusive. Mere possession of refined forensic data from the crime lab is no guarantee that the data can provide the clarity required by the fact finders, who must reach a decision of innocence or guilt.

One might ask, "What else is there?" The answer is simply context and interrelationship. As Rynearson and Chisum remarked, the interpretive value of evidence is a function of time and surroundings. It is only when we take the pieces of the crime scene puzzle and put them in some order or form that meaning is derived. Until then, the pieces of the puzzle are just that, pieces. Any single piece, in and of itself, may support any number of subjective theories. By putting the pieces together and placing them in a context with one another, we arrive at true understanding. The vast majority of the crime scene investigator's efforts at documentation are accomplished for the specific purpose of capturing this scene context.

Unfortunately, many crime scene investigators are content to go to a scene and simply collect "things." Is the end-all of crime scene processing simply to effectively collect stuff? Is it enough that we clean up the mess and then hand all of the puzzle pieces to a jury, expecting them to make sense of it? The answer to these questions is no. Crimes beg questions. Who did this, and why, and how? Police have a specific responsibility to investigate crime and report their findings. So the burden of asking and answering these questions lies with the investigator, long before any trial is considered. Only by objectively answering these questions is it possible to achieve justice. The investigative purpose then is to make sense of all of the information that is developed.

Evidence comes to the investigation in two basic forms: it is either physical or it is testimonial. Anyone who has been an investigator for more than a day understands one simple truth about the difference between the two: people lie, people misperceive, and people get it wrong. Humans are subjective creatures and, as such, humans are not the best witnesses. Testimonial evidence, although important, is neither the strongest nor the most objective evidence. As early as 1924, J. Adams, in his introduction to the translated text of *Criminal Investigation*, spoke to this issue, stating:

> The trace [evidence] of crime discovered and turned to good account, a correct sketch be it ever so simple, a microscopic slide, a deciphered correspondence, a photograph of a person or object, a tattooing, a restored piece of burnt paper, a careful survey, a thousand more material things are examples of incorruptible, disinterested and enduring testimony from which mistaken, inaccurate and biased perceptions, as well as evil intention, perjury and unlawful cooperation are excluded. As the science of criminal investigation proceeds, oral testimony falls behind and the realistic proof advances; "circumstances cannot lie, but witnesses can and do."[1]

Of course, people can screw up anything, including objective evidence. The crime scene investigator or the fact finder can overstate the physical evidence, misrepresent it, or misunderstand it; but that is a problem associated with our human frailties and is not the fault of the evidence itself. Physical evidence — if properly collected, evaluated, and correlated — has the power to establish facts regarding an incident that are irrefutable by anyone. It is in evaluating the objective evidence for context and interrelationship that the second venue of analysis, the final step of the crime scene investigative process, occurs. This process is known as crime scene analysis.

The crime scene investigator accomplishes crime scene analysis or crime scene reconstruction in an effort to seek context from the physical evidence. Context is sought by correlating all of the evidence items to one another in an attempt to objectively describe the nature and order of the events that entail the incident being investigated. This is a difficult task and one that must follow a specific methodology. The difficulty lies in the tendency of the analyst to incorporate subjective considerations into the analysis. Although subjective behavior by crime scene investigators or forensic scientists is always dangerous, it is in this final step that subjectivity becomes the most dangerous. The crime scene investigator never has all of the pieces to the puzzle, thus there are always holes and fuzzy areas in which the analyst must try to understand the context of individual pieces of data. The desire to have closure — to have a complete understanding — will cause the investigator to try and fit all of the pieces of the puzzle into a neat and tidy theory. In doing so, subjectivity will creep into the process. It is only by applying established methods of crime scene analysis that the investigator can keep subjectivity at bay and produce an objective picture of the event.

As defined by the Association of Crime Scene Reconstruction, crime scene analysis is "the use of scientific methods, physical evidence, deductive and inductive reasoning and their interrelationships to gain explicit knowledge of the series of events that surround the commission of a crime."[2] The author and Tom Bevel described this process of crime scene reconstruction as "event analysis," defining event analysis as an in-depth crime scene reconstruction that employs scientific method to evaluate the physical evidence known to the analyst.[3] The specific purpose of the analysis is to gain explicit knowledge of the series of events that comprise a given incident and, when possible, to identify the most likely sequence of those events.

Crime scene analysis or event analysis uses a defined methodology to look at each piece of physical evidence, its interrelationship to the scene, and other items of evidence. From this, it attempts to define specific events that occurred during the course of the incident. Whenever possible, it goes one step further by adding order or sequence to those events. Note the word *attempts*. Crime scene analysis rarely provides an all-inclusive theory of the entire incident. As in the puzzle analogy, the crime scene investigator only has certain elements, specific pieces of the puzzle. By placing these pieces into some context, the analyst will provide a skeleton of the crime. But not all of the pieces will easily fit into the developing picture. It is not uncommon to find evidence of actions that the investigator knows happened, without being able to place them in the overall sequence. Nevertheless, this skeleton, however incomplete, will serve as an objective foundation on which all of the subjective information from the investigation can be considered.

It is critical to recognize that objective crime scene analysis will not answer each and every question. One of the most interesting aspects of crime scene analysis is that, if approached properly, it will become vaguer as it is refined by the analyst. Ironically, in becoming less specific, the analysis also becomes more accurate. The more the crime scene investigator challenges what s/he has included in the analysis, the more likely it is that the analyst will recognize subtle subjective inferences.

A History of the Concept of Crime Scene Reconstruction

The methods of crime scene analysis are not new to the investigation of crime. The basic methods described here have been included and described in investigative texts for over 100 years. As early as 1900, Hans Gross spoke of the necessity of reconstructing the crime through a meticulous examination and collection of facts. He warned the investigating officer that by heaping testimony upon testimony, the officer will "almost always be led astray and found wandering from the goal [the truth]."[4] Although Gross described his beliefs across his entire text and did not present them as a specific methodology, he discussed every aspect of our current beliefs. This included the necessity of making detailed crime scene observations, scientific examination of physical evidence in an effort to obtain as much objective data as possible and applying this information to specific questions regarding the crime in an effort to "reconstruct the occurrence, build up by hard labor a theory fitted in and coordinated."[5]

In 1933, Luke May wrote a manual entitled *Scientific Murder Investigation*. May went so far as to outline a very distinct series of questions that should be answered in the investigative process, but in leading his readers to these questions, he outlined the process of the investigation itself. May used a slightly different analogy, that of a building and the investigation, stating that without plan and direction, only the simplest of structures was possible. He likened the murder investigation to building a skyscraper; without planned effort and an underlying superstructure, successful completion of the investigation was impossible. May went on to state that the investigator must "develop other facts, correlating and interlocking to make a whole from apparently disassociated separate units."[6] May concluded that unless the investigator knew what to search for, there was little purpose behind the crime scene search. He warned of developing subjective personal theories and the all-too-common habit of trying to fit the pieces of the investigation into such theories rather than trying to obtain additional information that might lead to novel and more accurate theories. May felt that the true mark of the scientific investigator was one who could "work untiringly, obtaining facts upon which to predicate theories, changing his theories as the facts developed warrant."[7] As in the case of Gross, May did not spell out a specific step-by-step crime scene analysis methodology, but his beliefs set a clear foundation for such a methodology.

Edward Heinrich, also known as the "Wizard of Berkeley," is perhaps one of the first investigative authors to set out a specific crime scene analysis methodology. He commented correctly that one must first analyze the method of the crime before one could properly understand its purpose or hope to identify the criminal, a belief not lost on current day criminal profilers. Heinrich went so far as to describe analysis as "like a mosaic … every fact must be evaluated before it can be fit into the pattern. In that way every fact as it is developed and equated becomes a clue."[8] Heinrich's methodology included defining precisely what happened, where it happened, and when [in what order] it happened. All of this information, developed from the crime scene, would ultimately lead to the more subjective questions of why did it happen and who did it.

In 1933, H. Rhodes made the first case that crime scene analysis was a specific scientific process. In his text *Clues and Crime*, he indicated that the object of the crime scene evaluation was to decide specifically how the crime was committed and in what order the events occurred.[9] As with future authors, Rhodes felt that the scientific method was the underlying foundation of any such analysis.

The noted Dr. Paul Kirk, famous for his efforts in the Sam Shepherd case, was one of the first authors to refer to his work as "crime scene reconstruction." Dr. Kirk wrote *Crime Investigation* in 1953, and although he did not mention reconstruction directly, he made the case that the crime scene was the foundation of the criminal investigation and that field technicians (police officers and crime scene technicians) had to work side by side with scientists (forensic scientists at the crime lab) in order to unveil what physical evidence could describe about a given crime.[10] His application of these beliefs was evident in his affidavit in support of Dr. Shepherd, filed in April 1955.[11]

Between 1956 and 1978, Charles O'Hara's *Fundamentals of Criminal Investigation* was a standard reference utilized in criminal investigation courses. Like Kirk, O'Hara placed a significant emphasis on the objective value of physical evidence and its scientific evaluation. He went so far as to spell out a specific methodology for crime scene investigation. O'Hara described his process in terms of scientific method, stating that it involved:

- Painstaking, comprehensive collection of data
- Arrangement and correlation of that data
- Definition of issues and investigative questions
- Development of a hypothesis along the lines of the available data and subsequent resolution of any hypotheses
- Testing of the hypothesis and elimination, when possible, of contradicting hypotheses
- Testing of the final hypothesis before acceptance[12]

Although O'Hara broadened this "representative approach" to the entire investigation, including subjective aspects such as testimonial evidence, he agreed with Kirk and others that physical evidence and the crime scene shouldered a distinct responsibility in solving crime. He also made the case for conducting a separate crime scene reconstruction in an effort to determine the circumstances of the crime.[13]

James W. Osterburg, another noted criminal investigative author, made a specific association of the reconstruction process to the scientific method in his text *Criminal Investigation: a Method of Reconstructing the Past*. Osterburg was clear in his belief that physical evidence was the primary source of data from which any reconstruction should develop.[14]

Prior to 1997, one of the most defined methodologies for crime scene reconstruction was Chisum and Rynearson's text, *Evidence and Crime Scene Reconstruction*. Their particular methodology emphasized the importance of contextual information, a concept grounded in the belief that time and surroundings were a significant source of objective data. They suggested the use of logic pathways and the use of a "storyboard approach" in which specific events were mapped out once they were identified and then sequenced within the whole reconstruction.[15] If any criticism exists of this methodology, it would be that Chisum and Rynearson continued to incorporate subjective aspects of the investigation, such as intent and motive, into the early stages of the reconstruction process. They believed this information should be considered early on, rather than waiting until after defining the events through the evaluation of the physical evidence alone.

The noted Dr. Henry Lee would comment on the reconstruction issue both in his text *Crime Scene Investigation* and his subsequent text *Henry Lee's Crime Scene Handbook*. Lee advocated the use of scientific method as the specific means utilized in reconstruction. His process included five steps involving data collection, conjecture, hypothesis formation, hypothesis testing, and theory formulation.[16,17] Like many authors, Lee did not state categorically that reconstruction is based on physical evidence, but he made it clear that the primary data of any reconstruction was based on the evaluation of physical evidence.

Peter Lamb, of the U.K.'s Home Office Forensic Science Unit (FSU), defined the reconstructive process as involving four phases: information, observation, interpretation, and conclusions. Lamb described the information phase as considering the initial known information in an effort to define investigative questions. Lamb's observation phase involved the collection of specific data regarding the problem. The interpretation phase involved correlating the information and observations, challenging observations, and looking for valid hypotheses. The final conclusion phase is described as a matter of testing hypotheses and eliminating those that can be objectively eliminated.[18]

In 1997, the author in conjunction with Tom Bevel published *Bloodstain Pattern Analysis: with an Introduction to Crime Scene Reconstruction*, in which we presented a concise and specific methodology incorporating and drawing upon the previous efforts of many individuals.[19] This method of reconstruction is a distinct action confined to the objective evidence and conducted after all forensic analysis is complete.

Crime Scene Reconstruction Methodology

The basis of all crime scene reconstruction is, at its core, the scientific method. The scientific method follows a generally accepted five- to six-step process (depending upon the author) to collect and evaluate information regarding some subject. These steps include defining the problem or question to be resolved, collecting data to resolve the problem, developing a hypothesis, classifying and organizing data, testing the predictions of the hypothesis, and defining a conclusion (Figure 12.1). The scientific method helps us find answers to complex questions by providing form and direction to the search. The answer developed through the scientific method rarely claims to be absolute; rather, the scientific method provides the best explanation given the data. It is, however, an explanation arrived at with far less subjectivity. It has a clear and specific foundation that allows others to examine and evaluate for themselves. A reconstruction developed through scientific method is not based on opinions grounded in "because I think so." It always relies on specific data that others can see and independently consider.

This application of the scientific method is similar to the standard techniques applied in any criminal investigation. Even lacking training in research techniques, criminal investigators routinely define investigative questions, seek and weigh data, develop hypotheses, and make conclusions (Figure 12.2). The critical steps, however, lie between developing the hypothesis and defining the conclusion, which include classifying and organizing data and then testing predictions. These actions are often accomplished subconsciously or in a haphazard fashion by criminal investigators. When these steps are performed without an applied methodology, the reconstruction can quickly become subjective.

The methods of crime scene reconstruction can be applied in two specific circumstances to resolve investigative issues. In one fashion, the methods are utilized to reconstruct the entire incident (the crime) using the process known as event analysis. A full-scale event analysis considers all known data from the crime scene and involves the examination of all of the physical evidence in an attempt to establish specific actions of the incident and the order in which those actions occurred. Although this all-inclusive approach is oftentimes revealing, it is not always necessary given the investigative circumstances. Thus, in some instances a more discrete process is applied to data in an attempt to resolve a specific investigative question. The text will describe both techniques in some detail.

Scientific Method Used to Resolve a Specific Investigative Question

Oftentimes, a specific investigative issue will be all that is in question before the court. This issue may revolve around guilt or innocence or perhaps mitigation, but beyond this

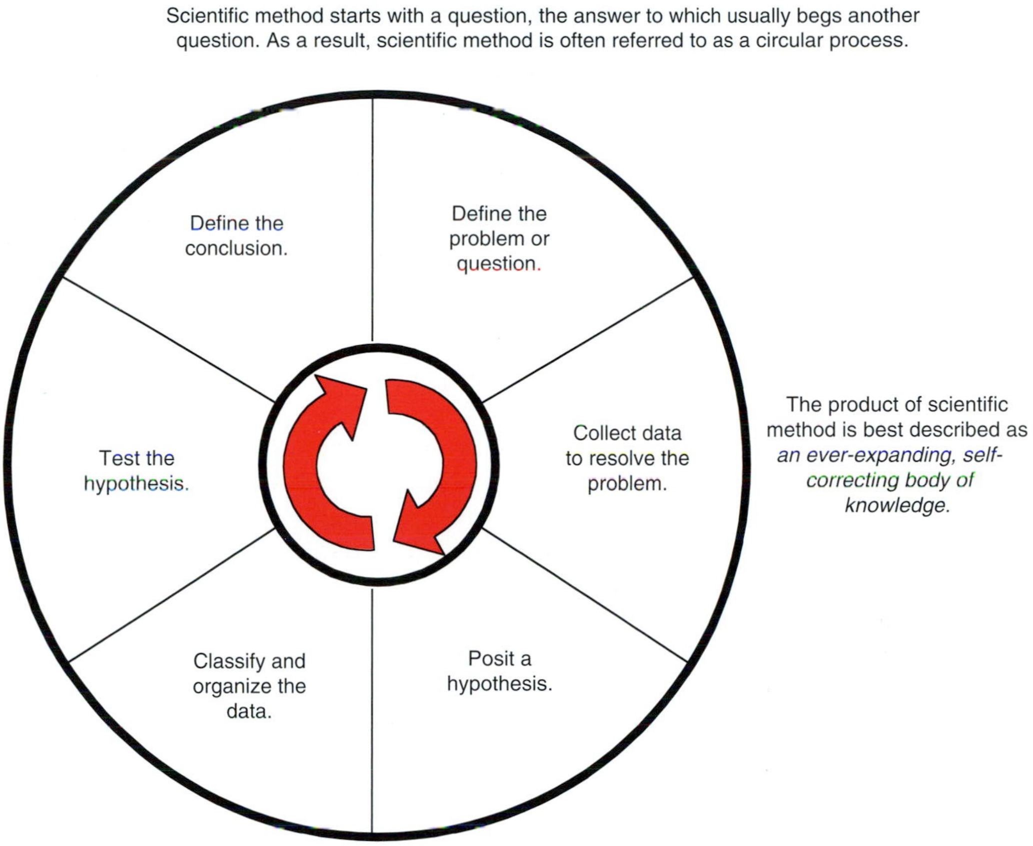

Scientific method starts with a question, the answer to which usually begs another question. As a result, scientific method is often referred to as a circular process.

Define the conclusion.

Define the problem or question.

Test the hypothesis.

Collect data to resolve the problem.

The product of scientific method is best described as *an ever-expanding, self-correcting body of knowledge.*

Classify and organize the data.

Posit a hypothesis.

Figure 12.1 Scientific method is the backbone of all analysis. It includes a six-step process that begins with a question and ends with a conclusion.

issue there will be little question as to what happened and how. In this instance, the crime scene analyst applies the scientific method in a very direct approach in an attempt to resolve the issue.

One of the most important aspects of using the scientific method is in knowing what the problem is. A problem ill-defined or too broad will reduce the probability of answering the issue. Therefore, the first concern is in knowing how to pose the question or realizing what subproblems must be answered before one can answer the ultimate question. For example, the question "Is this homicide or suicide?" is far too broad. To answer this question, the analyst must evaluate and answer a number of more precise questions, such as:

- How was the weapon employed?
- Can the final position of the weapon and the victim be explained?
- Can the injuries be self-inflicted?
- Is there any single injury that cannot be self-inflicted?

When an investigative question is posed correctly, there will be a discrete number of possible answers. These answers represent the array of viable solutions to the problem. For example, consider an investigative question of "Is the scene a dump site?" The possible answers are: yes, it is a dump site; or no, it is not a dump site. As posed, there are only

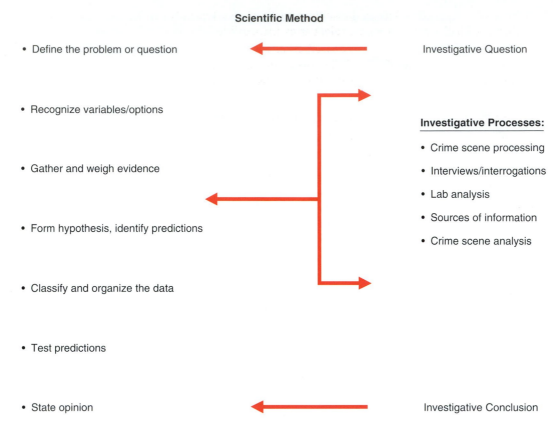

Figure 12.2 The methods employed by criminal investigators are an integral part of the scientific method. The primary difference is that the scientific method is always a well-thought-out and conscious effort.

two possible answers. If the question is "In what order were the weapons first utilized?" there may be any number of answers, depending upon the number of weapons involved.

To answer the investigative question, the analyst develops a hypothesis, an educated guess as to the answer. The development of the first hypothesis is often based on very limited knowledge. This hypothesis, however, will aid in the search for more data. The analyst looks at the situation and, based upon his or her interpretation of the scene and the evidence collected to that point, develops a belief as to what the answer to the question is. In other words, the analyst develops a conjecture. In order to evaluate this or any other hypothesis, the analyst must identify and consider predictions. With every hypothesis, there are predictions of what one might expect if the hypothesis were true. An underlying belief in reconstruction is that nothing just happens. There are events that led up to and follow any claimed action in the crime scene. The critical skill for the analyst is in recognizing these pre- and postevents, since they form the basis of any predictions. With a question and a hypothesis in mind, the analyst then looks for data that may allow him or her to test his or her predictions. Once the data necessary to resolve the question are collected, they must be organized and classified in order to understand their meaning. In this stage, the analyst evaluates how any one item of data may relate to any other. It is through this correlation of information that we are able to test a hypothesis and make a conclusion. In some instances, the predictions regarding a specific hypothesis may hold, and we will conclude that our hypothesis is possible. In others, the predictions may fail, requiring us to either revisit the hypothesis or reject it as impossible.

The scientific method is often described as a circular process, creating an ever-expanding, self-correcting body of knowledge on a subject. As this body of knowledge develops, the scientific method is best at eliminating possibilities rather than identifying the one and only answer. Therefore, in order to resolve an issue, the analyst will have to evaluate any viable hypothesis, test the predictions, and when appropriate, eliminate those that are unworkable. Only then can the analyst objectively conclude anything.

An important part of crime scene reconstruction is in knowing what the data prove or disprove. For example, the presence of a fingerprint on the trigger of a murder weapon in no way defines absolutely that the owner of that fingerprint was responsible for pulling the trigger during the murder. It may be compelling evidence, but one must consider other possibilities as well. An obvious possibility is that the individual picked the weapon up at the scene following its discharge, inadvertently leaving the print as it was handled. Both when testing predictions or in understanding and correlating data, the analyst must have a clear and precise understanding of what the data prove or do not prove. Inferences presented as data (e.g., Joe's fingerprint is on the trigger, thus Joe pulled the trigger) can lead the reconstruction to ruin. The analyst must identify the predictions, test them, and then define an overall conclusion based on the predictions. In some instances, this may require correlating only a few pieces of data, but in other instances, it may demand considering a significant number of data items.

Event Analysis — Reconstructing Entire Events

Figure 12.3 is a case example of an event-analysis worksheet, which is an effective format for dealing with and resolving specific investigative issues. On those occasions when a single investigative issue is in question, the use of the scientific method in combination with the event-segment worksheets is a functional and appropriate response. Oftentimes, particularly in homicide investigations where little, if anything, is known about the events that transpired, there is a need to reconstruct all of the events associated with the incident. This is a daunting task, demanding significant effort on the part of the analyst. Event analysis uses the scientific method as a backdrop while applying seven steps to identify (as fully as possible) the specific actions taken during an incident. Event analysis concentrates on objective evidence (the physical evidence) and only rarely concerns itself with subjective aspects such as witness testimony. The end result of the event analysis, however, will be compared in detail with testimonial evidence and investigative theories in an effort to determine whether they are valid statements or theories.

In order to understand event analysis, we must define three basic terms associated with the process. The "incident" in event analysis is the overall situation being investigated. In time, it may well be identified as a criminal act, but to refer to the incident as a crime prior to the analysis is, in some cases, putting the cart before the horse. Each incident is made up of macrocomponents, analogous to the chapters in a book. These chapters are referred to as "events." Events define gross aspects of the incident, such as approaching the scene, controlling the victims, killing the victims, etc. Without significant effort, these chapters can be defined at the scene by simply considering what the investigator observes. As a result of an in-depth analysis, they are later refined and adjusted to be more accurate. Each event is made up of "event segments," microcomponents of

Event Segment Analysis Worksheet

Investigative Question: Was the victim shot while under the truck?

Possible Hypothesis

A- The victim was shot while under the truck.

B- The victim was not under the truck when shot.

Data on Specific Event Segments

1. GSW right lateral chest, circumferential abrasion ring.
2. Track - right to left, front to back, neither up or down.
3. Bullet recovered (.380).
4. Wound is 51 inches from the heel.
5. Victim found supine, halfway under the truck.
6. One .380 shell casing on the victim s side of the fence.
7. Three .380 shell casings on far side of fence.
8. Only two defects perforate the entire fence from the far side.
9. Both trajectories are 60—50 in. up from the ground plane depending on elevation of the given position.
10. Both trajectories are relatively level trajectories with the ground plane.
11. Victim was upright at some point after bleeding began.
12. Victim s arm was up, aligned with the shoulders.

Information Relationships

Pertaining to Option A:

      The presence of a .380 casing (7) on the victim s side of the fence is somewhat consistent with a possible shooter located on the passenger side of the truck. The victim's position in the scene (6) combined with the evident trajectory through the body (1 and 2) is possible, given a round fired beneath the truck from the passenger s side. But such a trajectory demands the weapon be fired low to the ground.

Pertaining to Option B:

      The casings on the far side of the fence (8) and the evident defects in the fence (9) make it evident the shooter was still firing from the far side of the fence. They also allow for a mechanism of injury to the victim. But the trajectories of these defects (10) prevent any possible position in which the victim is low to the ground. The evident location of the wound (5) and the trajectories of the .380 rounds (10) perforating the fence are consistent with the victim being upright when shot. Combined with the wound track (2) all support an upright position. The three defects in the victim s shirt require that the victim s arm be upright and the cloth free hanging. These defects also are consistent with a standing victim. Finally, the bloodstain patterns indicate the victim was upright after beginning to bleed. This precludes the supine position as a wounding position and is consistent with the standing position.

Opinion as to the Most Probable Conclusion:

      Option B is the most probable; the victim was not under the truck when shot.

Figure 12.3   An event-analysis worksheet. This document is used to evaluate specific investigative issues. Such documents serve to capture the information relative to the issue (data on specific event segments) and how that information relates to other information (information relationships).

the event. Event segments are snapshots of specific moments in time, detailing specific actions that occurred.

The presence of physical evidence and a variety of interrelationships between items of evidence will speak to the existence of any given event segment. Event segments are always defined by specific data. The more event segments the analyst is able to define, the more accurately the analyst can describe the true nature of the event. Thus an event analysis is always reverse-engineered, beginning with the crime scene data and working backward to a conclusion. Event analysis is conducted after all forensic reports are completed and all available data have been collected. The steps used to produce this analysis are described below. A case example is included, but for the sake of brevity, the supporting documentation for the example is limited. Although the example will not demonstrate the overall scene analysis, it will illustrate the application of the process.

Step 1: Collect Data, Establish Likely Events

Walking into the scene, the crime scene analyst is bombarded with information. Throughout processing, additional information comes to light, all of which allows the investigator to understand the gross aspects of the analysis. For instance, in a close-in knife attack, it will be obvious that the perpetrator had to get close to the victim, even though the analyst may have no idea as to "how" that was done. As the scene is evaluated, areas where confrontations or a specific wounding occurred may be evident. This kind of information will speak to the existence of the event, even though the specifics of the event may still be lacking. The true function of events is the same as our analogous chapter of a book. They serve to break the reconstruction down into manageable parts, to which specific details can be associated and then worked, rather than trying to deal with all of the information as a single conglomerate.

Case Example: Defining Events

A husband returns home to find his wife dead on the floor of their bathroom (Figure 12.4). She is naked, with significant blunt trauma to the head and bearing signs of ligature strangulation around her neck. Ties belonging to the husband are beneath the body. There is a significant volume of blood in the scene, but all visible blood is confined to the area of the bathroom. The house shows no signs or indications that anyone has ransacked or searched it in any fashion, and nothing is missing. There is no evidence of disarray anywhere else in the home. The home security system is off, and the front door was unlocked upon the arrival of the husband. There are no bloodied weapons in the scene or unbloodied items that would be consistent with the blunt-force injuries.

Based upon the initial information presented, there are three events readily recognized: entry, strangulation assault, and final blunt-trauma assault. It is always possible that there are additional events, such as a search of the house or some other postincident behavior by the perpetrator. Lacking evidence of such activity, however, we confine ourselves to what the initial scene suggests until other evidence presents itself.

Step 2: Establish Event Segments from the Data Available

By considering all of the information available, the analyst begins to define specific aspects of the reconstruction. The order in which these event segments are identified is totally

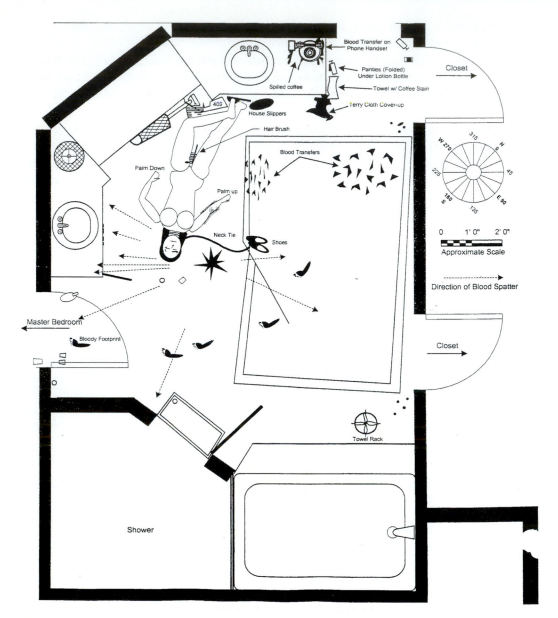

Figure 12.4 The crime scene sketch of the scene depicted in Figure 12.5 through Figure 12.8. (Figure courtesy of Oklahoma City Police Department Crime Scene Investigation Unit. With permission.)

random. Event segments are identified through evaluation of forensic reports, photographs, sketches, and examination of physical evidence. Oftentimes, when developing the event segments, the investigator will find it beneficial to work data regarding one area of the scene at a time. This will help reduce the randomness of developing the event segments and make it easier for the analyst to make sense of the bigger picture.

Event segments can be defined by the presence of specific evidence, by the interrelationships of that evidence, or by scientific analysis of that evidence. For example, in a shooting scene, a bullet recovered from the wall of a scene indicates a gunshot event associated with that area. The defect created by the bullet may point to a specific trajectory within the room. That trajectory, in consideration of the presence of ejected shell casings, may support the general location from which the gunshot was fired. The wound track identified in the ME's (medical examiner) report, of a perforating gunshot injury, along with the presence of a spatter pattern in the scene, may identify the orientation of the victim at that moment. Finally, an analysis of the casing and recovered bullet will at the very least identify the nature of the weapon involved. If specific weapons were seized, scientific analysis may identify or refute that a specific weapon was the wounding agent. Each of these items defines part of the snapshots of what transpired during the incident. Event segments are described by the analyst as objectively as possible, eliminating inference and any subjective association. Each will have a specific basis, grounded in physical evidence that allows the analyst to lay claim to its existence.

As every aspect of the physical evidence and scene is examined, any number of event segments may be discovered and documented. How many are discovered is a matter of how detailed the investigator is, how much evidence exists, and how well it was documented.

Case Example: Defining Event Segments

In reviewing the scene (See Figure 12.4 through Figure 12.8) and discussing the autopsy with the ME, we can establish the following event segments:

- The ties were obtained prior to alarming the victim.
- A spatter-producing event occurred low to the floor while the cabinet door was open.
- A significant volume of blood was deposited onto the floor, creating a coagulated pool.
- The white rug was displaced.
- The blood pool was disturbed.
- The hair dryer and towel were deposited on the floor.
- The lamp was deposited on the floor unplugged.
- The victim was left in her final position.
- The spray bottle was deposited on the lamp.
- The hairbrush was deposited on the lamp cord.
- The victim was struck multiple times with an unknown heavy object that had distinct angled edges (ME report).
- The victim was strangled from behind with a ligature, consistent with the ties, which would have immobilized her (ME report).
- The blunt-force weapon was removed from the scene.

These event segments may or may not be significant to the investigation, and they are developed in no specific order or with any association. Obviously, when dealing with the entire scene, the number of event segments would increase significantly.

Step 3: Define Associated Event Segments

As the event segments are developed, the analyst looks for associations between the various event segments and events. Once all of the segments are identified, the analyst reviews the entire product for any associations that may have been missed. It is here that events assist the reconstruction. The analyst makes associations of the various event segments to the events, breaking the mass of data into manageable chunks of information. Occasionally, specific event segments will be misidentified, or the analyst will not recognize what, if any,

Figure 12.5 A view of the bathroom. A significant volume of blood has pooled on the floor and was subsequently disturbed. (Figure courtesy of Oklahoma City Police Department Crime Scene Investigation Unit. With permission.)

Figure 12.6 Event segments defined by this area of the bathroom include a spatter event near the floor while the cabinet door was open. (Figure courtesy of Oklahoma City Police Department Crime Scene Investigation Unit. With permission.)

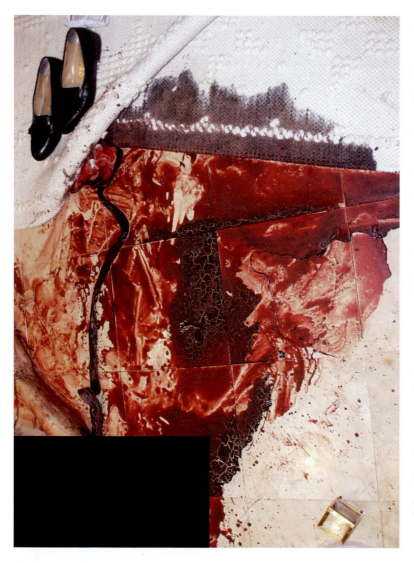

Figure 12.7 Event segments defined by this area include movement of the white rug after the pooling of the blood. (Figure courtesy of Oklahoma City Police Department Crime Scene Investigation Unit. With permission.)

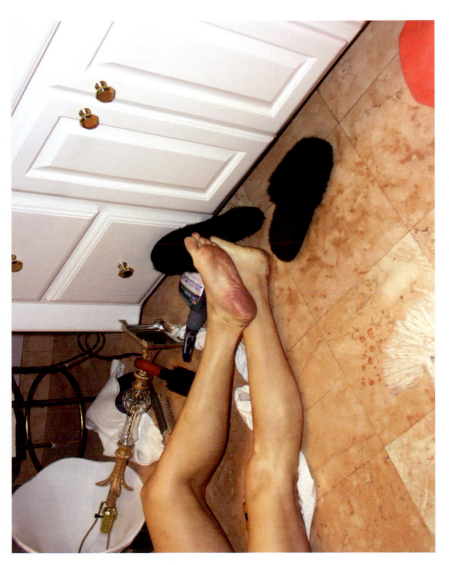

Figure 12.8 A significant number of relational and sequencing aspects are evident in this photograph. Consider the positions and layering evident by the lamp, the lamp cord, the hairbrush, the spray bottle, and the victim's final position. The hairdryer is located beneath the white towel at the top of the picture. (Figure courtesy of Oklahoma City Police Department Crime Scene Investigation Unit. With permission.)

association exists. As the process continues, misidentification of event segments will become evident, and their rightful place in the reconstruction will be found. In some instances, however, the analyst will have no idea as to how or in what manner the segment relates to the incident. There will be little doubt that the event segment occurred, but its context in the overall incident may not be understood.

Case Example: Define Associated Event Segments

After identifying the event segments, we must associate them with our events. As discussed, our definition of events may change in the light of additional information. In this scene, we need to add an event — postincident actions — to describe actions that clearly occurred subsequent to the murder. After making this change, we can identify the following associations.

- Strangulation assault
  The ties were obtained prior to alarming the victim.
  The hair dryer and towel were deposited on the floor.
  The lamp was deposited on the floor unplugged.
  The victim was left in her final position.
  The victim was strangled from behind with a ligature, consistent with the ties, which would have immobilized her (ME report).
- Final blunt-trauma assault
  A spatter-producing event occurred low to the floor while the cabinet door was open.
  A significant volume of blood was deposited onto the floor, creating a coagulated pool.
  The victim was struck multiple times with an unknown heavy object that had distinct angled edges (ME report).
  The blunt-force weapon was removed from the scene (sketch).
- Postincident actions
  The white rug was displaced.
  The blood pool was disturbed.
- Event segments that have no clear association
  The spray bottle was deposited on the lamp.
  The hairbrush was deposited on the lamp.

These last two segments may be associated with the initial assault, or they could be some form of postincident actions. Lacking a specific association, they are kept separate for the time being.

Step 4: Order and Sequence the Associated Event Segments

Reconstruction considers not only that specific actions occurred during a crime, but also the order in which they occurred. By considering a variety of data elements, this chronology of sequence between respective event segments can be identified. This sequencing information can be self-evident, or it can be quite subtle. For example, a wound must occur before bleeding can begin. Bleeding must occur before a bloodstain is deposited, and the bloodstain must exist before a subsequent action can disturb it. The sequence of wound, bleeding, deposition of blood is self-evident, but the subtle differences that may allow the analyst to recognize when the alteration of the bloodstain occurred may be anything but evident.

The chronology of event segments provides form to what would otherwise be a mass of information. This chronology of the event segments is defined in two ways: either as absolute chronology or relative chronology. Absolute chronology is related to timing aspects. When did the event segment occur? In this era of computer-aided dispatch (CAD) systems, there is often a wealth of information regarding when specific events occurred. For example, it is possible to compare the time of a 911 call with the background noise and description of what is occurring, creating an absolute chronology. Although not common, when evaluated, such information is often revealing. Relative chronology, on the other hand, is the sequencing of event segments in relation to one another. Relative chronology is the true backbone of the reconstruction. Relative chronology speaks only to what precedes or what follows a given segment, with no association to absolute time. Borrowing on concepts from archeology, the analyst considers the event segments in an effort to define those that must have preceded another event segment (known as *terminus ante quem*), those that must have followed another event segment (*terminus post quem*), and those that were likely simultaneous event segments (*terminus peri quem*). See Figure 12.9. Rarely will sequencing information exist that allows the technician to associate the order of each and every event segment with every other segment. In some fashion, however, the relative chronology of each known event segment will be evident in relation to at least one other segment. By combining these interrelationships, the analyst will develop a mosaic of logical order for the majority of the event segments (Figure 12.10).

Case Example: Ordering Associated Event Segments

After identifying and associating the event segments with an event, we examine the information in an effort to identify a sequence or chronology for the event segments. See Figure 12.11. The segments are ordered as follows:

B: Strangulation assault
1. The ties were obtained prior to alarming the victim.
2. The hair dryer and towel were deposited on the floor.
3. The lamp was deposited on the floor unplugged.
4. The victim was strangled from behind with a ligature, consistent with the ties, which would have immobilized her (ME report).
5. The spray bottle was deposited on the lamp.
6. The victim was left in her final position.
7. The hairbrush was deposited on the lamp.

Prior to assaulting the victim, the perpetrator must obtain the ties, so this takes the number one position, B1. The hair dryer and towel are not bloodied and are associated with the counter adjacent to where the victim is found laying. They take position B2. The victim was then strangled and immobilized, leading to her position on the floor. The positioning of the spray bottle beneath the victim's foot is very likely a simultaneous event to the final position of the victim. The hairbrush is on top of the lamp, so it arrived some time after the lamp was deposited on the floor, position B3.

C: Final blunt-trauma assault
1. A spatter-producing event occurred low to the floor while the cabinet door was open.
2. The victim was struck multiple times with an unknown heavy object that had distinct angled edges (ME report).

Defining Relative Chronology

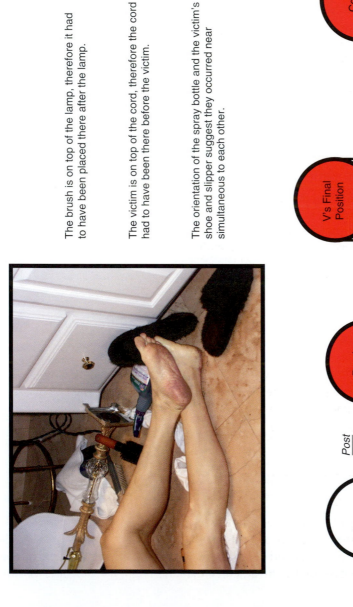

The brush is on top of the lamp, therefore it had to have been placed there after the lamp.

The victim is on top of the cord, therefore the cord had to have been there before the victim.

The orientation of the spray bottle and the victim's shoe and slipper suggest they occurred near simultaneous to each other.

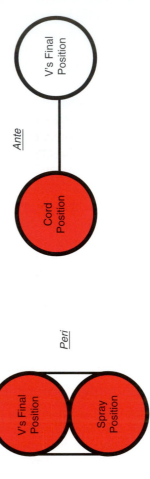

Figure 12.9 Relative chronology is defined by three associations. An action can precede another action (*terminus ante quem*); an action can follow another action (*terminus post quem*); two actions can be nearly simultaneous (*terminus peri quem*).

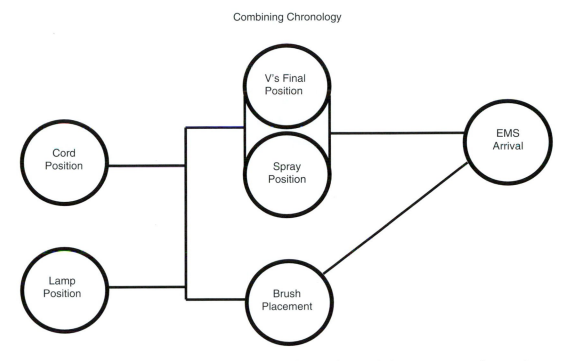

Figure 12.10 The most effective means of understanding and demonstrating relative chronology is to illustrate it graphically.

3. A significant volume of blood was deposited onto the floor, creating a coagulated pool.
4. The blunt-force weapon was removed from the scene.

Before spatter can occur, there must be a wound, but in this instance we may be looking at simultaneous events, given the position and immobilized victim. After wounding, a large volume of blood bled out into the scene, producing the pool. Sometime subsequent to the attack, the wounding agent was removed from the scene.

D: Postincident actions
1. The blood pool was disturbed.
2. The white rug was displaced.

The blood pool was exposed to the environment for some time prior to its disturbance. The pool has limits, indicating it extended to the original position of the rug and that the rug was saturated by the pool. The rug was then displaced to the northeast.

The relative chronology presented by this information is not a simple linear series of events (e.g., 1 through 5), and the only functional way to sort them out is to graph them, as seen in Figure 12.11.

Step 5: Audit the Information

From the moment that order between two or more event segments is defined until the completion of the report, the analyst constantly checks and challenges his or her beliefs. Auditing is the process of looking beyond the obvious to try and validate or refute previous conclusions. It is often the case that contradictory evidence suggests multiple variations

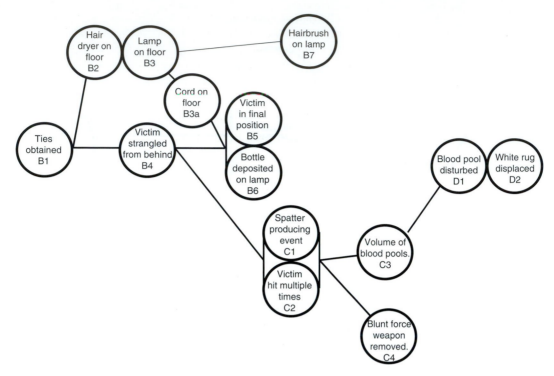

Figure 12.11   By combining the evident relationships between actions, the investigator can develop a mosaic of the overall incident. Although there is no specific relationship between the presence of the hair dryer (B2) or the lamp (B3) on the floor and the victim being strangled (B4), their relationship becomes evident through their shared relationship to the ties being obtained (B1) and the bottle deposited on the lamp (B6).

of order or even associations. Step 5 is a process that, once begun, really never stops. The addition or consideration of some new piece of data or data relationships may allow the analyst to better define a sequence or eliminate a sequence that was previously defined. The most important aspect of this step is to take a position completely opposite of your original opinion. Auditing only works when you actively try to prove yourself incorrect.

Step 6: Determine and Final-Order the Events

The reader may recall that a certain level of assumption was introduced when defining the events. Events are rarely defined by hard facts in the initial stages, yet they are often self-evident. After working through the event segments, the order and nature of the events will be far more evident. This may demand redefining the events or even reordering the events. The information derived from the event-segment analysis will provide the basis for reordering or revisiting the events.

Step 7: Flow-Chart the Overall Incident Based on the Event and Event-Segment Sequence

The incident is now in the form of specific actions, ordered and sequenced as effectively as possible. To validate and audit the analysis and to make it understandable to an audience, the analyst graphically charts out the reconstruction. Figure 12.11 is just a small part of the entire flowchart.

The end product of event analysis is a defined outline of what can objectively be concluded as having occurred during the incident. The only things included on the flow-chart are objective aspects. The analyst may have event segments or sequencing information that s/he believes is correct but cannot objectively establish. This information is not forgotten, as it may be helpful in developing an overall theory of the crime, but it is not included in the final flowchart.

Care must be taken to protect the objectivity of any crime scene analysis, particularly when the investigating officer is the one conducting the analysis. A crime scene analysis will define both factual evidence and opinion evidence. It is imperative that the analyst know the difference. From the photo in Figure 12.8, it is a fact that the lamp and cord were in their final position prior to the final positioning of the victim. There are no options. Whether the spray bottle and victim's final position are a simultaneous action is not an absolute fact, it is an opinion. The totality of the objective evidence suggests that they were simultaneous, but it is possible the bottle's positioning preceded the victim's final position. Granted this detail may not be of great importance, but it is still an opinion. To make the flowchart more objective, the two items could easily be separated, rather than presenting them as simultaneous.

Another aspect of maintaining objectivity is that the analysis report will, for the most part, be anonymous with regard to suspects. For example, given a circumstance where "Joe" is caught after a murder and a pair of boots in his possession have spatter containing the victim's DNA, Joe's name would not appear on the analysis. A resulting event segment might read, "The brown boots were in proximity to a forceful impact involving the victim." Granted "Joe" may well have been wearing the boots, but the analyst has no way of objectively establishing this. Thus, the crime scene analyst cannot invade the jury's domain of deciding guilt. This is true even if the investigator knows that statements made by "Joe" and other evidence implicate him. Additional care should be exercised when identification evidence is encountered that is associated with a suspect. Fingerprints, blood, or other body fluids may well establish the presence of the individual in the scene, but that does not tell us everything that they were doing at the time. The analyst cannot presume the nature of that presence. Let us continue the previous example and say that in the crime scene a bloody fingerprint is located. The fingerprint belongs to the suspect "Joe." Based on this evidence, a resulting event segment might read, "Subsequent to bloodshed, Joe was in contact with the victim's blood while present in the scene." Granted, the evidence against "Joe" is certainly starting to stack up, but the analyst has no *objective* evidence to prove that "Joe" was in the scene wearing the boots and killing the victim. Trust the jury to make sense of this. Unless some specific identification evidence places a suspect in the scene or associated with the evidence, the name of the suspect should not be included in the analysis report. When such evidence does exist, the analyst should use caution in claiming what the evidence proves the suspect was doing.

The use of event analysis is varied. First and foremost, it provides a backdrop that the investigative team can use to test investigative theories. It is also effective when used to evaluate testimony and confessions, helping to identify individuals who may not be telling all or telling the truth. It is important to remember that the scientific method is best for excluding things rather than identifying the one right answer. But exclusion always adds clarity. In evaluating a theory or statement, if the information presented contradicts the analysis, the theory or statement is excluded as having occurred in that particular fashion. Thus the theory must be reexamined, or the statement giver must be reinterviewed to understand the contradiction. If resolution is not possible, the theory or statement is invalid and excluded by the physical evidence.

On the other hand, the statement or theory may match up to each and every aspect of the known reconstruction. That does not prove that the theory or statement is the "one and only right answer." It merely establishes that the theory or statement is possible given the circumstances. Remember that a reconstruction routinely provides only a skeleton of facts about what transpired. There are always holes or blank spots, areas where there are no supporting data or facts to identify what transpired. Take the spray bottle in Figure 12.8. Why is it in the scene, and when was it placed there? For every person who might choose to look at that issue, there is an equal number of ways to fill in the answer. Was the bottle part of a postincident cleanup? Or was it placed there the day before and forgotten and is now simply a coincidental artifact? The totality of objective evidence would support either theory. Without specific facts to evaluate the issue, we cannot exclude either possibility. As a result, a reconstruction can routinely present a situation in which there may be any number of possible scenarios that, although similar, are also materially significant to the investigation in their differences.

This is the dilemma of reconstruction. In each and every case, we are presented with only so many pieces of the puzzle, and no matter how hard we work, there will always be blank spots. These blank spots will be of a nature that the analyst will have little, if any, idea as to the nature of the associated events. Forget concise theories; forget stories that play out from start to finish; this simply is not the case in crime scene analysis. But from the pieces presented, we have an obligation and duty to derive the most objective picture possible. The methodology of event analysis allows the investigator to create an objective picture of specific elements of the crime or incident. Armed with this information, the investigator can resolve issues relating to investigative theories; evaluate statements by witnesses, suspects, and victims; and, when necessary, provide a firmly grounded opinion in court of what took place.

Summary

The possession of data in no way implies an understanding of what that data really means. Collecting evidence and then failing to consider the context and interrelationships of the various items of evidence in the scene creates a similar circumference. Thus, the final step of crime scene investigation is to conduct an analysis. There are two forms of analysis. The first is conducted at the crime lab by the forensic scientist or technician. From this effort, more refined data regarding the evidence is established. Once this is complete, the second form of analysis — a crime scene analysis —is possible.

Crime scene analysis, crime scene reconstruction, and event analysis are synonymous. They refer to a process of evaluating objective evidence (the physical evidence and its context) in an effort to define specific actions that occurred. Once defined, these actions are considered against one another in an attempt to order and sequence them. The appropriate vehicle for conducting crime analysis has and always will be scientific method. Scientific method begins with a question, followed by a collection of data to resolve the question. The analyst puts forth a hypothesis, an educated guess as to the answer to the question. In order to test the hypothesis, the analyst must make predictions regarding the hypothesis and seek additional evidence in the scene that would corroborate or refute the hypothesis. After considering and testing all viable alternatives, the analyst defines a conclusion. In seeking answers, the more precise the question, the more likely it is that an objective answer can be found. The final product of a crime scene analysis is distinct from an investigative report. It deals only with objective evidence and what that evidence can define. Subjective aspects are excluded whenever possible from the crime scene analysis report.

Suggested Reading

Bevel, T. and Gardner, R.M., *Bloodstain Pattern Analysis: with an Introduction to Crime Scene Reconstruction*, 1st ed. CRC Press, Boca Raton, FL, 1997.

Nordby, J., *Dead Reckoning: the Art of Forensic Detection*, CRC Press, Boca Raton, FL, 2000.

Rynearson, J.M. and Chisum, W.J., *Evidence and Crime Scene Reconstruction*, J.M. Rynearson, Ed., Shingletown, CA, 1989.

Chapter Questions

1. What are the two venues in which analysis is accomplished?
2. Why are context and interrelationship so important to crime scene analysis?
3. Describe the steps involved in scientific method.
4. Crime scene analysis can be applied to two different issues. What are they?
5. Why is the manner in which an investigative question posed so important?
6. What is the difference between relative and absolute chronology?
7. What is the basis of any defined actions (event segments) that the crime scene analyst identifies?
8. When testing investigative conclusions using event analysis, what are the two possible results?

Notes

1. Gross, H., as translated by Adams, J., *Criminal Investigations: a Practical Textbook,* Sweet & Maxwell Ltd., London, England.
2. Association of Crime Scene Reconstruction, By-laws, www.acsr.org, 1995.
3. Bevel, T. and Gardner, R.M., *Bloodstain Pattern Analysis: with an Introduction to Crime Scene Reconstruction*, 2nd ed., CRC Press, Boca Raton, FL, 2001, pp. 45–50.
4. Gross, H., System der Kriminalistic, in *Criminal Investigation: a Practical Textbook*, Adam, J.C., Ed., Sweet Maxwell Ltd., London, 1924, pp. 37–38.
5. Gross, H., System der Kriminalistic, in *Criminal Investigation: a Practical Textbook*, Adam, J.C., Ed., Sweet Maxwell Ltd., London, 1924, p. 38.
6. May, L.S., *Scientific Murder Investigation*, Institute of Scientific Criminology, Seattle, WA, 1933, p. 9.
7. Ibid.
8. Block, E., *The Wizard of Berkeley,* Coward-McCann Publishing, New York, NY, 1958.
9. Rhodes, H., *Clues and Crime,* Mussery Publishing, London, England, 1933.

10. Kirk, P., *Crime Investigation,* Interscience Publishers, Inc., New York, NY, 1953.

11. Kirk, P.L., affidavit of Paul Leland Kirk, in the Court of Common Pleas, Criminal Branch, State of Ohio Cuyahoga County vs. Samuel H. Shepherd, No. 64571, Cuyahoga County, OH, Apr. 26, 1955.

12. O'Hara, C.E., *Fundamentals of Criminal Investigation,* 4th ed., Charles C. Thomas Publishing, Springfield, IL, 1976, pp. 20–21.

13. Op. cit., p. 58.

14. Osterburg, J.W., *Criminal Investigation: a Method of Reconstructing the Past,* Anderson Publishing, Cincinnati, OH, 1992, p. 194.

15. Rynearson, J.M. and Chisum, W.J., *Evidence and Crime Scene Reconstruction,* J.M. Rynearson, Ed., Shingletown, CA, 1989, pp. 100–108.

16. Lee, H.C., *Crime Scene Investigation,* Central Police University Press, Taiwan, 1994, pp. 198–200.

17. Lee, H.C., Palmbach, T., and Miller, M.T., *Henry Lee's Crime Scene Handbook,* Academic Press, San Diego, CA, 2001, pp. 276–281.

18. Lamb, P., The Murder of Carl Chauhan: Using BPA to Clarify Events, presentation to International Association of Bloodstain Pattern Analysts, Odessa, TX, Oct. 2003.

19. Bevel, T. and Gardner, R.M., *Bloodstain Pattern Analysis: with an Introduction to Crime Scene Reconstruction,* 1st ed., CRC Press, Boca Raton, FL, 1997.

Appendix A:
Crime Scene Equipment

What ultimately ends up in a unit's crime scene kit is very much a matter of personal preference and the organization's operational tempo. Nevertheless, to meet any crime scene processing task, an investigative unit should have the following items in some form or fashion, or have near-immediate access to such items on an on-call basis. If developing a "new" cache of equipment, begin with those items most often required and build the equipment kits up over time.

Once an established kit is in place (whether it is mobile or kept at the office), supervisors must initiate a recurring inventory and restocking procedure. This resupply should be scheduled at a minimum twice monthly. If resupply is left to the individual technician's discretion, the crime scene team is guaranteed to arrive on a significant scene missing critical items. Purchase and organize the equipment based on the way the unit operates and to meet the environmental conditions in which the unit operates.

Basic Kits

Fingerprint Kit

Regular and magnetic powders (light and dark colors or biochromatic)
Fiberglass brushes for each color of standard powder
Magnetic brushes
Fluorescent powder
Lifting tape (both standard and 2 to 3 in. wide)
Rough-surface lifting tape
Fingerprint-tape backing cards (white and black)
Hinge lifters (multiple sizes and colors of backing)
Palm adhesive lifters
Rubber or gel lifters
Silicone lifting material
Scissors
Sharp-point indelible pen
Postmortem print kit
Superglue (fuming wand, liquid, or cards)

Portable fuming chamber
Small-particle reagent

Photography Kit

35-mm SLR or large-format or digital camera with capability of:
    50-mm lens
    55- or 105-mm macro lens
    28-mm lens
Tripod
Shutter-release cable
Off-camera flash unit with diffuser
Duo-sync cord (minimum 3-ft length)
Reference scales including:
    ABFO scale
    6-in. white and black rulers
    Footprint scales or folding scale
    Adhesive measuring tape
    Millimeter scales for close-up photographs
    Adhesive numbers and letters
    Paper scales (1 to 96 in.)
Photo placards (both alpha and numeric)
Surveyor flags
High-visibility photo markers (e.g., Evipaq evidence markers)
Tape, clay, or reusable rubber adhesive compound (used to attach scales in odd positions)
Spare batteries (flash and camera)
ALS filters for camera lens (orange and yellow)
Photo gray card
Lens cleaner and paper
Video camera with strobe

Casting Kit

Dental stone (prepackaged in zip-lock–type containers)
Collapsible gallon water container
Expandable impression form
Spray sealant for loose soil conditions
Silicone evidence-casting material (e.g., Durocast or Microsil)
Clay (used to create dams for silicone casting on vertical surfaces)
Gelatin lifters
Footwear adhesive or rubber lifters
Fingerprint roller (clean, used solely for impression evidence)
Electrostatic lifting device and film
Flour sift
Indelible marking pen
Tape
Consider an alternative mixing container for dental stone (e.g., rubber or plastic bowl)

Mapping and Sketching Kit

Magnetic compass
Tape measures
    10 to 25 ft steel or fiberglass (×2)
    100 to 200 ft steel or fiberglass
    Wheel or rolling tape measure
    If available, infrared, laser, or sonic measuring device
Graph paper and clipboard
Writing tablets
Pens
Appropriate straight edges and templates (e.g., Berol templates)
Body and vehicle diagrams
Preprinted evidence measurement logs
Self-adhesive sticky note pads (2 × 2 in., 2 × 4 in.) (used to set reference points)
Bold markers
2-ft rebar sections (×2) (used to set datum points)

When using baseline techniques:
    100-ft-wide cloth tape measure
    Grading stakes

When using polar coordinates:
    Sighting transit or laser with tripod
    Stadia rod

When using grid techniques:
    Grading stakes
    Twine (used to align stakes or set grid in gravesites)
    Rigid grid for gravesites

Personal Protective Gear

Tyvek suits, sleeves, booties
Face masks or particle masks
Rubber gloves (heavy duty, nonpowdered)
Goggles
Work gloves
Knee pads
Heavy-duty clothes and boots for hazardous scenes (e.g., fire scenes)
Prewet hand towels (e.g., Clorox wipes)
Paper towel
Hand sanitizer
Portable eyewash station
Sunscreen/insect repellent
Biochemical gas mask with filters
Self-contained breathing apparatus (SCBA) gear if utilizing solvent-based techniques
    on scene

Scene-Integrity Equipment

Barrier tape
Rope/parachute cord
Crime scene screen
If possible, crime scene tent/cover (prevents overhead observation by media)

Evidence Collection Tools

Basic tool kit containing:
    Hammer
    Screwdrivers
    Socket set
    Pliers
    Crescent wrench
    Saws
Pry bar
Metal detector
Inspection mirror or bore scope
Glass cutter
Forceps
EMT utility scissors (they cut almost anything)
Single-edge razor blades
Sterile swabs
Sterile disposable pipettes
Sterile disposable scalpels
Square-bladed shovel
Sieve screens

Evidence Collection Containers

Paper envelopes:
    Small (change envelopes)
    Medium (letter sized)
    Large (manila)
Bags (paper):
    Small (lunch style)
    Large (grocery style)
Bags (plastic zip-lock–style, various sizes)
Large plastic bags (used to containerize bloody objects until they can be returned to a drying room)
Paper for creating pharmacist folds or glassine envelopes
Clean pill bottles
Clean plastic bottles, with screw-on lids
Clean pizza boxes (for storing ESLD lifts)

Indelible marking pens
Evidence tags
Butcher paper
Large, 3- to 4-in. clear adhesive lifting tape (used for recovering fiber and hair evidence)
Appropriate rape evidence recovery kits (both victim and suspect)
Unused paint cans (pint and gallon) with lids
Evidence tape
Cardboard boxes and plastic ties (used to stabilize and containerize weapons, knives, and similar objects)

Lighting Equipment

Utility work light (halogen) and stand
Flashlights with spare batteries
Drop light (e.g., mechanic's light)
Spare bulbs for all lighting devices
100-ft interior/exterior extension cord, with three-prong outlet
Alternative light source (e.g., blue light, FLS, or ALS)
Spare barrier-filter goggles for ALS

Additional Kits

Bloodstain Pattern Analysis/Enhancement Kit

Luminol
Black plastic sheeting (used for blacking out windows during luminol exams)
Leuco-crystal violet
Fluorescein
Presumptive blood test kits
5× loupe with millimeter scale
Scientific calculator
Protractor
Self-adhesive sticky note pads (2 × 4 in.) (used to mark and label bloodstain patterns)
Bold markers

Trajectory Analysis Kit

Trajectory rods
Centering guides
Angle finder
Plumbtesmo/Cupertesmo detection paper
10 × 10-in. white foam core square (used with laser trajectory kits)

Appendix B:
Risk Management

Throughout the text, there were repeated references to hazards and risks and the efforts needed to mitigate them. Risk is mitigated by implementing risk management. Risk management is not a euphemism for telling the crime scene team to "be careful out there." Risk management is a deliberate effort to identify hazards, assess the significance of those hazards, and then implement controls to mitigate the risk and reduce the probability of injury or harm. Risk management is employed across industry, the military, and other organizations as a method of increasing the safety of personnel.

Risk management has four basic tenets:

1. *Begin managing risk in the planning stages of an event:* Before one engages in a specific activity, it is useful to sit down in advance and identify potential hazards. When planners know and consider the hazards in advance, control measures are more deliberate and thought out more thoroughly, and thus they are more likely to resolve the risk. Hasty attempts to deal with a risk during an activity may or may not resolve the problem. Oftentimes, such spur-of-the-moment responses result in what the military refers to as being "overcome by events" (OBE).

2. *Accept no unnecessary risk:* Unnecessary risk is generally considered to be a willful engagement in a hazardous activity for which an obvious control measure exists. Driving a car without buckling the seat belt is an unnecessary risk. We all have to take our chances on the highways, but there is no rational reason for doing so without using readily available safety equipment. Entering a biohazard crime scene without using available protective gloves and suits is clearly an example of unnecessary risk.

3. *Make risk-management decisions at the right level:* Although supervisors are ultimately responsible for everything their subordinates do, there is no reason to allow less experienced subordinates to make critical decisions on managing risk. One might read into that statement and assume that risk management endorses micromanagement, where only the boss makes decisions. This is hardly the case. Risk management simply sets logical and appropriate levels of authority based on a full consideration of the nature of the risk. If the potential effect of a hazard is catastrophic, then an individual with the appropriate level of experience and training should decide how to respond to the risk. One would not allow a rookie officer to

make the green-light call for a SWAT sniper, any more than one would allow a young technician to independently decide that it was safe to enter an unstable building.

4. *Accept risk only when the benefits outweigh the costs:* In policing, much as in the military, real-life dangers are a part of the culture. The police cannot walk away from a hostage scene and say, "Not my problem," any more than they can say, "That scene is bloody and I'm not working it." The mission must be accomplished. Weighing risks and benefits demands a consideration of the mission and the necessity of activity. But even with a necessitating circumstance, some risks are simply too significant to take. An excellent crime scene example is the methamphetamine lab. The scene must be processed, but unless trained personnel are on scene, this is not a risk any sane supervisor is willing to chance.

These four tenets provide an underlying theory for risk management. Depending upon which authority you consult, risk management is accomplished in four to five practical steps. For the purposes of this text, the process will be presented in four steps:

Step 1. *Hazard identification:* Any activity poses some form of risk. Walking on the street, taking a bath, dancing — all have possible consequences. Work activities and certainly those involving hazardous environments have evident risks. Supervisors analyze the operations involved in their organization's mission by considering the normal course of personnel activities. From this analysis, they identify common forms of hazards that may be associated with these activities. Many of the hazards associated with crime scenes were discussed in Chapter 5. Inhalation hazards, biohazard exposure, and unstable structures are just a few of the obvious risks associated with scene processing. These hazards are considered in advance of the activity, as they are common to many scenes. Although preplanning is important, on-scene hazard identification is necessary as well and is an integral part of ongoing assessment of the crime scene. Unique situations and environments or other circumstances can result in new hazards not previously considered. Hazard identification requires constant vigilance.

Step 2. *Risk assessment:* Once a hazard is identified, it must be assessed for two specific issues. The first consideration is the potential effect of the hazard. Generally, hazard effects are classified as negligible, moderate, critical, or catastrophic. This classification speaks to the danger posed by the hazard to both personnel and the mission. The second consideration is how probable or likely it is that the hazard will occur. Typical classifications for probability include: frequent, likely, occasionally, seldom, unlikely. These two classifications can be combined to provide an overall risk assessment, as seen in Figure B.1. This matrix classifies the overall assessment of the risk in four values: extreme, high, medium, and low. Consider the example of the methamphetamine lab. Handled by untrained individuals, these scenes are literally bombs waiting to go off, so the hazard probability is likely. The hazard effect can be catastrophic to personnel. Together, these two classifications define an extreme risk.

Step 3. *Risk control and mitigation:* One cannot eliminate risks altogether, but by taking certain steps we can make most activities safer. Once a risk is identified, control measures are considered as a means of reducing the probability that the hazard

Risk Assessment Matrix

HAZARD PROBABILITY

HAZARD EFFECT	Frequent	Likely	Occasional	Seldom	Unlikely
Catastrophic	Extreme	Extreme	High	High	Medium
Critical	Extreme	High	High	Medium	Low
Moderate	High	Medium	Medium	Low	Low
Negligible	Medium	Low	Low	Low	Low

Figure B.1 Risk-assessment matrix. By considering both the likelihood that a given hazard will occur and the effect that the hazard would create, one can develop an overall risk assessment of the hazard. For instance, if the hazard were considered to be an event that seldom occurs but had a moderate effect, the overall risk assessment would be "low." On the other hand, if the hazard had a moderate effect but frequently occurred, the assessment would be "high." This assessment helps the supervisor decide where to place his/her priorities in reducing risks and to define at what level a risk-management decision can be made.

may occur, or of reducing the effect of the hazard on personnel. Control measures can be simple or elaborate, depending upon the nature of the hazard. As in the case of the methamphetamine lab, the control measure is simply to leave the scene and wait for a trained team.

Step 4. *Supervision of controls:* Control measures often include defined levels of decision authority specifying who can override a control measure or allow a procedure to go ahead in the face of the risk. For medium and low risks, the decision authority is generally low. As the risk assessment increases to high or extreme, the decision authority is usually placed at a much higher supervisory level. Returning to the methamphetamine lab example, the on-scene technician should not have the authority to override the control measure of "leave and wait for a trained team." If that decision were to be questioned and the control measure perhaps ignored, a much higher level of authority would have to make the decision because of the probable dangerous consequences of ignoring the control measure.

Risk-assessment and -control measures look good on paper, but risk management is accomplished only through supervision and leadership. Once a control measure has been identified and a level of decision authority has been defined, then everyone in the organization must be held accountable. If a control measure is put in place stating that "all personnel will wear appropriate PPE (personal protective equipment) in a biohazard scene," then everyone is expected to abide by the control measure. It is in the supervision step that risk management almost always fails. Supervisors will either ignore established control measures or release decision authority to subordinates. Far too often, this results in injury for a hazard that had previously been assessed and for which control measures had been identified.

From a practical perspective, many risk-management decisions are based on an operational analysis of the organization, and these decisions end up being incorporated into a set of standard operating procedures (SOPs). Of course, ad hoc risk management is still necessary for unique hazards that present themselves on scene, but these are dealt with by the appropriate supervisor. If necessary, the lessons learned from dealing with these unique hazards can be incorporated into the SOP or documented for future reference in the form of an after-action report.

Risk management is an absolute responsibility for supervisors at every level. If high-level supervisors (including the chief) fail to act on risk-management procedures, lower-level supervisors and certainly on-scene supervisors must take action. There is no excuse for sending crime scene personnel into hazardous situations without at least considering how to make the situation less dangerous. Risk management should be an integral part of an organization's mindset. Supervisors have a distinct responsibility to manage risk, but every member of the organization should recognize and use risk-management procedures. To accomplish this goal, risk management should be a part of in-service training for all officers.

Index[*]

---

[*]Page numbers in *italics* designate figures. *See also* cross-references designate related topics and more detailed lists of subtopics.